INTRODUCING POLITICAL PHILOSOPHY

INTRODUCING POLITICAL PHILOSOPHY

A POLICY-DRIVEN APPROACH

WILLIAM ABEL
ELIZABETH KAHN
TOM PARR
AND
ANDREW WALTON

OXFORD
UNIVERSITY PRESS

OXFORD

UNIVERSITY PRESS

Great Clarendon Street, Oxford, OX2 6DP,
United Kingdom

Oxford University Press is a department of the University of Oxford.
It furthers the University's objective of excellence in research, scholarship,
and education by publishing worldwide. Oxford is a registered trade mark of
Oxford University Press in the UK and in certain other countries

Published in the United States of America by Oxford University Press
198 Madison Avenue, New York, NY 10016, United States of America

British Library Cataloguing in Publication Data
Data available

Library of Congress Control Number: 2020947350

ISBN 978–0–19–878327–5

Printed in Great Britain by
Bell & Bain Ltd., Glasgow

For Marion Walton, who saw the start of this book, but sadly not the end.

INTRODUCTION

Should the state permit euthanasia? Should it prohibit recreational drug use? Should it ban hate speech? Should it condone, or even require, affirmative action policies in universities, in business, and in government? Should it permit private schools? Should it provide a basic income to its members? What leave arrangements should it offer to new parents? Should it grant members of minority groups exemptions from otherwise universal laws? Should judicial review constrain the decisions of a democratically elected government? Should the state shorten prison sentences? Should it ban intensive animal farming? How should it act to address climate change? Should an affluent state increase its overseas development aid? Should states have stricter immigration policies? When, if ever, should they intervene in the affairs of other states to prevent human rights abuses?

All of these questions have been prominent in political debate over the last fifty years, and there remains plenty of dispute about them at the start of the 2020s. Some readers may be most familiar with them in the context of Western Europe, North America, and Australasia. But their reach extends far beyond this. Brazil has among the most extensive affirmative action programmes in the world. States from Bolivia to South Korea have systems of judicial review. And the question of how to tackle climate change frequently hits the headlines almost everywhere. These issues remain high on the political agenda partly because they're divisive—that is, partly because there's deep and ongoing dispute about which public policies the state should adopt.

There's often disagreement about these matters because individuals endorse different moral views. Some readers might be surprised by this statement. It's sometimes claimed that politics is a morality-free zone—it's an arena rife with self-interest, slogans, cunning, malice, manipulation, and even trolling. These critics might see politics as merely a competition in which there are winners and losers; where laws are, at best, what serves the interests of the majority and, at worst, a tool of oppression. Some might think that morality has nothing to do with it.

We don't see it that way. This isn't because we deny that politics involves many or all of these vices. It's because we think that, despite this, morality must inform our thinking about political issues, including the public policies that the state should adopt. Even if it's not always immediately obvious, when we debate the justifiability of a particular public policy, we must rely on moral claims to defend our views.

This book contains chapters on the questions listed at the start of this Introduction. For each one, we highlight how disputes about the topic involve disagreements about moral values. As the chapter titles indicate, we link each policy to a philosophical topic, analysis of which is indispensable in determining how the state should act. For example, debates about drug policy require us to examine questions about paternalism; debates about affirmative action demand that we explore the wrongness of discrimination; and discussions of prison sentences must involve some investigation into the justification for state punishment. In this way, political arguments about public policy are an apt subject of philosophical analysis—or, in other words, they present a prime opportunity to do some *political philosophy*.

A central aim of this book is to introduce readers to political philosophy by theorizing about public policy. It does this as follows. In Chapter 1, we provide a preliminary outline of how to do political philosophy. We issue some brief remarks about the methods of political philosophy and the relevance of disputes about public policy. We recommend that readers begin with this chapter to get some understanding of the basics of the discipline. However, we maintain that the best way to learn about political philosophy is to see it in action. Therefore, our suggestion is to run through Chapter 1 briefly in the first instance, but then to return to it to hone understanding of the methods after having observed them in practice in the rest of the book.

In each of the remaining chapters, we draw on the tools of political philosophy to explore a distinct area of public policy. In each case, we identify some of the moral threads that run through the public policy debate; we explain the philosophical positions taken by the various sides; we introduce the academic literature that supports these positions; and we examine the strengths and weaknesses of the competing views.

To assist with these tasks, we develop an argument in favour of the position we think is the most plausible, and we criticize the arguments of those who reach other conclusions. Crucially, though, we don't do this because we want readers uncritically to accept our views. Rather, it's because we think that this is a good way for readers to learn about the discipline. In taking a position and criticizing the alternatives, we hope to demonstrate an aspect of good practice in political philosophy, namely taking a stance on the issue in question, arguing in favour of it, and defending it against the strongest objections.

In other words, above all else, what we want readers to take from this book isn't the particular conclusions that we reach. Instead, it's an understanding of how to use the tools of political philosophy to analyse the justifiability of competing public policies, as well as to construct an argument in defence of a policy and defend it against criticism. With this in mind, we see each chapter as demonstrating some skills that readers might emulate, rather than as gifting readers the correct answers. It's in this way that the book serves as an introduction to doing political philosophy.

REFLECTIONS

The idea of writing a book of this kind was first conceived a few years ago. When approaching its final stages, we thought it important to reflect on where we've reached, particularly in terms of the shortcomings of our final product. While there may be many, two especially important points come to mind.

One concern that drives each of the authors of this book in their research, writing, and teaching is the importance of using political philosophy to shine a spotlight on the injustices that so many individuals endure in the hope that doing so can contribute to real change. Perhaps it'll be clear that issues such as gender inequality, racial discrimination, and the mistreatment of sexual and religious minorities are pivotal to this book's design.

However, we're unsure about whether the policies on which we've focused are the best choices in this regard. At any rate, there are several policies on which we could have focused that we regret not having included. This includes chapters on the justifiability of racial profiling, on the legalization of sex work, and on whether firms may discriminate against customers on the basis of various characteristics. While we address disability in several chapters, we're sorry that this book contains no sustained discussion of the topic. Likewise, we're disappointed that there's almost no mention of mental health.

Furthermore, we're conscious that there's some lack of diversity among the scholars that we cite and with whom we engage in this book. As is the case with many disciplines, the views of middle-class white men receive disproportionate attention, to the detriment of members of every other group. This is a shame for multiple reasons, but especially because a consequence of this is that some topics don't receive the attention that they warrant.

Though we've made efforts to address this shortcoming, these have been hampered by one of the main aims of this text—introducing readers to some of the most influential ideas in political philosophy. As a matter of fact, and owing to the advantages that members of this group enjoy, many of these ideas come from authors who're socially and economically privileged. However, if we were to refuse to mention these viewpoints, we'd fail in our responsibility to expose readers to some of the ideas that are most central to the discipline.

Though we realize that one book can cover only so much ground, we believe it's vital to highlight these misgivings. These are the things on which we'd focus if we were to start this project again and it's our error not to have been more on the pulse here. We record our testament to the importance of doing better.

ACKNOWLEDGEMENTS

Since this book has taken longer than five years to put together, it's hard to remember everyone we should thank. The best we can do at this stage is to record various lists of individuals to whom we owe particular debts of gratitude.

We thank Meera Inglis for all of her incredible work putting together the online resources for this book. To have organized a body of teaching support materials of this order would have been impressive enough in any case, but to have tailored it so well to address the circumstances facing students and lecturers that arose in 2020 is nothing short of extraordinary.

For providing valuable comments on chapters of this book, for helpful conversation, and for academic support and advice throughout, we thank: Andreas Albertsen,

David Axelsen, Jess Begon, Paul Bou-Habib, Daniel Callies, Shuk Ying Chan, James Christensen, Stan Collymore, Maria Dimova-Cookson, Dimitris Efthimiou, Christopher Finlay, Tim Fowler, Dorothea Gaedeke, Mollie Gerver, Anca Gheaus, Siba Harb, David Held, Lisa Herzog, Jeff Howard, Meera Inglis, Tyler John, Peter Jones, Hwa Young Kim, Johannes Kniess, Bruno Leipold, Andy Mason, Tim Meijers, Søren Flinch Midtgaard, Chris Mills, Kian Mintz-Woo, Andres Moles, Mirjam Müller, Dan Nadasan, Erin Nash, Fay Niker, Jonathan Parry, Wouter Peeters, Katie Rickard, Antoinette Scherz, Liam Shields, Adam Slavny, Areti Theofilopoulou, Isa Trifan, Alex Volacu, Adam Warner, and Annette Zimmermann.

In similar vein, we thank a host of anonymous referees organized by Oxford University Press. Also, we're incredibly grateful to Sarah Iles, Emily Spicer, and Katie Staal for their wonderful editorial work and support.

We're grateful to Justice Everywhere Blog (justice-everywhere.org), where some sections of early drafts of several chapters were posted for pedagogical development.

We're lucky to have several academic influences who've inspired us and helped us learn how to do political philosophy. For this, we thank: Derek Bell, Kimberley Brownlee, Clare Burgum, Simon Caney, Paula Casal, Matthew Clayton, Rainer Forst, Stefan Gosepath, Dudley Knowles, Matt Matravers, Sue Mendus, Darrel Moellendorf, Serena Olsaretti, Martin O'Neill, Adam Swift, Victor Tadros, Andrew Williams, and Kerri Woods. Thanks also to the Justitia Amplificata Centre for Advanced Studies at Goethe University in Frankfurt, where Beth had a visiting fellowship for one month; the University Center for Human Values at Princeton University, where Tom was a visiting scholar for one year; and the Law and Philosophy Group at Universitat Pompeu Fabra, where Andrew was a visiting scholar for one semester. Special thanks go to PopWorld in Newcastle.

Finally, we owe huge thanks to families and friends that've supported us, nurtured our ideas, and helped us to enjoy both doing and setting aside our work. For Will, this is Debbie, Ian, Patrick, and Ben. For Beth, this is Charles, Hazel, John, Anna, El, Mum, Paul, Dad, Prue, and Ringo. For Tom, this is Emma, Ricki, John, Bruno, David, Hwa, Katie, and Dimple, with special thanks going to the late Yaki Meredith. For Andrew, this is: for the patter of Rosario, Matt, Dan, Seren, Kyle, John, Disco, Hwa, Sebi, and Emily; for the warmth of Marion, Roger, Suad, Saad, Noor, Amelie, Leila, Warda, Lutfi, Lina, Raad, Jess, Ahmed, Laura, Robert, Chloe, Lucy, and Thomas, and, for all her love and laughter, Maryam.

NOTE

During the production of this book one of the authors was in the employ of the Bank of England. Any views expressed are solely those of the author and so cannot be taken to represent those of the Bank of England.

BRIEF CONTENTS

Detailed Contents   xiii

About the Authors   xviii

Guide to Online Resources   xix

1   DOING POLITICAL PHILOSOPHY   1

2   EUTHANASIA AND FREEDOM   13

3   HATE SPEECH AND FREEDOM OF EXPRESSION   28

4   RECREATIONAL DRUGS AND PATERNALISM   45

5   AFFIRMATIVE ACTION AND DISCRIMINATION   62

6   SCHOOLS AND EQUALITY OF OPPORTUNITY   78

7   BASIC INCOME AND DISTRIBUTIVE JUSTICE   93

8   PARENTAL LEAVE AND GENDER EQUALITY   109

9   MINORITY EXEMPTIONS AND MULTICULTURALISM   126

10 JUDICIAL REVIEW AND DEMOCRACY   141

11 PRISON SENTENCES AND PUNISHMENT   156

12 INTENSIVE ANIMAL FARMING AND MORAL STATUS   172

13 ENVIRONMENTAL TAXES AND INTERGENERATIONAL JUSTICE   187

14 IMMIGRATION AND THE POLITICAL COMMUNITY   203

15 DEVELOPMENT AID AND GLOBAL JUSTICE   218

16 HUMANITARIAN INTERVENTION AND POLITICAL
    SELF-DETERMINATION   233

References   249
Index   270

DETAILED CONTENTS

About the Authors	xviii
Guide to Online Resources	xix

1 DOING POLITICAL PHILOSOPHY — 1

1.1 Introduction	1
1.2 What Is Political Philosophy?	2
1.3 Which Arguments?	5
1.4 Analysis in Political Philosophy	6
1.4.1 Argument Structure	6
1.4.2 Examples	7
1.4.3 Refining Moral Claims	8
1.4.4 Underlying Moral Claims	8
1.4.5 Kinds of Examples	9
1.5 From Arguments to Analysis and Back Again	10
1.6 Further Engagement in Political Philosophy	11

2 EUTHANASIA AND FREEDOM — 13

2.1 Introduction	13
2.2 The Freedom to Choose	15
2.2.1 Defining Freedom	15
2.2.2 The Value of Freedom	16
2.2.3 The Stability Qualification	17
2.3 'Assist Us to Live Not Die'	20
2.4 Doing, Enabling, and Allowing	22
2.5 The Slippery Slope	24
2.6 Conclusions	26

3 HATE SPEECH AND FREEDOM OF EXPRESSION — 28

3.1 Introduction	28
3.2 The Terrain of Expression	30
3.3 The Harm of Hate Speech	31
3.3.1 The Threat of Harm	31
3.3.2 The Climate of Hate	32
3.4 Arguments for Freedom of Expression	34
3.4.1 Autonomy	34
3.4.2 Speakers, Audiences, and Thinkers	36
3.4.3 Problems with State Regulation	37

3.5 Further Arguments for Restrictions 39
   3.5.1 Offensive Speech 39
   3.5.2 Dignity 41
3.6 Conclusions 43

4 RECREATIONAL DRUGS AND PATERNALISM 45

4.1 Introduction 45
4.2 The Landscape of Drug Policy 46
   4.2.1 Definitions 46
   4.2.2 The Paternalist Argument 47
4.3 Anti-Paternalist Arguments 48
4.4 Misinformed Choices 50
4.5 Bad Choices 52
   4.5.1 Addiction and Second-Order Preferences 52
   4.5.2 Autonomy and Overdose 56
4.6 Conclusions 59

5 AFFIRMATIVE ACTION AND DISCRIMINATION 62

5.1 Introduction 62
5.2 Three Kinds of Wrongful Discrimination 64
5.3 Discrimination and Affirmative Action 66
   5.3.1 Discrimination and Compensation 66
   5.3.2 Preventing Discrimination 67
   5.3.3 Why Affirmative Action? 68
5.4 Diversity and Integration 68
5.5 The Reverse Discrimination Objection 70
   5.5.1 Discrimination and Merit 71
   5.5.2 Discrimination and Equality 73
5.6 Effectiveness Objections 74
   5.6.1 The Off-Target Objection 74
   5.6.2 The Stigma Objection 75
5.7 Conclusions 76

6 SCHOOLS AND EQUALITY OF OPPORTUNITY 78

6.1 Introduction 78
6.2 Elite Private Schools and Equality of Opportunity 80
   6.2.1 Unfairness and Harm 81
   6.2.2 The Comparison with Elite Private Schools 81
6.3 Equality or Adequacy? 83
6.4 Equality Above All? 85
   6.4.1 Unrestricted Parental Licence 87
   6.4.2 Family Values 88
6.5 Do Schools Matter? 89
6.6 Conclusions 90

7   BASIC INCOME AND DISTRIBUTIVE JUSTICE   93

    7.1   Introduction   93
    7.2   The Effects of Basic Income   94
    7.3   The Significance of Income and Exit   97
          7.3.1   Justice as Fairness   97
          7.3.2   The Difference Principle and Basic Income   98
          7.3.3   Democratic Equality   100
          7.3.4   The Case for Basic Income   102
    7.4   The Problem of Non-Contributors   102
    7.5   The Problem with Taxation   105
          7.5.1   The Intuitive Problem   105
          7.5.2   The Theoretical Problem   106
    7.6   Conclusions   107

8   PARENTAL LEAVE AND GENDER EQUALITY   109

    8.1   Introduction   109
    8.2   The Gendered Division of labour   111
          8.2.1   Equality of Outcome   112
          8.2.2   Equality of Opportunity   113
          8.2.3   Harmful Effects   114
    8.3   Parental Leave Schemes   115
    8.4   Defending Mandatory Leave   117
          8.4.1   Conditional Leave   117
          8.4.2   Use It or Lose It Leave and Default Leave   118
          8.4.3   The Case for Mandatory Leave   120
    8.5   The Limits of Parental Leave   120
          8.5.1   Freedom in Family Life   120
          8.5.2   Beyond Parental Leave   122
    8.6   Conclusions   124

9   MINORITY EXEMPTIONS AND MULTICULTURALISM   126

    9.1   Introduction   126
    9.2   Cultures, Majorities, and Minorities   128
          9.2.1   Misrecognition   129
          9.2.2   Minority Equality   130
    9.3   The Bads of Multiculturalism   132
    9.4   Universal Compliance   134
    9.5   Exemption Fairness   136
    9.6   Conclusions   139

10 JUDICIAL REVIEW AND DEMOCRACY   141

    10.1 Introduction   141
    10.2 Rights   142
    10.3 The Role of Courts   144

10.4 Democracy 146
    10.4.1 Defining Democracy 146
    10.4.2 Judicial Review and Defences of Democracy 148
10.5 The Instrumental Defence of Democracy 148
    10.5.1 The Instrumental Defence 148
    10.5.2 The Instrumental Defence and Judicial Review 149
10.6 The Intrinsic Defence of Democracy 150
    10.6.1 The Intrinsic Defence 150
    10.6.2 Revisiting Disagreement 152
10.7 Conclusions 153

11 PRISON SENTENCES AND PUNISHMENT 156
11.1 Introduction 156
11.2 The Importance of Deterrence 159
    11.2.1 Outcomes and Deterrence 160
    11.2.2 Duties and Deterrence 161
11.3 Deterrence and Prison Sentences 163
    11.3.1 The Effects of Prison Sentences 163
    11.3.2 Proportionality 164
    11.3.3 The Case for Shorter Prison Sentences 165
11.4 Retributivism 166
11.5 Communicating Condemnation 168
11.6 Conclusions 170

12 INTENSIVE ANIMAL FARMING AND MORAL STATUS 172
12.1 Introduction 172
12.2 The Treatment of Animals 174
    12.2.1 Suffering and Killing 174
    12.2.2 Pain and Pleasure in Animals 175
12.3 Intensive Animal Farming 177
12.4 The Moral Community 180
    12.4.1 Fred's Experiment 181
    12.4.2 Reconsidering the Moral Community 182
12.5 Enforcing Better Treatment 183
12.6 Conclusions 184

13 ENVIRONMENTAL TAXES AND INTERGENERATIONAL JUSTICE 187
13.1 Introduction 187
13.2 Environmental Taxes 189
13.3 Intergenerational Duties 192
    13.3.1 Intergenerational Sufficiency 192
    13.3.2 Intergenerational Equality 193
    13.3.3 The Non-Identity Problem 194
13.4 Historical Emissions 196
13.5 The Impact of Environmental Taxes 199
13.6 Conclusions 201

14 IMMIGRATION AND THE POLITICAL COMMUNITY 203

14.1 Introduction 203
14.2 The Case for Open Borders 204
14.3 Is Migration A Luxury? 206
14.4 Brain Drain 209
14.5 The Harmful Effects of Immigration 212
    14.5.1 Security 213
    14.5.2 The Economy 214
    14.5.3 Culture 215
14.6 Conclusions 216

15 DEVELOPMENT AID AND GLOBAL JUSTICE 218

15.1 Introduction 218
15.2 Duties of Aid 219
15.3 The Causes of Poverty 221
    15.3.1 The Responsibility of the Poor? 221
    15.3.2 The Responsibility of the Affluent? 223
15.4 Does Charity Start at Home? 225
    15.4.1 Reciprocity and Political Power 226
    15.4.2 Special Duties and Priority 227
15.5 Is Aid Appropriate? 229
15.6 Conclusions 231

16 HUMANITARIAN INTERVENTION AND POLITICAL
SELF-DETERMINATION 233

16.1 Introduction 233
16.2 Universal Values 235
16.3 Political Self-Determination 237
    16.3.1 The Political Self-Determination Objection 238
    16.3.2 The Limits of Political Self-Determination 240
    16.3.3 A Radical Conclusion? 242
16.4 The Role of International Law 243
16.5 The Objection from Likely Failure 245
16.6 Conclusions 247

References 249
Index 270

ABOUT THE AUTHORS

Mr William Abel is a Senior Economist at the Bank of England, and he works on labour markets, housing, and consumer spending.

Dr Elizabeth Kahn is an Assistant Professor in Political Theory in the School of Government and International Affairs at Durham University, and she researches the relationship between structural injustices and the obligations of individuals.

Dr Tom Parr is an Associate Professor in Political Theory in the Department of Politics and International Studies at the University of Warwick, and he researches issues relating to egalitarianism, economic justice, and the future of work.

Dr Andrew Walton is a Senior Lecturer in Political Philosophy in the Politics Department at Newcastle University, and he researches issues in trade justice, economics ethics, and housing policy.

GUIDE TO ONLINE RESOURCES

Students and lecturers are further supported by online resources to encourage deeper engagement with the content:

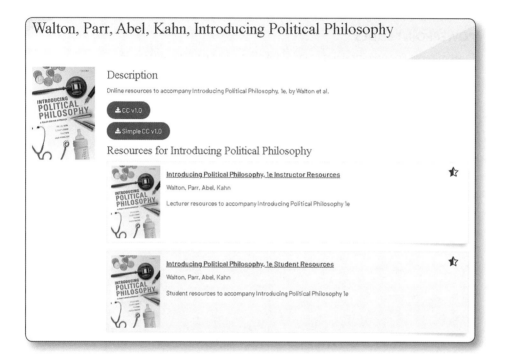

Walton, Parr, Abel, Kahn, Introducing Political Philosophy

Description

Online resources to accompany Introducing Political Philosophy, 1e, by Walton et al.

⬇ CC v1.0

⬇ Simple CC v1.0

Resources for Introducing Political Philosophy

Introducing Political Philosophy, 1e Instructor Resources

Walton, Parr, Abel, Kahn

Lecturer resources to accompany Introducing Political Philosophy 1e

Introducing Political Philosophy, 1e Student Resources

Walton, Parr, Abel, Kahn

Student resources to accompany Introducing Political Philosophy 1e

FOR STUDENTS

LINKS TO FURTHER READINGS AND RESOURCES

A carefully selected list of websites help to broaden your knowledge and understanding of policy areas and the philosophical arguments that influence them.

SELF-TEST QUESTIONS

Questions that help guide you through each chapter and identify the most salient points for learning and analysis.

FOR REGISTERED ADOPTERS

SEMINAR ACTIVITIES

Seminar activities designed to encourage students to engage further in discussions and debates.

TEACHING GUIDE

A Teaching Guide explains how to get the most out of the book's inside-out approach.

POWERPOINT SLIDES

Customizable PowerPoint slides to facilitate effective teaching preparation.

1

DOING POLITICAL PHILOSOPHY

SUMMARY

- In this chapter, we offer some remarks about how to do political philosophy.
- We identify the main aims and focus of the discipline, which centre on the moral claims at the heart of political arguments.
- We describe two tools in the practice of political philosophy. One of these involves arranging arguments in clear and organized terms, and the other involves the use of examples and thought experiments in the analysis of moral claims.
- We discuss how to employ these tools in the service of a political argument.
- We conclude by reflecting on the importance of these lessons for what follows in the rest of this book.

1.1 INTRODUCTION

Learning any new task is difficult. When someone first throws a dart, it's likely to miss the board. When someone starts to play the piano, it's hard to have both hands in the right place at the right time. And when someone begins a new language, it takes a while before it's possible to have even a simple conversation. Political philosophy is no different.[1] At the outset, it may be daunting. But it's also like these tasks in another respect. With some introduction, it's possible to learn the ropes swiftly and, pretty soon, it can become second nature. It's our aim in this chapter to open the door to this—to give the reader an idea of what political philosophy is all about, and to provide some tools to get going.

The chapter runs as follows. In section 1.2, we describe some of the main aims of political philosophy, showing that we can make progress with the subject by studying arguments about the justifiability of various public policies. In the remaining sections,

---

[1] Political philosophy is sometimes known as political theory, and some scholars use these terms interchangeably. For simplicity, we'll stick with political philosophy.

we discuss three features of this task. In section 1.3, we comment on *which* arguments political philosophers might consider. In section 1.4, we look at *how* to engage with these arguments. We emphasize the importance of two tools: arranging arguments in a format that clarifies the claims on which they rely, and using examples and thought experiments to assess them. In section 1.5, we explore how to deploy these skills. In section 1.6, we bring these elements together with some reflections on taking the next steps in political philosophy.

By no means do we aim to provide a complete commentary. There are several other useful methodological tools that political philosophers might employ, and the discipline can usefully draw on the insights of several closely related fields of study. We'll flag some leads of these kinds as the chapter proceeds, and close with some suggestions for further reading.

But, recognizing that we can't do justice to the full range of matters, the aim here is merely to introduce the subject, as well as to explain some of its common tools. Most importantly, this chapter provides some guidance on how to read and understand what follows in this book and to begin engaging with political philosophy. In short, our aim is to provide a starter kit for a first expedition.

1.2 WHAT IS POLITICAL PHILOSOPHY?

Politics is rife with disagreement. We take it that this claim is uncontroversial. But for evidence, we can consider the table of contents in this book. It lists fifteen areas of public policy, all of which are the subject of heated debate. We disagree about whether physician-assisted suicide should be legal; when, if ever, humanitarian intervention in other states is justifiable; and what conditions, if any, someone without work must meet in order to claim unemployment benefits or whether they should receive a basic income.

Some of these arguments are about *empirical claims*. These kinds of debates are about how things are, including the relationship between various factors. For example, one fear with legalizing physician-assisted suicide is that it'll increase the likelihood that an individual will be pressured by others into ending their own life. Disputes about this practice might arise because we disagree about the size of this risk, perhaps because we've different interpretations of the available data.

But not all disagreement is about empirical claims. To see this, let's imagine that we agree that the evidence clearly shows that legalizing physician-assisted suicide won't increase the risk of an individual being pressured by others into ending their life. Nevertheless, disagreement might persist. There may be dispute about whether it's ever morally permissible to commit suicide or for a physician to assist with this. Advocates of legalization might contend that it's up to the individual to decide whether to live or to die. They might hold that they've the right to choose for themselves. Meanwhile, opponents might argue that suicide disrespects the sanctity of life and that the state shouldn't condone it, let alone permit medical staff to aid and abet it. These aren't disputes about empirical matters. They're disagreements about how things should be because they're disagreements about the values, aims, and ideals that should guide public policy. They're arguments about *moral claims*.

It's sometimes thought that politics is all about empirical claims. It'll help to clarify this point with an example, so let's consider the policy of making unemployment benefits conditional on their recipient actively seeking work. Supporters of this policy might attempt to justify it by appealing to the idea that making unemployment benefits unconditional will result in shirking. This is to assert the following:

> *Empirical claim*: Making unemployment benefits unconditional will cause more individuals to refuse or avoid work.

In the public arena, debate about unemployment benefits often proceeds with exclusive focus on this claim, with disagreement centring on whether or not the available evidence supports it. Indeed, some think this is perfectly reasonable, holding that disagreement in politics should be all about empirical claims. After all, they're testable. They can be verified. In contrast, perhaps there's no way to test moral claims. Maybe they can't be proven or disproven.

It's worth making three points about this reasoning. First, whatever the merits of these ideas, identifying the distinction between empirical claims and moral claims is important. As we'll show, separating claims along these lines is useful for making clear exactly what ideas are involved in an argument, as well as how to evaluate them. Even if someone's view rests on only an empirical claim, it'd remain worthwhile to identify this claim, and to subject it to careful analysis. Considerable research has been undertaken around the empirical matters involved in many political arguments. It's important that we consult this research, and explore what it supports.

Second, it's a mistake to think that political arguments can rely upon empirical claims alone. Again, the example of unemployment benefits can make this clear. As a case against making these benefits unconditional, the components of this argument that we've identified so far are as follows:

> *Empirical claim*: Making unemployment benefits unconditional will cause more individuals to refuse or avoid work.
>
> *Conclusion*: The state shouldn't make unemployment benefits unconditional.

But there's something odd about this. The conclusion clearly involves a moral judgement. It's a position about how the state *should* act. But this is strange. How has the conclusion assumed this form, when it's derived from a claim that's strictly empirical? The answer is that this is an error. A conclusion with moral content can't be derived from purely empirical claims. As David Hume put it, we can't derive an 'ought' from an 'is'.[2]

---

[2] David Hume, *Treatise of Human Nature* (Oxford: Oxford University Press, 2000 [1739]), book 3, part 1.

The way in which many political arguments avoid making this error is that they rely on unspoken moral claims. For example, an opponent of unconditional unemployment benefits might in fact have in mind the following:

Moral claim: The state shouldn't enact policies that cause more individuals to refuse or avoid work.

Empirical claim: Making unemployment benefits unconditional will cause more individuals to refuse or avoid work.

Conclusion: The state shouldn't make unemployment benefits unconditional.

This argument no longer makes the mistake of deriving an 'ought' from an 'is'. Because it now contains a moral claim, we can reach a conclusion about what the state should do. But it's important to notice that it escapes the error only for this reason. So, while it may be common to believe that empirical claims are all there is or should be in politics, arguments can't avoid relying on moral claims.

This leads us to a third point. Not least because they're an indispensable part of any political argument, it's crucial that we assess its moral claims. To see this, let's consider a different claim:

Alternative moral claim: The state should enact policies that cause more individuals to refuse or avoid work.

If this claim is correct, the critic of making benefits unconditional has a problem. Since the argument relies on the exact opposite of the alternative moral claim, the truth of the alternative moral claim falsifies the conclusion. Indeed, it implies that the state should adopt entirely different policies. Given that so much hangs on which moral claims are correct, it's vital that we subject them to analysis.

Here, we've arrived at what political philosophy is all about. One of its main aims is to make the terms of political arguments precise, and to arrange them in an organized fashion. When someone takes the view that the state should make unemployment benefits unconditional, political philosophers want to know what claims they offer to support this conclusion. We look to distinguish empirical claims from moral claims, and to lay out the argument neatly.

Having done this, the next task is assessment. We might give some attention to the empirical claims. Insofar as political philosophers are keen to know whether an argument is forceful, it's important to determine whether the available evidence supports any relevant empirical claims. It's in this way that political philosophy connects with political science, as well as with a broader range of fields, including economics, sociology, and psychology.

But political philosophers are mostly concerned with exploring the moral claims of an argument, and the relationship between an argument's claims and its conclusion. It's here that the discipline connects to other parts of philosophy, particularly moral philosophy and logic. Methods from these fields provide useful insights into how to assess moral claims and the coherence of a line of reasoning. Political philosophy uses these tools to scrutinize political arguments.

1.3 WHICH ARGUMENTS?

Political philosophy involves considering political arguments. But this raises a question: *which* ones? In politics, as in so many areas of life, there's no shortage of arguments, all with different claims and conclusions about what we should value and what justifies the exercise of political power. How do we choose which views warrant our attention?

It's difficult to offer comprehensive guidance on this issue, but it's useful to make two points about how political philosophers approach the matter. First, we tend to emphasize the moral issues at the heart of political arguments. Sometimes, this means setting aside certain concerns. As we'll acknowledge at various points in this book, it's not always possible to discuss everything that's relevant to, say, whether the state should ban hate speech or have more open borders. Instead, we aim to engage with the moral claims at the centre of political debate about them.

Second, political philosophers focus on the most forceful things that can be said about these issues. The reason for this is simple. The best way to determine how to exercise political power is to consider the best arguments in favour of the various options, and to see which of these is the strongest.

Identifying which arguments are the most forceful isn't simple. Even after years in the discipline, it's easy to make mistakes about this. But one tip is to avoid generalizations about views. It's an unfortunate feature of contemporary politics that so many arguments target 'a party line' or the leanings of 'the left' or 'the right'. It's an even more unfortunate feature of both public and academic political discussion that so much is written in relation to 'isms'—liberalism, socialism, and so forth. This is a shame partly because such generalizations can be misleading. For example, they can associate liberals with free markets, or socialists with big government, even though some who identify as liberal are sceptical about free markets, and some who identify as socialist endorse decentralized political systems. Because of this, generalizations can create unhelpful divisions, obscuring what matters in political decision-making. This isn't whether arguments or their advocates are liberals, socialists, free marketeers, governmentalists, or otherwise. What matters is the plausibility of the claims made in support of particular courses of action.

In the light of this, we suggest that it's often best to start with the actual arguments offered by political philosophers and others involved in politics. It pays to consider their reasoning so as to get a handle on what can be said in support of various positions. This isn't to suggest that we should focus exclusively on these arguments. Sometimes, a view points in the right direction, without getting the details exactly right. To work with this fact, it's important that we make a charitable interpretation, considering the claims of others in their best possible light. Sometimes we might need to go beyond this, by adjusting their views slightly to make them as strong as possible. But, by building on the political arguments of others in these ways, we're likely to find the arguments most worthy of analysis.

1.4 ANALYSIS IN POLITICAL PHILOSOPHY

Across this book, we aim to familiarize the reader with two methods that political philosophers often employ to assess political arguments. As we indicated in the introduction to this chapter, we can't discuss all of the available tools in the kit.[3] We'll set aside the task of conceptual analysis, where political philosophers aim to define and to delineate concepts, such as liberty and equality. We'll also set aside other methodological tools that are used to analyse moral claims. To consider all of these ideas in an introduction to political philosophy would be overwhelming.

Instead, we'll focus on two tools that are both commonplace and easily accessible. One is a structure for presenting logical arguments, often known as a syllogism. The second is examples and thought experiments that are designed to test, modify, and justify moral claims.

1.4.1 ARGUMENT STRUCTURE

A syllogism is an argument that involves two claims that are supposed to lead to a conclusion. We can arrange all political arguments in this format. A virtue of doing so is that it can help us to see their terms very plainly. This is especially valuable since a common difficulty in assessing arguments is that the claims on which they rely are unclear, as is the relationship between them. Stating terms precisely makes things transparent, and this allows us to bring the argument into better focus.

Another important virtue of a syllogism is that it allows us to see one way in which to challenge an argument, namely by identifying errors in its logic. Let's consider the following argument against affirmative action, a version of which we discuss in Chapter 5:

Moral claim: The state should compensate any individual who's suffered wrongful discrimination.

Empirical claim: Affirmative action fails to compensate all those who've suffered wrongful discrimination.

Conclusion: The state shouldn't adopt affirmative action.

This argument brings to light a genuine concern. Fear that affirmative action misses the target is a common objection to its use. For example, while these measures may compensate women or black or minority-ethnic individuals who've been unjustly deprived of valuable opportunities, they often fail to assist working-class white men who've also suffered wrongful discrimination.

---

[3] For further discussion, see Adrian Blau (ed.), *Methods in Analytical Political Theory* (Cambridge: Cambridge University Press, 2017).

But laying out the syllogism of this argument helps us to identify a flaw in its reasoning. To see this, let's consider an alternative conclusion:

Alternative conclusion: The state should use affirmative action more widely.

According to this alternative conclusion, rather than abandon the use of affirmative action because it doesn't reach all appropriate targets, the state should expand the use of these measures so that they do. What's significant here is that the alternative conclusion would look no less appropriate at the end of the syllogism than the originally asserted conclusion. This is important because it means that the original conclusion doesn't follow from the moral claim and the empirical claim. These two claims could be true, and yet the conclusion could be false. This is sometimes called a *non-sequitur*, and detecting a non-sequitur can be a valuable means of challenging an argument.

A final virtue of placing an argument in a syllogism is that it allows us to crystallize its moral claim. This is helpful because it brings this component into focus, and it identifies where we should concentrate moral analysis.

1.4.2 EXAMPLES

As an entry point for discussing the tools of moral analysis, let's consider another argument that's sometimes used to oppose affirmative action:

Moral claim: The state shouldn't treat an individual differently in virtue of their socially salient characteristics, such as their race or gender.

Empirical claim: Affirmative action treats individuals differently in virtue of their socially salient characteristics.

Conclusion: The state shouldn't adopt affirmative action.

This is the *reverse discrimination objection* to affirmative action. It's the worry that these measures are objectionable in the same way as other forms of wrongful discrimination, namely they treat an individual differently based on their socially salient characteristics. For example, affirmative action might reserve a set of seats in parliament for those who're female, not male, or for those who're black, not white.

But we can put pressure on the moral claim in this argument. We can do this by reflecting on the plausibility of the claim in various examples. We can consider a scenario in which the moral claim has implications about what the state should do, and then compare this to our own intuitive judgements.

For instance, let's consider the rules by which the state issues driving licences. One rule that it applies concerns sight. In particular, it refuses driving licences to those who're blind. When it does this, the state treats an individual differently in virtue of a socially salient characteristic. Accordingly, the moral claim of the reverse discrimination objection implies that this is wrongful.

But many won't share the judgement that it's wrong for the state to deny driving licences to those who're blind. While it's true that this policy treats an individual differently in virtue of a socially salient characteristic, it doesn't seem wrong to do so in this case. This should lead us to doubt the plausibility of the moral claim and, in turn, this threatens to undermine the reverse discrimination objection.

1.4.3 REFINING MORAL CLAIMS

Faced with the problematic example that we've described, the advocate of the reverse discrimination objection has a few options. One is to abandon the moral claim, taking it to have been falsified. Another possibility is to modify the claim. One way to do this is as follows:

> *Revised moral claim*: The state shouldn't treat an individual differently in virtue of their socially salient characteristics, such as their race or gender, when these characteristics aren't relevant to the case at hand.

This claim is stronger than the previous one. Again, we can show this by using examples. The practice of denying driving licences to those who're blind isn't at odds with the revised moral claim. This is because sight bears on the capacity to drive, so the claim doesn't object to this rule. By contrast, let's imagine a case in which a less qualified male doctor is hired ahead of a more qualified female doctor, because the hiring committee prefers male to female or non-binary doctors. Many regard this kind of hiring decision as wrongful, and the modified moral claim can explain this reaction. It involves treating an individual differently in virtue of a characteristic that's irrelevant to the case at hand.

We don't need to end our assessment of the moral claim here. We can test it by comparing its implication with our intuitive judgements in further examples, and we should accept, reject, or modify the claim accordingly. In this way, we can continue our analysis, perhaps reaching a point where we've a plausible moral claim, or where we've found that no modification can resolve its problems, and so we should reject it.

1.4.4 UNDERLYING MORAL CLAIMS

Another way to extend our interrogation of a moral claim is to consider whether it's supported by any underlying reasoning that we should accept. We might ask: does this moral claim rely on a deeper conviction or a more overarching idea about how the state should act?

An advocate of the revised moral claim might contend that the state shouldn't treat an individual differently in virtue of their socially salient characteristics, such as their race or gender, when these characteristics aren't relevant to the case at hand *because this violates the demands of meritocracy*. On this view, the revised moral claim is supported by an underlying moral idea that applies to a much broader range of cases. We might state it as follows:

> *Underlying moral claim*: The state should award social positions to the best qualified candidate.

Again, identifying this claim in an argument can be useful for several reasons. It can help us to appreciate the moral ideas that underpin a line of reasoning, which we can then assess by exploring examples. In doing so, we can subject the argument to further testing. This can involve accepting, rejecting, or modifying the underlying moral claim as appropriate. In turn, this can give us grounds to endorse or discard the argument.

1.4.5 KINDS OF EXAMPLES

It's by this process of testing and revising moral claims by using examples that we can assess their plausibility. Some of the examples that we discuss in this book are drawn from the world around us, like the case of driving licences. However, sometimes good examples aren't so close to hand, as real-life scenarios can involve too much or too little detail to be helpful.

Let's take the topic of humanitarian intervention. There are many historical examples that we can use to explore whether a state abusing the human rights of its subjects gives others a just cause to intervene. For instance, we might reflect on whether the United Kingdom was justified in invading Iraq in 2003. However, this example is problematic in several ways. Not least among these is that the United Kingdom has a history of wrongful interference in the affairs of states in the Middle East. Because this may affect our judgement about whether the war in 2003 was justifiable, this may pollute our reasoning about whether human rights abuses provide a just cause for humanitarian intervention. In cases such as these, it can be helpful to use our imaginations a bit to purify an example. Perhaps we might consider whether it would've been justifiable to intervene under the assumption that the United Kingdom didn't have this history. Because operating in this way enables us to focus more precisely on the question at hand, this can be a useful exercise.

Occasionally, it can pay to be even more creative. Let's consider the following:

Green Button Experiment: A state is violating the rights of its subjects. A foreigner owns a fabulous machine that, if activated by pressing a green button, would instantly discontinue all rights violations. The green button will have no effects other than to block the rights violations.[4]

This example is entirely fictional. No such button really exists. But still, the example helpfully narrows our attention. By neutralizing other variables that bear on intervention, such as questions of likely effectiveness, it enables us to home in on the crux of the matter, where our intuitive judgements about what constitutes a just cause for humanitarian intervention are most informative. The general point is that, by suspending various features of real life to tailor examples to our purposes, we can sharpen our moral analysis. This technique is known as using a thought experiment.

---

[4] Fernando Tesón and Bas van der Vossen, *Debating Humanitarian Intervention: Should We Try to Save Strangers?* (Oxford: Oxford University Press, 2017), 45–9.

Specifying examples in a manner that's precisely tailored to assessing moral claims without being too far-fetched for us to pass any sensible judgement is a tricky art.[5] We must also be careful about the conclusions we draw from thought experiments, particularly when they're very fanciful.[6] For instance, if we assume away a history of wrongful interference, we can't use any subsequent insights to determine whether intervention is justifiable in cases where there's such a history. We need to build these factors back into our thinking somewhere along the way. Nonetheless, it can remain valuable to use thought experiments to assess moral claims, and our outline in this section gives a broad overview of how and why they're employed in political philosophy.

1.5 FROM ARGUMENTS TO ANALYSIS AND BACK AGAIN

So far in this chapter, we've identified which arguments warrant attention in political philosophy, highlighted the importance of arranging these arguments in a clear and precise manner, and introduced the tools with which to assess their moral claims. But there remains a question about what to do with these insights.

One central aim of political philosophy is to work up a view about which public policies the state should adopt. We can reason about moral values and their relationship to the exercise of political power in order to take a stance on what's the right course of action for the state to pursue. Sometimes, political arguments are *assertive*, seeking to defend a moral claim or public policy. Sometimes, they're *critical*, seeking to oppose or resist a view. In either case, it's important to be explicit about the conclusion of an argument, and also to elaborate which claims are necessary to get there and why these claims are plausible. Put in language that'll be familiar from maths lessons: show your answer *and* your working.

Another important part of this task is to consider opposing views. The questions that political philosophy explores are typically matters of controversy that arise from disputes about the demands of morality. As G. A. Cohen warns, advocates of a view often fall into the trap of thinking that those on the other side of the debate are 'obviously wrong', sometimes because 'they are wholly unable to conceive how people who

---

[5] For discussion, see Kimberley Brownlee and Zofia Stemplowska, 'Thought Experiments' in Blau (ed.), *Methods in Analytical Political Theory*, 21–45.

[6] Here, there's a more general debate about the extent to which theory should abstract from reality, at least if it aims to direct political action. For influential discussion, see Charles W. Mills, '"Ideal Theory" as Ideology', *Hypatia*, 20 (2005), 165–84; Onora O'Neill, 'Abstraction, Idealization, and Ideology in Ethics' in J. D. G. Evans (ed.), *Moral Philosophy and Contemporary Problems* (Cambridge: Cambridge University Press, 1987), 55–69; Laura Valentini, 'On the Apparent Paradox of Ideal Theory', *Journal of Applied Philosophy*, 17 (2009), 332–55; and Lea Ypi, *Global Justice and Avant-Garde Political Agency* (Oxford: Oxford University Press, 2011), part 1.

disagree with them could see things differently'.[7] But it's vital to appreciate the existence and merits of opposing views. As we describe in section 1.3, this involves discerning and properly exploring the arguments offered by political philosophers and others involved in politics, reading them charitably, and looking for their strongest version. Accordingly, doing political philosophy requires not only that we defend our own view, but also that we explain and challenge opposing arguments. Furthermore, we must make it obvious when we're doing this—at each point in the text, we must be clear about whether we're relying on an idea to advance the view that we endorse or to challenge the alternatives.

It flows from these comments that another practical skill in political philosophy concerns how to present a view. An example of this is to organize a text by presenting our own position in the earlier parts of a paper, and then identifying and challenging the alternatives in later sections. This kind of structure can make clear what claims and conclusions the text means to defend, as well as what opposing views it means to criticize.

Of course, there are many ways to present a political argument. These comments aren't to suggest that all political philosophy does or should follow the same template. They're intended as a guide to some important aspects of writing political philosophy, and to give some ideas about how to do this in practice. The chapters that follow present various models of this. As we noted in the Introduction to this book, the rationale for offering an argument in each chapter, rather than merely summarizing the debate as a textbook might, is to provide practical examples of how to do political philosophy. In this respect, they can be read as a means of extending the guidance offered here.

1.6 FURTHER ENGAGEMENT IN POLITICAL PHILOSOPHY

The purpose of this chapter is very much introductory. The aim was to provide a starter kit to familiarize readers with some of the most common features of the discipline. To this end, we've emphasized the importance of focusing on the moral ideas at the heart of political arguments, clarifying the claims of these views, and ordering them in a logical fashion. We've stressed the significance of adopting a clear position, engaging with the strongest contrasting views, and organizing a text to make a sustained argument. And we've outlined how we can use syllogisms, examples, and thought experiments to analyse views and assess their moral claims.

There are two ways to take things further. One is to explore more detailed and more wide-ranging commentary on the vast array of tools and techniques that political philosophy uses. At the end of this chapter, we provide some suggestions for further

---

[7] G. A. Cohen, *On the Currency of Egalitarian Justice, and Other Essays in Political Philosophy* (Princeton, NJ: Princeton University Press, 2011), 231–2.

reading that can guide this investigation. But perhaps more important than this is to begin engaging with political philosophy. As with many skills, much of the art is learned best by observing how it's practised and by attempting to do it yourself. The rest of this book provides a resource for this. It's an exercise in political philosophy and, as it unfolds, it attempts to draw attention to the tools we've identified here. Perhaps it'll be useful to return to this chapter to review some of its content. But more than anything, we suggest that readers use it as a springboard for doing political philosophy, and we invite them to take up this task in other chapters.

FURTHER READING

A good place to begin reading about the aims and important features of political philosophical writing is the chapter on 'How to Do Political Philosophy' in G. A. Cohen, *On the Currency of Egalitarian Justice, and Other Essays in Political Philosophy* (Princeton, NJ: Princeton University Press, 2011), 225–35.

An excellent and accessible introduction to the methods of political philosophy is Jonathan Glover's 'The Scope and Limits of Moral Argument' in his *Causing Death and Saving Lives* (London: Penguin, 1977), 22–35. A more detailed discussion of the use and construction of example cases is Kimberley Brownlee and Zofia Stemplowska, 'Thought Experiments' in Adrian Blau (ed.), *Methods in Analytical Political Theory* (Cambridge: Cambridge University Press, 2017), 21–45. A rigorous engagement on the use and place of examples in theorizing political philosophy is Frances Kamm, *Bioethical Prescriptions: To Create, End, Choose, and Improve Lives* (Oxford: Oxford University Press, 2013), part 5.

For more extensive discussions of methods in political philosophy, there's Christian List and Laura Valentini, 'The Methodology of Political Theory' in Herman Cappelen, Tamar Azabó Gendler, and John Hawthorne (eds), *The Oxford Handbook of Philosophical Methodology* (Oxford: Oxford University Press, 2016), 525–53. Another place to look is in Adrian Blau (ed.), *Methods in Analytical Political Theory*.

 For additional material and resources, including web links and self-test questions, please visit the online resources
www.oup.com/he/walton1e.

2

EUTHANASIA AND FREEDOM

SUMMARY

- In this chapter, we consider whether the state should permit an individual to end their own life. We argue that a doctor should be permitted to assist an individual to end their own life, as well as to intervene to hasten their death.
- We support this view by appealing to the value of freedom, specifically the freedom to choose how to live and die.
- We examine the claim that it's an affront to the sanctity of life for an individual to hasten their own death. We argue against this view.
- We consider but reject the claim that, even if a doctor may *allow* an individual to die, they may not *enable* the individual to end their own life or *intervene* to hasten their death.
- We explore the worry that it's wrong for the state to allow a doctor to assist an individual to end their life, since this increases the risk that some individuals will have their lives ended against their wishes. We present empirical evidence that assuages this worry.
- We conclude by outlining some implications of our argument for the design of public policy.

2.1 INTRODUCTION

In 2015, after years of heated debate and intense campaigning, the United Kingdom's House of Commons rejected the Assisted Dying Bill. This bill would've made it legal for a doctor (or a suitably qualified nurse) to enable a terminally ill, competent adult to end their own life.[1] In other words, the bill proposed to legalize some forms of *physician-assisted suicide*. In rejecting this practice, the United Kingdom aligns with the vast majority of states around the world. The exceptions include Albania, Colombia, Germany, Japan, and Switzerland, as well as parts of the United States. In these places, physician-assisted suicide *is* legal, but it remains highly controversial.

Physician-assisted suicide is only one way in which a doctor can hasten an individual's death. To appreciate the full range of cases, we must start by distinguishing between three ways in which a doctor may act. First, they can be *passive* by allowing an individual to die. In these cases, a doctor refrains from attempting to save an individual's

---

[1] *Assisted Dying (No. 2) Bill* [HC], Bill 7, 2015–16.

life. This occurs when a doctor honours an individual's 'Do Not Resuscitate' (DNR) request or their decision to decline life-extending treatment. Second, a doctor can *assist* an individual by enabling them to bring about their own death. This occurs when a doctor provides a patient with life-ending medication that the patient then self-administers. Third, a doctor can be *active* in hastening an individual's death by administering life-ending medication.

Additionally, we can distinguish between cases based on the kind of consent that an individual gives. First, there are cases in which the medical intervention is *voluntary*, meaning that it results from the patient's request. Second, there are cases in which the medical intervention is *involuntary*, meaning that the doctor either fails to consult the patient or overrules their wishes. And, third, there are cases in which the medical intervention is *non-voluntary*, meaning that the individual neither gives nor withholds their consent because they're unable to do so, typically because they're in a coma.

Based on these distinctions, we can construct Table 2.1, which illustrates the full range of cases in which a doctor hastens an individual's death:

Table 2.1 Types of interventions that hasten death

	Passive	Assisted	Active
Voluntary	(1)	(2)	(3)
Non-Voluntary	(4)	(5)	(6)
Involuntary	(7)	(8)	(9)

Cases (5) and (8) are impossible in practice. For case (5), this is because a doctor can't assist a patient to end their own life if the patient is *unable* to self-administer life-ending medication—say, because they're in a coma. For case (8), this is because a doctor can't assist a patient to end their own life if the patient is *unwilling* to self-administer life-ending medication.

In this chapter, we focus on cases (2) and (3). Case (2) involves physician-assisted suicide of the kind that would've been legalized under the Assisted Dying Bill, and around which there's considerable controversy. Case (3) involves *voluntary active euthanasia*, in which an individual may legally request that a doctor intervene on their behalf to hasten their death. This practice is even more controversial than physician-assisted suicide because the doctor seems to play a more integral role in ending life. Despite this concern, Belgium, the Netherlands, and Luxembourg permit this practice, as well as physician-assisted suicide, making them notable outliers in this respect. While we consider several of the other ways in which a doctor might act to hasten a patient's death, we do so primarily to illuminate our discussion of cases (2) and (3). We focus on these cases because of the philosophical questions that they raise and the political importance of answering them.

A recurring theme in debates about the justifiability of these practices relates to a conflict between two values. On the one hand, advocates of these policies appeal to the value of *freedom* and, in particular, to the judgement that an individual should be free to decide when and how to end their life. Indeed, a common refrain voiced by those who campaign for legalizing such practices is 'give me choice over my death'.[2] On the other hand, critics maintain that exercises of this freedom are an affront to the *sanctity of life*. This worry can take at least three forms. One is the claim that it's disrespectful to the sanctity of life for someone to hasten their own death. A second concern is that, even if a doctor is permitted to allow or enable a patient to die, the sanctity of the patient's life forbids the doctor from intervening actively to hasten death. A third worry is that legalizing physician-assisted suicide and voluntary active euthanasia makes it more likely that a patient's life will be ended without their consent. In this chapter, we explore these disputes by developing a freedom-based defence of legalizing physician-assisted suicide and voluntary active euthanasia in section 2.2, and then by responding to the three worries relating to the sanctity of life in sections 2.3, 2.4, and 2.5. In section 2.6, we discuss the policy implications of our findings.

We recognize that many further factors bear on whether the state should permit physician-assisted suicide and voluntary active euthanasia. For example, some think that it's a mistake to expect or require a doctor to end another's life, given the profession's commitment to saving lives.[3] There are also difficult questions surrounding what constitutes patient consent. For example, which mental faculties must an individual possess for their request for life-ending medication to be valid? For reasons of space, we set aside these interesting matters.

2.2 THE FREEDOM TO CHOOSE

The most forceful argument for legalizing physician-assisted suicide and voluntary active euthanasia rests on an appeal to the value of freedom.[4] We build this argument by defining freedom and relating this value to these end-of-life practices. We then add an important qualification.

2.2.1 DEFINING FREEDOM

We can represent claims about freedom by putting them in the following form: 'X is free from Y to do or be Z'. In this formulation, X refers to an agent, such as an individual. Z refers to a course of action or an outcome, such as ending one's life. And Y refers to

---

    [2] Ramzy Alwakeel, 'Assisted Dying Bill: MPs Vote Down Controversial Legislation as Protest Rages Outside Parliament', *Evening Standard*, 11 September 2015, available at http://www.standard.co.uk/news/uk/assisted-dying-bill-mps-vote-down-controversial-legislation-as-protest-rages-outside-parliament-a2945541.html.

    [3] Fiona Randall and Robin Downie, 'Assisted Suicide and Voluntary Euthanasia: Role Contradictions for Physicians', *Clinical Medicine*, 10 (2010), 323–5.

    [4] For examples, see Ronald Dworkin et al., 'Assisted Suicide: The Philosophers' Brief', *New York Review of Books*, 44 (1997), 41–7 and Jonathan Glover, *Causing Death and Saving Lives* (London: Penguin Books, 1990), chs 14–15.

an obstacle, such as the law, that prevents X from doing or being Z.[5] In states where physician-assisted suicide and voluntary active euthanasia are illegal, the law creates obstacles (Y) that prevent an individual (X) from choosing to end their life in one of these ways (Z).

Some disagreements about freedom are disagreements about which agents matter, what counts as an obstacle, and what courses of action or outcomes matter. For example, we might wonder whether an individual is *unfree* to cycle along the river if they've never learned to ride a bicycle. On some accounts, their lack of ability qualifies as an obstacle that renders them unfree. On other accounts, the only obstacle that could render them unfree is others' coercive interference in their choice. Though important for other debates, these discussions needn't concern us here. What matters for our purposes is a point on which there's agreement across rival accounts, namely that laws that prohibit physician-assisted suicide and voluntary active euthanasia deprive individuals of a freedom that they would enjoy if these practices were legalized.

Given this definition of freedom and, specifically, the way in which laws that prohibit conduct reduce an individual's freedom, we can make sense of the following claim:

Freedom empirical claim: Legalizing physician-assisted suicide and voluntary active euthanasia gives an individual freedoms to choose when and how they die.

2.2.2 THE VALUE OF FREEDOM

In order to reach a conclusion about the moral significance of the freedom empirical claim, we must supplement it with the following:

Freedom moral claim: An individual should be free to choose when and how they die.

To defend this claim, we must consider *why* an individual should be free to make these kinds of choices. We can make progress on this front by investigating the related idea that an individual should be free to choose how they *live*. The foremost avenue for defending this idea holds that an individual has a fundamental interest in pursuing the projects they choose, living by the values they endorse, and determining how to trade off between competing options. It's typical to support these claims by appeal to the importance of *autonomy*—that is, the condition of being the author of one's own life.

We can illustrate the value of autonomy by considering the following scenario.[6] Let's imagine that there's a team of experts who carry out detailed research on your lifestyle and the optimal course of action for you to enjoy a fulfilling life. Now let's also imagine that, if these experts were to make major life decisions for you (such as whether and whom to marry), then you would have a much more fulfilling life than at present. Despite this, we suspect that you'd be reluctant to give these experts this decision-making power. Indeed, we frequently object when we're deprived of the

---

[5] Gerald MacCallum, 'Negative and Positive Freedom', *The Philosophical Review*, 76 (1967), 312–34.
[6] Glover, *Causing Death and Saving Lives*, 81.

freedom to choose on even much more trivial matters, such as when neighbourhood committees or local councils regulate the colour we can paint our houses. The reason for this is that we place great significance on being free to author our own lives.

It's noteworthy that among the most important decisions we make about our lives are those relating to when and how we die.[7] Many individuals believe that the way in which they die should reflect the way they have lived, aligning with their fundamental convictions about what gives their lives meaning. In this way, an individual's freedom to choose when and how they die shares a lot in common with their freedom to live in accordance with their own values. This is why it's easy to understand an individual's reluctance to delegate choices that determine the timing and nature of their death to someone else, even an expert. It's on this basis that we believe each individual should be free to choose when and how to end their own life.

Drawing these ideas together, we can present the following argument for legalizing physician-assisted suicide and voluntary active euthanasia:

Freedom moral claim: An individual should be free to choose when and how they die.

Freedom empirical claim: Legalizing physician-assisted suicide and voluntary active euthanasia gives an individual freedoms to choose when and how they die.

Conclusion: The state should legalize physician-assisted suicide and voluntary active euthanasia.

This is the *freedom argument* for permitting physician-assisted suicide and voluntary active euthanasia.

2.2.3 THE STABILITY QUALIFICATION

The freedom argument seems to imply that the state should never create obstacles that prevent an individual from ending their life as they see fit. But, on reflection, this conclusion is too extreme. To see this, let's consider the case of Toby, an adult in great health, with excellent long-term social and economic prospects, but who's currently suffering from a temporary but severe case of unrequited love.[8] Gripped by the tragedy of his current situation, Toby expresses a belief that his life is no longer worth living and that he wishes to end it. However, since he can't face doing it alone, Toby would like a doctor to hasten his death for him. As we've stated it so far, the freedom argument implies that we've reasons to grant this request. After all, the argument claims that an individual should be free to choose the timing and nature of their death.

We believe that this would be an error and that we ought not to grant Toby's request. This implies that physician-assisted suicide and voluntary active euthanasia shouldn't be legal in cases of this kind. But how can an advocate of the freedom argument make sense of this? To answer this question, we need a principle that can distinguish between cases in which these practices should be legal and cases in which they shouldn't.

---

[7] Dworkin et al., 'Assisted Suicide'.   [8] Dworkin et al., 'Assisted Suicide'.

One possibility is to distinguish between cases on the basis of the *character* of an individual's preference to end their life. On the one hand, there are *fleeting* preferences, which are the wants and desires that an individual has 'in the moment'. On the other hand, there are *stable* preferences, which persist over time, reflecting their deeper value judgements. Stable preferences are 'second order', in the sense that they're preferences about preferences.[9] This distinction is important because there are cases in which we respect an individual's autonomy by frustrating some of their fleeting preferences in favour of their stable preferences. This may be true of someone who's addicted to cigarettes and who's trying to quit. In this case, we may respect their autonomy by withholding a cigarette from them, rather than by enabling them to satisfy the craving. We might say that they don't *really* want the cigarette—that is, because of its character, their preference for the cigarette lacks the kind of moral significance that stable preferences possess.

If this analysis is correct, then we might draw similar conclusions about Toby's struggles with unrequited love. On this view, we respect his autonomy by withholding the medical intervention he requests, rather than by satisfying this fleeting preference. Again, we might even say that he doesn't *really* want to end his own life. This move justifies restricting an individual's freedoms to choose when and how they die to instances that align with their stable preferences. We call this the *stability qualification*.

A complication with this analysis is that it can be difficult to know whether an individual's preference to end their life is stable or only fleeting. There are at least two options available. The first is to look to whether we can expect them to endorse our decision after the event.[10] In the case of someone who's addicted to cigarettes and who's trying to quit, we can expect that they'll later thank us for withholding a cigarette from them. This counts in favour of this course of action. Likewise, if we're confident that an individual who requests assistance to end their life would retrospectively endorse our decision to withhold that assistance, then we've good reason to do so. This is very likely to be the case for Toby. By contrast, we normally lack this confidence in the case of those with painful, terminal illnesses. This provides one method that we can use to distinguish between cases in which physician-assisted suicide and voluntary active euthanasia should be legal and cases in which they shouldn't.

Let's now turn to the second option, which is to maintain that there are some objective hallmarks of cases in which an individual's preference to end their life is stable, and not merely fleeting. These hallmarks can then serve as necessary conditions on the eligibility of an individual's request for physician-assisted suicide or voluntary active euthanasia.[11] For example, perhaps we can be confident that an individual's

[9] Harry Frankfurt, 'Freedom of the Will and the Concept of a Person', *Journal of Philosophy*, 68 (1971), 5–20.

[10] Dworkin et al., 'Assisted Suicide'. For further discussion, see Mollie Gerver, 'Denying Services to Prevent Regret', *Journal of Applied Philosophy*, 36 (2019), 471–90.

[11] For example, see Glover, *Causing Death and Saving Lives*, 183 and Tom Beauchamp, 'Justifying Physician-Assisted Deaths' in Hugh LaFollette (ed.), *Ethics in Practice: An Anthology, Fourth Edition* (Oxford: Wiley Blackwell, 2014), 85–91 at 89.

preference to end their life is stable only if their medical condition is 'extremely burdensome and the burden outweighs any benefits' and when 'pain management cannot be made adequate'.[12] To this, we might add cases of terminal illness where there's a prognosis of only some months left to live. An implication of this is that, if the state is to allow physician-assisted suicide and voluntary active euthanasia, then it should do so only if an individual's medical circumstances meet some specified conditions.

We've discussed two methods that we can employ to distinguish between cases in which an individual's request to end their life is stable, and so physician-assisted suicide and voluntary active euthanasia should be legal, and cases in which the request is only fleeting, and so these practices should be illegal. The first is to examine whether we can expect an individual to endorse our decision after the event. The second is to consult their medical circumstances. We might even combine these two, which generates the result that the state should legalize physician-assisted suicide and voluntary active euthanasia only in cases where both conditions are satisfied. We don't propose to select between these options.

In summary, we can state the freedom argument with the stability qualification as follows:

Qualified freedom moral claim: An individual should be free to choose when and how they die so long as they satisfy the stability qualification.

Freedom empirical claim: Legalizing physician-assisted suicide and voluntary active euthanasia gives an individual freedoms to choose when and how they die.

Conclusion: The state should legalize physician-assisted suicide and voluntary active euthanasia for instances in which an individual satisfies the stability qualification.

To conclude this section, we address the worry that placing certain conditions on when we grant an individual's request for physician-assisted suicide or voluntary active euthanasia risks insulting others who meet these criteria.[13] For example, let's consider the case of Noel Conway who campaigned for legal permission to end his life after living with motor neurone disease for several years.[14] The concern is that, if he were allowed this freedom, others might reasonably interpret the state as making a negative judgement about the worth of the lives of those living with this condition.

While we share these fears, we doubt that they're decisive. This is because, even if it's insulting to convey such a message, we believe it's also insulting to deny Noel Conway the freedom to determine the timing and nature of his death. This point is especially significant given that societies have long deprived those with various illnesses and disabilities the freedom to determine for themselves how to live and die. By denying

---

[12] Beauchamp, 'Justifying Physician-Assisted Deaths', 89.

[13] Susan Behuniak, 'Death with "Dignity": The Wedge That Divides the Disability Rights Movement from the Right to Die Movement', *Politics and the Life Sciences*, 30 (2011), 17–32.

[14] Kevin Rawlinson, 'Terminally Ill Man Loses High Court Fight to End His Life', *The Guardian*, 5 October 2017, available at https://www.theguardian.com/society/2017/oct/05/entombed-man-noel-conway-loses-high-court-fight-end-life.

everyone the option of physician-assisted suicide and voluntary active euthanasia, the state worsens that problem. And so, while we're sensitive to insulting messages that policies can send, we believe this speaks in favour of our view, and not against it.

2.3 'ASSIST US TO LIVE NOT DIE'

Our thesis is that, subject to the stability qualification, the state should legalize physician-assisted suicide and voluntary active euthanasia on the grounds that doing so gives an individual the freedom to choose the timing and nature of their death. However, some critics vehemently oppose the idea that it's valuable to allow an individual to exercise their freedom in this way—that is, by ending their own life. In reply to the advocates of legalization, critics rally around slogans such as 'assist us to live not die'.[15] The exact meaning of this phrase is somewhat ambiguous, but its implication is clear, namely that it's an affront to the sanctity of an individual's life to enable them to end it hastily, rather than to protect it.

We can motivate this position in different ways. An especially powerful justification locates the sanctity of life in some of the ideas about freedom that we use to defend physician-assisted suicide and voluntary active euthanasia. Along these lines, David Velleman contends that there's a tension between prizing an individual's freedom and approving of acts that undermine that freedom.[16] Central to this line of reasoning is the idea that an individual's free choices have value because they're the choices of someone who's *capable* of choosing freely. It's the fact that these choices have a particular source—namely, an individual capable of making free choices—that bestows a special kind of significance on them. On this view, there can be no such value in those options that terminate an individual's capacity to choose freely. To value these freedoms makes the mistake of valuing an individual's wishes while overlooking the very reason that those wishes have value.

In support of this analysis, Velleman gives the example of voluntary slavery.[17] It's widely accepted that individuals should lack the freedom to sell themselves into slavery, even voluntarily. By this, we mean that, if an individual signs a contract selling themselves to someone else, then this contract isn't morally binding. The state shouldn't enforce it. One reason for this conclusion is that, as a slave, an individual can't make any meaningful choices about their own life, and so it's an error to treat their decision to sell themselves into slavery as one that we should respect. Again, this is because valuing an individual's choice to sell themselves into slavery makes the mistake of valuing their wishes while overlooking the very reason that those wishes have value. Velleman maintains that the state has the same reasons to deny an individual the freedom to end their own life hastily, namely because, if they were to exercise this

---

[15] Not Dead Yet UK, 'Resources', available at http://notdeadyetuk.org/resources.

[16] J. David Velleman, 'A Right of Self-Termination?', *Ethics*, 109 (1999), 606–28.

[17] Velleman, 'A Right of Self-Termination?', 615 and 619–20.

option, they would undermine their own capacity to choose freely. If this is correct, then we should oppose physician-assisted suicide and voluntary active euthanasia for the same reasons that we oppose voluntary slavery.

We call this the *termination objection*, and we can state it as follows:

Termination moral claim: Because the capacity to choose freely is what gives value to an individual's choices, they shouldn't be free to terminate this capacity.

Termination empirical claim: Legalizing physician-assisted suicide and voluntary active euthanasia gives an individual freedoms to terminate their capacity to choose freely.

Conclusion: The state shouldn't legalize physician-assisted suicide or voluntary active euthanasia.

To defend our argument against the termination objection, we make three separate points.[18] First, from the perspective of the termination objection, there's nothing distinctive about physician-assisted suicide or voluntary active euthanasia. This creates difficulties. To see this, let's compare these practices with that of *voluntary passive euthanasia*, in which an individual refuses life-saving treatment or issues an advanced directive that forbids a doctor from resuscitating them. It's widely accepted that voluntary passive euthanasia should be legal, as it'd be wrong to compel an individual to receive medical treatment, perhaps including surgery, against their wishes. But, crucially, if we must oppose actions that undermine an individual's capacity to choose, then we'd need to reject this conclusion. Doing so strikes us as implausible.

A second point relates to the relevance of voluntary slavery in defending the termination moral claim. When an individual contracts into slavery, this constrains their freedom because it gives control of their choices to someone else. But, arguably, what's troubling about the case may not be that they no longer enjoy the freedoms they once did, but that there's someone else who makes choices for them. If so, the example supports only a narrower moral claim, something along the lines of the idea that an individual shouldn't be free to give permanent and complete control of their choices to someone else. This claim is irrelevant for theorizing about physician-assisted suicide and voluntary active euthanasia, where no such control is given to others. To be sure, in the cases with which we're concerned, doctors act in ways that affect the patient's capacity to choose, but this occurs at the discretion of the patient, and not at the discretion of the doctor.

This brings us to our third response, which is the most fundamental. Even if we sometimes have reasons not to assist an individual to act in a way that will undermine their capacity to choose, it's hard to believe that these reasons should always (or nearly always) prove decisive, as is required by proponents of the termination objection.

---

[18] We draw on Jeff McMahan, 'Human Dignity, Suicide, and Assisting Others to Die' in Sebastian Muders (ed.), *Human Dignity and Assisted Death* (Oxford: Oxford University Press, 2017), 13–29 and Frances Kamm, 'Physician-Assisted Suicide, the Doctrine of Double Effect, and the Ground of Value', *Ethics*, 109 (1999), 586–605.

To see why we think this, let's consider a soldier who throws themself onto a grenade knowing that, though this will kill them, it'll prevent their squadron from suffering serious but non-lethal physical harm. It's common to celebrate sacrifices of this kind. However, we'll struggle to account for this sentiment if we accept the termination moral claim, given that the soldier's actions undermine their capacity to choose. Moreover, if we're willing to allow that the soldier acts permissibly, as our intuitions suggest, then why not think that there are other cases in which it's permissible for an individual to end their own life, such as when they suffer from a painful, terminal illness? At any rate, such cases pose a serious challenge to the termination moral claim.

We believe that these three responses cast significant doubt on the plausibility of the termination objection.

2.4 DOING, ENABLING, AND ALLOWING

The freedom argument supports legalizing *both* physician-assisted suicide and voluntary active euthanasia. However, it's significant that, even among states that permit the former, very few permit the latter as well. Are there good grounds for treating these two practices differently?

The Assisted Dying Bill proposed that a doctor may *enable* an individual to hasten their death by preparing life-ending medication and by assisting them in self-administering that medication. But it emphasized that 'the final act of *doing* so must be taken by the person for whom the medicine has been prescribed', and that it did 'not authorize' the doctor 'to administer a medicine to another person with the intention of causing that person's death'.[19] This phrasing distinguishes voluntary active euthanasia from physician-assisted suicide on the basis of the kind of intervention that each involves.

Earlier, we distinguished three ways in which a doctor may intervene to hasten death. First, they can be *passive* by allowing an individual to die. This occurs with voluntary passive euthanasia, where the doctor merely allows death—say, by failing to resuscitate the patient. Second, they can *assist* an individual by enabling them to bring about their death. This is the case with physician-assisted suicide, where the doctor *enables* or *assists* the patient to hasten their death by supplying them with life-ending medication. Third, the doctor can be *active* in hastening an individual's death by administering life-ending medication. This is true of voluntary active euthanasia.

There may be important moral differences between allowing an individual to die, enabling them to die, and directly bringing about their death. Some think that these actions (dis)respect the sanctity of life in different ways, and that this has implications for which practices the state should legalize.[20] In particular, they maintain that the law

---

[19] Clauses (4) and (5) of the *Assisted Dying (No. 2) Bill* [HC], Bill 7, 2015–16 (emphasis added).

[20] John Keown, 'Against Decriminalising Euthanasia: For Improving Care' in Emily Jackson and John Keown (eds), *Debating Euthanasia* (Oxford: Hart Publishing, 2012), 87–101.

should adopt a more permissive attitude towards voluntary passive euthanasia than physician-assisted suicide and, similarly, that the law should adopt a more permissive attitude towards physician-assisted suicide than voluntary active euthanasia.

The distinction between allowing harm, enabling harm, and doing harm is a familiar one.[21] Let's suppose that we know an individual has drowned, and that we hear about three other individuals who were present. One individual supplied heavy weights, which a second individual tied to the victim before throwing them into the water. A third individual looked on at the events, refusing to come to the victim's rescue when they could have done so easily. Although we should feel uneasy about the actions of all three of these individuals, intuitively we condemn them to different degrees. We might think that allowing harm to happen can be very bad, but it isn't as bad as enabling that harm. Similarly, we might think that enabling harm can be very bad, but it isn't as bad as directly causing that harm.

Some philosophers reject these claims outright, maintaining that it's no worse to do harm than to enable it, and that it's no worse to enable harm than to allow it.[22] Though we've some sympathy for this move, we set it aside to make two narrower points. First, we can appeal to the distinction between allowing, enabling, and doing to condemn only those acts that are performed in relation to something bad. While we may condemn an individual for contributing to harm, we wouldn't condemn an individual on the grounds that they contributed to something fun, whether they allowed it, enabled it, or directly caused it to occur. This point is important since it reveals that, if the distinction between allowing, enabling, and doing is to bear on practices such as physician-assisted suicide and voluntary active euthanasia, then it must be that the acts involved are bad in some way. However, this is the very claim that our earlier arguments rebut.

Second, we must pay special attention to the context in which physician-assisted suicide and voluntary active euthanasia occur. Outside of the medical context, allowing something to occur might be akin to 'letting nature run its course', as opposed to intervening to alter this trajectory. But medical professionals are employed with a specific mandate, namely not to let nature run its course. This alters the moral significance of the distinction between doing, enabling, and allowing. As Dworkin et al. put it:

> it is certainly not permissible for a doctor to kill one patient in order to use his organs to save another . . . it would be equally impermissible for a doctor to let an injured patient bleed to death, or refuse antibiotics to a patient with pneumonia—in each case the doctor would have allowed death to result from a 'natural' process—in order to make his organs available for transplant to others.[23]

---

[21] Fiona Woollard, 'Doing vs. Allowing Harm', *Stanford Encyclopedia of Philosophy* (2016), available at https://plato.stanford.edu/entries/doing-allowing.

[22] For discussion, see Shelly Kagan, *The Limits of Morality* (Oxford: Clarendon Press, 1989).

[23] Dworkin et al., 'Assisted Suicide'. For further discussion, see Judith Jarvis Thomson, 'Physician-Assisted Suicide: Two Moral Arguments', *Ethics*, 109 (1999), 497–518.

Even if there's some moral difference between these two acts, it's hard to believe that the difference could be sufficiently large to justify treating them very differently in the eyes of the law—say, by criminalizing one but legalizing the other.

We reach a similar verdict when an individual wishes to end their life. For example, let's suppose that an individual who's terminally ill wants to die and so, at their request, we cease to administer medication that's keeping them alive. This kind of voluntary passive euthanasia is widely accepted. But now, let's consider two variations in which the individual needs medication to hasten their death. In the first, they can self-administer the medication. In the second, they need a doctor to do so. It seems hard to believe that there's a serious moral difference between these three cases. What really matters is whether the patient wishes to die, as well as whether the stability qualification is satisfied.[24] On this basis, we contend that, if the state should legalize voluntary passive euthanasia, as is surely the case, then the state should also legalize physician-assisted suicide and voluntary active euthanasia.

2.5 THE SLIPPERY SLOPE

We now shift our attention to a different objection. One version of this objection utilizes the alleged fact that legalizing physician-assisted suicide and voluntary active euthanasia will endanger the lives of those who're already vulnerable. More specifically, an individual with deteriorating health may feel pressured—and, indeed, may *be* pressured—to end their life to relieve their family of financial and emotional burdens where they wouldn't have done so otherwise.[25] These issues are important, but we set them aside. We do this to concentrate on a more pressing version of the objection, which claims that, if the state legalizes these practices, then a likely consequence is that we'll see a rise in *non-voluntary euthanasia* and *involuntary euthanasia*. Non-voluntary euthanasia is where a patient neither gives nor withholds their consent because they're unable to do so, typically because they're in a coma. Involuntary euthanasia is where a doctor either overrules the patient's consent or fails to consult the patient's preferences. To oppose legalizing physician-assisted suicide and voluntary active euthanasia on these grounds is to endorse the *slippery slope objection*.[26]

It bears noting that an advocate of a slippery slope argument aims to identify a countervailing consideration, rather than to deny that their opponent has any point at all. In our case, a critic who offers this objection needn't contend that there are no good reasons to legalize physician-assisted suicide and voluntary active euthanasia. They maintain that, if there are such reasons, these are defeated by concerns relating to non-voluntary and involuntary euthanasia. In order to establish this, they must

---

[24] Dworkin et al., 'Assisted Suicide' and Glover, *Causing Death and Saving Lives*, 185.

[25] Margaret Battin, 'Voluntary Euthanasia and the Risks of Abuse: Can We Learn Anything from the Netherlands?', *Law, Medicine and Health Care*, 20 (1992), 133–43.

[26] For discussion of an array of slippery slope objections, see James Rachels, *The End of Life: Euthanasia and Morality* (Oxford: Oxford University Press, 1986), 172–3.

demonstrate both the *plausibility* of the claim that we're on a slippery slope and that the countervailing consideration is sufficiently *important* to defeat any other reasons we have.

To evaluate the slippery slope objection, we first examine the empirical evidence. Currently physician-assisted suicide and voluntary active euthanasia are legal in the Netherlands under an act passed in 2001, but such practices have been ongoing since 1984, when the Dutch Supreme Court ruled that a doctor wouldn't be prosecuted so long as they followed strict guidelines. Opponents of this decision contend that it led to abuse.[27] A basis for this objection is a study known as the Remmelink Report, which indicated that approximately 1,000 deaths per year occurred 'without the explicit and persistent request' of the patient. Though the report isn't clear about this, it's very likely that nearly all of these deaths were cases of non-voluntary euthanasia rather than involuntary euthanasia. Even so, this is a troubling result, which might be thought to provide some support for the slippery slope objection.

On this basis, we can state the objection as follows:

Slippery slope moral claim: The state should minimize non-voluntary euthanasia and involuntary euthanasia.

Slippery slope empirical claim: Legalizing physician-assisted suicide and voluntary active euthanasia increases the likelihood of non-voluntary euthanasia and involuntary euthanasia.

Conclusion: The state shouldn't legalize physician-assisted suicide or voluntary active euthanasia.

This argument fails for two reasons. First, the evidence we've cited doesn't support the slippery slope empirical claim.[28] To defend this claim, we'd need to compare end-of-life statistics in the Netherlands with those from another state where the only relevant difference is that doctors practising physician-assisted suicide and voluntary active euthanasia are threatened with prosecution.[29] We're unaware of any study that provides such analysis.

Moreover, the findings of a number of later studies cast further doubt on the slippery slope empirical claim. For example, one report from the Netherlands reveals that, between 1995 and 2010, there was a consistent decline in both the number and proportion of estimated deaths without the explicit and persistent request of the patient.[30] Again, this data doesn't establish any causal link between the design of policy and the number of deaths. However, at least in the absence of more robust evidence to the

[27] John Keown, 'Euthanasia in the Netherlands: Sliding Down the Slippery Slope?', *Notre Dame Journal of Law, Ethics & Public Policy*, 9 (1995), 407–48 at 437–47.

[28] Penney Lewis, 'The Empirical Slippery Slope from Voluntary to Non-Voluntary Euthanasia', *Journal of Law, Medicine, and Ethics*, 35 (2007), 197–210.

[29] Peter Singer, 'Making Our Own Decisions about Death', *Free Inquiry*, 25 (2005), 36–8.

[30] Bregje Onwuteaka-Philipsen et al., 'Trends in End-of-Life Practices Before and After the Enactment of the Euthanasia Law in the Netherlands from 1990 to 2010: A Repeated Cross-Sectional Survey', *The Lancet*, 380 (2012), 908–15.

contrary, it does suggest that we can dispel fears that legalizing physician-assisted suicide and voluntary active euthanasia leads us down a slippery slope.

Second, there's a mismatch between the slippery slope objection's moral claim and
its conclusion. To repeat an earlier point, an advocate of a slippery slope objection
must show not only that a course of action leads to a bad outcome, but also that this
bad outcome makes the course of action worse than the alternative. In our case, to
establish the conclusion that the slippery slope warrants opposing physician-assisted
suicide and voluntary active euthanasia, the moral claim must be that minimizing
non-voluntary euthanasia and involuntary euthanasia should take precedence over
granting individuals freedoms to determine when and how to end their lives. Given
the importance of this freedom to an individual, especially when they're suffering
unbearably, we think that proponents of this objection must say more to defend
this claim.

2.6 CONCLUSIONS

Our arguments imply that, subject to the stability qualification, the state should legalize
physician-assisted suicide and voluntary active euthanasia on the grounds that doing
so gives an individual freedoms to choose when and how they die. We've also demonstrated that we can defend this stance against those who claim that legalizing such
practices is an affront to the sanctity of life.

There are different models of legalization.[31] For example, in European states where
physician-assisted suicide or voluntary active euthanasia are available, it's common to
demand that an individual has a terminal illness or that they're experiencing unbear-
able suffering with no prospect of improvement. By contrast, where physician-assisted
suicide is legal in the United States, it's normally available to only those who have
a terminal illness with less than six months to live. Our comments on the stability
requirement may provide a starting point for thinking about this issue. There are also
different monitoring systems. While in Europe, an independent commission must
verify compliance with the relevant laws, this isn't the case in the United States. It's
possible that the case for an independent monitoring system stems from worries that
motivate the slippery slope objection, and our analysis of this topic might inform the
design of policy in this regard. Nothing we've said in this chapter can settle which
of these models is more appropriate, but our discussion identifies some of the most
important considerations to which we must be attentive when deliberating about this
matter and, more generally, the legal status of physician-assisted suicide and voluntary
active euthanasia.

---

[31] Samantha Halliday, 'Comparative Reflections upon the Assisted Dying Bill 2013: A Plea for a More
European Approach', *Medical Law International*, 13 (2013), 135–67.

FURTHER READING

Two excellent overviews of the debate around legalizing physician-assisted suicide and voluntary active euthanasia are Katherine Smits, *Applying Political Theory: Issues and Debates* (Basingstoke: Palgrave, 2009), ch. 7 and Robert Young, 'Voluntary Euthanasia', *Stanford Encyclopedia of Philosophy* (2019), available at http://plato.stanford.edu/entries/euthanasia-voluntary.

For an influential text in favour of legalizing these practices, a good starting point is Ronald Dworkin et al., 'Assisted Suicide: The Philosophers' Brief', *New York Review of Books*, 44 (1997), 41–7. For opposing views, a good entry point is J. David Velleman, 'Against the Right to Die' in Hugh LaFollette (ed.), *Ethics in Practice: An Anthology, Fourth Edition* (Oxford: Wiley Blackwell, 2014), 92–100. For a more detailed treatment of the termination objection, we suggest J. David Velleman, 'A Right of Self-Termination?', *Ethics*, 109 (1999), 606–28. And, for detailed treatment of the slippery slope objection, see John Keown, 'Euthanasia in the Netherlands: Sliding Down the Slippery Slope?' in John Keown (ed.), *Euthanasia Examined: Ethical, Clinical, and Legal Perspectives* (Cambridge: Cambridge University Press, 1995), 261–96.

For rigorous engagement with these objections, excellent reads are Judith Jarvis Thomson, 'Physician-Assisted Suicide: Two Moral Arguments', *Ethics*, 109 (1999), 497–518; Frances Kamm, 'Physician-Assisted Suicide, the Doctrine of Double Effect, and the Ground of Value', *Ethics*, 109 (1999), 586–605; and Penney Lewis, 'The Empirical Slippery Slope from Voluntary to Non-Voluntary Euthanasia', *Journal of Law, Medicine, and Ethics*, 35 (2007), 197–210.

 For additional material and resources, including web links and self-test questions, please visit the online resources **www.oup.com/he/walton1e**.

3

HATE SPEECH AND FREEDOM OF EXPRESSION

SUMMARY

- In this chapter, we consider when, if ever, a state should restrict hate speech.
- We show that political disputes about this topic are part of broader disagreements about the limits of freedom of expression.
- We make a case for restricting hate speech when, and on the grounds that, it incites or makes more likely harm to particular members of society.
- We consider whether some familiar justifications for freedom of expression provide a persuasive case against our view, exploring arguments that appeal to autonomy, individual interests in expression, and the dangers of granting the state regulatory power. We contend that none of these justifications supports the protection of hate speech.
- We examine an argument that the state should restrict hate speech when, and on the grounds that, it causes offence, and that this justifies more extensive regulation than we propose. We respond by demonstrating several flaws in this argument.
- We express greater sympathy for the view that the state should restrict hate speech when, and on the grounds that, it threatens individuals' dignity, but maintain that this doesn't give us reason to extend regulation much beyond what we already propose.
- We conclude by sketching the kinds of hate speech legislation that our arguments support.

3.1 INTRODUCTION

In 2013, the Canadian Supreme Court ruled on a case in which Bill Whatcott distributed flyers associating individuals who're gay with various diseases and with paedophilia.[1] In 2006, the Danish judiciary reviewed a newspaper's publication of a cartoon depicting the Muslim Prophet Mohammad with a bomb concealed in his turban.[2] In 2016, police in Huntington, Cambridgeshire investigated flyers that were posted through letterboxes

---

[1] Richard Madan, 'Anti-Gay Flyers Violated Hate Law, Supreme Court Rules', *CTV News*, 27 February 2013, available at https://www.ctvnews.ca/canada/anti-gay-flyers-violated-hate-law-supreme-court-rules-1.1173807.

[2] Nicholas Watt, 'Danish Paper Sorry for Muhammad Cartoons', *The Guardian*, 31 January 2006, available at https://www.theguardian.com/media/2006/jan/31/religion.saudiarabia.

reading 'Leave the EU, no more Polish vermin'.[3] And, in 2017, the United States' laws on free expression were questioned when, at a Unite the Right rally in Charlottesville, protesters chanted anti-Semitic and anti-Muslim slogans and waved Nazi symbols.[4] These cases raise the question: when, if ever, should the state restrict hate speech?

Many states have laws to this effect. In the United Kingdom, the Public Order Act 1986 prohibits speech, writing, signs, and other visible representation that's 'threatening, abusive or insulting' or that's designed to stir up 'hatred against a group of persons . . . defined by reference to colour, race, nationality . . . or ethnic or national origins'.[5] Further legislation applies to acts that express hatred on grounds of sexual orientation or religion.[6] Similar laws exist in many other parts of the world, including Canada, India, New Zealand, South Africa, and across the European Union.[7]

But the legal regulation of hate speech isn't universally endorsed. This is because some believe that these laws violate individuals' *freedom of expression*. There's almost no legislation of this kind in the United States, where the constitution's First Amendment protects very generous entitlements to freedom of expression. Moreover, even those who believe that hate speech calls for some regulation disagree about its details. For example, in 2012, critics launched a campaign to alter the details of the Public Order Act, arguing that the law 'should not be used to protect us from having our feelings hurt' and that we should 'accept that the risk of insult is a fair price to pay for living in a society which values free speech'.[8] The campaign was successful and, as a result, the Public Order Act was amended so that it's no longer a crime to act insultingly.[9]

In this chapter, we explore these disagreements by developing a defence of hate speech regulation. In section 3.2, we construct a framework for thinking about these issues. In section 3.3, we make a case for restricting hate speech when, and on the grounds that, it incites or increases the likelihood of harm to certain groups in society. Then, we defend this case against challenges from two directions. In section 3.4, we consider arguments against restricting hate speech. These arguments appeal to familiar ideas about the value of free expression, namely that it serves the interests of speakers, audiences, and thinkers, and that there's danger in granting states the power to restrict it. In section 3.5, we consider objections from the opposite direction, which, if correct, might justify more extensive regulation. We consider whether the state should restrict hate speech when, and on the grounds that, it causes offence or threatens individuals' dignity. We argue that none of these challenges gives us reason to alter our

---

[3] Kate Lyons, 'Racist Incidents Feared to Be Linked to Brexit Result', *The Guardian*, 26 June 2016, available at https://www.theguardian.com/politics/2016/jun/26/racist-incidents-feared-to-be-linked-to-brexit-result-reported-in-england-and-wales.

[4] Joel Gunter, 'A Reckoning in Charlottesville', *BBC News*, 13 August 2017, available at https://www.bbc.co.uk/news/world-us-canada-40914748.

[5] *Public Order Act 1986 (c64).* [6] *Racial and Religious Hatred Act 2006 (c1).*

[7] For a summary, see Katherine Smits, *Applying Political Theory: Issues and Debates* (London: Palgrave, 2009), ch. 8. [8] Reform Section 5, 'Victory', available at http://reformsection5.org.uk.

[9] *Crime and Courts Act 2013 (c22).*

claims about hate speech regulation to any great extent. In section 3.6, we explore the implications of our discussion for the design of hate speech policy.

3.2 THE TERRAIN OF EXPRESSION

We begin by issuing four clarifications that are central to understanding disputes about hate speech. First, we employ a broad understanding of expression that includes any public 'act that is intended by its agent to communicate to one or more persons some proposition or attitude'.[10] This includes all forms of verbal communication. But it also extends beyond this, so as to include printed or visual media, artwork, music, social media, and so forth. Our focus on 'public' expression means that we can set aside more complex cases involving private acts of communication, such as a conversation within one's own home.

Second, an expression is hateful if and only if it satisfies three conditions: (i) the act must single out an individual or group of individuals on the basis of some socially salient characteristic, such as their race or religion; (ii) it must ascribe to this individual or group of individuals some repugnant quality, such as them being criminal or diseased, or, more generally, it must treat them as an object of contempt; and (iii) it must cast its target as an unwelcome presence and an appropriate object of hostility.[11] Though each of these conditions is subject to a range of interpretations, this account of what it means for expression to be hateful suffices for our purposes, not least because it's broadly in line with how laws often treat this matter.

Third, we can measure the extent to which expression is free by considering what *obstacles*, if any, stand in the way of an individual saying, writing, or otherwise communicating something. We elaborate this understanding of freedom in Chapter 2. For example, in the present context, we might wonder whether someone is unfree to express their views if no broadcaster is willing to grant them airtime.[12] In this chapter, we restrict our attention to those obstacles that the state can place directly in front of an individual to limit their expression. One way for the state to do this is by making certain forms of expression illegal. But there are also more subtle tools at its disposal. For example, a state might cordon off protest marches, require them to take a particular route, or demand that they're authorized in advance. All of these actions limit an individual's freedom of expression by placing obstacles in front of them. Crucially, this doesn't settle the matter of whether states *should* act in these ways. All we mean to establish is that the extent to which expression is free is a matter of the obstacles that stand in someone's way.

---

[10] Thomas Scanlon, 'A Theory of Freedom of Expression', *Philosophy & Public Affairs*, 1 (1972), 204–26 at 206.

[11] Bhikhu Parekh, 'Hate Speech: Is There a Case for Banning?', *Public Policy Research*, 12 (2006), 213–23 at 214.

[12] Joshua Cohen, 'Freedom of Expression', *Philosophy & Public Affairs*, 22 (1993), 207–63 at 215–17.

Finally, we can distinguish two ways in which a state might restrict free expression: through content-based policies or through means-based policies.[13] Content-based policies aim to restrict expression based on its viewpoint or subject matter. This includes measures designed to restrict the expression of particular political outlooks or the discussion of particular topics, for example. By contrast, means-based policies aim to restrict particular methods or avenues of expression. This includes measures intended to limit the times or days on which a protest can take place. As we hope is clear from the examples with which we began this chapter, our concern here is with content-based policies.

Drawing these strings together, we can restate our central question as follows: should the state place obstacles in front of an individual that limit their ability to communicate publicly ideas that single out individuals on the basis of some socially salient characteristic, labelling them with some repugnant quality or as an object of contempt, and an unwelcome presence that's an appropriate target for hostility? We begin to answer this question by developing a case in favour of the state taking such action.

3.3 THE HARM OF HATE SPEECH

Many restrictions on expression are uncontroversial. For example, there's little objection to preventing an individual from distributing pornographic images of children. Likewise, it's widely seen as justifiable to restrict expression when this is necessary to prevent physical harm. John Stuart Mill is one of the most ardent defenders of freedom of expression, but even he recognizes this limit, famously concluding that we ought not to allow someone to proclaim that corn dealers are starvers of the poor in front of an angry mob gathered near the corn dealer's house.[14] In this section, we develop an argument for restricting hate speech that proceeds from such concerns.

3.3.1 THE THREAT OF HARM

As Mill notes, one problem with making accusations about corn dealers in front of an angry mob is that this act of expression constitutes 'a positive instigation to some mischievous act'.[15] The issue is that this speech threatens harm. In this case, we've an example of *incitement*, in which an individual encourages others to commit a crime.[16] To clarify this point, let's consider the following case:

Incitement: Simeon provokes Wilson who, as a result, attacks Temi.

It's true that Simeon doesn't lay a finger on Temi. But Simeon's act remains seriously morally wrong because of the causal role it plays in the harm that Temi suffers.

---

[13] Cohen, 'Freedom of Expression', 213.

[14] John Stuart Mill, 'On Liberty' in John Gray (ed.), *John Stuart Mill: On Liberty and Other Essays* (Oxford: Oxford University Press, 1991 [1859]), 62.

[15] Mill, 'On Liberty', 62.   [16] Scanlon, 'A Theory of Freedom of Expression', 210–11.

Even states with permissive laws on freedom of expression prohibit speech of this kind. For example, the United States' Supreme Court has ruled on several occasions that incitement isn't permitted even under the First Amendment. The reason such acts of expression are so widely condemned is that they have a foreseeable negative impact on the victims who're at risk of harm as a result. We call this the *harm condition*, and it's significant for our purposes since this is the main way in which incitement is morally bad.

This gives us an initial basis on which to defend restrictions on hate speech, such that when hate speech incites, we've a strong reason for restricting it. However, this justification isn't unique to hate speech. Indeed, there's a sense in which the classification of expression as hateful needn't even enter discussion here. Our concern with incitement supplies us with a reason to restrict *any* expression that precipitates harm, whether or not it targets members of a socially salient group with contempt and hostility.

It's plausible that expressions of hate involve incitement of a particularly egregious kind such that we should attach harsher punishment to those who violate relevant laws.[17] But we can also construct a more specific case for restricting hate speech by building on the harm condition in another way.

3.3.2 THE CLIMATE OF HATE

In *Incitement*, Simeon's actions play a direct causal role in the harm that Temi suffers. But it's also possible for conduct to play a similar causal role in a more diffuse way. Let's consider a revised version of the case:

> *Incitement 2*: Wigbert spreads the message that Islam is an extremist religion and that it's vital to extinguish its threat from our society. Upon hearing these messages, Quail comes to believe that it's appropriate to harass Muslims, and she sets fire to Aisha's house.

In this case, the link between Wigbert's speech and the harm experienced by Aisha is more indirect than in the initial example of incitement. Nonetheless, a clear link remains and, because of this, acts such as these also meet the harm condition.

The broader relevance of this point turns on the fact that hate speech tends to increase the likelihood of harm being inflicted on members of socially salient groups.[18] When an individual spreads a message that associates members of these groups with repugnant qualities—that they're criminals, diseased, or bestial, for example—and that they're unwelcome and an appropriate target of hostility, the likelihood that they will be wronged by others increases. If a member of a socially salient

---

[17] Christopher Heath Wellman, 'A Defence of Stiffer Penalties for Hate Crimes', *Hypatia*, 21 (2006), 62–80.

[18] Parekh, 'Hate Speech', 217–19 and Alexander Brown, 'The Racial and Religious Hatred Act 2006: A Millian Response', *Critical Review of International Social and Political Philosophy*, 11 (2008), 1–24 at 13–15.

group is, because of this affiliation, seen by others as a criminal, they may treat them with a greater-than-average degree of suspicion in their daily lives, they may be more inclined to treat them violently or to damage their property, or they may discriminate against them in the labour market or in housing selection.

In some cases, the regular and persistent spread of hate speech may create a 'climate of hate'—that is, a social environment in which a member of some group experiences the loathing and animosity of others, who perceive themselves to be morally superior to them and who fail to show appropriate concern for their fate. Again, this might increase the danger to their person and property and the likelihood of discrimination, and give rise to the possibility of social segregation, in which members of some groups are socially cut off from the rest of society. In the worst cases, those exposed to hate speech use their vote to support unjust policies that marginalize or exclude members of various socially salient groups and, in doing so, call on the power of the state to enforce this climate of hate on its victims.

Based on these considerations, we can formulate the following argument:

Harm moral claim: The state should place obstacles in front of conduct that causally contributes to others suffering harm.

Harm empirical claim: Hate speech causally contributes to others suffering harm.

Conclusion: The state should restrict hate speech.

We call this the *harm argument* for restricting hate speech.[19]

Although critics oppose this argument for a variety of reasons, it's notable that few do so by disputing its claims. The harm moral claim is powerfully intuitive, and it's almost universally supported across a wide range of views regarding the purposes and limits of the exercise of political power.

The harm empirical claim is difficult to prove beyond doubt, because it's hard to isolate the specific causal role of hate speech in diffuse harms. But there are several reasons to think the claim is plausible. Most immediately, there's evidence suggesting that exposure to hate speech increases our susceptibility to the effects of implicit biases.[20] As we explain in Chapter 5, such biases have an important bearing on the likelihood of discrimination, and several other harms perpetrated against members of socially salient groups. Additionally, in the few studies that isolate the role of hate speech in causing violence, the evidence strongly supports the harm empirical claim.[21]

---

[19] It's worth recording that others make a similar argument in support of prohibiting certain forms of pornography, particularly those that place women in a degrading or abused role, on the grounds that pornography of this kind increases the risk of violence against women. See Andrea Dworkin, *Pornography: Men Possessing Women* (London: Women's Press, 1981) and Catherine A. MacKinnon, *Only Words* (Cambridge, MA: Harvard University Press, 1996).

[20] Andres Moles, 'Expressive Interest and the Integrity of Hate Speakers', *Politics in Central Europe*, 6 (2010), 18–38 at 22–4.

[21] For example, see David Yanagizawa-Drott, 'Propaganda and Conflict: Evidence from the Rwandan Genocide', *The Quarterly Journal of Economics*, 129 (2014), 1947–94.

Bringing these claims together sets forth our case for restricting hate speech. For the reasons we've given, we believe that the claims of this argument are plausible and that its case for restricting hate speech is forceful. Though critics tend to accept the various components of this argument, what they often contest is whether these claims support the conclusion we defend. This pressure is applied to the harm argument in both directions. Some argue that, even though hate speech is harmful, freedom of expression is sufficiently valuable that the state must protect it nonetheless. By contrast, others argue that there are further reasons to restrict hate speech, and that we can justify even more extensive regulations on expression than we propose. In sections 3.4 and 3.5, we consider these possibilities.

3.4 ARGUMENTS FOR FREEDOM OF EXPRESSION

Those opposed to restricting hate speech tend to advance two distinct lines of reasoning in response to the harm argument. First, they claim that the value of freedom of expression is such that the harms of hate speech are a price we must pay to respect individuals' fundamental interests in free speech. One way to motivate this argument is to appeal to individuals' interest in autonomy. An alternative way is to appeal to a broader array of interests we have in writing, vocalizing, or otherwise communicating our views to an audience and in hearing, reading, or witnessing others' acts of expression. Second, critics might claim that, even if it wouldn't violate such interests and so the case against hate speech has some appeal, it's a problem to give states these regulatory powers. We consider these arguments in turn.

3.4.1 AUTONOMY

Roughly speaking, an individual enjoys autonomy if and only if they're the author of their own life. We elaborate on this idea in Chapters 2 and 4. For present purposes, it suffices to draw attention to one component of autonomy, namely the moral importance of an individual being 'sovereign in deciding what to believe and in weighing competing reasons for action'.[22] According to Thomas Scanlon, this interest generates a strong presumption against placing obstacles in the way of certain kinds of expression.[23] This is because such obstacles shape and limit the flow of information on which an individual can make judgements about what to believe and how to act.

This makes a particularly powerful case in favour of freedom of expression because it has appeal even if an environment without such obstacles isn't conducive to developing *true* beliefs. An individual who sees themselves as sovereign can't reasonably complain if, in this environment, their beliefs are false, because nobody has interfered

---

[22] Scanlon, 'A Theory of Freedom of Expression', 215.
[23] Scanlon, 'A Theory of Freedom of Expression', esp. 206–22.

with the flow of information they receive. In this case, they must see it as their own responsibility to form beliefs based on the evidence that's freely available to them. Accordingly, we might expect that the interest in autonomy provides a good reason not to restrict hate speech. It's an individual's responsibility to make judgements about the merits of the views to which they're exposed and about the acceptability of acting in ways that are harmful to others. Even if hate speech plays a role in precipitating harm, an individual's interest in being sovereign in deciding what to believe and how to act must take precedence.

It's important to specify precisely how this thesis might be thought to challenge the harm argument. One thing to notice is that it doesn't dispute the harm moral claim— that is, the claim that the state should place obstacles in front of individuals undertaking actions that will causally contribute to others suffering harm. Instead, what it does is qualify this claim in a certain way. We can clarify this as follows:

> *Autonomy-qualified harm moral claim*: The state should place obstacles in front of conduct that causally contributes to others suffering harm, unless this would violate the interest an individual has in being sovereign in deciding what to believe and how to act.
>
> *Autonomy empirical claim*: Restricting hate speech violates an individual's interest in being sovereign in deciding what to believe and how to act.
>
> *Conclusion*: The state shouldn't restrict hate speech.

One problem with this argument is that it's unclear why we should accept the autonomy-qualified harm moral claim. While it's true that an individual has an interest in autonomy, they also have an interest in not suffering harm. This latter interest is particularly significant in cases where hate speech threatens personal safety or makes someone vulnerable to discrimination. It's certainly not obvious that an individual's interest in autonomy defeats their interest in avoiding these harms.[24] Thus, we might reasonably conclude that there's no compelling reason to qualify the harm moral claim to only those forms of expression that don't violate autonomy.

Furthermore, we believe that there's reason to doubt the autonomy empirical claim. As detailed above, hate speech has the effect of enhancing individuals' implicit biases. It has this effect partly when and because it tends to bypass their cognitive capacities, contaminating their beliefs without rational reflection. In this respect, we might think that some hate speech sets back (rather than furthers) an individual's sovereignty over what they believe, since it may not engage their rational capacities. If so, then restricting hate speech might offer a mechanism through which to protect autonomy in the light of the threats to rational reflection that hate speech poses.

---

[24] Susan Brison, 'The Autonomy Defence of Free Speech', *Ethics*, 108 (1998), 312–39 at 328–9 and Caleb Yong, 'Does Freedom of Speech Include Hate Speech?', *Res Publica*, 17 (2011), 385–403 at 400.

3.4.2 SPEAKERS, AUDIENCES, AND THINKERS

The argument in section 3.4.1 appeals to a specific interest in having access to others' expression. A related but distinct defence of freedom of expression refers to a much wider array of interests. These fall into three categories.

First, *speakers* have interests in voicing their views.[25] Among other things, an individual has an interest in expressing their ethical and political convictions using a range of media, including speeches, writings, and public displays, such as protest marches and campaigns, as well as in producing art in the many forms it can take. Those who engage in these acts often do so to articulate views or feelings about what they take to be significant aspects of human interest. They may do this for a range of reasons: because they wish to bear witness or give testimony by sharing what they feel is an important experience of their own; because they feel an obligation to speak for or promote a just cause; or simply because they wish to declare their position to the public. What unites this list is that all of these activities involve an individual pursuing their 'expressive interests'—that is, their interest 'in being able to call something to the attention of a wide audience'.[26]

Second, *audiences* have interests in hearing the views of others.[27] Specifically, an individual has an interest in being amused, seeing aesthetically pleasing spectacles, being informed about religious and political matters, knowing the variety of products that we can purchase, and so on. It's easy to see how freedom of expression can serve these interests. From art to journalism to advertising, others' verbal and visual expressions are a significant medium through which an individual can develop and fulfil their comedic, aesthetic, religious, political, and consumer interests.

Third, both speakers and audiences have interests as *thinkers*.[28] The core idea here is that expression is a means of conveying to others one's mental contents. Because of this, it's a crucial tool for understanding a speaker's thoughts and ideas. Free expression is therefore vital if an individual is to develop a clear understanding of others' outlooks, which in turn is pivotal if they're to form valuable relationships with others. In other words, we might think that freedom of expression enables individuals to communicate honestly about matters of moral significance and to cooperate in ways that do justice to these concerns.

We recognize that a concern for each of these interests provides some reason not to place obstacles in front of free expression and, because of this, each puts pressure on the harm argument for restricting hate speech. Some advocates of these ideas maintain that the state must even protect speech that labels members of various socially salient groups as objects of contempt and appropriate targets of hostility. This is because even

---

[25] Cohen, 'Freedom of Expression', 224–8 and Thomas Scanlon, 'Freedom of Expression and Categories of Expression', *University of Pittsburgh Law Review*, 40 (1978), 519–50 at 521–3.

[26] Scanlon, 'Freedom of Expression and Categories of Expression', 521.

[27] Scanlon, 'Freedom of Expression and Categories of Expression', 524.

[28] Seana Shiffrin, *Speech Matters: On Lying, Morality, and the Law* (Princeton, NJ: Princeton University Press, 2014), ch. 3.

these acts of expression can serve speaker, audience, and thinker interests in the discussion of religious and political matters.[29] For example, in the case of the Danish cartoons, it might be that the authors intended to offer sincere commentary on the relationship between certain features of Islam and the violent conduct of some members of that religion. It might also be that audiences have some interest in considering the possibility of such a relationship.

However, we doubt that the concerns that motivate this response to the harm argument justify allowing a very wide range of hateful expression. This is because a great deal of hate speech does little or nothing to advance the interests of speakers, audiences, or thinkers.[30] For example, it's difficult to see what value is served by allowing acts of expression that imply that there's a close link between being gay and paedophilia, or between a particular nationality and rodents. For this reason, and at least with respect to more extreme forms of hate speech, we think that the harm argument survives in the face of a concern with the interests of speakers, audiences, and thinkers.

The general lesson of this analysis is that we've little reason, if any, to protect expression that's of *low value*. The significance of this should already be familiar from a range of other cases in which free speech isn't protected. For example, we've strong reasons to allow advertising given that it helps speakers to publicize their products and enables audiences to become informed about the various options available to them. However, with a concern for these interests in mind, it's clear that we should restrict *false* advertising. This is because this practice sets back (rather than serves) the interests of consumers. Similarly, we can reformulate the harm argument for restricting hate speech with the qualification that the state might be under a duty to protect even harmful expression if it serves speaker, audience, and thinker interests. But since hate speech tends not to serve these interests to any meaningful degree, this qualification rarely comes into effect, and so the conclusion of the harm argument is largely untouched.

3.4.3 PROBLEMS WITH STATE REGULATION

A final defence of freedom of expression focuses on the dangers of granting states the power to restrict it. To elaborate this worry, we begin with one of the most famous defences of free speech, developed by Mill.[31] Mill claims that an environment of free expression ensures that true (or partially true) views are heard, and that we consider the variety of reasons that count in favour of and against different positions. One way to understand this argument aligns with Scanlon's claim that free speech serves an interest in sovereignty over what to believe. As we've already discussed this possibility, we set it aside in order to focus on an alternative interpretation of the argument. This holds that, even if individuals' autonomy and their interests as speakers, audiences, and thinkers aren't served well by an environment of free speech, we should expect things to be even worse when states enjoy the power to restrict expression.

---

[29] Cohen, 'Freedom of Expression', 236–7.
[30] Yong, 'Does Freedom of Speech Include Hate Speech?', 394–8.   [31] Mill, 'On Liberty', ch. 2.

Three considerations support this worry.[32] First, even well-intentioned state officials are *fallible*, meaning that they may make honest mistakes about what kinds of regulations on expression best serve the interests we've identified. Thus, even if it's morally justifiable to restrict hate speech in theory, perhaps in practice it's better not to have policies of this kind.

Second, there's a danger of *regulatory chill*. This term refers to the phenomenon whereby certain restrictions on expression cause individuals to be less expressive in domains that aren't covered by the restrictions. This might result from the fact that legal regulation (or other forms of restriction) can be vague and imprecise, such that an individual may be unsure whether or not some public act of communication falls foul of the law. Preferring to play safe, individuals might respond to this by self-censoring to a level that exceeds the intentions of policymakers. Because of this, otherwise reasonable restrictions on expression might predictably dampen our social environment in ways that seriously damage the interests of speakers, audiences, and thinkers.

Third, hate speech regulation brings the possibility of *abuse of power*. This occurs when states enjoy the legal authority to extend restrictions on expression beyond what's morally justifiable. Abuse of power is especially problematic when the state can repress political criticism or stifle disagreement. Again, this will likely jeopardize the interests of speakers, audiences, and thinkers.

These considerations suggest the following *freedom of expression objection* to restricting hate speech:

> *Freedom of expression moral claim*: The state should protect an individual's interests in being sovereign in deciding what to believe, as well as individuals' interests as speakers, audiences, and thinkers.
>
> *Practicality empirical claim*: Given the dangers of fallibility, regulatory chill, and abuse of power, an individual's interests are better served if the state doesn't place obstacles in front of expression.
>
> *Conclusion*: The state shouldn't restrict hate speech.

It's possible to raise doubts about the practicality empirical claim. For our purposes, it's sufficient to emphasize that, for this argument to challenge the case for restricting hate speech, we must refine its claims. This is because advocates of the harm argument don't seek to obstruct expression in general. To supply an objection to this argument, we must specify the empirical claim in the following way:

> *Hate speech practicality empirical claim*: Given the dangers of fallibility, regulatory chill, and abuse of power, an individual's interests are better served if the state doesn't place obstacles in front of *hate* speech.

We doubt that this claim is plausible. One reason for this tracks a point we made earlier, namely that hateful expression can enhance individuals' implicit biases, contaminating

---

[32] Cohen, 'Freedom of Expression', 232–4.

their beliefs without rational reflection. When exposed to hate speech, we're therefore more likely to form false beliefs about a wide variety of social and cultural facts.[33] A second reason to doubt this claim draws on the possibility that we can specify legislation in a way that's sufficiently precise, such that, while it restricts expression, the dangers of fallibility, regulatory chill, and abuse of power aren't serious ones. One reason to think this is possible is that many of the states we listed in section 3.1 have hate speech regulations that are roughly in line with those supported by the harm argument. As far as we can tell, there's little reason to think that, in virtue of this, these states furnish legal environments less amenable to individuals' interests in expression than states that lack these regulations, such as the United States. Devising regulation sufficiently precise to limit the dangers we've described is undoubtedly a tricky task and one that warrants careful oversight, but the existence of hate speech legislation that manages this gives us confidence to doubt the hate speech practicality empirical claim.

3.5 FURTHER ARGUMENTS FOR RESTRICTIONS

Having responded to those who oppose restricting freedom of expression, we now turn our attention to whether there are *additional* grounds on which to restrict hate speech and, if so, whether these can justify even more extensive regulations than we propose. We focus on two possibilities: that the state should restrict hate speech when and because it causes offence; and that the state should restrict hate speech when and because it tarnishes the public reputation of those it targets.

3.5.1 OFFENSIVE SPEECH

Offensive speech is expression that's shocking to one's ethical or moral sensibilities. Many forms of hate speech have effects of this kind. For example, let's take the case in which a Danish newspaper published a cartoon depicting the Muslim Prophet Mohammad with a bomb concealed in his turban. This caused widespread outrage, as many Muslims (as well as others) were deeply upset by this association of Islam with terrorism.

Offence is experienced as something that's bad for an individual. It's true that the negative effects of offensive speech on an individual's feelings are generally much less morally serious than the negative effects of the threat of harm to their physical safety. But, arguably, the underlying moral worry has a similar character, namely that acts of expression of both kinds have a foreseeable negative impact on the victims who're at risk of (emotional or physical) harm as a result. If correct, this reveals a further way in which the harm condition may be satisfied. It's on this basis that Joel Feinberg concludes that 'It is always a good reason in support of a proposed criminal prohibition that it would probably be an effective way of preventing serious offence . . . to

---

[33] Andres Moles, 'Autonomy, Free Speech and Automatic Behaviour', *Res Publica*, 13 (2007), 53–75.

persons'.[34] This argument for restricting hate speech is the *argument from offence*, and we can state it as follows:

> *Offence moral claim*: The state should place obstacles in front of conduct that causes offence.
>
> *Offence empirical claim*: Hate speech causes offence.
>
> *Conclusion*: The state should restrict hate speech.

As Feinberg acknowledges, one difficulty with this argument is that the case for regulation is weaker, and perhaps even vanishes entirely, when those who're offended could easily have avoided being exposed to the expression.[35] It makes a moral difference that those offended by the Danish cartoons could simply have refrained from looking at them. This conclusion is important since it reveals how it isn't always necessary to restrict hate speech in order to prevent offence. Instead, the state might ensure that those who're likely to be offended enjoy reasonable opportunities to avoid offensive displays. Returning to a distinction that we drew in section 3.2, the state can sometimes ensure hate speech doesn't cause offence through means-based policies that restrict particular methods or avenues of expression, rather than through content-based policies that restrict expression because it causes offence.

Of course, some methods of communication can make avoidance impossible. When flyers are plastered all over a town, it may be nearly impossible for an individual to avoid seeing them. Moreover, there may be cases in which it's not enough merely to avoid being exposed to hateful expression. For example, even if an individual doesn't look at the Danish cartoons, they may be offended by their publication, or perhaps by the knowledge that others have seen them. In these cases, the argument from offence might retain some appeal.

A further difficulty concerns the offence moral claim.[36] Perhaps the most fundamental worry is that offence as such doesn't seem to provide any reason to restrict expression. Part of the concern here is that some individuals are offended when there's no reasonable basis for this. For example, some find it offensive to see gay couples holding hands in the street. But it's hard to see that this offence gives us *any* reason to prevent this conduct.

Indeed, even if offence were to provide some reasons for restriction, these will likely be outweighed given that some offensive speech may have properties that make its expression worth protecting. For one thing, some offensive speech can do a considerable service to the interests of speakers, audiences, and thinkers. For example, let's consider the musical comedy, *The Book of Mormon*, which satires the beliefs and practices of Mormon missionaries. While this show caused a great deal of offence to many

---

[34] Joel Feinberg, *The Moral Limits of the Criminal Law, Volume 2: Offense to Others* (Oxford: Oxford University Press, 1985), 1.

[35] Feinberg, *Offense to Others*, 61.

[36] Peter Jones, 'Religious Belief and Freedom of Expression: Is Offensiveness Really the Issue?', *Res Publica*, 17 (2011), 75–90.

Mormons (as well as to many Christians more broadly), the play served the interests of its producers and viewers by disseminating religious commentary and comedic entertainment. In other words, while it might be true that much *hate speech* is of low-value expression, the broader category of *offensive speech* contains many forms of expression that aren't of low value. Therefore, restricting speech on the basis that it causes offence seriously threatens speaker, audience, and thinker interests, and we believe that this counts strongly against doing so.

It bolsters this point to note that individuals can be easily offended and offended by a considerable range of things. Several religions find the basic tenets of other religions offensive, when those religions hold different views about who is (not) a prophet or the son of God, and politicians frequently claim that they're offended by political criticism. If the state were to restrict expressions of these kinds because they cause offence, the upshot would be intolerance and a challenge to freedom of conscience and democracy. Moreover, in such an environment, the dangers of fallibility, regulatory chill, and abuse of power loom large.

Perhaps needless to say, we're not suggesting that all arguments for restricting hate speech incur these worries. Our point is that these objections apply to the claim that the state should restrict expression on the grounds that it causes offence and, therefore, that we should reject arguments for hate speech regulations that rely on the offence moral claim.

3.5.2 DIGNITY

A distinct argument for restrictions on hate speech appeals to the moral importance of *dignity*.[37] An individual lives with dignity when they have moral standing equal to that of others, and some argue that the state should restrict hate speech when and because it threatens this equal moral standing.

To elaborate this idea, we begin with a slightly different one: many countries have laws against libel and slander that aim to protect individuals' reputations. For example, there are laws that allow a politician to sue those who broadcast false claims that damage their public image. This might happen if a newspaper wrongly alleges that a politician has embezzled funds or had extra-marital affairs. These laws disincentivize news outlets from making false claims of these kinds and, in doing so, they protect individuals from smears that would unjustly undermine their reputations in the eyes of the general public.

In a similar fashion, we can understand dignity as requiring a kind of public reputation. An individual lives with dignity when they're regarded by others as an equal member of their community, and so entitled to respect and equal protection under the law. Without this reputation, their dignity is threatened. This bears on the justifiability

---

[37] Mari J. Matsuda, 'Public Response to Racist Speech: Considering the Victim's Story', *Michigan Law Review*, 87 (1989), 2320–81 and Jeremy Waldron, *The Harm of Hate Speech* (Cambridge, MA: Harvard University Press, 2012), ch. 5.

of restricting hate speech in a straightforward fashion. Just as libel and slander can undermine the public image of a politician, so too hate speech can damage the reputation of members of various groups. For example, Nazi posters that depict Jews and Muslims as sub-human convey a message that these individuals aren't equal members of the community. The same goes for acts of expression that depict individuals who're gay as paedophiles, and perhaps also for cartoons that associate the Muslim Prophet Mohammad with terrorism. These are examples of *group libel*.

One risk with group libel is that an individual whose dignity is threatened will experience the dangers associated with a climate of hate. They may be subject to violence, discrimination, and so on. Conceived of in this way, the present argument aligns neatly with the harm argument, both in its concerns and its conclusions. Alternatively, we might think that it matters that an individual's dignity is threatened irrespective of whether this produces the threat of harm. On this view, an individual is wronged when and because they're the target of hate speech that undermines their equal moral standing in the community as such. Based on this, we can compose a distinct argument for restricting hate speech, calling it the *argument from dignity*:

> *Dignity moral claim*: The state should place obstacles in front of conduct that threatens dignity.
>
> *Dignity empirical claim*: Hate speech threatens dignity.
>
> *Conclusion*: The state should restrict hate speech.

Critics contest both claims of this argument. Some challenge the dignity moral claim on the basis that group libel can serve speaker, audience, and thinker interests.[38] For reasons we've outlined, we doubt that this is true for group libel that involves hate speech, which is distinctly low value. Critics also challenge the dignity empirical claim, questioning whether it's really hate speech that threatens individuals' dignity. Those who favour this line of reasoning argue that hate speech is a symptom of underlying attitudes towards members of various socially salient groups, and that it's these attitudes (not their expression) that threaten dignity.[39] Even if this is correct, as we emphasized in sections 3.3 and 3.4, hate speech can shape individuals' attitudes, making them more likely to regard others not as their moral equals. Thus, we believe that this challenge overlooks the full range of ways in which hate speech threatens dignity.

However, even if the argument from dignity succeeds, we suspect that it doesn't justify regulations that are much more extensive than those supported by the harm argument. This is because there's considerable overlap between the kinds of speech that contribute to a climate of hate and the kinds of speech that threaten dignity. Advocates of the argument from dignity may not be troubled by this result. After all, the authors who advance this view are merely exploring reasons for regulation, and they don't seek to challenge our analysis. But for our purposes, what matters is that the

---

[38] Cohen, 'Freedom of Expression', 236–7.

[39] Robert Mark Simpson, 'Dignity, Harm, and Hate Speech', *Law and Philosophy*, 32 (2013), 701–28.

present argument doesn't support more extensive regulation than we've defended, and we believe it isn't in tension with our view in any serious way.

3.6 CONCLUSIONS

Three headlines emerge from our analysis in this chapter. The first is that the state has a strong reason to restrict hate speech. This means that it should place obstacles in front of an individual that limit their ability to communicate ideas that single out individuals on the basis of a socially salient characteristic, labelling them with some repugnant quality or as an object of contempt, and an unwelcome presence that's an appropriate target for hostility. The reason for this is that hate speech raises the likelihood that members of the targeted groups will suffer harm.

The second and third conclusions relate to the design of hate speech regulation. As we noted in section 3.5, there are several reasons to reject offence-based restrictions on freedom of expression. One implication of this is that we should avoid specifying hate speech regulation in a way that suggests a concern with offence. It's for this reason that we agree with the critics of the United Kingdom's Public Order Act (mentioned in section 3.1), who successfully campaigned to amend the law on the grounds that we should 'accept that the risk of insult is a fair price to pay for living in a society which values free speech'.

Finally, as we also noted in section 3.5, the argument from dignity supports conclusions that are somewhat similar to those we endorse. This is because speech that threatens others' dignity is likely to contribute to a climate of hate in which members of some socially salient groups face an increased risk of violence, discrimination, and so on. Moreover, even if this weren't the case, such that we should restrict hate speech that tarnishes individuals' public reputations without producing these effects, we suspect that this will not justify regulations that are much more extensive than those that we support. Thus, we can conclude that the central scope of regulation should be to place obstacles in front of hate speech when and because it's likely to cause harm to members of socially salient groups.

FURTHER READING

A good overview of the moral considerations surrounding freedom of expression and hate speech regulation is Katherine Smits, *Applying Political Theory: Issues and Debates* (Basingstoke: Palgrave, 2009), ch. 8.

For further reading on justifications of freedom of expression, it's worth beginning with the canonical defence of the position in John Stuart Mill, 'On Liberty' in John Gray (ed.), *John Stuart Mill: On Liberty and Other Essays* (Oxford: Oxford University Press, 1991 [1859]). For more detailed contemporary work, important texts are Thomas Scanlon, 'A Theory of Freedom of Expression', *Philosophy & Public Affairs*, 1 (1972), 204–26; Thomas Scanlon,

'Freedom of Expression and Categories of Expression', *University of Pittsburgh Law Review*, 40 (1978), 519–50; and Joshua Cohen, 'Freedom of Expression', *Philosophy & Public Affairs*, 22 (1993), 207–63. Each of these three texts includes some discussion of permissible restrictions on expression, but generally lean against restricting hate speech.

For a detailed objection to the case these authors make against restricting hate speech, see Susan Brison, 'The Autonomy Defence of Free Speech', *Ethics*, 108 (1998), 312–39. For other arguments in defence of restricting hate speech, an important text is Joel Feinberg, *The Moral Limits of Criminal Law, Volume 2: Offense to Others* (Oxford: Oxford University Press, 1985), chs 1–3. Good pieces on the arguments from harm and dignity are Jeremy Waldron, *The Harm of Hate Speech* (Cambridge, MA: Harvard University Press, 2012); Bhikhu Parekh, 'Hate Speech: Is There a Case for Banning?', *Public Policy Research*, 12 (2006), 213–23; Mari J. Matsuda, 'Public Response to Racist Speech: Considering the Victim's Story', *Michigan Law Review*, 87 (1989), 2320–81; and Caleb Yong, 'Does Freedom of Speech Include Hate Speech?', *Res Publica*, 17 (2011), 385–403.

For critical discussion of the argument from offence, clear analysis is offered in Peter Jones, 'Religious Belief and Freedom of Expression: Is Offensiveness Really the Issue?', *Res Publica*, 17 (2011), 75–90. Another helpful text is Waldron, *The Harm of Hate Speech*, ch. 5. For critical discussion of the argument from dignity, an excellent article is Robert Mark Simpson, 'Dignity, Harm, and Hate Speech', *Law and Philosophy*, 32 (2013), 701–28.

As we highlight in footnote 19, several of the issues and arguments considered in this chapter have also been discussed at length in relation to the regulation of pornography. For further reading on freedom of expression and pornography, see Rae Langton, 'Speech Acts and Unspeakable Acts', *Philosophy & Public Affairs*, 22 (1993), 293–330; Catherine A. MacKinnon, *Only Words* (Cambridge, MA: Harvard University Press, 1996); and Hugh Lafollette (ed.), *Ethics in Practice: An Anthology, Second Edition* (London: Blackwell, 2002), chs 35–38.

 For additional material and resources, including web links and self-test questions, please visit the online resources **www.oup.com/he/walton1e**.

4

RECREATIONAL DRUGS AND PATERNALISM

SUMMARY

- In this chapter, we explore whether it's justifiable for a state to discourage an individual from using recreational drugs. We focus on paternalist arguments—that is, arguments that appeal to the idea that a state may intervene in an individual's life for their own good.
- We argue against the justifiability of these policies, except in some extreme cases.
- After defining our terms, we offer three arguments for the anti-paternalist claim that a state may not intervene in an individual's life for their own good. These are that there's value in an individual acting autonomously; that it's disrespectful to intervene in an individual's life for their own good; and that an individual is a better judge of their interests than the state. We contend that each of these considerations provides some reason to oppose paternalist drug policies.
- We then examine whether it's justifiable for a state to intervene in an individual's life for their own good when that individual is misinformed about the options. We conclude that, in the case of recreational drugs, the appropriate response to misinformation is to educate an individual about the effects of drugs, rather than to discourage their use.
- We consider whether a state may act paternalistically to discourage an individual from making choices that risk addiction or overdose. While we recognize that this is sometimes the case, we draw on empirical evidence to show that this result has only limited relevance for the regulation of recreational drug use.
- We conclude by outlining some implications of our argument for the design of drug policy.

4.1 INTRODUCTION

In nearly every state across the world, there are laws and policies that discourage recreational drug use. Although several states have recently legalized the use of cannabis for recreational purposes, this remains an outlier position, both in terms of the number of states to make this move and in terms of the fact that their treatment of cannabis (in comparison with other drugs) is an exception to the rule.

In this chapter, we focus on the argument that policies that discourage recreational drug use are justifiable because they reduce harm to users. This isn't the only way in which these policies are defended, but it's an especially interesting one for two reasons. First, the argument plays a prominent role in public discussions about drug policy. For example, the United Kingdom's 2017 Drug Strategy explicitly notes that 'Drugs are illegal because . . . analysis has shown they are harmful to human health'.[1] Second, arguments of this kind are the subject of notable philosophical controversy. This is because these arguments are *paternalist*, in the sense that they purport to justify the state's intervention in an individual's life for their own good. Critics contend that this is a grave error. For example, the Drug Policy Alliance campaigns fervently against prevailing drug policies on the grounds that states ought to respect 'the sovereignty of individuals over their own minds and bodies'.[2] Our aim is to investigate the foundations of this dispute and, in doing so, to shed light on whether it's justifiable for a state to enact paternalist policies that discourage individuals from using recreational drugs. Our conclusion is that paternalist arguments for existing drug policies are seriously inadequate, and so the case for these policies is much weaker than many of us assume.

This chapter proceeds as follows. In section 4.2, we clarify the nature and scope of our analysis, and briefly describe the paternalist case for discouraging recreational drug use. In section 4.3, we survey three arguments in defence of *anti-paternalism*— that is, the idea that the state shouldn't intervene in an individual's life for their own good. These arguments generate strong reasons to doubt the justifiability of policies that discourage recreational drug use. In section 4.4, we respond to the claim that it's justifiable for the state to intervene in an individual's life when that individual is misinformed about the options available to them. In section 4.5, we engage with the idea that it's justifiable for the state to intervene in an individual's life when they would otherwise act in a way that risks addiction or overdose. We argue that neither of these claims undermine our main conclusion regarding the unjustifiability of policies that discourage recreational drug use. In section 4.6, we reflect on the implications of our analysis for policy.

4.2 THE LANDSCAPE OF DRUG POLICY

In order to frame our arguments, two sets of preliminaries are in order.

4.2.1 DEFINITIONS

We begin by making four points that clarify the subject of our investigation. First, we use the term 'drugs' to refer to psychoactive substances. These are substances that, when consumed or administered, affect the user's mental capacities. This definition is a broad

---

[1] HM Government, '2017 Drug Strategy', available at https://assets.publishing.service.gov.uk/government/uploads/system/uploads/attachment_data/file/628148/Drug_strategy_2017.pdf, 16.

[2] Drug Policy Alliance, 'About the Drug Policy Alliance', available at http://www.drugpolicy.org/about-us/about-drug-policy-alliance.

one, ranging from caffeine to cocaine, which says nothing about the legality, harmfulness, or addictiveness of those substances.

Second, our main concern is with drug *use* and, therefore, with policies that affect when and how individuals consume drugs. In the course of our analysis, we touch on related policies, such as those that affect when and how individuals produce and sell drugs. Some of these raise distinctive questions of their own.[3] However, we're concerned with these issues here only insofar as they bear on the justifiability of policies that target drug use.

Third, we focus on the use of drugs for *recreational* purposes, rather than on the medical or therapeutic use of these substances. We acknowledge that the line between these categories is sometimes blurry, such as when an individual uses drugs to relieve stress, but we hope that this rough distinction is clear in a large enough range of cases that this complication isn't too damaging to our conclusions. Our reason for restricting our attention to the recreational use of drugs is that this is the activity around which there's the most political and philosophical controversy.

Fourth, our interest is in the justifiability of policies that *discourage* individuals from using drugs recreationally. One way in which the state can do this is by imposing criminal penalties on those who engage in this activity. But there are other options too. For example, the state might run public education programmes designed to instil distaste for drug use, or support initiatives whose purpose is to cultivate an interest in healthy living. Another possibility is for the state to impose criminal penalties on individuals who produce or sell drugs. Though this policy affects when and how individuals use drugs only indirectly, via the influence it has on the supply of drugs, its aim would still be to discourage drug use if it were enacted with this justification in mind. There are crucial differences between these policies, such that some are much more difficult to justify than others. For example, it might be more difficult to justify imprisonment than taxation. However, for our purposes, what matters is what these policies have in common, namely that they discourage individuals from using drugs recreationally. Our goal is to investigate whether this *aim* is a justifiable one and, in particular, whether it's justifiable for the state to discourage individuals from using drugs recreationally for the user's benefit.

4.2.2 THE PATERNALIST ARGUMENT

Those who defend policies that discourage individuals from using recreational drugs often point to the harmful consequences of this activity for drug users. It might appear as though those who voice this point mean to assert only an empirical claim:

Recreational drug use empirical claim: Recreational drug use harms drug users.

---

[3] Douglas Husak and Peter de Marneffe, *The Legalization of Drugs: For and Against* (Cambridge: Cambridge University Press, 2005), 96–105.

However, in order to generate a conclusion regarding how the state should act, we must supplement this with a moral claim. This gives rise to the *paternalist argument*, which is as follows:

> *Paternalist moral claim*: The state should discourage an individual from acting in ways that are harmful to themself.
>
> *Recreational drug use empirical claim*: Recreational drug use harms drug users.
>
> *Conclusion*: The state should discourage an individual from using drugs recreationally.

By fleshing out the paternalist argument in this way, we can distinguish two sets of objections to it. One set challenges the paternalist moral claim. These objections come from those who maintain that states shouldn't intervene in an individual's life for their own good. A second set targets the recreational drug use empirical claim, holding either that recreational drug use isn't harmful to drug users, or that it's much less harmful than is commonly believed. We consider each of these points in what follows.

4.3 ANTI-PATERNALIST ARGUMENTS

There are many activities that few states discourage despite them being harmful to their participants. This includes a variety of contact sports, such as boxing and American football, as well as several extreme sports, such as race car driving and mountaineering. It's true that some commentators call for more extensive regulations to protect the safety of these sports' participants. This is a point to which we'll return in section 4.6. But it's significant that few believe that the state should generally dissuade an individual from participating in these activities. This should prompt us to scrutinize the paternalist moral claim, according to which the state ought to discourage an individual from acting in ways that are harmful to themself. We do this by offering three arguments against paternalism, which together explain why we should oppose policies that discourage an individual from using recreational drugs.

First, some paternalist policies alter the *freedoms* available to individuals. As we explain in Chapter 2, whether an individual is free to do something depends on the obstacles they face. Making an action illegal places an obstacle in front of an individual, and so this can reduce their freedom. This suggests an initial argument for anti-paternalism, namely one that appeals to the value of autonomy. We also discuss this idea in greater detail in Chapter 2, as well as later in this chapter. For the moment, it suffices to note that it's *intrinsically* valuable for an individual that they be free to set and pursue their own plans in life, which includes having the freedom to choose the activities in which they engage, at least so long as these plans don't wrong others. Stated in this way, the idea isn't that this freedom is the most effective *means* to advance an individual's interests (although we return to an argument along these lines presently). Rather, this freedom to choose is valuable *in itself*—there's value in an individual being free to choose that's independent of the value of what they choose.[4] The upshot of this is that we've a reason to ensure that an individual is free to choose the activities in which they engage and, therefore, also a reason to oppose policies that strip them of this freedom. We call this the *autonomy argument* for anti-paternalism.

We acknowledge that this argument might not supply us with reasons to condemn all measures that reduce an individual's freedom. In particular, even if an appeal to autonomy can plausibly explain what's wrong with criminalizing recreational drug use, it's more difficult to see how it can explain what's wrong with discouraging their use in other ways, such as by adopting taxes that merely raise the price of these goods. If this is correct, then the autonomy argument will provide us with stronger reasons to oppose some anti-drugs policies than others.

A second argument holds that it's wrong for the state to interfere in an individual's life for their own benefit because this treats them as if they lack the capacity to set and pursue their own plans in life. Treating an individual in this way is *disrespectful*, and wrong for this reason.[5] For our purposes, it's especially important to note that policies may be disrespectful in this way even when they enhance, rather than reduce, an individual's freedom.[6] For example, it may be disrespectful for the state to subsidize safer activities, in an effort to incentivize an individual to turn away from more dangerous ones, if the motivation for this were that this individual lacked the capacity to set and pursue their own plans in life. Even though the state doesn't restrict anyone's freedom—indeed, it enhances their options by subsidizing safer activities—this policy may remain objectionable because of the disrespect it conveys. It's for this reason that we characterize paternalism and anti-paternalism in terms of interference in an individual's life, rather than the restriction of freedom. These ideas make up the *disrespect argument* in favour of anti-paternalism.

Third, John Stuart Mill defends anti-paternalism on the grounds that an individual is likely to be a better judge of their own interests than the state. He writes,

> with respect to his own feelings and circumstances, the most ordinary man or woman has the means of knowledge immeasurably surpassing those that can be possessed by anyone else [and so] the strongest of all the arguments against the interference of the public with purely personal conduct is that, when it does interfere, the odds are that it interferes wrongly, and in the wrong place.[7]

We can add to this that an individual is likely to be not only a better judge than the state of what's in their interests, but also of how to serve and protect those interests. This is because, since they're likely to have much more information than the state about their own tastes and preferences, it's overwhelmingly likely that the best way to serve and protect those interests is by giving them the power to make the decisions that affect

---

[4] Joseph Raz, *The Morality of Freedom* (Oxford: Clarendon Press, 1986), chs 14–15.

[5] Jonathan Quong, *Liberalism without Perfection* (Oxford: Oxford University Press, 2010), ch. 3.

[6] Quong, *Liberalism without Perfection*, 75 and 102.

[7] John Stuart Mill, 'On Liberty' in John Gray (ed.), *John Stuart Mill: On Liberty and Other Essays* (Oxford: Oxford University Press, 1991 [1859]), 85 and 92.

their own life, rather than by having the state make these decisions on their behalf. This is the *better judge argument* in favour of anti-paternalism.

We've stated each of these arguments briefly, and we recognize that a complete defence of them requires some refinement. In the ensuing sections, we make some progress on this front. But for now, it's useful to bring these ideas together by returning to the case of recreational drug use. In section 4.2.2, we outlined the paternalist argument for discouraging an individual from using recreational drugs. It runs as follows:

Paternalist moral claim: The state should discourage an individual from acting in ways that are harmful to themself.

Recreational drug use empirical claim: Recreational drug use harms drug users.

Conclusion: The state should discourage an individual from using drugs recreationally.

In this section, we've cast doubt on this argument by challenging the paternalist moral claim. We've done this by offering three reasons in favour of anti-paternalism: that there's value in an individual acting autonomously; that it's disrespectful to intervene in an individual's life for their own good; and that an individual is a better judge of their interests than the state. These arguments support the conclusion that the state shouldn't intervene in an individual's life for their own good. And so, just as it's valuable for an individual to be free to choose between a life of artistic pursuits, playing or watching sport, religious devotion, or any of a great many other things, so too it's valuable for them to be free to choose whether or not to indulge in recreational drug use.[8]

It's notable that even proponents of paternalism tend not to reject the claims we've advanced here, at least not in a wholesale way. Instead, it's more common to qualify the paternalist moral claim in ways that accommodate the objections, but leave room for some paternalism. More specifically, these advocates of the paternalist argument contend that our commitment to anti-paternalism has *limits*, and that these limits create room in which to defend paternalist policies that discourage recreational drug use. In the following sections, we explore two arguments of this kind, which focus on different ways that an individual's choices may not serve the values that support anti-paternalism.

4.4 MISINFORMED CHOICES

One doubt about the case for anti-paternalism derives from the fact that an individual may be misinformed about the options available to them, as well as the consequences of each of those options.[9] The case of recreational drug use illustrates this nicely. Drug

[8] Douglas Husak, *Drugs and Rights* (Cambridge: Cambridge University Press, 1992), ch. 2.
[9] Robert Goodin, 'Permissible Paternalism: Saving Smokers from Themselves' in Hugh LaFollette (ed.), *Ethics in Practice: An Anthology, Second Edition* (Oxford: Blackwell Publishing, 2002), 307–12 at 309.

users often fail to appreciate the likelihood of addiction, the severity of the burdens that this might generate, and the health risks involved with using various drugs.

This is important for three reasons, each relating to an argument from section 4.3. First, if an individual isn't fully aware of what an activity involves and the risks associated with it, then they're less likely than otherwise to act in ways that align with their interests. In extreme cases, this may compromise their abilities to such an extent that they're no longer a better judge than the state of what choices best serve their interests. Second, for the same reasons, misinformation reduces the value of autonomy that's realized when an individual is free to choose their life plan. What matters for autonomy is that an individual is free to choose in an informed way about the activities in which to engage. Third, though its disrespectful for the state to treat an individual as if they lack the capacity to set and pursue their own plans when they possess this capacity, it may not be disrespectful for the state to treat them in this way when they lack the relevant capacity—say, because they lack access to some crucial information.

In support of these ideas, it may help to consider the following case:

> *Bridge*: Brayden wants to visit his friend, but the only way to get there is by crossing a dangerous bridge. Brayden believes that there's only a 1 per cent probability that the bridge will collapse and, because of this, he decides to cross. However, Alisha knows that there's a 10 per cent probability that the bridge will collapse.[10]

In this case, it's plausible that Alisha should intervene in Brayden's decision. What explains this result is that Brayden misunderstands the risks involved. In a similar vein, proponents of the paternalist argument might contend that policies that discourage recreational drug use are justifiable for the same reason, namely in response to the fact that an individual may be misinformed about the consequences of recreational drug use.

With this in mind, we might propose the following *argument from misinformation*:

> *Misinformation moral claim*: The state should intervene in an individual's life for their own good when they're misinformed about their options.

> *Misinformation empirical claim*: Many individuals are misinformed about the consequences of recreational drug use.

> *Conclusion*: The state should discourage an individual from using drugs recreationally.

In response to this argument, we make two points. First, it's important to note that this isn't an argument in favour of paternalist policies as such. It doesn't justify discouraging an individual from using recreational drugs *on the grounds that this is harmful to drug users*. It's the fact that an individual misunderstands the risks of using drugs recreationally that justifies intervening in their life, not the risks themselves. Intervening in an individual's life when they lack sufficient information to make informed decisions is

---

[10] This case is modified from one discussed in Mill, 'On Liberty', 106–7.

sometimes called *soft paternalism*. What we hope is clear is that soft paternalism differs significantly from the kind of paternalist interventions into an individual's life for their own benefit that we've considered so far.

Second, we believe that the appropriate response to misinformation isn't to discourage an individual from engaging in this activity. Instead, it's to ensure that they're made fully aware of the consequences of each of the options available to them. In *Bridge*, the appropriate response to Brayden's misinformation is for Alisha to inform Brayden that there's a 10 per cent probability that the bridge will collapse, and then allow him to make his own decision. It becomes justifiable for Alisha to prevent Brayden from crossing only when this isn't possible or when it's very costly to do so.

This result is important because it shows that the conclusion of the argument from misinformation doesn't follow from its claims. More specifically, it suggests that we should aim to ensure that those who use drugs are aware of the associated risks, rather than to enact policies whose purpose is to discourage individuals from engaging in this activity. There are many ways in which the state could achieve this. One possibility is to run a public education programme that outlines the consequences of recreational drug use. Another is for the state to introduce 'drug licences' that users can acquire only after passing an exam that tests knowledge of the relevant risks. Policies of this kind aren't paternalist since their aim is merely to educate drug users about the consequences of their choices, and not to reduce recreational drug use.

4.5 BAD CHOICES

A distinct argument for paternalist policies is more threatening to our view. Here, the worry isn't that an individual may be misinformed. It's that even an individual who's fully informed might choose badly. Indeed, they might even select an option (or maybe a series of options) that's *very* bad for them, perhaps seriously threatening their health and life. When there's a serious risk of this kind, many think we should restrict an individual's choices or override their decisions for their own good.

Arguments along these lines are common in discussions of drug policy, as we often fear that an individual who chooses to use drugs for recreational purposes may become addicted or risk overdosing. We discuss these possibilities in turn.

4.5.1 ADDICTION AND SECOND-ORDER PREFERENCES

Drug addiction involves being unable to control one's frequent and repeated use of a substance.[11] Typically, this is due to an individual's previous use of the substance causing them to experience a strong impulse to return to it, with the likely effect that this'll jeopardize their pursuit of other activities. Evidence of this process comes from

[11] National Health Service, 'Addiction: What Is It?' (2015), available at https://www.nhs.uk/live-well/healthy-body/addiction-what-is-it.

research that explores the effects of powdered cocaine.[12] Some studies show that, after exposure to cocaine, rodents will quickly self-administer the drug to the detriment of almost all other activities, including eating, sleeping, and sex. Other studies reveal that cocaine use can affect users' cognitive abilities, leading to lower attention span, lower motivation, and increased impulsivity.

Although advocates of paternalist drug policies regularly cite such information as if it alone makes the case, our investigation requires that we go further. In particular, we must ask: what moral concerns does addiction raise?

One concern is that those who're addicted will act in ways that fail to serve their own preferences.[13] At first glance, this might sound strange because, when an addicted drug user uses a drug, they satisfy a preference for consuming it. But things aren't that straightforward. Although they might act in accordance with this preference, they might simultaneously frustrate others. One way in which this can occur is if they have a preference not to satisfy their preference to use drugs. This is an example of a *second-order preference*—that is, a preference about one's preferences.

In these cases, it's less obvious that our concern for an individual's autonomy, our respect for their capacity to make decisions about their own life, and their position as the best judge of their interests speak against discouraging them from acting on their immediate urge to use the drug—that is, their *first-order preference*. Instead, we might think that the best way in which to serve these values is to discourage them from satisfying their first-order preference, and therefore assist them to satisfy their second-order preference. This is plausibly the case if an individual's second-order preferences are more stable and less fleeting than their first-order preferences, and thus better track what they regard as in their interests. In Chapter 2, we draw on this idea to explain why we should deny the option of euthanasia to an individual with great life prospects who momentarily claims that they wish to die because of a severe case of unrequited love. We may think that similar considerations support discouraging recreational drug use.

This analysis suggests the following possibility:

Revised paternalist moral claim: The state should discourage an individual from acting in ways that frustrate their second-order preferences.

Formulated in this way, we find this claim unpersuasive. This is because there are many cases in which an individual acts in ways that frustrate their second-order preferences, but where it looks inappropriate for the state to interfere in their life. For example, some individuals wish that they could read more novels than they do but, when the opportunity arises, the temptation to relax in front of the television proves too great. Despite this, few conclude that the state should be in the business of assisting these individuals to read more novels. It's in the light of counterexamples such as these that we believe

---

[12] Gabriel Horn et al., 'Brain Science, Addiction, and Drugs', *The Academy of Medical Sciences* (2008), available at https://acmedsci.ac.uk/file-download/34265-524414fc8746a.pdf, 77–81.

[13] Goodin, 'Permissible Paternalism', 309–10.

that those drawn to arguments that rely on claims about second-order preferences need to specify their moral claim more precisely.

One response to this concern is to appeal to the *extremity* of the mismatch between first-order preferences and second-order preferences. In this respect, there's an important difference between recreational drug use and reading fewer novels than one would like. In particular, the former affects many more areas of an individual's life, and to a much greater extent, than the latter. It's true that it may be bad for an individual's intellectual development for them to read fewer novels than they wish but, unlike with recreational drug use, the effects of this don't contaminate other areas of their life, such as personal relationships or their employment status.

It's tempting to think that the implication of this is that the state should discourage an individual from acting in ways that are detrimental to various *objectively valuable* aspects of their life, such as health, family, and work. Perhaps this is what distinguishes recreational drug use from failing to read as many novels as one wishes. However, we think it's a mistake to draw this conclusion. Chiefly, this is because this result sits uncomfortably with the argument we're currently considering, which emphasizes the moral significance of second-order *preferences*.

We believe that the relevant distinction between the two cases is as follows. With respect to recreational drug use, the tension between an individual's first-order preference to use a drug and their second-order preference not to do so is stark, not least because of how this seriously frustrates their preferences regarding other aspects of their life. But with respect to reading fewer novels than one wishes, the tension between an individual's first-order preferences and their second-order preferences is much less severe. This suggests the following argument:

Second-order preferences paternalist moral claim: The state should discourage an individual from acting in ways that seriously frustrate their second-order preferences.

Second-order preferences empirical claim: Recreational drug use seriously frustrates users' second-order preferences.

Conclusion: The state should discourage an individual from using drugs recreationally.

We call this the *second-order preferences argument* for paternalist drug policies.

We've some sympathy for this argument, and we believe that the three defences of anti-paternalism—namely, those that refer to the value of autonomy, respect for capacity to choose, and the idea that an individual is a better judge of their own interests than the state—have reduced appeal when the claims of the second-order preferences argument are satisfied. This gives us some reason to discourage recreational drug use.

Having said that, two further points limit this conclusion. First, the argument's empirical claim is plausible in the case of only *some* drugs. It might be correct that the recreational use of heroin and crack cocaine seriously frustrates a user's second-order preferences. However, we don't see the same risks, or at least not to any comparable degree, with the recreational use of other drugs.[14] The point isn't that users of these drugs don't become addicted. Rather, the point is that the effects of their use are less likely than with heroin and crack cocaine to contaminate other areas of an individual's life about which they care, such as personal relationships or employment status. Because of this, the second-order preferences argument applies in only a limited range of cases.

Second, it's vital to bear in mind that the extent to which recreational drug use frustrates a user's second-order preferences is a contingent matter that's determined by the institutions, policies, and laws that we have in place. It's not that recreational drug use unavoidably seriously frustrates an individual's second-order preferences. To see this, let's consider the example of someone who's very wealthy, such that their regular drug use poses no threat of making them homeless, where it might have done so if they'd been on the poverty line. What this example reveals is that the conclusion of the second-order preferences argument doesn't immediately follow from its claims, since there may be ways to reduce the extent to which recreational drug use frustrates a user's second-order preferences. For instance, one reason that recreational drug use poses a threat of homelessness is that it's a common requirement of rental agreements and homeless shelters that tenants don't use certain drugs. If the state were to prohibit landlords and shelters stipulating this requirement, it'd reduce the extent to which recreational drug use risks the possibility of homelessness. We believe that this is a more appropriate response to the concerns identified by proponents of the second-order preferences argument.

Some might doubt that the state can reform our institutions, policies, and laws such that recreational drug use never seriously frustrates a user's second-order preferences, particularly in the case of more extreme drugs. We're unsure about this. Our hunch is that we shouldn't rule out the possibility that, in a suitably reformed world where those who use drugs recreationally incur many fewer social and legal sanctions than at present, recreational drug use might not seriously frustrate a user's second-order preferences, and so the second-order preferences argument loses its bite. However, we recognize that it's difficult to cite evidence for this claim, and we acknowledge that we should tread cautiously in advocating a move in this direction in case our confidence on this point is misplaced.

Nonetheless, we believe our remarks remain salient because, even if it's true that the second-order preferences argument supplies us with strong reasons to discourage recreational drug use, our reservations about this argument should guide the design of the policies in this domain. In particular, we should favour policies that reduce (and certainly don't increase) the extent to which recreational drug use frustrates a user's second-order preferences. This is important because many commonly employed anti-drug policies, such as criminal penalties, clearly aren't conducive to this goal. This is because they jeopardize family relationships and trigger clauses that make it difficult

---

[14] David Nutt, Leslie King, and Lawrence Philips, 'Drug Harms in the UK: A Multicriteria Decision Analysis', *The Lancet*, 376 (2010), 1558–65.

for those who use drugs to find work and housing. If our arguments are persuasive, then what this suggests is that a more appropriate response to the fact of drug addiction is to provide greater support and rehabilitation for drug users. We regard this implication of our view as a welcome result.

4.5.2 AUTONOMY AND OVERDOSE

In some extreme cases, a further concern with addiction isn't merely that it seriously frustrates a user's second-order preferences, but also that it strips the user of the capacity for autonomy. The idea here is that addiction can render an individual unable to author their life to any meaningful degree. This threatens one of our arguments for anti-paternalism since it seems to imply that the value of autonomy counts in favour of limiting an individual's opportunities to use drugs recreationally rather than against doing this. This is because, for an individual to make choices about how to live, it's necessary that they enjoy the mental capacities to do so, and this might not be the case if they're highly addicted to a substance.

We think there's little mileage in this view. This is because, for both short-term and long-term drug users, there's ample evidence that the overwhelming majority of individuals who use drugs recreationally aren't addicted to such an extent that this jeopardizes their autonomy. For example, one major study found that, of 8 million individuals who used powdered cocaine in 1988, only 10 per cent said that they'd used it once or more per week, and only 3 per cent said that they'd used it daily.[15] This finding is in line with heroin and crack cocaine use, where even those with addictions tend to give up in the end, often in order to pursue other activities, such as to raise a family. For these reasons, we think it's a stretch to believe that a serious concern with recreational drug use is the threat it poses to users' autonomy.

A related worry with recreational drug use focuses on how it can endanger an individual's life. This is the risk of death by overdose. Of course, the risk of death is a threat to autonomy in the sense that, when someone dies, they lose their autonomy. Still, we think it makes sense to treat death differently given that this kind of threat to autonomy is somewhat distinct from the threat supposedly posed by addiction.

Arguments that appeal to the risk of fatal overdose offer a promising basis on which to justify paternalist drug policies since our reasons to protect an individual's life are very strong. It's true that we've some grounds to endorse anti-paternalism, but it's plausible that these must give way when an individual's life is in danger.[16] For example, even if it's disrespectful for the state to interfere in an individual's life for their own benefit, this moral concern appears insignificant when interference is necessary to protect their life.

One complication is that the state doesn't have reasons to discourage *all* activities that threaten an individual's life. After all, whenever someone uses a treadmill, there's

---

[15] Cited in Husak, *Drugs and Rights*, 123–4.
[16] Peter de Marneffe, 'Avoiding Paternalism', *Philosophy & Public Affairs*, 34 (2006), 68–94.

some chance that they'll slip, hit their head, and die. The risks are even higher when they go mountain walking or skydiving. But still, few of us believe that the state should discourage these activities. Rather, it's plausible that the state should restrict its attention to only those activities that pose a sufficiently serious threat of death.

These clarifications are important because they bear on the justifiability of policies whose purpose is to discourage an individual from using recreational drugs. In particular, they suggest that we must present an *overdose argument* for paternalist drug policies as follows:

> *Overdose moral claim*: The state should discourage an individual from acting in ways that seriously endanger their life.
>
> *Overdose empirical claim*: Recreational drug use seriously endangers the lives of drug users.
>
> *Conclusion*: The state should discourage an individual from using drugs recreationally.

There are two ways to challenge this argument. Some contest the overdose moral claim, insisting that, so long as an individual acts autonomously and with accurate information about the choices they face, then it's up to them if they wish to risk their life.[17] This may be unwise or wasteful but, arguably, it's no business of the state to discourage lifestyle choices of this kind. We set this challenge aside to focus on issues with the overdose empirical claim.

To measure the risk of death by overdose from recreational drug use, we must look to the *toxicity* of a drug. This refers to the 'narrowness of the window between the dose used to procure a desired effect ("pharmacological dose") and the dose that might result in death from overdose ("lethal dose")'.[18] From this, we can calculate a drug's *safety ratio*, which refers to the ratio of the lethal dose to the pharmacological dose. This means that, the lower the safety ratio, the greater the risk of overdose. The Academy of Medical Sciences reports that safety ratios for common recreational drugs vary considerably: heroin has a ratio of 6, cocaine has a ratio of 15, and cannabis has a ratio of greater than 1,000.

These figures give an initial reason to doubt the overdose empirical claim, at least as a general assertion about recreational drug use. The likelihood of consuming a thousand times more of a substance than one needs to produce the desired effect is extremely low. Perhaps even consuming six times more of a substance than one needs to produce the desired effect isn't a mistake that many of us are likely to make.

It's important to note that the circumstances of some recreational drug use might make the mistake more likely. For example, it can be difficult for the consumer to know the concentration or purity of the substance that they're taking. When someone

---

[17] Though he isn't concerned with overdose in particular, arguments that support this position are developed in Joel Feinberg, *The Moral Limits of the Criminal Law, Volume 3: Harm to Self* (Oxford: Oxford University Press, 1986), especially chs 1–3.

[18] Horn et al., 'Brain Science, Addiction, and Drugs', 76–7.

uses multiple drugs or multiple doses, the calculations can become more difficult and the effects can blur their judgements about how much they've already taken and about the amount to place in any dosage. However, many of these distortions are due to the fact that the use of most recreational drugs is illegal, and so the market for these drugs is unregulated. It's possible that we could reduce the risk of fatal overdose by legalizing and regulating the recreational use of drugs. Perhaps some serious risks would remain, especially for drugs with a low safety ratio, such as heroin. But even if so, we've reason to doubt that the overdose empirical claim is plausible in the case of most drugs.

To support this further, let's turn to some empirical evidence. One complication is that it's notoriously difficult to generate clear data on the number of deaths that result from individuals using drugs recreationally. A crude measure is to compare the number of recreational drug users with the number of deaths where drug use is recorded on the death certificate. In the United Kingdom in 2005–6, it's estimated that there were 39,000 heroin users, 776,000 cocaine users, and 2.8 million cannabis users.[19] In 2005, there were 2,762 deaths where drug use was mentioned on the death certificate, and 842 of these cases involved heroin, 176 involved cocaine, and nineteen involved cannabis.[20] Bringing these figures together might seem to suggest that heroin is associated with the death of roughly one in forty-six users each year, that cocaine is associated with the death of roughly one in 4,400 users each year, and that cannabis is associated with the death of roughly one in 150,000 users each year.[21]

However, we should treat these figures as considerable overestimations for at least two reasons. First, the number of users doesn't distinguish between regular users and those who tried the drug only once. For this reason, the estimation of, say, 776,000 cocaine users in the United Kingdom is likely to be seriously misleading. For a more accurate understanding of the risk of fatal overdose, it'd be better to compare the number of times a drug was used with the number of deaths where drug use was recorded on the death certificate. Unfortunately, we lack this information, but we know it'll be much higher than the number of users, since many of those who have used a drug have done so more than once. Second, it's also important that the vast majority of cases in which drug use is recorded on the death certificate involve the use of more than one drug.[22] This skews the statistics because the risk of fatal overdose may be serious for two drugs combined, but perhaps not for either independently of the other. Nonetheless, both of these drugs would be mentioned on the death certificate, which leads to the risk of double counting the threats that using these drugs poses.

[19] Stephen Roe and Louise Man, 'Drug Misuse Declared: Findings from the 2005/6 British Crime Survey, England and Wales', *Home Office Statistical Bulletin* (2006), available at http://webarchive.nationalarchives.gov.uk/20110220105210/rds.homeoffice.gov.uk/rds/pdfs06/hosb1506.pdf.
[20] Office of National Statistics, 'Report: Deaths Related to Drug Poisoning—England and Wales, 1993–2005', *Health Statistics Quarterly*, 33 (2007), 84.
[21] For similar findings in the United States, see Husak, *Drugs and Rights*, 96.
[22] Horn et al., 'Brain Science, Addiction, and Drugs', 75.

Our reading of the empirical data is that, while some recreational drug use, notably heroin, might involve a serious risk of fatal overdose, it's unclear that the risks associated with most drugs are sufficiently high to justify discouraging an individual from using them recreationally. Even on higher estimates of the risk of death associated with the recreational use of cannabis and powdered cocaine, these activities are much less hazardous than race car driving, boxing, and many extreme sports.[23] Given this, there's a dilemma facing those who advocate for policies whose purpose is to discourage recreational drug use on the grounds that this activity seriously risks fatal overdose. On the one hand, we might think that the risks an individual takes when using drugs recreationally are sufficiently serious as to warrant state action. If this is the case, then consistency would seem to require that the state also take a stand against other activities that involve similar risks. On the other hand, we might think that, since the risks associated with, say, extreme sports are insufficient to warrant state action, then the same should apply with respect to most recreational drug use.

4.6 CONCLUSIONS

Our main aim in this chapter has been to argue for the anti-paternalist idea that the state shouldn't intervene in an individual's life for their own good, and to show that this counts against the justifiability of paternalist policies whose purpose is to discourage an individual from using drugs recreationally. In this respect, our conclusions are very radical. They extend even beyond the claims of those who believe that the state should decriminalize recreational drug use. Our more extreme view is that it shouldn't discourage their use in any way.

However, our conclusions are limited in two important respects. First, we haven't argued that the state should treat all drugs the same or that it shouldn't adopt various other kinds of regulations. Importantly, in section 4.5, we acknowledged that there may be reasons that warrant excepting heroin and crack cocaine from what we recommend about recreational drug use more generally. Moreover, our arguments hint at several other qualifications. Given we appeal to values such as autonomy and the idea that an individual is a better judge of their own interests than the state, the case for age limits on drug use seems plausible. In section 4.4, we emphasized the importance of comprehensive education about recreational drug use and, in section 4.5, we showed that the importance of an individual being able to align their actions with their second-order preferences speaks in favour of adopting policies that are conducive to this end. In cases where the drugs in question are particularly liable to debilitating addiction, we suggested that encouraging other lifestyles and supporting rehabilitation are preferable to criminal penalties, and similar considerations might support significant advertising restrictions.

---

[23] Husak, *Drugs and Rights*, 95–6.

All of this is to say that it's crucial to understand our rejection of paternalist policies in this domain as taking place within a wider context of arguments for an appropriate policy environment.

Second, our focus has been on paternalist justifications for discouraging recreational drug use. As we noted in section 4.1, paternalism isn't the only motivation for policies that reduce recreational drug use. One important issue to consider is whether this activity harms others, such as the family members of drug users, and whether this harm can provide a justification for the kinds of policies we're considering. Such investigation must consider other moral ideas, such as the relationship between freedom and harm to others that we discuss in Chapter 3. Accordingly, we can't conclude that we should reject policies that discourage recreational drug use. Instead, what our analysis suggests is that we should reject arguments for these policies that rely on paternalist justifications.

FURTHER READING

For a good overview of the concept of paternalism, there's Jessica Begon, 'Paternalism', *Analysis*, 76 (2016), 355–73. And, for a philosophical overview of contemporary drug policy, there's Jonathan Wolff, 'Harm and Hypocrisy: Have We Got It Wrong about Drugs?', *Public Policy Research*, 14 (2007), 126–35.

For further reading on drug policy, a good place to begin is with the debates between Douglas Husak's arguments for the legalization of drugs and Peter de Marneffe's arguments against this. Accessible pieces include Douglas Husak, 'In Favor of Drug Decriminalization' and Peter de Marneffe, 'Against the Legalization of Drugs' in Andrew I. Cohen and Christopher Heath Wellman (eds), *Contemporary Debates in Applied Ethics, Second Edition* (Chichester: Wiley Blackwell, 2014), 333–57. For extended treatment, see Douglas Husak and Peter de Marneffe, *The Legalization of Drugs: For and Against* (Cambridge: Cambridge University Press, 2005).

For empirical evidence of the consequences of drug use, some useful recent reports are David Nutt, Leslie King, and Lawrence Philips, 'Drug Harms in the UK: A Multicriteria Decision Analysis', *The Lancet*, 376 (2010), 1558–65; Gabriel Horn et al., 'Brain Science, Addiction, and Drugs', *The Academy of Medical Sciences* (2008), available at https://acmedsci.ac.uk/file-download/34265-524414fc8746a.pdf; and Nicola Singleton, Rosemary Murray, and Louise Tinsley (eds), 'Measuring Different Aspects of Problem Drug Use: Methodological Developments', *Home Office Online Report* (2016), available at http://webarchive.nationalarchives.gov.uk/20110218135832/rds.homeoffice.gov.uk/rds/pdfs06/rdsolr1606.pdf.

For further reading on paternalism, an excellent discussion of prominent positions is provided in Jonathan Quong, *Liberalism without Perfection* (Oxford: Oxford University Press, 2010), ch. 3. For another defence of anti-paternalism, an important text is John Stuart Mill, 'On Liberty' in John Gray (ed.), *John Stuart Mill: On Liberty and Other Essays* (Oxford: Oxford University Press, 1991 [1859]). Another excellent piece that examines a related issue is Seana

Shiffrin, 'Paternalism, Unconscionability Doctrine, and Accommodation', *Philosophy & Public Affairs*, 29 (2000), 205–50.

For defences of paternalism, there's Peter de Marneffe, 'Avoiding Paternalism', *Philosophy & Public Affairs*, 34 (2006), 68–94 and Sarah Conly, *Against Autonomy: Justifying Coercive Paternalism* (Cambridge: Cambridge University Press, 2012).

 For additional material and resources, including web links and self-test questions, please visit the online resources **www.oup.com/he/walton1e**.

5

AFFIRMATIVE ACTION AND DISCRIMINATION

SUMMARY

- In this chapter, we argue that affirmative action is sometimes justifiable. We use the term 'affirmative action' to refer to policies beyond anti-discrimination law that directly regulate selection procedures to enhance the representation of members of various socially salient groups, such as those based on gender, race, and ethnicity.
- We outline an argument in support of affirmative action by distinguishing three prominent forms of wrongful discrimination and by showing that affirmative action is the appropriate response to the past and present wrongful discrimination suffered by members of socially salient groups.
- We add a second argument for affirmative action that appeals to the importance of enhancing diversity and social integration.
- We consider and respond to an objection that maintains that affirmative action is itself wrongfully discriminatory.
- We examine worries about the effectiveness of affirmative action. Proponents of these objections claim that affirmative action fails to achieve its intended aims and that its use is sometimes stigmatizing. We make several points to dispel these concerns.
- We conclude by reflecting on the implications of our argument for the design of affirmative action policies.

5.1 INTRODUCTION

'[T]he world in which affirmative action policies were initiated was a world where a great many prestigious institutions and professions were almost exclusively enclaves of upper-class White men'.[1]

Although the world to which this statement refers is the 1970s, its central point remains apt today. In almost all states, women and members of particular racial and ethnic groups are systematically under-represented among politicians, business-leaders, and

---

[1] Luke Charles Harris and Uma Narayan, 'Affirmative Action as Equalizing Opportunity: Challenging the Myth of "Preferential Treatment"' in Hugh LaFollette (ed.), *Ethics in Practice: An Anthology, Fourth Edition* (Oxford: Wiley Blackwell, 2014), 449–59 at 449.

other advantaged social positions. The same is true of those who're disabled and for those who're gay. For example, of the United Kingdom's 650 MPs, only 34 per cent are women, 10 per cent are black and minority ethnic (BME), 0.8 per cent are disabled, and 7 per cent are openly lesbian, gay, bisexual, or transgender (LGBT).[2] All of these figures are lower than the percentage of the overall population that these groups comprise.

In response to facts like these, various states enact *anti-discrimination* policies that prohibit excluding individuals from education, training, and jobs on the basis of their gender, race, ethnicity, disability, or sexual orientation.[3] These policies also permit organizations to adopt measures, such as outreach and targeted advertising, to encourage members of various groups to pursue careers in which they're currently under-represented.

Some states go even further than this, by permitting or requiring the use of *affirmative action*. These policies are distinctive because they permit or require selectors to consider a candidate's membership of a particular group to play a role in the selection procedure.[4] One example of this is to use *quotas*, such that a selector must ensure that the percentage of those selected who're members of an under-represented group surpasses some threshold. For example, quotas might govern the minimum number of women holding political positions. We find policies of this kind in many countries throughout the world, including Argentina, Greece, Nepal, Poland, Portugal, Rwanda, and Slovenia.[5] Other quotas regulate the minimum number of women on the boards of large companies (which is a policy pioneered in Norway but that has now spread to many other countries) and ensure that the percentage of a firm's workforce with disabilities exceeds some threshold (which has been a long-standing practice in Germany).[6] Advocates of these policies argue that these are suitable means of rectifying the under-representation of members of these groups, particularly given that a central cause of this under-representation is the past and present wrongful discrimination suffered by these individuals.

However, because these policies give weight to a candidate's membership of a socially salient group in selection procedures, critics contend that these policies themselves involve wrongful discrimination. This objection holds that, because affirmative action permits selectors to treat applicants differently according to their gender, race, ethnicity, disability, or sexual orientation, these policies are wrongful in much the same way as the past and present discrimination that advocates of affirmative action

[2] 'Election 2019: Britain's Most Diverse Parliament', *BBC News*, 17 December 2019, available at https://www.bbc.co.uk/news/election-2019-50808536.

[3] For example, see the United Kingdom's *Equality Act 2010*.

[4] For discussion, see L. W. Sumner, 'Positive Sexism', *Social Philosophy & Policy*, 5 (1987), 204–22 at 208.

[5] For example, see Drude Dahlerup and Lenita Freidenvall, 'Electoral Gender Quotas and their Implementation in Europe', *Study for the European Parliament* (2013), available at http://www.europarl.europa.eu/RegData/etudes/note/join/2013/493011/IPOL-FEMM_NT(2013)493011_EN.pdf, 6–9.

[6] For discussion of the former, see Věra Jourová, 'Gender Balance on Corporate Boards: Europe Is Cracking the Glass Ceiling', *European Commission* (Brussels: European Commission, 2016), 6–7. For discussion of the latter, see Anke Stock, 'Affirmative Action: A German Perspective on the Promotion of Women's Rights with Regard to Employment', *Journal of Law and Society*, 33 (2006), 59–73 at 69–70.

deride. In order to assess this complaint, we must consider when and why discrimination is wrongful.

In this chapter, we argue that affirmative action is sometimes justifiable. In section 5.2, we distinguish three prominent forms of wrongful discrimination. In sections 5.3 and 5.4, we offer two arguments in support of affirmative action, one concerning past and present wrongful discrimination and the other concerning the importance of diversity and social integration. In section 5.5, we outline the objection that affirmative action itself constitutes a form of wrongful discrimination. We respond by showing that, on an attractive account of what makes discrimination wrongful, this objection fails. In section 5.6, we draw on empirical evidence to respond to critics who maintain that these policies are ineffective. In section 5.7, we conclude by elaborating on the policy implications of our arguments.

5.2 THREE KINDS OF WRONGFUL DISCRIMINATION

Jo is a low-level employee at a warehouse. She applies for a promotion, but the job goes to a much less-experienced colleague. Over the course of many years, she tries again several times, but is always unsuccessful. Jo asks her employers whether there's some particular reason that she has failed to land a promotion, but she gets no answer. Reflecting on the fact that those promoted ahead of her have tended to be white and tended to be men, Jo begins to wonder if she has been treated this way because she's a black woman.

Jo is the victim of wrongful discrimination if she has indeed been treated worse than other employees on account of her race, or her gender, or both. The example helps us to identify two defining features of wrongful discrimination.[7] First, it's *comparative*: it involves receiving worse treatment than others. Second, this inferior treatment occurs because the victim is, or is believed to be, a member of a *socially salient group*. We define a group as socially salient if and only if membership or perceived membership of it has a significant impact on social interactions across a wide range of contexts.[8] Among others, this includes gender, racial, and ethnic groups, as well as those relating to disability and sexual orientation. What's useful about this definition is that it doesn't assume that those contained within a group identify as members of that group, share any particular objective trait or characteristic, or fall into any sort of natural kind or category. For our analysis, what matters is that they're treated differently as a result of being a member or being perceived as a member of a socially salient group.

Discrimination can occur in several ways. First, it can occur as a direct result of the discriminator's judgements or behaviour. The classic example of this is *direct cognitive discrimination*, which occurs when the discrimination is motivated by conscious beliefs. Jo is a victim of direct cognitive discrimination if her employers rejected her

---

[7] Kasper Lippert-Rasmussen, *Born Free and Equal?* (Oxford: Oxford University Press, 2013), 16.
[8] Lippert-Rasmussen, *Born Free and Equal?*, 30.

applications for promotion out of animosity, dislike, or indifference to women or black employees, or because they believe that members of these groups lack the qualities required for leadership.[9]

Second, discrimination can also result from implicit biases—relatively unconscious and automatic features of prejudiced judgements and behaviour. Jo is a victim of *direct non-cognitive discrimination* if her employers rejected her applications because they implicitly associate women or black employees with low-level employment, or if they systematically underestimate the talents of these individuals, or don't see them as a good fit for promotion. Evidence suggests that implicit biases such as these are pervasive.[10] They occur in individuals of all genders, and even in instances where the presence of such biases is explicitly denied by those who possess them. Moreover, these biases affect our judgements and behaviour in a variety of ways that can have significant effects on the lives of their victims.[11]

Third, discrimination can occur when, without a justified purpose, selection criteria disproportionately disadvantage members of socially salient groups.[12] This is *indirect discrimination*. This form of discrimination needn't involve any conscious or unconscious bias. It can happen when selection criteria don't directly refer to members of socially salient groups, but nonetheless pose greater hurdles for them. A landmark example of this kind occurred in 1971, when Duke Power were taken to the Supreme Court over their policy requiring their employees to have a high school diploma in order to apply for promotion.[13] By unanimous decision, the Court ruled that this policy was indirectly discriminatory and illegal. The Court reached this verdict on the basis of two facts. First, the policy severely disadvantaged black employees, because these individuals were much less likely to have a high school diploma than white employees due to the history of racial oppression, including school segregation. Second, since this policy didn't serve any 'business necessity', the resulting disadvantage was disproportionate. Since then, we've seen countless further instances of indirect discrimination. For example, in 2017, the European Court of Justice condemned the Greek police force's height requirement as indirectly discriminatory on the grounds that it disproportionality disadvantaged women.[14] If similar facts hold in Jo's case, then she too is a victim of indirect discrimination.

---

[9] Lippert-Rasmussen, *Born Free and Equal?*, 41.

[10] Brian A. Nosek et al., 'Pervasiveness and Correlates of Implicit Attitudes and Stereotypes', *European Review of Social Psychology*, 18 (2007), 36–88.

[11] Anthony G. Greenwald and Linda Hamilton Krieger, 'Implicit Bias: Scientific Foundations', *California Law Review*, 94 (2006), 945–67 and Christina Friedlaender, 'On Microaggressions: Cumulative Harm and Individual Responsibility', *Hypatia*, 33 (2018), 5–21.

[12] Lippert-Rasmussen, *Born Free and Equal?*, 55.

[13] Tarunabh Khaitan, 'Indirect Discrimination' in Kasper Lippert-Rasmussen (ed.), *The Routledge Handbook to the Ethics of Discrimination* (London: Routledge, 2017), 30–41 at 31.

[14] Squire Patton Boggs, 'Height Requirements, Police Officers and Discrimination: A Short Story', *Employment Law Worldwide*, 13 December 2017, available at https://www.employmentlawworldview.com/height-requirements-police-officers-and-discrimination-a-short-story.

There are also other forms of wrongful discrimination.[15] But we take these three to be the most common and the most relevant to our purposes in this chapter. Our next task is to relate these to arguments in favour of affirmative action.

5.3 DISCRIMINATION AND AFFIRMATIVE ACTION

There are two common ways to defend affirmative action by appealing to the discrimination suffered by members of socially salient groups. One strategy draws on the idea that affirmative action *compensates* for discrimination. The other appeals to the idea that these policies *prevent* further discrimination. We consider the foundations of these arguments before turning to their connection to affirmative action.

5.3.1 DISCRIMINATION AND COMPENSATION

In the very recent past, members of many socially salient groups were denied a fair start in life, access to good jobs, and the right to vote, as well as various other legal protections that have long been afforded to members of advantaged social groups. Against this backdrop, some defend affirmative action on the grounds that it compensates for these injustices.[16]

One way in which to flesh out this argument is by appeal to the idea that affirmative action compensates *groups* that are victims of historical injustices. On this view, affirmative action can be justifiable because it compensates, say, women for the historical discrimination that deprived them of education and employment opportunities. This argument relies on the claim that groups (as opposed to the individuals who comprise these groups) can be wronged, and that it's appropriate to compensate groups (as opposed to particular individuals) for these historical injustices. This claim is controversial.[17]

In the light of this, another option is to view affirmative action as a means of compensating the *individual* victims of historical injustices. These are the individuals who comprise the socially salient groups with which we're concerned. But, at this point, a problem arises. This relates to the fact that many of the beneficiaries of affirmative action aren't the same individuals who suffered the injustices that these policies compensate. Most of the victims of the very worst instances of gender and racist discrimination are no longer alive, and those who're alive are no longer of working age, or otherwise situated to receive the benefits of affirmative action. For example, most

---

[15] Lippert-Rasmussen, *Born Free and Equal?*, ch. 3.

[16] Kasper Lippert-Rasmussen, 'Affirmative Action, Historical Injustice, and the Concept of Beneficiaries', *Journal of Political Philosophy*, 25 (2017), 72–90 and Judith Jarvis Thomson, 'Preferential Hiring', *Philosophy & Public Affairs*, 2 (1973), 364–84.

[17] George Sher, 'Justifying Reverse Discrimination in Employment', *Philosophy & Public Affairs*, 4 (1975), 159–70 at 160.

of those who lived through the legal racial segregation of schools in the United States are dead, and those who aren't are more likely to be drawing their pension than applying for university places or hitting the labour market. Because of this, critics might maintain that this defence of affirmative action mistakenly justifies compensating members of socially salient groups for injustices that they didn't suffer.

In response to this, we make two points. First, we shouldn't overlook the fact that members of socially salient groups continue to suffer wrongful discrimination. There are *some* adults alive who attended racially segregated schools, and there are many others who've been the victims of discriminatory selection procedures in education, employment, and politics. Second, these individuals also suffer the *consequences* of past injustices. For example, many BME children grow up in poor neighbourhoods with high crime rates and inadequate schools, at least partly as a result of the historical discrimination suffered by previous generations.

Viewed with this in mind, the case for affirmative action isn't premised on the idea that the state should compensate present-day members of socially salient groups for the historical injustices suffered by their ancestors. Instead, the argument rests on the idea that it should compensate these individuals for the injustices that they themselves have suffered in the recent past. The consequences of these injustices may not be as severe as those faced by previous generations, but they're still significant and call for compensation.

5.3.2 PREVENTING DISCRIMINATION

This result leads us to a second argument for affirmative action, according to which policies of this kind are justifiable as a means of combating *ongoing* discrimination against members of socially salient groups. Advocates of this argument highlight that female, BME, disabled, and LGBT candidates are victims of ongoing discrimination in education, employment, and politics. They then contend that affirmative action is an appropriate means to prevent this discrimination or, at least, to prevent discrimination from having such damaging effects.[18]

Let's return to the case of Jo, a black woman consistently denied promotion. Given the pervasiveness of prejudice and implicit bias against female and black applicants, we might be confident that, in the absence of any other explanation, Jo's employment prospects have been set back by discrimination. There's ample evidence that such barriers occur.[19] For example, members of socially salient groups are consistently rated more negatively both on paper and in interview than other applicants with the same

---

[18] Elizabeth Anderson, *The Imperative of Integration* (Princeton, NJ: Princeton University Press, 2010), 144–8; Harris and Narayan, 'Affirmative Action as Equalizing Opportunity', 451–4; and Kasper Lippert-Rasmussen, 'The Ethics of Anti-Discrimination Policies' in Annabelle Lever and Andrei Poama (eds), *The Routledge Handbook of Ethics and Public Policy* (London: Routledge, 2018), 267–80 at 270–2.

[19] David Neumark, 'Experimental Research on Labor Market Discrimination', *Journal of Economic Literature*, 56 (2018), 799–866.

credentials. There's also evidence that female and black applicants suffer indirect discrimination. An instance of this is that both recruitment and promotion often operate via word-of-mouth networks, which disadvantages those currently under-represented in advantaged social positions. In short, there are several ways in which Jo's institutional structure and her employer's assessment of her suitability for promotion may be biased against her. This gives us some reason to use policies that prevent discrimination or mitigate its effects.

5.3.3 WHY AFFIRMATIVE ACTION?

Why think that affirmative action is an appropriate mechanism through which to compensate for historical discrimination or to prevent ongoing discrimination? In particular, why directly regulate selection procedures rather than benefit victims of wrongful discrimination in other ways, such as with cash transfers? The answer is that affirmative action brings about an outcome that more closely resembles the one that would've existed had there been no wrongful discrimination. The crucial point here is that, if wrongful discrimination deprives an individual of employment opportunities, then affirmative action is appropriate because these policies aim to provide them with the *same* employment opportunities they would've enjoyed in the absence of wrongful discrimination.[20] For example, if fewer women than otherwise are selected for promotion because of implicit biases, then we might employ a quota that ensures women aren't under-represented in more senior roles to prevent this kind of wrongful discrimination or its effects.

Drawing all of this together makes the following case for affirmative action:

Discrimination moral claim: The state should prevent wrongful discrimination and compensate its victims when it occurs.

Discrimination empirical claim: Affirmative action prevents wrongful discrimination and compensates the victims when it occurs.

Conclusion: The state should allow or require the use of affirmative action.

We call this the *discrimination argument* for affirmative action.

5.4 DIVERSITY AND INTEGRATION

Let's now turn to a rather different defence of affirmative action, which appeals to the role that these policies can play in advancing various socially desirable goals. One version of this argument focuses on the value of *diversity* within the organizations that use affirmative action.[21] Let's consider the case of universities. Part of the purpose of a

---

[20] Sher, 'Justifying Reverse Discrimination in Employment', 161–5.
[21] Barbara Bergmann, *In Defence of Affirmative Action* (New York: Basic Books, 1996), ch. 1.

university is to provide its students with an educational experience that enables them to live well-rounded lives. Though perhaps not impossible, it's plainly more difficult for a university to succeed in this respect if the vast majority of its staff and students are alike in terms of gender, race, ethnicity, disability, and sexual orientation. This goal is more achievable at a university that's more diverse in terms of students and faculty. Diversity also increases the likelihood that otherwise neglected areas of research, such as those relating to the categories we've mentioned, will be addressed by students and staff. Additionally, greater diversity is likely to increase the range of methods and perspectives that are brought to bear on topics.[22] Similar points apply in other contexts. For example, studies reveal that increased diversity within firms can enhance performance, improving revenue and returns on investments.[23]

A second version of this argument focuses on how diversity in education, employment, and politics can improve *social integration*.[24] One avenue for this is by providing role models for students from under-represented groups. Discussing the case of universities in the United States in the 1970s, Judith Jarvis Thomson writes,

> The proportion of black and women faculty members in the larger universities (particularly as one moves up the ladder of rank) is very much smaller than the proportion of blacks and women in the society at large—even, in the case of women, than the proportion of them amongst recipients of Ph.D. degrees from those very same universities. Black and women students suffer a constricting of ambition because of this. They need to see members of their race or sex who are accepted, successful, professionals. They need concrete evidence that those of their race or sex *can* become accepted, successful professionals.[25]

This is supported by empirical studies that reveal how having a mentor of the same gender or race can influence how women and members of racial minorities choose their occupations.[26]

Indeed, as Elizabeth Anderson notes, increasing diversity in advantaged social positions benefits social integration in many ways:

> [It] helps people learn to cooperate across racial lines, breaks down racial stigmatization, interracial discomfort, and habits of segregation, makes decision makers more aware of and accountable for the impact of their decisions on all racial groups, and invigorates democratic exchange in civil society.[27]

---

[22] Alison Wylie, 'Why Standpoint Matters' in Robert Rigueroa and Sandra Haring (eds), *Science and Other Cultures: Issues in Philosophies of Science and Technology* (London: Routledge, 2003), 26–48.

[23] Sara Fisher Ellison and Wallace Mullin, 'Diversity, Social Goods Provision, and Performance in the Firm', *Journal of Economics & Management Strategy*, 23 (2014), 465–81.

[24] Ronald Dworkin, *Sovereign Virtue: The Theory and Practice of Equality* (Cambridge, MA: Harvard University Press, 2000), chs 11–12 and Anderson, *The Imperative of Integration*, 148–53.

[25] Thomson, 'Preferential Hiring', 367 (emphasis in original).

[26] For example, see Michael Kofoed and Elizabeth McGovney, 'The Effect of Same-Gender and Same-Race Role Models on Occupational Choice: Evidence from Randomly Assigned Mentors at West Point', *Journal of Human Resources*, 54 (2019), 430–67.

[27] Anderson, *The Imperative of Integration*, 149.

These points count in favour of affirmative action, which offers a straightforward means by which to enhance diversity and social integration. For example, quota policies that govern the number of places at university for BME applicants, the percentage of a firm's workforce with disabilities, or the minimum number of women holding political positions advance these goals in education, employment, and politics. We can state this case for affirmative action as follows:

> *Diversity and integration moral claim*: The state should improve diversity and social integration in various contexts, including education, employment, and politics.
>
> *Diversity and integration empirical claim*: Affirmative action improves diversity and social integration.
>
> *Conclusion*: The state should allow or require the use of affirmative action.

We call this the *diversity and integration argument* for affirmative action.[28]

5.5 THE REVERSE DISCRIMINATION OBJECTION

At this stage, critics will be quick to press an objection. We're rightly outraged by the way in which those who discriminate wrongfully use categories such as gender and race to deprive individuals of opportunities for education and employment, and to enter political life. This is partly why the case for affirmative action is so compelling. But critics maintain that these policies should outrage us in much the same way, since they also deprive individuals of various opportunities by categorizing them according to things like their gender and race. In this way, affirmative action might seem to be merely another instance of wrongful discrimination. This is the *reverse discrimination objection*.

This objection features prominently in an important legal case concerning the use of affirmative action.[29] In the 1970s, the School of Medicine at University of California, Davis had a policy of reserving sixteen of its one hundred yearly places for minority students. Allan Bakke, a white applicant, was twice rejected from this programme. Bakke had good test scores. Indeed, they were better than some of those attained by students who were offered the reserved places. However, his application wasn't strong enough for him to secure one of the remaining eighty-four places on the course. Bakke challenged the University over the decision and, in due course, the case made its way to the Supreme Court, where it was ruled that the University's policy violated the constitution's main discrimination injunction: the equal protection clause of the 14th Amendment.

---

[28] We can distinguish arguments for affirmative action based on claims about diversity from those based on claims about social integration, such that a proponent of affirmative action may be sympathetic to one of these arguments but not the other. For example, see Anderson, *The Imperative of Integration*, 141–4 and 148–53. We set aside this subtlety.

[29] For details of this case, see Ronald Dworkin, 'The Rights of Allan Bakke' in Hugh LaFollette (ed.), *Ethics in Practice: An Anthology, Fourth Edition* (Oxford: Wiley Blackwell, 2014), 443–8 at 443.

In support of this judgment, Justice Lewis Powell stated that 'distinctions between citizens solely because of their ancestry are, by their very nature, odious'.[30] Such classification is precisely what the 14th Amendment was designed to prohibit and, he argued, 'equal protection cannot mean one thing when applied to one individual and something else when applied to a person of another color'.[31]

We can motivate this objection in two distinct ways. The first holds that classifying an applicant according to their membership of a socially salient group is objectionable because this violates the demands of meritocracy. Let's call this the *meritocracy objection*. The second version of the objection holds that classifying an applicant according to their membership of a socially salient group is objectionable because this fails to recognize the equal treatment to which they're entitled regardless of their gender, race, ethnicity, disability, and sexual orientation. Let's call this the *equal treatment objection*. We consider these arguments in turn.

5.5.1 DISCRIMINATION AND MERIT

The principle of meritocracy holds that we should award goods such as education, employment, and political office to the best qualified applicant. One way in which to defend this principle is by appealing to the idea that the best qualified applicant *deserves* to be selected, such that they're wronged if a less qualified applicant is selected ahead of them.[32] An alternative way in which to defend this principle is by appealing to the idea that, since everyone has an interest in tasks being carried out in an efficient manner, each individual has an interest in tasks being carried out by the applicant who's most qualified.[33] On this view, it's not the best qualified applicant who's wronged when a hospital appoints someone other than the most qualified doctor; it's everyone, who'll enjoy less good treatment as a result.

It's easy to see why the use of affirmative action is thought to violate this principle. After all, in the case of Allan Bakke, it was acknowledged that Bakke had better test scores than those achieved by some applicants who were offered the School's reserved places. Louis Pojman puts the concern as follows:

> What is wrong about discrimination against blacks is that it fails to treat black people as individuals, judging them instead by their skin colour rather than their merit. What is wrong about discrimination against women is that it fails to treat them as individuals, judging them by their gender, not their merit. What is equally wrong about Affirmative Action is that it fails to treat white males . . . as individuals, judging them by *both their race and gender*, instead of their merit.[34]

---

[30] *Regents of the University of California v. Bakke*, 438 U.S. 265 (1978).

[31] *Regents of the University of California v. Bakke*, 438 U.S. 265 (1978). See also Carl Cohen, 'Who Are Equals?' in Steven Cahn (ed.), *The Affirmative Action Debate, Second Edition* (Oxford: Routledge, 2002), 95–102.

[32] David Miller, *Principles of Social Justice* (Cambridge, MA: Harvard University Press, 1999), chs 8–9.

[33] Norman Daniels, 'Merit and Meritocracy', *Philosophy & Public Affairs*, 7 (1978), 206–23.

[34] Louis Pojman, 'The Case Against Affirmative Action' in Hugh LaFollette (ed.), *Ethics in Practice: An Anthology, Fourth Edition* (Oxford: Wiley Blackwell, 2014), 433–42 at 439 (emphasis in original).

We offer two replies. First, let's return to the discrimination argument for affirmative action. This argument sees affirmative action as the appropriate response to the past and present discrimination suffered by members of socially salient groups. Given this discrimination, advocates of this argument maintain that it's our *current* admissions and hiring procedures that violate the principle of meritocracy, and that affirmative action is actually a means through which to correct this fault.[35] To illustrate, let's consider the idea that affirmative action can help to prevent wrongful discrimination by correcting for implicit and institutional biases against women and members of racial and minority ethnic groups. Insofar as a selector's decisions are hindered by these biases, then they're not meritocratic in the first place. Viewed in this way, affirmative action aims to align admissions and hiring procedures with the principle of meritocracy, rather than violate it.

Similarly, with respect to the claim that affirmative action can compensate the victims of wrongful discrimination, while it's true that these individuals may not be the best qualified, this is sometimes the case only because their chances to develop their abilities have been set back by this discrimination. The additional barriers faced by members of some socially salient groups are another reason that many of our practices fail to adhere to the principle of meritocracy. Basing selection decisions solely on an applicant's qualifications is akin to judging who's the fastest by looking at who crossed the finish line first without considering whether all runners started from the same place. Affirmative action can correct this error.

Let's now turn to our second reply, which targets the fact that the meritocracy objection relies on an unduly narrow conception of merit.[36] To see this, let's contrast two students, one black and one white, who achieve identical exam results. Both students apply to university, but there's only one place left on the course. At the university in question, black students are under-represented. Is there some sense in which the black student is better qualified than the white student? We think so. After all, whereas the two students contribute equally to the academic environment, the black student is better able than the white student to advance the university's goal of having a racially diverse student population. Making this point in relation to the Bakke case, Ronald Dworkin writes:

> There is no combination of abilities . . . that constitutes 'merit' in the abstract; if quick hands count as 'merit' in the case of a prospective surgeon, this is because quick hands will enable him to serve the public better . . . If a black skin will . . . enable another doctor to do a different medical job better [perhaps because it will enhance a particular aspect of medical practice or create role models], then that black skin is by the same token 'merit' as well.[37]

Some respond to this by claiming that it's unfair to penalize an individual, such as Bakke, for something for which they're not responsible, such as their race or ethnicity. The problem with this response is that there's a host of other factors that influence a student's suitability for further study for which they're not responsible. To some extent, this is true even

---

[35] Harris and Narayan, 'Affirmative Action as Equalizing Opportunity', 453–4.
[36] Dworkin, 'The Rights of Allan Bakke', 446–7.   [37] Dworkin, 'The Rights of Allan Bakke', 446.

with respect to academic ability. A student can work more or less hard, and this will no doubt affect their results, but genetic and social factors also play a role. Because of this, even test scores can penalize an individual for something for which they aren't responsible. The upshot of this is that, if we're willing to allow an individual's intelligence to affect their 'merit', then we must also allow their membership of a socially salient group to do the same.

5.5.2 DISCRIMINATION AND EQUALITY

One concern with broadening the idea of merit in the way that we've suggested is that it permits selectors to make admissions and hiring decisions in accordance with an individual's membership of a socially salient group. Proponents of the equal treatment objection are troubled by this move.[38] The worry is that, by awarding goods in a way that's sensitive to these facts, we fail to recognize the equal treatment to which an individual is entitled regardless of their gender, race, ethnicity, disability, and sexual orientation. Isn't it a paradigmatic example of discrimination to treat an individual better or worse than others in virtue of their membership of a socially salient group?

However, it's precisely this point that demonstrates the weakness of the equal treatment objection. To appreciate why, let's start with the fact that it's only individuals who're sighted, and not those who're blind, who may hold driving licences. This is an example of a policy that classifies an individual according to their membership of a socially salient group, and then uses this information to grant or deny them a particular benefit, namely the permission to hold a driving licence. Clearly, however, this policy is justifiable. This is a case of discrimination, but it isn't *wrongful* discrimination.

There's considerable debate about when and why discrimination is wrong.[39] One prominent position holds that discrimination is wrongful when it expresses the disrespectful message that members of one socially salient group aren't morally equal to others in their society.[40] Part of what makes this view attractive is that it plausibly distinguishes between acts of discrimination that are objectionable and those that are innocent. The policy of denying driving licences to those who're blind doesn't display the disrespectful message that these individuals are morally inferior. In contrast, what we find so problematic about denying women the vote, for example, is that this *did* send the disrespectful message that women are second-class citizens, or perhaps not even citizens at all. The same is true for signs on courtroom doors that say 'men only' in a context where women have traditionally been denied access to legal professions.[41] This account also speaks readily to paradigmatic cases of racial discrimination, where 'exclusion by race was in itself an insult, because it was generated by and signalled contempt'.[42]

---

[38] Cohen, 'Who Are Equals?', 96–9.

[39] For an overview, see Andrew Altman, 'Discrimination', *Stanford Encyclopedia of Philosophy* (2015), available at https://plato.stanford.edu/entries/discrimination.

[40] Dworkin, 'The Rights of Allan Bakke', 447–8 and Deborah Hellman, *When Is Discrimination Wrong?* (Cambridge, MA: Harvard University Press, 2011).

[41] Hellman, *When Is Discrimination Wrong?*, 5–7.   [42] Dworkin, 'The Rights of Allan Bakke', 447.

If we adopt this account—namely, that discrimination is wrongful when it expresses disrespectful messages of this kind—the charge that affirmative action constitutes wrongful discrimination is untenable. When a company reserves seats on its boards for women, this doesn't carry the disrespectful message that men are morally inferior to women. It'd border on parody to suggest that the policy that denied Bakke his place at the University of California, Davis expressed contempt for white applicants. Affirmative action designed to address past and present discrimination and to enhance diversity and social integration doesn't have this wrong-making feature, and so we believe the use of such policies isn't vulnerable to the equal treatment objection.

5.6 EFFECTIVENESS OBJECTIONS

So far, we've focused on the moral credentials of affirmative action. However, to complete our defence of the use of these policies, we must show that they work. We achieve this by responding to two objections regarding their effectiveness.

5.6.1 THE OFF-TARGET OBJECTION

The first objection states that affirmative action is ineffective because it misses the target, in the sense that it tends to advantage those who face comparatively little discrimination, while failing to assist those who fare worse in this regard. One worry is that policies designed to improve the representation of women in advantaged social positions may benefit only those women from wealthier backgrounds, rather than women who're poor and tend to suffer more seriously at the hands of wrongful discrimination. In addition, this policy might take opportunities away from men from more disadvantaged backgrounds. Similarly, in the United States, some critics point out that, though affirmative action has succeeded in increasing the representation of black students in universities, these individuals tend to come from backgrounds as elite as their white peers.[43] This is the *off-target objection*.[44]

This objection has some force. But we believe it fails for two reasons. First, though we acknowledge that affirmative action often misses the target in the sense described, the implication of this isn't that the state should prohibit the use of affirmative action. Rather, what this suggests is that the state needs to support its more extensive use and, in particular, take extra steps to increase the likelihood that affirmative action targets the appropriate beneficiaries. For example, one response may be to use quotas to improve the representation of individuals from low-income families in advantaged social positions. The general point is that, while it might be fair to criticize a policy for being too blunt, the best response to this is to sharpen the tool, not abandon it.[45]

---

[43] For discussion of this trend, see Richard H. Sander, 'Class in American Legal Education', *Denver University Law Review*, 88 (2011), 631–82.   [44] Pojman, 'The Case Against Affirmative Action', 438–9.

[45] Lippert-Rasmussen, 'The Ethics of Anti-Discrimination Policies', 274 and Thomson, 'Preferential Hiring', 382.

Second, even setting this aside, the fact that affirmative action misses some of its targets isn't enough to condemn its use. This is because affirmative action may remain justifiable so long as it's better than the alternative, in which various forms of discrimination are allowed to prevail, and diversity and social integration are neglected.

5.6.2 THE STIGMA OBJECTION

A distinct objection to affirmative action holds that the use of these policies is unjustifiable because it's *stigmatizing*.[46] One version of this objection emphasizes the fact that affirmative action might strengthen the disposition to see others as members of a socially salient group and to regard and treat them differently on this basis. This would be the case if black doctors were perceived as less competent than their white counterparts because of the assumption that they've been the beneficiaries of affirmative action. In other words, affirmative action may lead to an increase in *external stigma*.

A second concern is that affirmative action might insult its beneficiaries. To illustrate this point, let's suppose that some women are hired partly in order to meet a quota, and that this sends a message to these and other women that affirmative action is necessary for them to succeed. In this context, the worry is that a beneficiary of these policies may be unsure of the grounds of their accomplishments, especially if they think that this may be questioned by others. A related danger is that they may feel that affirmative action belittles them along with their achievements. These are examples of *internal stigma*.

We can state the *stigma objection* in the following manner:

Stigma moral claim: It's wrong to cause internal or external stigma to members of socially salient groups.

Stigma empirical claim: Affirmative action causes internal and external stigma to members of socially salient groups.

Conclusion: The state should prohibit the use of affirmative action.

One weakness of this objection is that there's no clear evidence with which to verify the stigma empirical claim. On the one hand, some small-scale experiments suggest that participants view women who're beneficiaries of affirmative action as less competent than their counterparts even when there's evidence that they performed similarly.[47] On the other hand, a study of law schools in the United States found that race-based affirmative action had no impact on black students' assessment of their own professional abilities, or on peers' perception of those abilities.[48]

---

[46] Carl Cohen, 'Why Race Preference Is Wrong and Bad' in Carl Cohen and James Sterba, *Affirmative Action and Racial Preference* (Oxford: Oxford University Press, 2003), part 3.

[47] Madeline Heilman, Caryn Block, and Peter Stathatos, 'The Affirmative Action Stigma of Incompetence: Effects of Performance Information Ambiguity', *Academy of Management Journal*, 40 (1997), 603–25.

[48] Angela Onwuachi-Willig, Emily Houh, and Mary Campbell, 'Cracking the Egg: Which Came First—Stigma or Affirmative Action?', *California Law Review*, 96 (2008), 1299–352.

Fortunately, it's not necessary for us to evaluate this data to refute the stigma objection. It's sufficient to point out that its claims don't support its conclusion. Evidence from the United States suggests that the performances of employees recruited as a result of affirmative action are broadly indistinguishable from those who don't benefit from these policies.[49] This suggests that there's no empirical basis for the belief that these individuals are weaker performers than their peers. Given this fact, the appropriate way to deal with internal and external stigma (if indeed it is a problem) isn't by abandoning affirmative action, but instead by educating individuals about how their beliefs on these matters aren't supported by the evidence.

5.7 CONCLUSIONS

Affirmative action is highly controversial, and it's sometimes rejected by those who're otherwise sympathetic to measures whose purpose is to enhance the representation of members of various socially salient groups in education, employment, and politics. Our aim in this chapter has been to dispel this scepticism. We outlined two arguments in favour of affirmative action, which appeal to the fact that it's an appropriate way to compensate for and prevent wrongful discrimination and that it can promote diversity and social integration. To bolster our defence, we've also responded to several philosophical and empirical concerns. Together, we believe that this constitutes a strong case for the use of affirmative action in some circumstances.

This doesn't close the issue. Our focus here has been on the use of quotas in general, but these policies admit of variation. For example, quotas can be more or less demanding. There may also be instances in which other forms of affirmative action are more suitable than quotas. We must be alive to the possibility that different kinds of wrongful discrimination and the various concerns we have about diversity and social integration provide us with reasons to favour one form of affirmative action over another. In some contexts, it might be better to require selectors to lower the entry requirements for applicants from under-represented groups. These important matters warrant further exploration. But our contribution in this chapter has been to show how we can proceed with this task, knowing that affirmative action is sometimes justifiable.

---

[49] Harry Holzer and David Neumark, 'What Does Affirmative Action Do?', *Industrial and Labour Relations Review*, 53 (2000), 240–71 and Jesse Rothstein and Albert Yoon, 'Affirmative Action in Law School Admissions', *University of Chicago Law Review*, 75 (2008), 649–714.

FURTHER READING

Good overviews of the moral and legal disputes that bear on the justifiability of affirmative action are Katherine Smits, *Applying Political Theory: Issues and Debates* (Basingstoke: Palgrave, 2009), ch. 4 and Robert Fullinwider, 'Affirmative Action', *Stanford Encyclopedia of Philosophy* (2017), https://plato.stanford.edu/entries/affirmative-action.

An accessible defence of the use of affirmative action is Luke Charles Harris and Uma Narayan, 'Affirmative Action as Equalizing Opportunity: Challenging the Myth of "Preferential Treatment"' in Hugh LaFollette (ed.), *Ethics in Practice: An Anthology, Fourth Edition* (Oxford: Wiley Blackwell, 2014), 449–59. And an accessible critique is Louis Pojman, 'The Case Against Affirmative Action' in Hugh LaFollette (ed.), *Ethics in Practice: An Anthology, Fourth Edition* (Oxford: Wiley Blackwell, 2014), 433–42.

For extended arguments in support of the justifiability of affirmative action, excellent starting points are L. W. Sumner, 'Positive Sexism', *Social Philosophy & Policy*, 5 (1987), 204–22 and Judith Jarvis Thomson, 'Preferential Hiring', *Philosophy & Public Affairs*, 2 (1973), 364–84. A more advanced defence is Kasper Lippert-Rasmussen, *Making Sense of Affirmative Action* (Oxford: Oxford University Press, 2020). For an extended argument against the use of policies of this kind, see Carl Cohen, 'Why Race Preference Is Wrong and Bad' in Carl Cohen and James Sterba, *Affirmative Action and Racial Preference* (Oxford: Oxford University Press, 2003), 3–190.

For further discussion of the wrongness of discrimination, we recommend Kasper Lippert-Rasmussen, *Born Free and Equal?* (Oxford: Oxford University Press, 2013); Deborah Hellman, *When Is Discrimination Wrong?* (Cambridge, MA: Harvard University Press, 2011); and Sophia Moreau, *Faces of Inequality: A Theory of Wrongful Discrimination* (Oxford: Oxford University Press, 2020).

 For additional material and resources, including web links and self-test questions, please visit the online resources **www.oup.com/he/walton1e**.

6

SCHOOLS AND EQUALITY
OF OPPORTUNITY

SUMMARY

- In this chapter, we explore the value of equality of opportunity and assess its implication for the design of the school system, arguing for the radical conclusion that the state should prohibit elite private schools.
- We begin by outlining how elite private schools create inequalities in prospects between children, and we develop an account of why this is morally problematic.
- We analyse a challenge to our argument that comes from those who reject equality of opportunity in favour of educational adequacy. We respond by commenting on the counterintuitive implications of the latter, and by further examining the values that underpin the conception of equality of opportunity that we favour.
- We consider the possibility that it's wrong for the state to prohibit elite private schools because this interferes too much in family life. We offer a framework for assessing which choices we should protect on these grounds, and we argue that the choice to send one's child to an elite private school doesn't fall in this set.
- We investigate the claim that prohibiting elite private schools is unlikely to have any significant effect on equalizing opportunities between children. We suggest that the empirical evidence doesn't support this worry.
- We conclude by reflecting on the implications of our arguments for the design of the school system.

6.1 INTRODUCTION

A child's education has a significant impact on their emotional, physical, and intellectual development. When done well, education enables a child to develop their talents and positions them to make wise choices, enabling them to live a flourishing life. Because it can provide an array of important goods, it's one of the key responsibilities of parents and the state to guarantee that each child receives a good education. In particular, parents have a moral duty to ensure that *their own children* are suitably educated and the state has a moral duty to ensure that *all* children enjoy good opportunities to prosper. Although these objectives will often align, they're sometimes in conflict.

This tension plays a pivotal role in public debate about the following question: should the state prohibit elite private schools? In response to the United Kingdom's Labour Party's 2019 campaign for abolition, critics argue that 'it is the most natural instinct in the world to want to do the best for your children, and those parents who send their sons and daughters to [elite private] schools are making a legitimate choice'.[1] The choice benefits the children because elite private schools tend to operate with budgets that are much greater than those in state schools and, as a result, students at elite private schools enjoy smaller classes and superior resources and technology.[2] Defenders of this choice contend not only that the state should permit this kind of *parental partiality* but also that these actions are laudable, reflecting a valuable parent–child relationship.

However, those who believe that the state should prohibit elite private schools express concern at the fact that these benefits accrue to only *some* children, namely those whose parents are willing and able to pay for them to receive such an education. This is problematic because it violates *equality of opportunity*. This is the idea that children should enjoy similar prospects for success in the competition for advantaged social positions (such as in the competition for higher education and in the labour market) regardless of their family background. The general worry with elite private schools is that they allow some parents, especially high-earning parents with more disposable income, to confer educational advantages on their children that other children will not enjoy, especially those from poorer backgrounds. For example, in the United Kingdom, students who attend elite private schools are three times more likely to attend a highly selective university and, although these students account for only 7 per cent of the school population, they make up 74 per cent of the country's top judges, 61 per cent of its top doctors, 51 per cent of its leading print journalists, and 32 per cent of MPs.[3] Summarizing this concern, the Labour Party write, 'young people's opportunity to flourish and fulfil their potential is still determined by the size of their parents' bank balance'.[4]

In this chapter, we explore these disputes by defending the claim that the state should prohibit elite private schools. In section 6.2, we elaborate on the appeal of equality of opportunity to construct an initial case against elite private schools. We reinforce this case in section 6.3, where we respond to those who reject equality of

[1] Barnaby Lenon, 'Abolishing Private Schools Would Not Improve Education', *The Times*, 18 July 2019, available at https://www.thetimes.co.uk/article/abolishing-private-schools-would-not-improve-education-ww2rhdzj8.

[2] Chris Belfield, Claire Crawford, and Luke Sibieta, *Long-Run Comparisons of Spending Per Pupil Across Different Stages of Education* (London: Institute for Fiscal Studies, 2017).

[3] Department for Education, *Widening Participation in Higher Education, England, 2013/2014 Age Cohort* (2016) and Philip Kirby, 'Leading People 2016', *The Sutton Trust* (2016), available at https://www.suttontrust.com/research-paper/leading-people-2016.

[4] Richard Adams, 'Abolish Eton: Labour Groups Aim to Strip Elite Schools of Privilege', *The Guardian*, 9 July 2019, available at https://www.theguardian.com/education/2019/jul/09/abolish-eton-labour-groups-aim-to-strip-elite-private-schools-of-privileges.

opportunity in favour of educational adequacy. In section 6.4, we reply to those who maintain that denying parents the option of sending their child to an elite private school interferes too much in family life. In section 6.5, we assess the claim that, since schooling isn't the major determinant of a child's prospects, prohibiting elite private schools is unlikely to have any significant effect on equalizing opportunities. In section 6.6, we summarize the discussion and reflect on some of the implications of our arguments for the design of the school system.

Before moving on, we offer two clarifications. First, our interest in this chapter is in *elite private schools*—that is, fee-paying schools that don't receive funding from the state and that generally provide better-than-average education that increases their students' prospects of success in the competition for advantaged social positions. We can distinguish elite private schools from grammar schools, which are selective but not fee-paying, as well as from religious schools, which aim to cultivate various religious convictions in their students. Both grammar schools and religious schools raise distinct considerations that we lack the space to address in detail here.

Second, we must be careful not to confuse our question—should the state prohibit elite private schools?—with another closely related one: if the state permits elite private schools, is it morally permissible for parents to send their child to such a school? These two questions are distinct and, in principle, we might supply different answers to each of them. For example, we can imagine someone maintaining that, even though the state should abolish elite private schools, parents are morally permitted to make use of them while they continue to exist. There's nothing more incoherent about this position than holding that, even though the state should legally prohibit the private ownership of firearms, an individual is morally permitted to own firearms until such legislation comes into effect. We don't mean to express sympathy for either of these views, or even to claim that these cases are strictly analogous. We mean to highlight only that we might provide different answers to these two kinds of questions without contradiction, and that our concern in this chapter is exclusively with whether the state should prohibit elite private schools.[5]

6.2 ELITE PRIVATE SCHOOLS AND EQUALITY OF OPPORTUNITY

We explore the reasons that motivate critics of elite private schools by first considering a hypothetical example, and then connecting this with the case of schooling.

---

[5] For discussion of the moral permissibility of sending a child to an elite private school when it does exist, see Adam Swift, *How Not to Be a Hypocrite: School Choice for the Morally Perplexed Parent* (London: Routledge, 2003), part 2.

6.2.1 UNFAIRNESS AND HARM

Let's consider the following:

> *Race*: Savannah and Chantin compete in a race. The winner receives a financial reward, and the loser gets nothing. Chantin consistently runs faster than Savannah in practice, and in response Savannah's parents supply their daughter with a performance-enhancing drug. As a result of taking the drug, Savannah wins the race.[6]

It's clear that something morally problematic occurs here, relating to the fact that, because Savannah takes the drug provided by her parents, Chantin enjoys worse prospects of success than Savannah. In particular, there's no *equality of opportunity* between the two: Chantin suffers a disadvantage in comparison with Savannah. It might not always be objectionable for there to be inequality of opportunity. For example, if Savannah had improved her performance by training harder, then perhaps we wouldn't object to her enjoying greater prospects of victory than Chantin. However, *Race* is different. In this case, the disadvantage that Chantin suffers in comparison with Savannah stems from the fact that Savannah enjoys access to a performance-enhancing drug that's denied to Chantin without any good reason.

In this case, the inequality of opportunity between Savannah and Chantin is morally bad for two reasons. First, we believe it's *unfair* that Chantin enjoys less valuable prospects than Savannah through no fault or responsibility of her own.[7] It's morally bad that Chantin's opportunities in life are less valuable than Savannah's, where this is due to Chantin's parents' inability or unwillingness to supply her with a performance-enhancing drug. This is because this is something for which we can't hold Chantin responsible. Second, the inequality of opportunity should trouble us because Chantin's life doesn't merely continue as it would've done otherwise, had Savannah not taken the drug. In particular, had Savannah not used the drug, Chantin would've won the race and received the financial reward. In this respect, the disadvantage that Chantin suffers in comparison with Savannah also reduces Chantin's prospects of success, both in terms of the race itself and the benefits she'd then receive. In other words, Chantin is *harmed* by the inequality of opportunity. Again, we might not object to this harm if Savannah had earned her victory, perhaps as a result of training harder, but this isn't true in the case we're considering.

6.2.2 THE COMPARISON WITH ELITE PRIVATE SCHOOLS

There are three features of *Race* that make it interestingly similar to elite private schools.[8] First, just as Savannah and Chantin compete for financial reward, students compete for advantaged social positions in higher education and in the labour market. Second,

---

[6] This example mirrors the queue-jumping example in Swift, *How Not to Be a Hypocrite*, 24.

[7] What would we say if the inequality of opportunity stemmed from some other feature of her circumstances for which she has no responsibility, such as if Chantin inherited shorter legs from her parents? We discuss questions of this kind in Chapter 7.

[8] Harry Brighouse and Adam Swift, *Family Values: The Ethics of Parent-Child Relationships* (Princeton, NJ: Princeton University Press, 2014), 127–8.

through the education that students receive at elite private schools, these individuals are normally better equipped than they would be otherwise for academic study, as well as for performing well in exams and in interviews. Because of this, attending an elite private school boosts a student's chances of securing a place at a prestigious university and it enhances their employment opportunities. In this way, elite private schools confer comparative advantage in the competition for advantaged social position on their students, producing inequality of opportunity between these students and those who attend other schools. Third, if the greater prospect of those at elite private schools stemmed from the fact that these students worked harder than those at other schools, then perhaps we wouldn't object. However, this isn't the case. Instead, the inequality of opportunity is, at least in part, attributable to the fact that students at elite private schools enjoy additional opportunities that are denied to others without any good reason.

As with *Race*, this inequality of opportunity is morally problematic for two reasons. First, it's *unfair* that students from other schools enjoy less valuable prospects than students from elite private schools through no fault or responsibility of their own. Second, this inequality of opportunity *harms* students who don't attend elite private schools, since these students fare less well than otherwise in the competition for advantaged social positions. As Harry Brighouse and Adam Swift observe, the crucial point is that, when a child attends an elite private school, this

> does not leave untouched, but rather is detrimental to, those other children's prospects in the competition for jobs and associated rewards . . . [I]f some children are getting it and others are not, then those who aren't are not just worse off than the others; they are worse off than they would have been if the others had not been getting it.[9]

To clarify why this is the case, it helps to note that education is a *positional good*, such that its value to any given student depends partly on how much they possess of it in comparison with how much other students possess.[10] This is because what matters most when someone applies to a university or for a job is how they fare in comparison with other applicants. If a student at an elite private school receives educational benefits that push them ahead of a student from a state school who would otherwise have been ahead in the competition, then the state school student is *harmed* because they'll be one place lower than they otherwise would have been. It's in this way that the presence and use of elite private schools reduces others' prospects of success.

Together, the unfairness of the inequality of opportunity and harm that it causes form the basis of a case for prohibiting elite private schools.[11] It's on these grounds that we might formulate the following argument:

> *Equality of opportunity moral claim*: Because of its unfairness and harmfulness, no individual should suffer worse prospects than anyone else in the competition for advantaged social positions in virtue of their family background.

[9] Brighouse and Swift, *Family Values*, 128.
[10] Harry Brighouse and Adam Swift, 'Equality, Priority, and Positional Goods', *Ethics*, 116 (2006), 471–97.
[11] For further arguments, see Swift, *How Not to Be a Hypocrite*, 34–46.

Elite private schools empirical claim: Students who don't attend elite private schools suffer worse prospects in virtue of their family background in comparison with those who do.

Conclusion: The state should prohibit elite private schools.

We call this the *equality of opportunity argument* in favour of prohibiting elite private schools.

6.3 EQUALITY OR ADEQUACY?

One important challenge to this argument targets its moral claim. Critics contend that, although it *seems* that we should oppose inequalities in children's life-prospects, this conviction is a mistake. Rather, our concern should be to ensure that each child receives an adequate education—an education necessary for them to live a decent life. This is consistent with inequality of opportunity. On this view, it doesn't matter that those who attend other schools suffer worse prospects than those who attend elite private schools, so long as each child receives an education that's sufficiently good.

We can flesh out the reasoning in support of this objection in several ways. One version claims that, though we've reasons to favour equality, the chief requirement of this is that each individual is able to *relate* to others as their moral equal.[12] Those who endorse this outlook argue that what matters is that no one is oppressed, excluded, or dominated. That is, no one should fear being looked down on by others. These aims require that children receive an education, part of the purpose of which is to develop their skills so that they can participate in society as moral equals. A component of this is that each child receives the training necessary for them to find gainful employment on reasonable terms. But, to achieve this, we needn't realize equality of opportunity for advantaged social positions. The fact that some suffer worse prospects than others isn't morally problematic so long as those with the worst prospects can still live good lives and find decent jobs. We can call this the *adequacy objection* to the equality of opportunity argument. Its central claim is as follows:

Adequacy moral claim: All that matters is that each individual should receive an education that's sufficient for them to participate in society as a moral equal.[13]

If correct, the adequacy objection would undermine the equality of opportunity argument for prohibiting elite private schools. Of course, those who favour this option might oppose these schools for *other* reasons, such as on the grounds that these schools might heighten segregation and, in this way, increase the risk of oppression, exclusion,

[12] Elizabeth Anderson, 'Fair Opportunity in Education: A Democratic Equality Perspective', *Ethics*, 117 (2007), 595–622 and Debra Satz, 'Equality, Adequacy and Education for Citizenship', *Ethics*, 117 (2007), 623–48. See also Harry Frankfurt, 'Equality as a Moral Ideal', *Ethics*, 98 (1987), 21–43.

[13] Anderson, 'Fair Opportunity in Education', 615.

and domination.[14] However, even if so, what this reveals is that the state should enact policies whose purpose is to counteract the segregation caused by elite private schools, not prohibit them.

With proponents of the adequacy moral claim, we agree that it's vital that each child receives an education that's sufficiently good that they can live a decent life. However, we deny that this is all that matters.[15] To see this, let's imagine a world in which the adequacy moral claim is satisfied, such that everyone enjoys an adequate education, though there's inequality of opportunity between children from richer and poorer social backgrounds. Now, let's suppose that a state inherits a large windfall that it must spend on education and that, wherever it invests this sum, it'll not undermine the adequacy of the education that anyone receives. What should the state do with the funds? Our firm intuition is that this state is morally required to improve the prospects of those children who're worse off in the competition for advantaged social positions. But advocates of the adequacy moral claim can't make sense of this judgement. Indeed, if this claim is correct, then there would be nothing wrong in using the resources to enhance the education of those whose prospects are already better than average. This strikes us as implausible. In our opinion, it makes more sense to look to mitigate the inequality of opportunity between children of different family backgrounds, as the equality of opportunity moral claim suggests.

We can deepen this analysis by distinguishing two notions of equality of opportunity.[16] When we introduced this idea, we suggested that what matters is that no child should suffer worse prospects than anyone else in the competition for advantaged social positions in virtue of their family background. This is *fair equality of opportunity*. This notion is distinct from a separate understanding that holds that, when we allocate advantaged social positions, we should do so only on the basis of an applicant's suitability—that is, on grounds of competence, ability, or other aspects of fittingness—and not on the basis of characteristics, such as race or gender, that are irrelevant to any applicant's merit. This is *meritocratic equality of opportunity*.

Advocates of the adequacy objection tend to support meritocratic equality of opportunity, but the reason for this has little to do with the alleged unfairness and harmfulness of inequality of opportunity. Instead, according to these scholars, our reason to favour meritocratic equality of opportunity is that this promotes *efficiency*. The crucial point is that, when we fail to appoint on the basis of an applicant's suitability, we risk appointing someone who's less qualified for the position, and therefore who'll need more training to bring them up to speed. Because we could've avoided bearing these costs, we should regard this use of the resources as wasteful. From the perspective of meritocratic equality of opportunity, all that matters is that we find the right

[14] Elizabeth Anderson, 'Rethinking Equality of Opportunity: Comment on Adam Swift's How Not to Be a Hypocrite', *Theory and Research in Education*, 2 (2004), 99–110 at 105–9.

[15] Harry Brighouse and Adam Swift, 'Educational Equality versus Educational Adequacy: A Critique of Anderson and Swift', *Journal of Applied Philosophy*, 26 (2009), 117–28 at 125–6.

[16] John Rawls, *A Theory of Justice, Revised Edition* (Cambridge, MA: Harvard University Press, 1999), 57–65.

applicant for the role. And, as Elizabeth Anderson points out, to this extent, 'how they came to be that way is of no concern'.[17]

It's here that we think the adequacy objection loses much of its appeal. Our sense is that, above and beyond a concern with efficiency, we've further reasons to condemn inequalities of opportunities between individuals, such that it can make a moral difference how an applicant acquired their qualifications. More specifically, we retain the intuition that it's morally bad when, through no fault or responsibility of their own, students at other schools suffer worse prospects than students from elite private schools in much the same way that it's morally bad when, through no fault or responsibility of their own, female students suffer worse prospects than male students. This verdict holds up in the face of the efficiency-based rationale of meritocratic equality of opportunity, and it's because of this that we favour fair equality of opportunity.

6.4 EQUALITY ABOVE ALL?

Let's recall:

> *Equality of opportunity moral claim*: Because of its unfairness and harmfulness, no individual should suffer worse prospects than anyone else in the competition for advantaged social positions in virtue of their family background.

Another objection to this claim is that it condemns too much, implausibly restricting parents' freedom to treat their child in ways that are highly valuable. To elaborate this point, let's consider the following. Reading bedtime stories can be a source of great joy for parents and children alike. Many adults have fond memories of their own childhood that involve being read their favourite stories, perhaps even with comedic voices or theatrical accompaniments. These sessions are also a prized and valued part of the day for many parents, and they enhance the parent–child relationship in a way that's vital for a child's development and well-being. Intuitively, it seems that we should laud such activities and that, when a child is denied bedtime stories, we've reason for sadness and regret. Indeed, we might think that part of what's so objectionable about existing labour markets is that many parents are effectively forced to work during evenings and at weekends, and are deprived of opportunities to spend this valuable time with their child.

However, a problem arises because bedtime stories are educationally beneficial. In particular, they have a significant impact on a child's cognitive development. Accordingly, a child who's denied bedtime stories is less well equipped than a child who's read them in the competition for advantaged social positions.[18] In other words, when parents read their child a bedtime story, they confer on them an advantage that upsets equality of opportunity, just as with the advantage conferred by elite private schools. This creates *unfairness*: a child who's denied bedtime stories enjoys worse

---

[17] Anderson, 'Rethinking Equality of Opportunity', 102.

[18] Annette Lareau, *Unequal Childhoods* (Berkeley, CA: University of California Press, 2003).

prospects than a child who's read them, and this inequality arises through differences in family background. Moreover, reading bedtime stories isn't neutral in its effects on other children. It reduces others' prospects in the competition for advantaged social positions, thereby *harming* them.

Combining this empirical point with the equality of opportunity moral claim gives rise to the following argument:

> *Equality of opportunity moral claim*: Because of its unfairness and harmfulness, no individual should suffer worse prospects than anyone else in the competition for advantaged social positions in virtue of their family background.
>
> *Bedtime stories empirical claim*: Children who aren't read bedtime stories suffer worse prospects in virtue of their family background in comparison with those who're read bedtime stories.
>
> *Conclusion*: The state should prohibit bedtime stories.

This presents defenders of the equality of opportunity argument against elite private schools with a dilemma. Given the parallels, consistency seems to require either that we *accept* the equality of opportunity argument and thus the state should prohibit bedtime stories, or that we *reject* the equality of opportunity argument and thus the state should permit elite private schools.

Advocates of elite private schools might seize on this result, contending that it's outrageous to prohibit parents from reading bedtime stories to their child. They can also broaden the point by highlighting that there's a range of parental conduct that we've reason to protect and even to celebrate, even though it upsets equality of opportunity.[19] If this is right, then it's not at all clear that the fact that elite private schools create unequal opportunities between children provides us with a decisive reason to prohibit them. We call this the *bedtime stories defence* of elite private schools.

One reason that this line of argument is forceful is that it draws attention to instances in which equality of opportunity should give way to other values. Defenders of elite private schools can use this point to justify a variety of conduct that upsets equality of opportunity by claiming that, because these actions are morally alike (elite private schools are like bedtime stories in this respect), the state must treat them similarly. This is a powerful move because it takes a view that critics of elite private schools share (about the permissibility of bedtime stories) and uses a demand for consistency to settle a case where the permissibility of conduct is under dispute (about elite private schools).

In order to assess this defence of elite private schools, we need to examine the reasons for permitting parents to read bedtime stories to their child. In what follows, we consider two possibilities. The first appeals to a general permission for parents to benefit their child. The second appeals to a subtler concern with building valuable parent–child relationships. We argue that neither of these provides a firm basis on which to defend elite private schools.

---

[19] Satz, 'Equality, Adequacy and Education for Citizenship', 634.

6.4.1 UNRESTRICTED PARENTAL LICENCE

We often hear that it's parents' prerogative to do the best that they can for their child. When we discover that parents have arranged for their daughter to take piano lessons, hired her a maths tutor, or moved her to a school where she's more likely to flourish, we may be inclined to think that they're 'doing right by their child'. This might suggest the following:

> *Unrestricted parental licence moral claim*: Parents are permitted to provide the best upbringing that they can for their child.

One way to motivate this claim is to appeal to the general idea that an individual should be free to use their own time and money as they wish.[20] On this view, parents can use their wealth to purchase whatever they want—fast cars, a nice house, or good food— and spend their days however they think suitable—reading their child a story, playing football with them, or helping them learn a foreign language. Given that parents may use their resources in these ways, why not also allow them to purchase an elite private education for their child, or indeed anything else that might benefit them?[21] To permit some of these activities and not others seems arbitrary.

While we recognize that parents should enjoy some prerogative to benefit their child and that a reason for this might derive from the general freedoms they should enjoy, we deny that this supports the unrestricted parental licence moral claim. The problem is that the permissions this claim grants are too extensive to be plausible. To see why we think this, let's consider the real-life example of Wanda Holloway, whose daughter lost out on a spot in her school's cheerleading squad.[22] In an attempt to secure her daughter a place in the squad, Holloway hired a hitman to murder the mother of a rival cheerleader, hoping that the rival would be too grief-ridden to compete.

Even though Holloway was simply using her wealth to purchase what she wished, in a way that she thought would provide her daughter with the best upbringing, her actions were clearly very seriously wrong. Our repulse at this case indicates that, whatever parents may do for their child, their remit has limits. At the very least, we need to revise the moral claim along the following lines:

> *Restricted parental licence moral claim*: Parents are permitted to provide the best upbringing that they can for their child within reasonable moral limits.

However, stated in this way, this claim is too general to be illuminating. More specifically, if we're to make sense of its demands, then we need to know what are the 'reasonable moral limits' that parents must respect. Reflecting on the case of Holloway, a natural way to flesh out this idea is to say that parents may act however they wish so long as they don't *harm* others. But the problem with this view is that it's much too extensive. This

---

[20] Robert Nozick, *Anarchy, State, and Utopia* (New York: Basic Books, 1974), ch. 7.
[21] Anderson, 'Rethinking Equality of Opportunity', 104.
[22] Brighouse and Swift, *Family Values*, 115.

is because, as we've pointed out, even reading bedtime stories to a child harms other children who're denied them by upsetting equality of opportunity. For this reason, we can't appeal to harm alone to identify the reasonable moral limits of parents' conduct. Since harm occurs in the case of Holloway, when parents send their child to an elite private school, and when parents read their child a bedtime story, we need further moral analysis to determine where we should draw the line between those harms that the state should permit and those that it should prohibit. So, let's turn to an argument that helps us make progress on this front.

6.4.2 FAMILY VALUES

An alternative justification for parents' permission to read bedtime stories to their child, which would hold despite this harming other children in the competition for advantaged social positions, refers to the interests of both parties in securing *familial relationship goods*.[23] These are goods that parents and children realize through developing and sustaining caring and intimate relationships within loving families. These familial relationship goods explain why parenting can be so meaningful: because it provides access to something distinctively valuable that's impossible to attain elsewhere, including in other kinds of relationships, such as close friendships. These goods also provide a strong rationale for permitting parents to engage in activities that benefit their child. Even if some such activities upset equality of opportunity, we think this is a price that we should be willing to pay, since the value of familial relationship goods outweighs this loss.

This result is important for it helps us to understand why the state should permit parents to read bedtime stories to their child. It's because this activity is important for realizing familial relationship goods and because, in this case, we attach greater value to the realization of these goods than we do to the equality of opportunity that this activity threatens. To elaborate this point, Harry Brighouse and Adam Swift note that, when a parent reads their child a bedtime story, they're doing several things:

> He is intimately sharing physical space with his child; sharing with her the content of a story selected by one of them; providing the background for future discussions; preparing her for her bedtime and, if she is young enough, calming her; reinforcing the mutual sense of identification . . . . He is giving her exclusive attention in a space designated for that exclusive attention at a particularly important time of her day.[24]

The familial relationship goods realized in this experience offer a plausible explanation for why we're uncomfortable with prohibiting bedtime stories, as well as several other activities in which parents engage to benefit their child.

---

[23] Harry Brighouse and Adam Swift, 'Legitimate Parental Partiality', *Philosophy & Public Affairs*, 37 (2009), 43–80 at 51–9.
[24] Brighouse and Swift, *Family Values*, 125.

But it's consistent with this to maintain that activities that lack such goods aren't worthy of protection. Making this point, Brighouse and Swift write,

> Think of a parent who invests all possible resources in securing competitive advantage for his child: perhaps, say, sending her to an expensive private school designed to optimize her chances in the competition for well-rewarded and interesting jobs, investing in a trust fund, and interacting with her on the basis of judgments about how best to develop her human capital. These activities are not protected by the considerations we have invoked concerning the value of the family. In normal circumstances at least, none of these is essential for the important goods distinctively made available by the familial relationship.[25]

On this analysis, we should tolerate the inequality of opportunity that's a necessary consequence of allowing parents to read bedtime stories because this activity is crucial for the realization of familial relationship goods. However, we ought not to tolerate the inequality of opportunity that arises from allowing parents to send their child to an elite private school, since this activity is *not* crucial for the realization of familial relationship goods, and so it's not amenable to the same kind of justification. In the latter case, what remains is the disruption to equality of opportunity and, without the counterweight of familial relationship goods, we believe that the balance of reasons speaks in favour of prohibiting elite private schools.

This point helps us to delineate the reasonable moral limits within which parental licence must remain. Of the various ways in which parents can benefit their child, those that harm others are unjustifiable unless they realize familial relationship goods. This line of reasoning explains why we should treat the case of Holloway and elite private schools differently to bedtime stories. Although the last of these activities disrupts equality of opportunity, it has the benefit of realizing familial relationship goods. By contrast, the other two involve only their respective harms. Thus, reading bedtime stories falls within the reasonable moral limits of parental licence, while Holloway's actions and elite private schools don't. By making this move, we can retain an objection to elite private schools without reaching the implausible conclusion that the state must also prohibit bedtime stories.

6.5 DO SCHOOLS MATTER?

We now consider another response often offered to critics of elite private schools. One component of the equality of opportunity argument is the following claim:

Elite private schools empirical claim: Students who don't attend elite private schools suffer worse prospects in virtue of their family background in comparison with those who do.

---

[25] Brighouse and Swift, *Family Values*, 125.

Here, we consider the view that this empirical claim attributes too much significance to the role of elite private schools. This view gains force by appealing to considerations raised by the bedtime stories defence, particularly the fact that being read bedtime stories is educationally beneficial for a child, such that a child who's read bedtime stories is better equipped than a child who's denied them in competition for advantaged social positions. Indeed, we might think that the evidence supports more than this: that activities such as reading bedtime stories, and various other influences that relate to family background, are the *major* determinant of a child's life-prospects. Given this evidence, Debra Satz writes, 'it is difficult to understand why an advocate of . . . equality . . . would focus on school funding issues'.[26] The suggestion is that prohibiting elite private schools would have only a minimal effect on equalizing children's prospects. This is the *ineffectiveness objection*.

In reply to this objection, it's important to note that we don't need to overstate the elite private schools empirical claim. It may be true that the school that a child attends isn't the only determinant of their prospects, nor may it be even the major determinant. However, it's uncontroversial that it plays *some* role. As we noted in section 6.1, children who attend elite private schools are over-represented in advantaged social positions. Statistical research shows that those who attend elite private schools are a third more likely to secure well-rewarded and interesting jobs than children from similarly wealthy families from similar neighbourhoods who attended other schools.[27] There's also robust evidence that, even when they occupy the same jobs and we control for the university they attended, the subject they studied, and the degree classification they received, those who attend elite private schools earn an average of 6 per cent more.[28]

This data isn't to suggest that other background factors aren't also important. Nor is the data sufficiently granular to say precisely what determines a child's prospects in comparison with those of others. But the data does indicate that children who attend elite private schools tend to fare better than similarly situated children at other schools. This is all that's necessary to make a case for prohibition. In other words, to defuse the ineffectiveness objection, critics of elite private schools needn't hold that prohibiting them would be sufficient to ensure equality of opportunity. They need to claim only that it'd make some difference to our pursuit of this goal.

6.6 CONCLUSIONS

The most direct conclusion to follow from the analysis in this chapter is the case for prohibiting elite private schools. Although we haven't considered all of the arguments for and against this view, we've demonstrated that a concern for equality of opportunity

---

[26] Satz, 'Equality, Adequacy and Education for Citizenship', 633.

[27] Lindsey Macmillan, Claire Tyler, and Anna Vignoles, 'Who Gets the Top Jobs? The Role of Family Background and Networks in Recent Graduates Access to High-Status Professions', *Journal of Social Policy*, 44 (2015), 487–515.

[28] Claire Crawford and Anna Vignoles, 'Heterogeneity in Graduate Earnings by Socio-Economic Background', *Institute for Fiscal Studies Working Paper W14/30* (2014), available at https://www.ifs.org.uk/uploads/publications/wps/WP201430.pdf.

supports it and we've responded to several of the most powerful objections offered in reply. We don't doubt that there'll be serious political opposition to our proposal, given that many influential figures, including politicians, attended such schools and send their children to them now. Yet, we've given impetus to the case, and put the onus on defenders of elite private schools to counter our view.

There are also notable implications beyond this. One is that, even if *prohibiting* elite private schools isn't feasible, other reforms might be available, such as removing their tax-free status or introducing quotas at universities that cap intake from them. To the extent that these measures would reduce the comparative advantage conferred by elite private schools, and improve equality of opportunity, they're reforms supported by our arguments in this chapter. Similarly, there are implications for the design of the broader education system. There are other ways that parents' wealth can influence schooling and there are other kinds of schools that upset equality of opportunity between children. Our arguments speak to the importance of reducing or restricting these effects, ensuring that education is equal across postcodes and regions and, more generally, mitigating the effect of family background on children's prospects. We've accepted that some such effects may be justifiable if they derive from activities that secure familial relationship goods. But, when this isn't the case, we've a strong justification for regulating conduct that upsets equality of opportunity.

FURTHER READING

A good overview of the moral importance of equality of opportunity and its bearing on education is Liam Shields, Anne Newman, and Debra Satz, 'Equality of Educational Opportunity', *Stanford Encyclopedia of Philosophy* (2017), available at https://plato.stanford.edu/entries/equal-ed-opportunity. There's also a good introductory discussion to the conflict between equality of opportunity and parental partiality in Adam Swift, *Political Philosophy: A Beginners' Guide for Students and Politicians* (Cambridge: Polity, 2001), part 3.

For those wanting to delve deeper into the justifiability of elite private schools, a good place to start is with Adam Swift, *How Not to Be a Hypocrite: School Choice for the Morally Perplexed Parent* (London: Routledge, 2003), part 1. For contrasting views, it's useful to read Elizabeth Anderson, 'Rethinking Equality of Opportunity: Comment on Adam Swift's How Not to Be a Hypocrite', *Theory and Research in Education*, 2 (2004), 99–110 and Debra Satz, 'Equality, Adequacy, and Education for Citizenship', *Ethics*, 117 (2007), 623–48, as well as the response in Harry Brighouse and Adam Swift, 'Educational Equality Versus Educational Adequacy: A Critique of Anderson and Satz', *Journal of Applied Philosophy*, 26 (2009), 117–28. For further discussion, there's a special issue dedicated to this in *Theory and Research in Education*, 2 (2004).

For further studies of equality of opportunity, a good place to begin is the taxonomy provided in John Rawls, *A Theory of Justice, Revised Edition* (Cambridge, MA: Harvard University Press, 1999), 57–78. A good overview of this literature is offered in Richard Arneson, 'Equality of Opportunity', *Stanford Encyclopedia of Philosophy* (2015), available at https://plato.stanford.edu/entries/equal-opportunity and an accessible account of the arguments in favour of various conceptions of equality of opportunity is outlined in Janet Radcliffe Richards, 'Equality of Opportunity', *Ratio*, 10 (1997), 253–79.

For further reading on the practicalities of achieving equality of opportunity, there's Brian Barry, *Why Social Justice Matters* (Cambridge: Polity, 2005), part 2; Véronique Munoz Dardé, 'Is the Family to Be Abolished Then?', *Proceedings of the Aristotelian Society*, 99 (1999), 37–56; Andrew Mason, 'Equality, Personal Responsibility, and Gender Socialisation', *Proceedings of the Aristotelian Society*, 100 (2000), 227–46; and Seana Shiffrin, 'Race and Ethnicity, Race, Labor, and the Fair Equality of Opportunity Principle', *Fordham Law Review*, 72 (2004), 1643–75.

 For additional material and resources, including web links and self-test questions, please visit the online resources **www.oup.com/he/walton1e**.

7
BASIC INCOME AND DISTRIBUTIVE JUSTICE

SUMMARY

- In this chapter, we defend basic income. This policy requires the state to make regular cash payments to each member of society, irrespective of their other income or wealth, or willingness to find employment.
- We start by describing three effects of basic income. The first is that it'll raise the incomes of the least advantaged. The second is that it'll protect against the threats of exploitation and abuse. The third is that it'll remove one obstacle to finding employment.
- We explain the significance of these effects by drawing on ideas about distributive justice, emphasizing the relevance of John Rawls's *justice as fairness* and Elizabeth Anderson's *democratic equality*.
- We consider and respond to an objection that alleges that an individual who receives a basic income without being willing to find employment fails in a duty of reciprocity to those who produce their society's wealth.
- We explore the claim that we should reject basic income because it'd require the state to interfere with the lives of those who'd be taxed to fund it. We contend that it's a mistake to oppose taxation in such a wholesale way.
- We conclude by reflecting on the economic sustainability of basic income.

7.1 INTRODUCTION

It's standard policy around the world for the state to provide financial support to economically disadvantaged members of its society. One example of this is *unemployment benefits*, whereby a jobseeker can claim regular cash payments from the state to assist them in hard times. These schemes typically operate with two parameters. First, a claimant's entitlement to benefits is *means-tested*, meaning that only those whose income or wealth is below some threshold may receive the payments. In most systems, the level of benefit varies in accordance with how far below the threshold an individual falls.[1]

---

[1] Philippe Van Parijs and Yannick Vanderborght, *Basic Income: A Radical Proposal for a Free Society and Sane Economy* (Cambridge, MA: Harvard University Press, 2017), 16–17.

Second, the receipt of these benefits is *conditional* on the claimant exhibiting a willingness to find employment. States often deny unemployment benefits to individuals who're unable to prove that they're seeking employment, those who decline job offers, and those who've voluntarily resigned from a previous post.

In recent years, many states have applied these parameters more stringently, in some cases requiring claimants to undertake unpaid work placements in order to continue receiving their payments.[2] But this is only one part of the story: there's also been a backlash against this, with growing support for the idea that each individual should enjoy a *basic income*. In contrast to unemployment benefits, this policy has two distinguishing features. First, a claimant's entitlement to basic income is *universal*, as opposed to means-tested, which means that these benefits don't vary in accordance with the level of income and wealth that they receive from other sources. Second, the receipt of these benefits is *unconditional*, and so they're granted independently of whether the claimant exhibits any willingness to find employment. Trials of this policy are underway in several states, including Finland and Kenya, and basic income is on the political agenda in various other places.[3]

What underlies many disputes about the terms on which states should make benefits available are disagreements about the proper distribution of social and economic resources between individuals. These are disagreements about the demands of *distributive justice*. For example, whereas some believe that each individual is entitled to cash support from the state because it's morally imperative that they can live a decent life, even if they're unwilling to search for employment, others protest that basic income seems to provide 'something for nothing'. Our aim in this chapter is to shed light on claims such as these by looking to their moral foundations.

We do this by arguing in defence of basic income. In section 7.2, we describe some of the likely effects of this policy. In section 7.3, we provide support for it by drawing on two influential accounts of distributive justice. In section 7.4, we respond to the concern that basic income is objectionable because it provides benefits to those who're unwilling to contribute to their society. In section 7.5, we consider and reject a criticism to the proposal that targets the fact that it'd have to be funded through taxation. In section 7.6, we conclude.

7.2 THE EFFECTS OF BASIC INCOME

One effect of providing an individual with regular cash payments is that it gives them the funds to support themselves and their projects. Most obviously, basic income ensures that each individual has the money to purchase the most essential goods, such as food, clothing, shelter, and so forth, at least if the payments are sufficiently generous.

---

[2] Evelyn Z. Brodkin and Flemming Larsen, 'Changing Boundaries: The Policies of Workfare in the U.S. and Europe', *Poverty & Public Policy*, 5 (2013), 37–47.

[3] For an overview of these trials, see Van Parijs and Vanderborght, *Basic Income*, ch. 6.

More generally, basic income increases the opportunities available to its beneficiaries since, with more financial resources, they can do more things.

To put the same point another way, one consequence of basic income is that it enhances individuals' freedom. To understand the relationship between an individual's income and their freedom, let's suppose that Jinjing wants a mountain bike to explore the hills. She enjoys the *formal* freedom to purchase a bike so long as she's legally permitted to do so. But that's little consolation if she can't afford it. By providing an individual with more resources, basic income turns this formal freedom into a *real* freedom.[4] Now, she isn't merely formally free to purchase a bike, she also has the means to do so. We call this the *income effect*.[5]

It bears mentioning that this effect will not be uniform across all individuals. For one thing, a modest basic income is likely to make an enormous difference to the real freedom of someone on the poverty line, but little difference to the very wealthy. For another, how it effects the net income and wealth of anyone depends on the tax system that funds it. If the revenue is generated by increasing taxes on high earners, they may be less wealthy overall, despite their basic income. Because of this, and depending on how it's designed, basic income could be *progressive*, meaning that it benefits the poor more than the rich, and *redistributive*, meaning that it takes resources from the rich and gives them to the poor.

A further effect of basic income is that it reduces an individual's dependence on other sources of income by bolstering their exit options. When the state withholds unemployment benefits from those who choose to leave their posts, the option of resigning is unaffordable to many employees, including most of those with lousy jobs and unscrupulous bosses. This puts considerable bargaining power in the hands of an employer, who knows that, because workers lack an effective exit option, they needn't improve wages or working conditions to attract or retain employees.

By contrast, basic income provides a kind of strike fund, such that employees can credibly threaten to resign unless their wages or working conditions improve. Consequently, we should expect this policy to improve the quality of individuals' work lives, and especially so for the least advantaged. This is because, while basic income may add little to the bargaining power of the highest earners, whose talents are scarce or who've influential connections, it'll empower those without these attributes to be more selective in their choice of employment.[6]

Indeed, not only does it protect against the tyranny of bosses, but it also guards against the tyranny of husbands. In the same way that basic income enhances the bargaining power of disadvantaged employees, so too it improves the circumstances of women who'd be financially dependent on their partners otherwise, and thus who agree to live with others under disagreeable conditions. This can include abusive

[4] Philippe Van Parijs, *Real Freedom for All: What (If Anything) Can Justify Capitalism?* (Oxford: Oxford University Press, 1995), ch. 1.

[5] Philippe Van Parijs, 'A Basic Income for All' in Philippe Van Parijs, Joshua Cohen, and Joel Rogers (eds), *What's Wrong with a Free Lunch?* (Boston, MA: Beacon Press, 2001), 14.

[6] Van Parijs and Vanderborght, *Basic Income*, 22.

relationships and other circumstances in which one individual's interests are neglected. In this way, basic income 'provides a modest but secure basis on which the more vulnerable can stand'.[7] We call this the *exit option effect*.

It's vital to note that the levels of the income effect and the exit option effect depend on the size of the payments to which an individual would be entitled under the policy. We support a generous basic income that would realize these effects to a considerable extent. However, even if the income isn't enough to give an individual the option to withdraw from the labour market entirely, it'll still improve their bargaining power both at work and at home by reducing their dependence on others.

A final effect of basic income relates to the *unemployment trap*. This term refers to the phenomenon whereby it's not financially rational to find employment since the removal of an individual's means-tested unemployment benefits, along with their newly incurred work-related expenses, would offset their wages. Because of this, individuals face a clear disincentive to work when benefits are means-tested. The incentives not to enter the labour market are even greater given other difficulties, such as uncertainty about how long the job may last, and the complexity of re-establishing unemployment benefits afterwards.[8]

One effect of basic income is that it'll greatly reduce this obstacle to finding employment. If an individual's entitlements are universal, rather than means-tested, then they'll not diminish when they find work. Any earnings that they receive will only increase their income. As a result, it'd be financially rational for even those with low and/or uncertain earnings to find employment. We call this the *unemployment trap effect*.

This effect refers specifically to the financial incentives to work. It doesn't follow from this that we should expect to see employment soar following the introduction of basic income. There are other determinants of unemployment, and the policy may strengthen some of these. In particular, we might expect that some individuals will withdraw entirely from the labour market, choosing instead to live solely off of their basic income. If this were a popular choice, then the net effect of the policy would be to reduce the number of those in employment. Nonetheless, providing universal, rather than means-tested, benefits does remove one obstacle to finding employment that's faced by those without work.

Defenders of basic income appeal to each of these three effects to show that this policy is preferable to unemployment benefits. However, critics tend to focus their objections on the unconditional nature of basic income, complaining about the fact that it provides cash payments to those who display no willingness to find employment. Since the income effect and exit option effect speak most directly to this feature, it's these on which we focus.

---

[7] Van Parijs, 'A Basic Income for All', 20. See also Anca Gheaus, 'Basic Income, Gender Justice, and the Costs of Gender-Symmetrical Lifestyles', *Basic Incomes Studies*, 3 (2008), 1–8.

[8] Van Parijs and Vanderborght, *Basic Income*, 18–19.

7.3 THE SIGNIFICANCE OF INCOME AND EXIT

In order to build our case for basic income, we'll now embed these points about the policy's effects within two accounts of distributive justice. We begin with John Rawls's *justice as fairness* and then proceed to Elizabeth Anderson's *democratic equality*. Even though these frameworks support distinct accounts of the demands of distributive justice, each provides us with strong reasons to endorse basic income.

7.3.1 JUSTICE AS FAIRNESS

Rawls's aim is to devise a set of principles that can guide us in choosing among the possible institutional arrangements under which individuals live.[9] This makes it a conception of *social* justice, concerned with the basic structure of society—its constitution, legal and economic system, various policies and regulations, and so forth.[10] These institutions have a pervasive impact on an individual's prospects, determining their rights, their duties, and the general circumstances in which they'll grow up and live. For this reason, it's important to consider how the basic structure distributes the various benefits and burdens of social cooperation.

Rawls's argument develops in two stages. First, he claims that we should develop principles of social justice by considering which principles individuals would select in a hypothetical situation that he terms the *original position*.[11] Here, we're to imagine representatives who're charged with the task of agreeing on principles that further the interest of their respective clients, but who lack particular information about their clients' characteristics, including their socioeconomic class, natural talent, gender, race, psychological propensities, and conception of what it means to live well. In other words, the representatives must choose principles of justice from behind a *veil of ignorance*.[12] Accordingly, the representatives are unable to bias the choice of principles to suit their client's particular traits, and so they must adopt principles that'll be favourable in any eventuality.

Second, Rawls turns his attention to the content of the principles that representatives in the original position would select. He indicates that they'd identify an index of *social primary goods*. These goods refer to all-purpose means that each individual wants or needs in order to participate freely and equally in social cooperation, whatever their characteristics or interests.[13] Rawls identifies five such social primary goods: (i) certain basic rights and liberties, such as freedom of thought and conscience; (ii) freedom of movement and of occupational choice; (iii) positions of power and responsibility in society; (iv) income and wealth; and (v) the social bases of self-respect.[14]

---

[9] John Rawls, *A Theory of Justice, Revised Edition* (Cambridge, MA: Harvard University Press, 1999), xi–xii.

[10] Rawls, *A Theory of Justice*, 6.   [11] Rawls, *A Theory of Justice*, 11, 15–19, and 102–68.

[12] Rawls, *A Theory of Justice*, 11.

[13] John Rawls, *Justice as Fairness: A Restatement* (Cambridge, MA: Harvard University Press, 2001), 58–9 and Rawls, *Justice as Fairness*, 57.   [14] Rawls, *Justice as Fairness*, 57.

We can call this set of goods Rawls's *currency* of distributive justice. It's his account of the goods that we should use to judge each individual's level of advantage for the purpose of determining a proper distribution of social and economic resources.

Armed with this currency, Rawls argues that the representatives in the original position would settle on the following principles, which constitute *justice as fairness*:

Principle of Basic Liberties: Each individual is to have an equal right to the most extensive total system of equal basic liberties compatible with a similar liberty for all, including freedom of expression, freedom of association, the right to vote, and so forth.

Principle of Fair Equality of Opportunity: Social and economic inequalities are to be arranged so that they are attached to offices and positions open to all under conditions of fair equality of opportunity.

Difference Principle: Social and economic inequalities are to be arranged so that they are to the greatest benefit of the least advantaged.[15]

Justice as fairness prioritizes the first principle over the second principle, and the second principle over the third principle. Moreover, this priority is lexical. This means that we may not violate the principle of basic liberties for the sake of the principle of fair equality of opportunity; and, similarly, we may not violate the principle of fair equality of opportunity for the sake of the difference principle.[16]

With these three principles, and their ordering, Rawls believes he has constructed a theory of justice that's both *liberal* and *egalitarian*. Justice as fairness is liberal in the sense that it gives an account of the importance of individuals' basic rights and their priority over other considerations. It's egalitarian in the sense that it integrates these basic rights with principles that condemn social and economic inequalities that violate fair equality of opportunity or fail to be to the greatest benefit of the least advantaged.

There are several ways in which justice as fairness might bear on the case for basic income. One possibility is to draw on basic income's exit option effect to establish a positive link between this policy and Rawls's remarks about the importance of freedom of occupational choice and the social bases of self-respect.[17] We're sympathetic to this point, but we'll postpone its discussion until we get to the work of Elizabeth Anderson in section 7.3.3. Before this, we'll focus on the connection between the income effect and Rawls's difference principle.

7.3.2 THE DIFFERENCE PRINCIPLE AND BASIC INCOME

The difference principle condemns all inequalities in the distribution of social primary goods, except those that maximally benefit the position of the least advantaged. Rawls offers two arguments for the appeal of this principle. Both begin by establishing an

---

[15] Rawls, *Justice as Fairness*, 42.   [16] Rawls, *Justice as Fairness*, 43.
[17] Simon Birnbaum, 'Radical Liberalism, Rawls and the Welfare State: Justifying the Politics of Basic Income', *Critical Review of International Social and Political Philosophy*, 12 (2010), 495–516.

equal distribution of goods as the default. He then outlines when and why we may depart from this baseline.

The first argument proceeds from the original position. Rawls contends that the representatives would be immediately drawn to an equal distribution of social primary goods. This is because, as a result of the veil of ignorance, these representatives aren't able to identify principles that'll bring any special advantage to their clients. Likewise, they've no reason to accept any special disadvantages. The upshot is equality. As Rawls puts it, 'since it is not reasonable ... to expect more than an equal share ... and it is not rational ... to agree to less ... the sensible thing is to acknowledge as the first step a principle of justice requiring an equal distribution'.[18]

The second argument emerges from a shortcoming of the principle of fair equality of opportunity. This principle holds that no individual should suffer worse prospects than others in virtue of various characteristics, such as the class into which they're born.[19] We discuss aspects of this principle in various other parts of this book. The justification for this principle is that it's unfair to allow an individual's prospects to depend on social contingencies, such as whether they're born into a rich family or a poor one. But if we're concerned by inequalities that are a product of these kinds of social contingencies, then so too we should be concerned with inequalities that are a product of natural contingencies, such as someone's natural talents. This is because the natural lottery is as morally arbitrary as the social lottery.[20] Rawls recognizes that the appropriate response to this similarity is, as a first step, 'to suppose that all social primary goods, including income and wealth, should be equal: everyone should have an equal share'.[21]

Having identified two reasons to favour an equal distribution, Rawls then makes his next move. He argues that we must take seriously the fact that, when inequalities increase economic efficiency by providing an incentive for industry and innovation, these inequalities can increase the total supply of social primary goods that we can distribute between individuals. For this reason, it's unreasonable to insist on an equal division. Instead, we may accept inequalities 'so long as these improve everyone's situation, including that of the least advantaged'.[22] In this way, the difference principle combines a concern for equality with a concern for economic efficiency.

There's a clear connection between this line of reasoning and basic income. In particular, since low earners seem to be among the least advantaged, it's their circumstances that we've most reason to improve. Basic income works for their benefit via its income effect—that is, it enhances their real freedom by increasing the cash at their disposable. As we've explained, we can also design the policy so that it's progressive and redistributive, transferring resources from those with the most to those with less.

---

[18] Rawls, *A Theory of Justice*, 130.   [19] Rawls, *A Theory of Justice*, 63.

[20] Rawls, *A Theory of Justice*, 64. This insight inspires other accounts of distributive justice, including Ronald Dworkin, *Sovereign Virtue: The Theory and Practice of Equality* (Cambridge, MA: Harvard University Press, 2000), esp. ch. 2.

[21] John Rawls, *Political Liberalism* (New York: Columbia University Press, 1996), 281.

[22] Rawls, *Political Liberalism*, 282, and Rawls, *A Theory of Justice*, 71.

Given the way in which this would use inequalities in the distribution of social primary goods to benefit the least advantaged, it's plausible that basic income is one of
the logical conclusions of Rawls's arguments. Indeed, as Philippe Van Parijs writes, the
'Difference Principle appear[s] to recommend . . . that one should introduce such an
income at the highest sustainable level'.[23]

Despite this seemingly straightforward connection, Rawls was embarrassed by the
implication that the difference principle might support basic income. We'll return to
his worries in section 7.4. Before that, let's turn our attention to an alternative account
of distributive justice.

7.3.3 DEMOCRATIC EQUALITY

Central to Elizabeth Anderson's account of *democratic equality* is the conviction that
we should be concerned with 'equality as a social relationship'.[24] To appreciate what this
means, it's useful to reflect on historical societies in which individuals occupied distinct
ranks in a social hierarchy, such as when individuals were designated as masters or
servants. Anderson argues that the chief commitment of those who value equality must
be to abolish hierarchies of this kind. As part of this, we must look to establish a 'social
order in which persons stand in relations of equality'.[25]

We should oppose several types of unequal social relations.[26] Exploitative relations,
in which some individuals are able to take advantage of others' vulnerabilities, provide
one such example. The master–servant relationship is a classic instance of this, as is
the case of an employer who can get away with offering poor wages under terrible
working conditions because they know that their employees must accept this offer
in order to put food on the table. Another example is relations of domination, where
one individual has so much power over others that they can direct others' actions at
whim.[27] This kind of domination occurs between tyrants and their subjects, as well
as between men and women in patriarchal societies like our own. Drawing on a rich
variety of examples, Anderson concludes that we should aim for a society where 'no
one need bow and scrape before others or represent themselves as inferior'.[28]

In focusing on relations between individuals, rather than on the distribution of
social and economic resources, it might be thought that democratic equality offers
a rival to justice as fairness and, in particular, the difference principle. But our view
is that democratic equality provides a complementary reason to care about society's

---

[23] Philippe Van Parijs, 'Why Surfers Should Be Fed: The Liberal Case for an Unconditional Basic Income',
Philosophy & Public Affairs, 20 (1991), 101–31 at 105.

[24] Elizabeth Anderson, 'What Is the Point of Equality?', *Ethics*, 109 (1999), 287–337 at 313.

[25] Anderson, 'What Is the Point of Equality?', 313.

[26] Anderson, 'What Is the Point of Equality?', 312–14 and Iris Marion Young, *Justice and the Politics of
Difference* (Princeton, NJ: Princeton University Press, 1990).

[27] For discussion, see Philip Pettit, *Republicanism: A Theory of Freedom and Government* (Oxford: Clarendon
Press, 1997).   [28] Anderson, 'What Is the Point of Equality?', 313.

distribution of resources.[29] This is because, as Anderson rightly points out, 'certain patterns in the distribution of goods may be instrumental to securing [equal] relations'.[30]

Having said this, the two accounts diverge in at least two ways. First, democratic equality adopts a different *currency* of distributive justice. Rather than social primary goods, defenders of democratic equality tend to emphasize the importance of each individual's *capabilities*.[31] Drawing on the work of Amartya Sen and Martha Nussbaum, those who favour this approach focus on whether an individual can achieve particular ends, such as being appropriately nourished, being gainfully employed, and having physical and mental well-being.[32] The capabilities that are especially important are those that are necessary for an individual to participate in social, economic, and political life as an equal member of a democratic society.[33] This is why it's called 'democratic equality'.

Second, advocates of democratic equality are concerned with individuals' circumstances in a distinctive way. In Rawls's view, equality holds centre stage. The difference principle permits inequalities, but only when these are maximally beneficial to the least advantaged. By contrast, democratic equality is a *sufficientarian* view, which aims to ensure that each individual has enough. As Anderson writes, our aim is 'not effective access to equal levels . . . but effective access to levels . . . sufficient to stand as an equal in society'.[34]

In some cases, this underlying concern with sufficiency provides us with reasons to favour equality. For example, to stand as an equal when voting in an election, a sufficient number of votes might be an equal amount of votes. On this view, if one individual enjoyed a greater number of votes than others, this wouldn't merely be unequal, it'd effectively deprive others of enough. But in many spheres of life, equality doesn't play such a special role. What matters is that everyone has enough food, shelter, clothing, and medical care, not that everyone's access to these goods is equal.

Though these disagreements between the difference principle and democratic equality are important for other disputes about distributive justice, they're not important for our purposes. Instead, the thing to highlight is that democratic equality seems to provide us with reasons to favour basic income. This is because it's one means—and perhaps even the best means—to ensure that each individual has sufficient access to nourishment, housing, and so forth, without the risk that they might fall into a position where they must bow and scrape before others to survive.[35]

---

[29] Andres Moles and Tom Parr, 'Distributions and Relations: A Hybrid Account', *Political Studies*, 67 (2019), 132–48.   [30] Anderson, 'What Is the Point of Equality?', 313–14.

[31] Anderson, 'What Is the Point of Equality?', 316–17.

[32] Amartya Sen, 'Equality of What?' in *The Tanner Lecture on Human Values* (Cambridge: Cambridge University Press, 1980), 197–220 and Martha Nussbaum, *Women and Human Development: The Capabilities Approach* (Cambridge: Cambridge University Press, 2000).

[33] Anderson, 'What Is the Point of Equality?', 317–18.

[34] Anderson, 'What Is the Point of Equality?', 318 and 317–19.

[35] Martin Luther King, Jr., *Where Do We Go from Here: Chaos or Community* (Boston, MA: Beacon, 2010 [1967]).

In addition to this, democratic equality casts new light on the value of basic income's exit option effect. When subject to exploitation from an employer, an individual with a basic income has a strike fund on which they can rely if they need to threaten to resign unless their wages or working conditions improve. And, when subject to the domination of her husband, a wife has the means to separate from an abusive relationship. Part of the appeal of basic income is that it provides a means of exiting oppressive relations of many kinds.

Intriguingly, like Rawls, Anderson indicates discomfort with the idea that her favoured account of distributive justice might lend support to basic income. Because of this, she also distances herself from this conclusion. We turn our attention to their concerns shortly, but first let's summarize our conclusions so far.

7.3.4 THE CASE FOR BASIC INCOME

We can bring the points of the preceding subsections together by stating the *distributive justice argument* for basic income as follows:

> *Distributive justice moral claim*: The state should improve the circumstances of the least advantaged and work to ensure that no one suffers oppressive social relations.

> *Basic income empirical claim*: Via its income effect and exit option effect, basic income improves the circumstances of the least advantaged and works to ensure that no one suffers oppressive social relations.

> *Conclusion*: The state should introduce basic income.

7.4 THE PROBLEM OF NON-CONTRIBUTORS

Both Rawls and Anderson are concerned at the fact that proponents of basic income are willing to give a share of the resources amassed through social cooperation to those who've freely chosen not to contribute to their production. In support of this objection, Anderson suggests that we should view the economy as a 'system of cooperative, joint production' and that, on this understanding, it can't be that anyone could have an entitlement to 'receive goods without . . . having an obligation to produce them'.[36] Because of this, an individual's entitlement to cash payments from the state must be '*conditional* on participating in the productive system'.[37] As Rawls imaginatively puts it, 'those who surf all day off Malibu must find a way to support themselves and would not be entitled to public funds'.[38]

Notwithstanding these claims, neither Rawls nor Anderson devote much attention to basic income in particular. For this reason, it makes sense to turn to the work of

---

[36] Anderson, 'What Is the Point of Equality?', 321.
[37] Anderson, 'What Is the Point of Equality?', 321 (emphasis added).
[38] Rawls, *Justice as Fairness*, 179.

others who develop this line of argument in further detail. There are several options available.[39] But the most powerful of these holds that it's *unfair* to those who produce society's wealth for the state to give a portion of this to those who've not contributed to its production.[40] It's the same intuition that's provoked by instances of free-riding, such as when someone rides the tram without buying a ticket or enjoys the advantages of street lighting, law enforcement, and national defence while avoiding their taxes.

One version of this view states that we shouldn't ask from an individual more than they can give. We can require only that each individual does their bit. While for some, this'll be a lot, for others, it'll be not much at all. This trades on the idea that an individual's entitlement to a given share of social and economic resources depends on them discharging a corresponding duty to make a productive contribution. The problem is that someone who fails to discharge this duty unfairly uses others as a means to achieving their own ends. This treats them in an offensively instrumental way. This is the *reciprocity objection* to basic income.[41] If persuasive, it means that the state has strong reasons to withhold cash payments from those unwilling to search for employment, with the effect that we should favour conditional unemployment benefits over basic income.

In effect, this means that advocates of this objection reject the distributive justice moral claim in favour of this revised version of it:

> *Revised distributive justice moral claim*: The state should improve the circumstances of the least advantaged and work to ensure that no one suffers oppressive social relations, on the condition that these individuals contribute to their society.

There are three reasons to resist this amendment. First, even if there's a duty to contribute, it's not the only thing with which we should be concerned when designing a system of benefits. For example, we've very strong reasons to avoid stigmatizing and humiliating individuals, as is often the case in means-tested systems, and to avoid demeaning them, as is often the case if the receipt of benefits is conditional on the claimant proving that they're unable to find employment.[42] Furthermore, there remains the worry that, with unemployment benefits, many individuals face an unemployment trap or lack any exit option, which consigns employees to poor wages and working conditions. These concerns alone may be sufficient to defeat any worries we might have about basic income's vulnerability to the reciprocity objection.

The deeper point to which this response alludes is that the context in which we presently operate makes a significant difference to how stringently we should insist on an individual discharging their duty to contribute. In a society characterized by severe injustice, when an individual's circumstances are especially bad, it makes no sense to

[39] Stuart White, 'Reconsidering the Exploitation Objection to Basic Income', *Basic Income Studies*, 1 (2006), 1–17.

[40] Stuart White, 'Liberal Equality, Exploitation, and the Case for an Unconditional Basic Income', *Political Studies*, 45 (1997), 312–26 at 317–20.

[41] White, 'Liberal Equality, Exploitation, and the Case for an Unconditional Basic Income', 319.

[42] Stuart White, 'What's Wrong with Workfare?', *Journal of Applied Philosophy*, 21 (2004), 271–84 at 278–9.

talk of reciprocity at all. This is because this individual benefits from social cooperation to such a small degree that they can be under no duty to contribute in return.[43]
Even if we should seek a society in which benefits are provided only conditionally to
those who're willing to search for employment, basic income might still be justifiable
given the injustice already suffered by many of society's least advantaged.

Second, even if we should demand that everyone contributes, it's far from obvious
that the appropriate response to those who fail to act in this way is to withdraw cash
payments. It's significant that almost no one contends that we may withdraw an individual's entitlements to other kinds of benefits, such as to healthcare or police protection. Why think that we should treat cash payments any differently, especially given
that they provide the basic funds on which to live? The tough challenge for advocates
of the reciprocity objection is to explain why, though it'd clearly be wrong to deny non-
contributors benefits such as police protection, it'd be fine to withdraw cash payments.

Third, the reciprocity objection relies on a problematic assumption about who's
entitled to the benefits of social cooperation.[44] In order for the objection to impugn
basic income, it must be that those who've contributed to the creation of society's
wealth own them in their entirety. If this weren't the case, then we wouldn't be morally
barred from redistributing some of these resources. But there are several reasons to
doubt that those who've contributed to the production of these resources are the sole
owners of these goods.

It's significant that the social and economic resources at the state's disposal aren't
the result of only contemporary cooperation. A host of other factors play a pivotal role,
including natural resources, inherited information and technology, and the labour of
many thousands of past generations.[45] Because of this, each society has a range of assets
over which contributors have no special claim. If these are the resources that the state uses
to fund basic income, then it can't be unfair if they go towards those unwilling to work.

It adds to this that many employees earn employment rents. This term refers to the
part of an employee's earnings that exceed what would've been necessary to induce
them to take the job. If someone would've accepted the offer at £8 per hour but, because
of market inefficiencies, they happen to earn £10 per hour, then the employment rent
is £2 per hour. It's unclear why those employees who're lucky enough to benefit from
such rents have any greater claim to them than anyone else.[46] In this way, employment
rents are similar to society's natural resources. Again, this means that it can't be unfair
if the state were to redistribute a portion of these rents to those unwilling to work.

We don't take these responses to establish either that there's no duty to contribute,
or that reciprocity is irrelevant to the case at hand. Rather, our claim is that we shouldn't
revise the distributive justice moral claim in the way that the critics suggest and that

---

[43] Tommie Shelby, 'Justice, Work, and the Ghetto Poor', *The Law & Ethics of Human Rights*, 6 (2012), 71–96.
[44] Paul Bou-Habib and Serena Olsaretti, 'Liberal Egalitarianism and Workfare', *Journal of Applied Philosophy*,
21 (2004), 257–70 at 263–7.   [45] Van Parijs, 'Why Surfers Should Be Fed', 117–21.
[46] Van Parijs, 'Why Surfers Should Be Fed', 121–5.

concerns that rely on these ideas have much less force against the case for basic income than is assumed.

7.5 THE PROBLEM WITH TAXATION

Any policy, including basic income, that requires the state to redistribute resources will be challenged by those who oppose using taxation for this purpose. These critics ask: if those who're taxed have a genuine entitlement to their income and wealth, how can it be justifiable for the state to take resources from them and use these to provide benefits for others? Let's call this the *entitlement objection*.

In defending basic income, we appealed to the following:

Distributive justice moral claim: The state should improve the circumstances of the least advantaged and work to ensure that no one suffers oppressive social relations.

An advocate of the entitlement objection needn't deny that a fairer distribution of social and economic resources is a laudable goal. Rather, their problem with this moral claim concerns the state's role in bringing this about, as they insist that it's simply not within the state's appropriate remit to act in this way. We'll discuss this objection in two stages, beginning with its intuitive appeal, and then exploring its foundations.

7.5.1 THE INTUITIVE PROBLEM

Let's consider the following example, which is devised by Robert Nozick:

Wilt Chamberlain: Let's suppose that there's an initially just distribution of resources—say, an equal amount of wealth for each person. We call this distribution *D1*. Now let's imagine that a basketball star, Wilt Chamberlain, signs a contract in which he gets 25 cents of each ticket purchased to watch his team. The season starts, and fans attend his team's games, each time giving 25 cents of their admission price to Chamberlain. These consumers are excited to see him play, and it's worth the total admission price to them. Let's suppose that in one season 1 million people attend his games and, as a result, there's a new distribution in which Chamberlain has gained $250,000 more than he had at *D1*. We call this distribution *D2*.[47]

Is *D2* unjust? Intuitively, the answer is 'no'. At the very least, it seems wrong for the state to take resources from Chamberlain to benefit others. After all, in the initial scenario, *D1*, each individual enjoys their fair share of resources, and the distribution changed through voluntary transfers alone. To put this another way, we might rhetorically ask: how can it be permissible for the state to tax Chamberlain's income when this effectively amounts to denying each spectator the power to transfer to him 25 cents from their own justly held resources?

---

[47] Robert Nozick, *Anarchy, State, and Utopia* (New York: Basic Books, 1974), 160–1.

As Nozick writes, whatever our redistributive aims—whether to improve the position of the least advantaged or to secure democratic equality—we can't achieve this 'without continuous interference with people's lives'.[48] Any attempt to change the distribution of social and economic resources, including to return to *D1*, requires the state to undo the choices that individuals make about how to use their money.

While there's much to admire in this creative argument, it doesn't prove as much as Nozick claims. This is for at least two reasons.[49] First, even if *Wilt Chamberlain* shows that individuals should enjoy discretion over how they use their resources when an inevitable consequence of this is *some* level of social and economic inequality, it doesn't follow that we must accept *all* such inequalities.[50] To see this, let's consider a revision of the case, in which Chamberlain accrues so much wealth that he can easily meddle in politics, subverting democratic processes to produce the results he desires. If this is what *D2* involves, then it's much less clear that it'd be wrong for the state to get involved.

Second, Nozick brushes over an important detail of the case, namely that, in virtue of his fortune in the natural lottery, Chamberlain enjoys many more valuable opportunities than others. When we place a spotlight on this feature, the example loses much or all of its intuitive force. Perhaps Nozick is correct to claim that it'd be a mistake for the state to take resources from Chamberlain if the spectators were as fortunate as him in the natural lottery, but chose to watch basketball rather than profit from their talents. But if the opportunities available to the spectators are much less valuable than those available to Chamberlain, then the case for redistribution seems stronger. For this reason as well, an appeal to *Wilt Chamberlain* is insufficient to support the entitlement objection.

7.5.2 THE THEORETICAL PROBLEM

Given these issues, let's turn to some other of Nozick's arguments. Among his most controversial and influential claims is that 'taxation of earnings from labor is on a par with forced labor'.[51] This is because, when the state taxes an individual's pay, then during the period of time in which an individual is earning income that'll be taxed away, they're effectively working for free. If income is taxed at 30 per cent, then an individual's earnings over a ten-hour shift are as if they worked seven hours for themselves, followed by three hours for the state. It's on this basis that Nozick concludes that income tax is morally equivalent to conscription.

To evaluate this claim, it's useful to distinguish two interpretations of it. The first is the idea that taxation *forces* an individual to work for a period for the benefit of others. In various places, Nozick appears to have this concern in mind. For example, he

---

[48] Nozick, *Anarchy, State, and Utopia*, 163.

[49] For other objections, see G. A. Cohen, *Self-Ownership, Freedom, and Equality* (Cambridge: Cambridge University Press, 1995), chs 1–3 and 9–10.

[50] Cohen, *Self-Ownership, Freedom and Equality*, 25–8.   [51] Nozick, *Anarchy, State, and Utopia*, 169.

claims that 'seizing the results of someone's labor is equivalent to seizing hours from him and *directing him to carry on various activities*'.[52] But if this is his complaint, then it misses the mark as there are crucial differences between income tax and conscription. Taxation doesn't compel anyone to work, nor does it compel anyone to work at a particular task or for a particular amount of time. Instead, it merely means that, if someone *chooses* to work, then the state will confiscate some portion of their income. In this way, income tax parallels those traffic laws that hold that, if someone chooses to drive, then they must do so according to the rules of the road.

Alternatively, Nozick might mean to oppose taxation on the grounds that even placing conditions on the terms on which an individual may work restricts their opportunities. In other places, Nozick seems sympathetic to this view, suggesting that each individual has a deep moral interest in 'shaping his life in accordance with some overall plan'.[53] But this interpretation threatens to undermine the entitlement objection even more thoroughly.[54] This is because the interest in shaping a life according to some overall plan, whereby it's problematic when the state denies an individual valuable opportunities, amounts to a concern with real freedom. And, as we explain in section 7.2, a concern for real freedom is what motivates many defenders of basic income. The idea is that, if one is committed to improving individuals' real freedoms, then this counts in favour of redistributing resources via taxation rather than against it. It's in the light of this that the entitlement objection fails.

7.6 CONCLUSIONS

Our analysis of basic income has focused on its relationship to the demands of distributive justice, emphasizing the appeal and relevance of the difference principle and democratic equality. Rather than rehearse our arguments, we conclude by making two remarks about the economic sustainability of the policy.

First, the costs of basic income have been carefully calculated in a range of contexts and, though there's some disagreement, many of these studies reveal optimistic results.[55] For example, in 2013, the United Kingdom's Citizen's Income Trust proposed a modest basic income.[56] This would've been costly to fund, but it'd also have facilitated considerable savings, as the system of unemployment benefits could be scrapped.[57] These savings are likely to be substantial as, though unemployment benefits are withheld from those unwilling to search for employment, it's very costly to identify these individuals.

---

[52] Nozick, *Anarchy, State, and Utopia*, 172 (emphasis added).   [53] Nozick, *Anarchy, State, and Utopia*, 50.

[54] Samuel Scheffler, 'Natural Rights, Equality, and the Minimal State' in Jeffrey Paul (ed.), *Reading Nozick* (London: Wiley Blackwell, 1982), 148–68.

[55] For an overview, see Van Parijs and Vanderborght, *Basic Income*, ch. 6.

[56] Citizen's Income Trust, 'Citizen's Income: A Brief Introduction' (2013), available at http://citizensincome .org/wp-content/uploads/2016/03/Booklet-2013.pdf.

[57] Citizen's Income Trust, 'Citizen's Income', 8–9.

Second, even if the concerns about economic sustainability are more serious than we've suggested, then this needn't mean that we should rule out the policy completely. Instead, perhaps the most sensible way to proceed is to trial it, maybe paying individuals only a very modest amount. As we noted in section 7.1, various states are considering basic income pilots. This strikes us as a wise move and, given our arguments in this chapter, something that warrants our support.

FURTHER READING

For an introduction to basic income and some supporting arguments, a good starting place is Philippe Van Parijs, 'Basic Income: A Simple and Powerful Idea for the Twenty-First Century', *Politics & Society*, 32 (2004), 7–39. For more extended discussion see Philippe Van Parijs and Yannick Vanderborght, *Basic Income: A Radical Proposal for a Free Society and Sane Economy* (Cambridge, MA: Harvard University Press, 2017). Meanwhile, for an excellent overview of the political philosophy literature on basic income, see Juliana Uhuru Bidadanure, 'The Political Theory of Universal Basic Income', *Annual Review of Political Science*, 22 (2019), 481–501.

For further exploration of the morality of unemployment benefits, there's an informative debate between Stuart White and his critics. We recommend starting with Stuart White, 'Liberal Equality, Exploitation, and the Case for an Unconditional Basic Income', *Political Studies*, 45 (1997), 317–20 and Stuart White, 'What's Wrong with Workfare?', *Journal of Applied Philosophy*, 21 (2004), 271–84. Responses include Philippe Van Parijs, 'Reciprocity and the Justification for Basic Income: Reply to Stuart White', *Political Studies*, 45 (1997), 327–30 and Paul Bou-Habib and Serena Olsaretti, 'Liberal Egalitarianism and Workfare', *Journal of Applied Philosophy*, 21 (2004), 257–70.

Much of this material refers to more general disputes about the demands of distributive justice. For a general overview of work on distributive justice see Julian Lamont and Christi Favor, 'Distributive Justice', *Stanford Encyclopedia of Philosophy* (2017), available at https://plato .stanford.edu/entries/justice-distributive. Furthermore, there's a very clear and accessible introduction to the thinking of John Rawls and Robert Nozick among other theorists of distributive justice in Will Kymlicka, *Contemporary Political Philosophy: An Introduction, Second Edition* (Oxford: Oxford University Press, 2002), 53–75 and 102–27 respectively.

 For additional material and resources, including web links and self-test questions, please visit the online resources **www.oup.com/he/walton1e**.

8

PARENTAL LEAVE AND GENDER EQUALITY

SUMMARY

- In this chapter, we defend the radical view that the state should legally require all parents to take a substantial period of parental leave following the birth or adoption of a child.
- We begin by identifying the various ways in which the current distribution of paid employment and household work is gendered, showing how women and men tend to play different roles in these domains.
- We consider three reasons to worry about these trends. The first contends that these gendered patterns of paid employment and household work are intrinsically unjust. The second holds that these trends are objectionable if they arise from unequal or different opportunities. The third opposes them on the grounds that they negatively affect the interests of women, men, and children. Together, these arguments provide us with strong reasons to challenge the gendered division of labour.
- We explain how different kinds of parental leave schemes can serve this goal, criticizing those that are likely to reproduce the current pattern of paid employment and household work. We argue that we should favour schemes that encourage a more equal division of labour between women and men.
- We defend a proposal that legally requires all parents to take a substantial period of parental leave. Though radical, we believe that this strikes the right balance between advancing gender equality and respecting other considerations relating to the family.
- We respond to the concern that our proposal interferes too greatly with parental freedom, as well as to the worry that it neglects the wider structures that perpetuate gender injustice.
- We conclude by discussing the implications of our arguments for the design of parental leave schemes and for the broader landscape in which these policies are nested.

8.1 INTRODUCTION

A glaring fact of contemporary society is the *gendered division of labour*, where the kind and amount of work that men do differs from the kind and amount of work that women do. Across Organisation for Economic Co-operation and Development (OECD) states in 2019, there was an average difference of 13 per cent between the median wages of women and men.[1] Even though it's long been the norm for both parents in a heterosexual couple to engage in some form of paid employment, women are still less likely than men to be employed, and vastly less likely to be employed full-time.[2] Women also tend to undertake far more unpaid care work and domestic labour than men.[3] When we compare the combined time that individuals spend working in the labour market and carrying out unpaid household work, women's total number of work hours far outstrips the total of their male counterparts in almost all countries.[4]

How should the state respond to this gendered division of labour? Policymakers employ a variety of tools, including: (i) laws that prohibit workplace discrimination against women; (ii) working time regulations designed to reduce the length of the work day or work week; (iii) measures that reduce the cost of professional childcare and childhood education; and (iv) parental leave policies that require employers to offer parents time off work after the birth or adoption of a child.

Here, we focus on *parental leave* policies because these bring to the fore several important moral disagreements relating to how the state should respond to the gendered division of labour. The practice of taking time off from work to care for a child has a particularly gendered history and, even today, it remains considerably more common among women than men. Recent research indicates that this fact explains much of the gender pay gap: following the birth of a child, mothers tend to see their wages and earnings decline substantially in comparison with fathers, as well as those who choose to forgo parenthood.[5]

In the light of this information, it's not surprising that many believe that parental leave policies must play a vital role in promoting greater *gender equality*. For example, in support of its 2015 Shared Parental Leave scheme (which allows parents to share up to fifty-two weeks away from work following the birth or adoption of a child), the government of the United Kingdom asserted the hope that this will 'create more equity in the workplace and reduce the gender penalty resulting from women taking long periods of time out of the workplace on maternity leave'.[6] But changes to parental leave policies have been met with considerable resistance. Some claim that it's not the business of the state to intervene in family life.[7] Others contend that it's a mistake to obsess

[1] OECD, 'Gender Wage Gap' (2020), available at https://data.oecd.org/earnwage/gender-wage-gap.htm.

[2] OECD, 'Gender Brief' (2010), available at http://www.oecd.org/els/family/44720649.pdf, 12.

[3] OECD, 'Gender Brief' (2010), available at http://www.oecd.org/els/family/44720649.pdf, 15.

[4] OECD, 'Time Spent in Paid and Unpaid Work, by Sex' (2018), available at https://stats.oecd.org/index.aspx?queryid=54757.

[5] Henrik Kleven, Camille Landais, and Jakob Egholt Søgaard, 'Children and Gender Inequality: Evidence from Denmark', *American Economic Journal: Applied Economics*, 11 (2019), 181–209. See also Henrik Kleven, Camille Landais, Johanna Posch, Andreas Steinhauer, and Josef Zweimüller, 'Child Penalties Across Countries: Evidence and Explanations', *AEA Papers and Proceedings*, 109 (2019), 122–6.

[6] Department for Business, Innovation, and Skills, 'Explanatory Memorandum to the Shared Parental Leave Regulations' (2014), available at https://www.legislation.gov.uk/uksi/2014/3050/pdfs/uksiem_20143050_en.pdf.

[7] Daniel Mitchell, 'Why Parental Leave Is None of the Government's Business', *Foundation for Economic Education*, 30 March 2019, available at https://fee.org/articles/why-parental-leave-is-none-of-the-government-s-business.

over the details of parental leave policies, when there are much more fundamental and far-reaching matters to resolve in the fight against gender injustice.[8]

In this chapter, we explore these debates by developing an argument for the radical conclusion that the state should make it *mandatory* for all parents to take a substantial period of leave from work following the birth or adoption of a child. We proceed as follows. In section 8.2, we analyse what's morally objectionable about the existing gendered division of labour. In section 8.3, we distinguish three categories of parental leave schemes and show how these relate to the gendered division of labour. We argue that this background provides us with a strong reason to favour policies that promote a more egalitarian division of labour, and, in section 8.4, we show that this counts in favour of mandatory parental leave. In section 8.5, we consider and respond to the concern that this proposal wrongly interferes with parental freedom, as well as to the worry that it misjudges what's important in the struggle for gender equality. In section 8.6, we conclude.

One final note is in order before we begin. Our main focus in this chapter is on families with two heterosexual parents. Crucially, this *doesn't* reflect a belief that this arrangement is in any way superior to the other forms that a family can take. We strongly oppose such a view. We focus on families with two heterosexual parents only because these are environments in which the traditional gendered division of labour is most likely to be reproduced. It's for this reason that philosophical analysis of this unit in particular is important.[9] Because of this choice of topic, our analysis concerns only one aspect of gender justice, namely between women and men, meaning that we set aside questions of justice for those who're non-binary.

8.2 THE GENDERED DIVISION OF LABOUR

Let's begin with the following claim:

> *Gendered division of labour moral claim*: The state should combat the gendered division of labour.

This view is widely endorsed, but what reasons can we offer in its support? To answer this question, let's explore three accounts of what's wrong with the gendered division of labour.

---

[8] Christina Castellanos Serrano and David Drabble, 'Shared Parental Leave to Have Minimal Impact on Gender Equality', *The Tavistock Institute*, May 2014, available at https://www.tavinstitute.org/news/shared-parental-leave-minimal-impact-gender-equality.

[9] Gina Schouten, *Liberalism, Neutrality, and the Gendered Division of Labor* (Oxford: Oxford University Press, 2019), 3–5.

8.2.1 EQUALITY OF OUTCOME

One view appeals to the idea that the state should ensure that there're no significant patterns of association between an individual's gender and their income or social position.[10] This claim provides us with the theoretical resources to condemn a state governed solely by men, for example. This is intuitive. One reason that we might worry about such an arrangement is instrumental: it's very likely that this state will represent the interests of women poorly. But we might also think it's wrong in a more direct way, regardless of its effects, when members of one gender hold a much greater proportion of powerful, higher-status, and higher-earning jobs.

Critics of equality of outcome maintain that this is a mistake, such that we ought not to view gender equality in the distribution of income and social positions as an important goal in itself. One reason in support of this criticism appeals to the idea that differences in employment and household work are unproblematic from the point of view of justice so long as they result from individuals' *voluntary* choices.[11] When this is the case, perhaps it's not the state's business to intervene. John Rawls expresses some sympathy with this position, holding that 'a liberal conception of justice may have to allow for some traditional gendered division of labour—assume, say, that this division is based on religion—provided that it is fully voluntary and does not result from or lead to injustice'.[12]

A defender of equality of outcome can respond by invoking the idea that we've strong reasons to restrict individuals' voluntary choices when these harm others. To illustrate, it might be that the gendered division of labour leads women to suffer greater discrimination, perhaps because this tightens the common association of women and household work. If that's the case, then we've reason to challenge the choices that sustain the gendered division of labour, even if these are fully voluntary.[13]

An alternative response is to maintain that it's beside the point to suppose that the gendered division of labour emerges from voluntary choices. Instead, the division results from choices that are constrained in a large number of important ways. Laws, social norms, unconscious biases, and economic inequalities structure the opportunities available to women, men, and non-binary individuals, with the predictable consequence that the choices made in this context sustain the gendered division of labour.[14] This leads us nicely to a second moral concern.

---

[10] Anne Phillips, 'Defending Equality of Outcome', *Journal of Political Philosophy*, 12 (2004), 1–19.

[11] Brian Barry, *Culture and Equality: An Egalitarian Critique of Multiculturalism* (Cambridge: Polity Press, 2001), 93.

[12] John Rawls, *Collected Papers* (Cambridge, MA: Harvard University Press, 1999), 599.

[13] Linda Barclay, 'Liberal Daddy Quotas: Why Men Should Take Care of the Children, and How Liberals Can Get Them to Do It', *Hypatia*, 28 (2013), 163–78 at 170.

[14] Clare Chambers, *Sex, Culture, and the Limits of Choice* (University Park, PA: Penn State University Press, 2008).

8.2.2 EQUALITY OF OPPORTUNITY

In Chapters 5 and 6, we explore the idea of equality of opportunity in considerable detail across a range of contexts. Here, it suffices to consider a widely accepted version of the idea that motivates an objection to the gendered division of labour. This holds that the state should ensure that no individual's prospects differ from those enjoyed by others in virtue of their gender.[15]

How does this moral claim bear on the statistics with which we began regarding the gendered division of labour? After all, they don't immediately establish that women endure worse *opportunities* in the labour market than men. It's conceivable the current distribution of paid employment and household work could arise from a background in which women and men enjoy equality of opportunity.

For several reasons, we believe this explanation for the gendered division of labour is highly implausible. This is because women tend to face additional obstacles in the competition for employment that aren't faced by men, while men tend to face additional obstacles in undertaking household work that aren't faced by women. These obstacles can take a variety of forms.[16] Powerful social norms can make some choices costlier for members of one gender than another. For example, if a woman is likely to experience social disapproval when she takes a promotion, then she faces an additional barrier that men don't face. Similarly, if there's a social norm against a man acting as the primary caregiver to a child, then he faces an obstacle not faced by women. Over time, these norms may even shape the ambitions of women and men, increasing the likelihood that women will prefer some things and men will prefer others.[17]

This is consistent with the idea that women and men act rationally in making different choices with regards to paid employment and household work. For example, where women tend to earn less than men, the financial incentive for mothers to drop out of the labour market in order to care for a child is much stronger than it is for fathers.[18] In this case, the difference in opportunities exists not because of differences in others' expectations of how women and men should act, but because of the economic incentives that parents face.

It's important to note that our analysis doesn't rely on the claim that the total array of opportunities available to women are *less valuable* than those available to men. This claim is rejected by those who emphasize that caregivers tend to be rewarded with better opportunities to form the bonds of intimacy with their child.[19] Our claim is more basic: no individual's prospects should *differ* from those enjoyed by others in virtue of their gender. Equality of opportunity is violated whenever women face obstacles not faced by men, and whenever men face obstacles not faced by women.

---

[15] Susan Moller Okin, *Gender, Justice, and the Family* (New York: Basic Books, 1989), chs 5 and 8.

[16] Anca Gheaus, 'Gender Justice', *Journal of Ethics & Social Philosophy*, 6 (2012), 1–24.

[17] For discussion, see Clare Chambers, 'Are Breast Implants Better Than Female Genital Mutilation? Autonomy, Gender Equality and Nussbaum's Political Liberalism', *Critical Review of International Social and Political Philosophy*, 7 (2004), 1–33.

[18] Okin, *Gender, Justice, and the Family*, 5.

[19] Schouten, *Liberalism, Neutrality, and the Gendered Division of Labor*, 104.

8.2.3 HARMFUL EFFECTS

A third basis on which to object to the gendered division of labour refers to its harmful effects on the interests of women, men, and children. We've already noted that women shoulder a greater quantity of work and tend to receive lower pay than men. This means that women usually enjoy less time and have fewer resources at their disposal than men. This creates greater financial dependence of women on men. This dependence is problematic to the extent that it gives men power over their partners, because they have discretion over the amount of resources their partners enjoy and the conditions according to which these resources are granted. In this way, the dependence of women on men increases the risk of maltreatment, abuse, and poverty.[20]

A further concern with existing arrangements is that many fathers lack the time to nurture their familial relationships because they spend so many hours in paid employment, and very few hours caring for their children. In this way, fathers miss out on what's arguably one of life's most valuable goods: loving and intimate relationships with one's close family. This loss is particularly morally significant if, as some evidence suggests, engaging in a fairer share of care work within the family has positive effects on men's emotional development.[21] In families with separated parents, this problem is likely to be even more acute. This is because the mother is much more likely to have custody of a child, and the father may see their child only occasionally.

Finally, children who grow up within families where mothers take on the majority of household work and where fathers spend little time at home miss the benefits of having a second parent involved in their upbringing. This is significant because a child is likely to be better off in a system in which they have access to multiple sources of care rather than one in which a single caregiver has a monopoly of parental authority over them.[22] The crucial thought is that the law and a parent's moral sensibilities aren't perfectly reliable mechanisms for guaranteeing the protection of a child's interests. And so, to minimize the chance of abuse, it makes sense to add another adult into the mix who has some responsibilities for the child. Furthermore, domestic arrangements are *schools of justice*, such that they have pervasive effects on a child's beliefs regarding gender roles and what they regard as a just distribution of work between parents.[23] We must be sensitive to the formative effects of family life on a child when reflecting on the significance of the gendered division of labour.

---

[20] Okin, *Gender, Justice, and the Family*, ch. 7.

[21] Alan Hawkins and Tomi-Anne Roberts, 'Designing a Primary Intervention to Help Dual-Earner Couples Share Housework and Child Care', *Family Relations*, 41 (1992), 169–77 and Kipling Rasmussen et al., 'Increasing Husbands' Involvement in Domestic Labor: Issues for Therapists', *Contemporary Family Therapy*, 18 (1996), 209–23.

[22] Anca Gheaus, 'Childrearing with Minimal Domination: A Republican Account', *Political Studies* (forthcoming).

[23] Okin, *Gender, Justice, and the Family*, 17–23. See also Gina Schouten, 'Citizenship, Reciprocity, and the Gendered Division of Labor: A Stability Argument for Gender Egalitarian Political Interventions', *Politics, Philosophy, and Economics*, 16 (2017), 174–209.

This range of harmful effects on women, men, and children is important because it reveals something distinctively objectionable about a society in which individuals' opportunities are structured by their gender. It's not merely that women face obstacles to opportunities that aren't faced by men, and vice versa, but also that the resulting opportunity sets for women, men, and children are less valuable than they might be otherwise. In other words, combating the gendered division of labour not only addresses the intrinsic unfairness of women's and men's opportunity sets being structured by their gender, it also enhances the value of those opportunity sets, as well as those of children.

8.3 PARENTAL LEAVE SCHEMES

We build a bridge from the preceding discussion to parental leave schemes by categorizing these schemes according to their relationship to gender equality: those that are equality-impeding, equality-enabling, and equality-promoting.[24]

Equality-impeding parental leave schemes are those that incentivize mothers and fathers to take on traditional gender roles, which in turn impedes efforts to mitigate or eliminate the gendered division of labour. An example of this is the system in place in the United Kingdom prior to 2015, where mothers were entitled to fifty-two weeks of leave, half of which was paid, while fathers were entitled to only two weeks' paid leave.[25] Schemes such as these are problematic for precisely the reasons we've outlined. For example, they violate the demands of equality of opportunity by offering different opportunities to individuals according to their gender. These schemes incentivize mothers to take on a much greater share of care work and domestic labour, and therefore they pose a very serious threat to the interests of everyone involved: mothers, fathers, and children.

Equality-enabling parental leave makes it possible for fathers to engage in more caregiving, but it doesn't incentivize families to take up this option. What's distinctive about such schemes is that they provide parents with the flexibility to settle on arrangements that work for them. The United Kingdom's Shared Parental Leave is an example of this, as it provides parents with fifty-two weeks' paid leave to share between them.

In terms of the concerns we've outlined, these schemes are an improvement on equality-impeding parental leave. But they aren't vastly better. This is because, though they provide greater flexibility, evidence suggests that parents are likely to come to arrangements that sustain the existing gendered division of labour. This is because of the informal ways in which our opportunities are shaped. Even when

---

[24] Harry Brighouse and Erik Olin Wright, 'Strong Gender Egalitarianism', *Politics & Society*, 36 (2008), 360–72 at 361–2.

[25] *The Paternity and Adoption Leave Regulations 2002*, available at http://www.legislation.gov.uk/uksi/2002/2788/contents/made.

parents can share leave, there's a greater incentive for mothers rather than fathers to take it, given prevailing social norms. Empirical evidence confirms these concerns, with only 1 per cent of fathers taking a substantial period of leave under the new scheme in the United Kingdom.[26] Against a background with these pressures, equality-enabling schemes continue to furnish women and men with opportunities that differ based on their gender and, in this way, these schemes harm women, men, and children.

Finally, let's turn to *equality-promoting* parental leave, which actively encourages fathers to engage in more caregiving and promotes more gender-egalitarian practices. These incentives can vary in character and strength. Here are four models:

> *Use it or lose it leave* provides periods away from work to both parents individually, which they may elect to take as they see fit. Each parent is entitled to, say, six months of leave, but this is lost if the parent doesn't opt in. This policy is in place in several states, including Iceland, Norway, and Sweden, where they're known as 'daddy quotas'.[27]

> *Default leave* provides periods away from work to both parents individually, for which they're automatically enrolled. But parents may opt out of this if they wish, thereby losing this entitlement.

> *Conditional leave* provides a period away from work to parents jointly, but each may take only as much leave as the other. For example, if the father takes three months of leave, then the mother must take three months as well.

> *Mandatory leave* requires that all parents take a period away from work.

We support the use of equality-promoting schemes. These are justified partly in virtue of the inadequacies of equality-impeding and equality-enabling parental leave. Equality-promoting schemes aim to ensure that the opportunities available to individuals don't differ because of their gender. This is true in the formal sense that each parent enjoys the same opportunities to take leave. Moreover, these schemes are sensitive to the wide array of costs that can structure opportunities. In attempting to mitigate the effect of these costs, there's reason to believe that schemes of this kind will be more successful in combating the gendered division of labour, thereby reducing the harmful effects associated with it.

This case for equality-promoting parental leave has its critics. But, since some of the most serious objections figure in debates about which of its versions is the most attractive, we'll approach these issues by defending one proposal in particular.

---

[26] Figures from My Family Care, 'Shared Parental Leave: Where Are We Now?' (2016), available at https://www.myfamilycare.co.uk/resources/white-papers/shared-parental-leave-where-are-we-now.

[27] OECD, 'Parental Leave: Where Are the Fathers?' (March 2016), available at https://www.oecd.org/policy-briefs/parental-leave-where-are-the-fathers.pdf.

8.4 DEFENDING MANDATORY LEAVE

Under the mandatory scheme, all parents would be legally required to take a substantial period of parental leave following the birth or adoption of a child. Although there are various ways to construct a scheme of this kind, let's consider a version that requires both parents to take six months away from employment to care for their child.

The simple case in support of mandatory leave is that it directly and firmly addresses the concerns relating to gender equality that motivate our analysis in this chapter. The mandatory scheme furnishes women and men with the same opportunities: having a child means taking six months away from employment to undertake childcare responsibilities, regardless of one's gender. The incentives that mothers and fathers face are protected from the influence of social and economic pressures. Social expectations around family roles can't influence the amount of leave that each parent takes, and it's not an option for the mother to take a greater amount of leave to retain the financial benefits of the father's pay, for example. A further attractive feature of the proposal is that it removes the incentive for employers to hire men rather than women on the grounds that women may be more likely than men to take time away from employment in order to meet the demands of parenting.

Insofar as the scheme addresses these concerns, we can expect it to alter the gendered division of labour. More specifically, it should result in a more even distribution of employment and childcare between genders, women and men being more evenly represented across full- and part-time employment, and a smaller gender pay gap. This will reduce the extent to which we observe patterns of association between an individual's gender and their income or social position. In turn, this will ameliorate the harmful effects of these patterns on mothers, fathers, and children. These considerations give us strong reasons to endorse mandatory leave.

An obvious objection to this policy is that it deprives parents of choice and flexibility about how they structure their family arrangements. We'll tackle this objection later in the chapter. However, to build towards this, it may help for us to explore several ways in which mandatory leave is superior to its alternatives.

8.4.1 CONDITIONAL LEAVE

Among other equality-promoting schemes, conditional leave is the most similar to mandatory leave. This proposal grants a period away from work to the parents jointly, but it requires that each parent take the same amount.[28] For example, if the state jointly provides parents with twelve months of leave, they might decide to take six months each, but if one parent wishes to take only three months, the other parent must do the same.

There's something very attractive about this proposal. Ensuring that parents take the same amount of time away from employment is likely to have similar effects to

---

[28] Brighouse and Olin Wright, 'Strong Gender Egalitarianism'.

mandatory leave in terms of equalizing opportunities between mothers and fathers, and reducing the gendered division of labour and the associated harms. Moreover, it has the additional benefit of achieving this while preserving an element of flexibility, where parents can take a shorter period of leave if they wish.

However, whatever the merits of granting parents more freedom, we believe that conditional leave approaches this in the wrong way.[29] The clearest difficulty is that the increased flexibility it grants parents as a pair comes at the price of a problematic lack of flexibility for parents as individuals. To illustrate this concern, let's consider a scenario in which a mother wishes to take six months of leave, but the father adamantly refuses to take anything more than one month. In this case, the mother can't take longer than one month, and she must either go back to work or give up her employment to spend time with her child. If she chooses the latter, conditional leave wouldn't achieve some of its gender-egalitarian aims. Perhaps more importantly, however such situations unfold, they make mothers' opportunities dependent on the will of fathers. Few concerned with improving the position of women vis-à-vis men will find this acceptable. Even if there are drawbacks to mandatory leave's restrictions, it lacks this troubling feature.

Two further concerns flow from this. First, because the leave is conditional, there's likely to be a net loss in terms of time devoted to parental care. Spending time with one's child, particularly in their early years, is of great value to both parents and the child. But, in the scenario described in the previous paragraph, the total period of leave is only two months. Not only is this less than the full year that could've been taken, it's less than what would've been taken if the leave weren't conditional. In fact, it's less than what's taken under many equality-impeding schemes. Again, in comparison to our proposal for mandatory leave, where parents would take a combined twelve months, this is a significant loss.

Second, because conditional leave can generate such disagreements between parents, there's a danger that it can cause or exacerbate tension within families. Although separation and relationship disharmony might not always be matters of state concern (or, indeed, even always a bad thing), it seems undesirable to adopt a proposal that's likely to fuel them.

8.4.2 USE IT OR LOSE IT LEAVE AND DEFAULT LEAVE

Both use it or lose it leave and default leave offer each parent a substantial period away from work that's independent of the other partner's choice. This avoids the difficulties associated with conditional leave. Moreover, these schemes provide more flexibility than mandatory leave by making the period of leave that they offer optional. In use it or

---

[29] These criticisms follow Anca Gheaus and Ingrid Robeyns, 'Equality-Promoting Parental Leave', *Journal of Social Philosophy*, 42 (2011), 173–91 at 177–81. See also Barclay, 'Liberal Daddy Quotas', 174–5.

lose it schemes, each parent must opt in.[30] In default schemes, each parent is automatically enrolled but may opt out.[31]

Our concern with these proposals is that the greater freedom that they afford parents means that they're less likely than mandatory leave to deliver returns when it comes to gender equality. This is most obvious in the case of use it or lose it schemes. Set against the social and economic background of gender roles that we've described, it's unlikely that reserving a period of leave for fathers will result in them taking it. Empirical studies confirm this fear. In Sweden, where two months of parental leave are reserved specifically for fathers, 40 per cent take no leave at all, and over 60 per cent use less than the two months reserved for them.[32] South Korea and Japan display similar trends.[33]

Default leave might fare better, as there's ample evidence that individuals are inclined to take the default option.[34] This might be because choosing the default involves fewer costs. For example, it involves less time considering the options and less effort than pursuing the alternative. Or, it might be because the default is perceived to have the state's support. Whatever the mechanisms, there's persuasive evidence of conformity to the default across a range of contexts. For example, whereas rates of organ donation in states with opt-in systems range from 4 to 28 per cent, in states with opt-out systems they range from 85 to 100 per cent.[35]

Despite this, it's far from obvious that we can transfer these findings to the case of parental leave. Organ donation, and the other cases in which defaults are effective, are subject to far less powerful social and financial incentives than gender roles and parental leave arrangements. The evidence from Sweden, South Korea, and Japan that we've already mentioned lends weight to this concern. Although these aren't default schemes, the fact that fathers rarely use leave allocated to them gives some reason to fear that the (relatively minor) costs of opting out will not deter them.

All in all, our concern is that, while use it or lose it leave and default leave may provide greater incentives for fathers to take time away from work than at present, they aren't sufficiently powerful to realize the benefits to gender equality that mandatory leave offers.

---

[30] Janet Gornick and Marcia Meyers, 'Creating Gender Egalitarian Societies: An Agenda for Reform', *Politics and Society*, 36 (2008), 313–49 and Barclay, 'Liberal Daddy Quotas'.

[31] Gheaus and Robeyns, 'Equality-Promoting Parental Leave', 182–6.

[32] Barbara Bergmann, 'Long Leaves, Child Well-Being, and Gender Equality', *Politics and Society*, 36 (2008), 350–9 at 352.

[33] Willem Adema, Chris Clarke, and Valérie Frey, 'Paid Parental Leave: Lessons from OECD Countries and Selected US States', *OECD Social, Employment, and Migration Working Papers*, No. 172 (2015), available at http://dx.doi.org/10.1787/5jrqgvqqb4vb-en.

[34] Gheaus and Robeyns, 'Equality-Promoting Parental Leave', 183–4. Gheaus and Robeyns draw on Eric Johnson and Daniel Goldstein, 'Do Defaults Save Lives?', *Science*, 302 (2003), 1338–9 and Richard Thaler and Cass Sunstein, *Nudge: Improving Decisions about Health, Wealth and Happiness* (New Haven, CT: Yale University Press, 2008).   [35] Johnson and Goldstein, 'Do Defaults Save Lives?'.

8.4.3 THE CASE FOR MANDATORY LEAVE

We can bring these points together by stating the *gender justice argument* for mandatory leave as follows:

Gendered division of labour moral claim: The state should combat the gendered division of labour.

Balancing moral claim: The state should adopt a parental leave scheme that combats the gendered division of labour without exacerbating women's dependence on men, worsening childcare, or damaging relationship harmony.

Mandatory leave empirical claim: Mandatory leave combats the gendered division of labour to a greater extent than use it or lose it leave or default leave. Unlike conditional leave, it does this without exacerbating women's dependence on men, worsening childcare, or damaging relationship harmony.

Conclusion: The state should adopt mandatory leave.

8.5 THE LIMITS OF PARENTAL LEAVE

Having developed our case in favour of mandatory leave, we now address two concerns that are sometimes pressed against reformers of parental leave. Both of these concerns pertain to how these schemes sit within the larger moral landscape. On the one hand, there are those who hold that interventions on this front transgress important interests in freedom and flexibility in family life. On the other hand, there are those who hold that addressing gender equality requires us to look far beyond the design of parental leave schemes. We discuss these concerns in turn.

8.5.1 FREEDOM IN FAMILY LIFE

It's a common objection to redesigning parental leave that doing so interferes too much in family life. As we noted in section 8.2, Rawls expects that a society committed to religious freedom may have to allow families to follow traditions that maintain the gendered division of labour. Concern for various other freedoms may push towards the same conclusion.

We must be clear about what proponents of this criticism claim. They're not against *any* interventions in family life. For example, Rawls is clear that allowing families to organize in ways that maintain the gendered division of labour is subject to the condition that it 'does not result from or lead to injustice'.[36] This clause permits, and justice surely requires, interventions in the home designed to prevent domestic abuse, for example. The thrust of the criticism is subtler than a general objection to regulation.

---

[36] Rawls, *Collected Papers*, 599.

The thought is more to the effect that we should balance our reasons to intervene in the home against our reasons to create space for freedom in family life. Following Gina Schouten, we might say that this amounts to a 'presumption in favor of enacting the gentlest intervention sufficient to accomplish the objective in question'.[37] Let's call this the *freedom presumption*.

We might incorporate this point into one of the claims of our argument as follows:

Revised balancing moral claim: The state should adopt a parental leave scheme that combats the gendered division of labour without exacerbating women's dependence on men, worsening childcare, damaging relationship harmony, or unduly interfering with individuals' freedom.

When the view is revised in this way, advocates of alternative schemes might contend that their favoured model better accords with this claim. Indeed, Anca Gheaus and Ingrid Robeyns defend default leave precisely on grounds that they believe it strikes the best balance between the relevant concerns.[38] This argument might hold up even if default leave were somewhat less effective than mandatory leave in securing gender equality. Advocates of alternative schemes might claim that they'll be only slightly less effective in this respect, and that this cost is a reasonable price to pay for preserving greater freedom.

Our response to this objection is to insist that we find the inverse of this statement more plausible, namely that mandatory leave restricts freedom only a little more than its alternatives and that this is a reasonable price to pay for gender equality. To motivate this response, let's consider the following. First, if mandatory leave gives each parent six months away from work, it's true that what it asks for isn't a trivial amount of time. But neither is this such a vast stretch in the course of most lives. It's very different to requiring five years of parental leave, for example. In this regard, it's not especially burdensome.

Second, it's important to recognize that mandatory leave doesn't deprive individuals of a broad range of valuable opportunities in the same way that prison does. Nor does it strip individuals of their freedom of religion or association. Indeed, it doesn't even remove the option of having a family, having a job, or combining the two in a particular way. All it does is place a clause on parenting that isn't especially limiting. Since this is a clause already faced by (most) women, it might actually be better to say not that it *places* this clause, but that it *equalizes* the placement of this clause.

Third, this clause involves something that many parents value. Again, it's not asking them to undertake a stretch in prison. It asks that they spend a period of time caring for their child, an experience that many parents cherish, and one that many parents regret when they've missed it.

---

[37] Gina Schouten, 'Restricting Justice: Political Interventions in the Home and in the Market', *Philosophy & Public Affairs*, 41 (2013), 357–88 at 379.

[38] Gheaus and Robeyns, 'Equality-Promoting Parental Leave', 174 and 182–8.

Finally, let's not overlook the fact that this is optional. Mandatory leave doesn't make parental leave mandatory. It merely makes parental leave mandatory for those who choose to have a child. Those who prefer not to spend six months on leave remain entirely free to do so by choosing not to have a child.

It adds to these considerations that the benefits of mandatory leave are considerable ones. One aspect of this is something that we've stressed already, notably that we doubt that the effects on gender equality of other schemes will be only slightly less than those that result from mandatory leave. Thus, when we permit the option of having a child without taking time away from employment, we see significant inequalities between genders and harmful effects on the interests of mothers, fathers, and children.

Drawing these points together, we might phrase our analysis in the following terms: what mandatory leave demands is merely that everyone who chooses to have a child must act in a way that's not especially arduous and that doesn't generate grave consequences for others. It's true that this limits parents' freedom, but we think that's fair enough. For example, when prohibiting racist hiring decisions, we limit employers' freedom. This loss (if it can even sensibly be called a loss) is justified on grounds of racial equality. Similarly, while mandatory jury service restricts how someone can use their time, this can be easily justified given the importance of securing a fair trial. Our core point is that restrictions that are limited in length and scope, as well as conditional, and that are designed to advance significant ends aren't unquestionably problematic.

To put the point another way, we're sympathetic to the freedom presumption, according to which the state should enact the gentlest intervention sufficient to accomplish the objective in question. But we believe that mandatory leave meets this test. At any rate, we believe it's a gentle enough intervention given its comparative advantage in our pursuit of gender equality. In this respect, even if we accept the revised balancing moral claim, mandatory leave strikes us as a more appealing option than the alternatives.

8.5.2 BEYOND PARENTAL LEAVE

The main appeal of making parental leave mandatory is because of its effects on gender equality. But resting our case on this promise seems to make it vulnerable to another worry. More specifically, perhaps we're placing too much weight on the potential of parental leave. Let's call this the *objection from misplaced focus*.

This objection stems from the idea that, when theorizing about gender, we must be careful to do so with appropriate comprehensiveness. Nancy Fraser highlights the problem as follows. If we attempt to advance gender equality by improving women's access to paid employment, then this may result in women shouldering a double shift, in which they perform a day's work in the office followed by another day's work when they return home. However, if we attempt to advance gender equality by providing greater recognition and support for household work, then we risk preserving the gendered division of labour and the associated harms.[39] According to Fraser, the issue is that neither of these approaches gets to the heart of the problem. Instead, what's demanded of us is the 'wholesale restructuring of the institution of gender', where we 'dismantle those roles and their cultural coding'.[40] Others elaborate similar problems, stressing that the most familiar approaches to gender justice neglect the inequality of power that precedes and shapes gender roles, ignore the myriad ways in which women are rendered dependent on men, and overlook the asymmetry of power between women and men at home and in the labour market.[41] Critics of mandatory leave might harness this reasoning to contend that our proposal makes this error.

One way in which to develop this point is to hold that many attempts to advance gender equality are ineffective or even counterproductive if pursued in isolation from other policies. For example, when Eva Feder Kittay objects to the United States' *Family and Medical Leave Act*, she acknowledges that it's important that parents be granted periods away from employment to look after their child.[42] But her concern is that the policy doesn't provide adequate financial support for those who'd like to do this. This is certainly an important concern, which we've not addressed with respect to our proposal. But we can accommodate this worry by agreeing with Kittay that it's imperative that parental leave is funded generously.[43]

A similar strategy is available in response to the concern that even a carefully designed parental leave scheme would be unlikely to have drastic effects on the gendered division of labour, since it speaks to such a brief period of individuals' lives. In particular, we believe that mandatory leave should go hand in hand with a raft of further policies, including generously funded childcare. In short, we agree that parental leave reform shouldn't happen in isolation from other policies.

Given this feature of our view, the objection from misplaced focus threatens our defence of mandatory leave only if it's a mistake to focus on such policies at all. To support this line of criticism, an opponent might draw on the idea that it's an error to work *within* a system that's inherently gender unjust, rather than pursue the more radical agenda of 'wholesale restructuring'.

We think that an objection along these lines would misunderstand the nature of our proposal, which may bring about systematic change of this kind. Fraser contends that, as part of this wholesale restructuring of the institution of gender, the state

---

[39] Nancy Fraser, 'After the Family Wage: Gender Equality and the Welfare State', *Political Theory*, 22 (1994), 591–618 at 604 and 608–9.   [40] Fraser, 'After the Family Wage', 612.

[41] Catherine A. MacKinnon, *Feminism Unmodified: Discourses on Life and Law* (Cambridge, MA: Harvard University Press, 1987), ch. 2 and Eva Feder Kittay, *Love's Labour: Essays on Women, Equality, and Dependency* (New York: Routledge, 1999), part 2.   [42] Kittay, *Love's Labour*, 133–46.

[43] This raises an interesting question about who should pay for the costs of this. We lack space to explore this matter here. For discussion, see Sandrine Blanc and Tim Meijers, 'Firms and Parental Justice: Should Firms Contribute to the Cost of Parenthood and Procreation?', *Economics & Philosophy*, 36 (2020), 1–27; Paula Casal and Andrew Williams, 'Rights, Equality, and Procreation', *Analyse & Kritik*, 17 (1995), 93–116; and Serena Olsaretti, 'Children as Public Goods?', *Philosophy & Public Affairs*, 41 (2013), 226–58.

must 'induce men to become more like most women are now—that is, people who do primary care work'.[44] But, crucially, this is exactly the kind of result that we should expect to flow from mandatory leave. In this way, our proposal coheres nicely with the views of proponents of radical change. Indeed, it's tough to see how we could restructure the institution of gender without reforming policies that affect parental care.

8.6 CONCLUSIONS

Our central claim in this chapter is that the state should legally require all parents to take a substantial period of leave following the birth or adoption of a child. The justification for this policy is that it'd address several moral worries relating to the gendered division of labour, while being sensitive to women's dependence on men, childcare, and relationship harmony, and without interfering with individuals' freedom too greatly.

In section 8.5, we suggested that this proposal must be generously funded and form part of a suite of policies designed to advance gender equality. There's not been space to defend these further claims fully. Likewise, there are several other aspects to discussions of parental leave that we've not addressed. One of these concerns the effect of these schemes on birth rates. Another relates to whether we must modify mandatory leave in the case of single parents, separated parents, or families with more than two parents. But we believe that the task of adjusting our conclusions in the light of these complexities is a manageable one. In any case, given the strong reasons that support mandatory leave, it's a task that we should give serious attention.

FURTHER READING

To explore the demands of gender equality and its implications for the gendered division of labour, it's worth beginning with Susan Moller Okin's *Gender, Justice, and the Family* (New York: Basic Books, 1989). This is an accessible text that frames much subsequent research on these matters. An excellent recent contribution is Gina Schouten, *Liberalism, Neutrality, and the Gendered Division of Labor* (Oxford: Oxford University Press, 2019).

Good overviews of the work in this field are Clare Chambers, 'Gender' in Catriona McKinnon (ed.), *Issues in Political Theory, Third Edition* (Oxford: Oxford University Press, 2015), 265–88; Anca Gheaus, 'Gender and Distributive Justice' in Serena Olsaretti (ed.), *Oxford Handbook of Distributive Justice* (Oxford: Oxford University Press, 2018); and Will Kymlicka, *Contemporary Political Philosophy, Second Edition* (Oxford: Oxford University Press, 2002), ch. 9.

For further reading on the demands of gender equality, Okin's book remains a significant contribution. Others include Richard Arneson, 'What Sort of Sexual Equality Should Feminists Seek?', *Journal of Contemporary Legal Issues*, 9 (1998), 21–36; Anca Gheaus, 'Gender Justice', *Journal of Ethics and Social Philosophy*, 6 (2011), 1–24; Anne Phillips, 'Defending Equality of

---

[44] Fraser, 'After the Family Wage', 611.

Outcome', *Journal of Political Philosophy*, 12 (2004), 1–19; and Ingrid Robeyns, 'When Will Society Be Gender Just?' in Jude Brown (ed.), *The Future of Gender* (Cambridge: Cambridge University Press, 2007), 54–74.

For further reading on parental leave, there's Linda Barclay, 'Liberal Daddy Quotas: Why Men Should Take Care of the Children, and How Liberals Can Get Them to Do It', *Hypatia*, 28 (2013), 163–78; Harry Brighouse and Erik Olin Wright, 'Strong Gender Egalitarianism', *Politics & Society*, 36 (2008), 79–92; and Anca Gheaus and Ingrid Robeyns, 'Equality-Promoting Parental Leave', *Journal of Social Philosophy*, 42 (2011), 173–91.

Beyond parental leave, a good overview of a broader range of topics relating to gender equality is Sally Haslanger et al., 'Topics in Feminism', *Stanford Encyclopedia of Philosophy* (2012), available at https://plato.stanford.edu/archives/sum2018/entries/feminism-topics.

 For additional material and resources, including web links and self-test questions, please visit the online resources **www.oup.com/he/walton1e**.

9

MINORITY EXEMPTIONS AND MULTICULTURALISM

SUMMARY

- In this chapter, we argue that there's a narrow range of cases in which the state should grant members of minority groups exemptions from laws and policies that apply to others.
- We show that social and economic institutions tend to favour the preferences of those who share the majority culture, with the result that a member of a minority group often faces additional burdens in complying simultaneously with the law and the demands of their culture or religion. We draw on this to propose an initial case for minority exemptions.
- In the remaining sections, we look at the limits of this argument to shed light on the range of cases in which the state should grant such exemptions.
- We argue that the state shouldn't grant exemptions that would legally permit an individual to cause harm to others. This argument counts against the justifiability of several highly contested exemptions, which would allow harm to women, children, and animals.
- Next, we consider the idea that, since all justifiable laws and policies require universal compliance, the state should grant no minority exemptions. Though we believe this states the case too strongly, we show that this line of reasoning can support further restrictions on which exemptions the state may allow.
- Finally, we reflect on the claim that a member of a minority group should bear the costs of their own beliefs, rather than have the state relieve this burden through an exemption. We argue that, though there is some mileage in the idea that motivates this objection, there are various ways advocates of exemptions can respond.
- We conclude by drawing together the various strings of our argument to produce an account of when the state should grant a minority exemption.

9.1 INTRODUCTION

In almost all states, there are a variety of cultural or religious groups, but one is dominant in terms of numbers. For example, a majority of Europe's population are Christian or follow Christian traditions, such as celebrating Christmas, while smaller numbers are Muslim, Jewish, Hindu, Sikh, Buddhist, and Pagan. In the past, being a member of a majority group brought a host of legal privileges, such as prioritized access to education.

But, in recent times, states have sought to rectify the disadvantages imposed on members of minority groups by applying the law equally to majorities and minorities alike.

Some states go even further than this, maintaining that we should grant exemptions to members of minority groups from otherwise universally applicable laws and policies. Here are some examples of *minority exemptions*.[1] In the United Kingdom, a turban-wearing Sikh is exempt from the legal requirement to wear a crash helmet when motorcycling and to wear a hard hat on a construction site. A Jewish storeowner is exempt from regulations on Sunday trading hours. And both Jewish and Muslim slaughterhouses are exempt from regulations on the humane slaughter of animals. In the United States, a member of the Native American Church is permitted to use peyote, which is a hallucinogenic drug whose use ordinarily carries a heavy prison sentence. And Amish parents may remove their children from compulsory education at around thirteen years old, rather than keep them in school until at least sixteen, as other parents must.

The justification for these exemptions sees them as part of a political programme of *multiculturalism*, which aims to treat members of minority groups fairly when designing and applying laws and policies. Other measures that form part of this agenda include: (i) policies that guarantee state funding for minority cultural events, practices, buildings, and festivals; (ii) policies that enhance the representation of members of minority groups in positions of advantage, such as at university, in business, or in government; (iii) policies that protect individuals from various forms of hate speech; and (iv) policies that support the voices of minorities in public arenas, such as through arts funding for minority projects. Because we explore some of these issues in our discussions of hate speech (Chapter 3) and affirmative action (Chapter 5), we set them aside here to focus on minority exemptions.

Advocates of minority exemptions contend that these policies can play a pivotal role in levelling the playing field, correcting for the fact that many existing laws and policies aren't neutral in their effects on the lives of members of different cultural and religious groups. For example, we might attempt to justify the exemption from the legal duty to wear a crash helmet by referring to the fact that it's much more difficult for turban-wearing Sikh men to comply with this law than it is for followers of other religions, such as Christianity. However, exemptions such as these encounter significant public and political resistance. According to one line of reasoning, we should oppose the idea that an individual's cultural or religious convictions can entitle them to exemptions from the law. On this view, if it's justifiable to require motorcyclists to wear crash helmets, then we should expect everyone to comply with this law. In recent years, several European states, including Germany, France, and Denmark, have moved closer to this position by either rejecting exemptions of this kind or narrowing the range of cases in which they apply. To be clear, the dispute isn't over whether states should aim to treat members of minority groups fairly when designing and applying

---

[1] Bhikhu Parekh, *Rethinking Multiculturalism: Cultural Diversity and Political Theory* (Basingstoke: Palgrave Macmillan, 2006), ch. 1.

laws and policies. Rather, it's whether minority exemptions offer an appropriate means of achieving this goal.

In this chapter, we explore these issues by developing an argument in support of minority exemptions in only a narrow range of cases. Our position is a moderate one that bridges the two sides of the debate. In section 9.2, we outline some ways in which it can be more burdensome for members of minority groups to comply with laws and policies that are attuned to the interests of more dominant groups, and we use this to build an initial case for minority exemptions. We then consider three responses, and explore whether any of these justifies narrowing the range of justifiable exemptions. In section 9.3, we argue that the state shouldn't allow exemptions that would permit harm to others. In section 9.4, we identify a further set of laws and policies that require universal compliance. In section 9.5, we consider but reject the view that, though members of minority groups bear additional burdens in comparison with members of other groups, these aren't sufficient to justify an exemption. In section 9.6, we draw these strands together to produce a framework for assessing the justifiability of various exemptions. We conclude that states should allow some minority exemptions, but reject many others.

9.2 CULTURES, MAJORITIES, AND MINORITIES

Arguments for granting exemptions to members of minority groups often begin with accounts of the ways in which members of majority groups use their political influence to support social and economic institutions that serve their own interests. This can occur in several ways. First, even though many states have attempted to eradicate the historical privileges enjoyed by members of majority groups, they sometimes overlook laws and policies that achieve the same effect but in less obvious ways. Second, even with the best intentions, policymakers can make the mistake of designing laws and policies with the norms and interests of the majority culture in mind. Third, many societies have a conception of 'the common good'—a shared ideal of their society that influences its population's practices, as well as the laws and policies that govern them. The ideas that infuse this conception of the common good often reflect the commitments and traditions of the majority ahead of members of minority groups. The same is true of the social and economic institutions that arise from this conception of the common good.[2]

To illustrate these points, let's consider the fact that businesses tend to adopt a work week that fits comfortably with the days and times of worship of the cultural majority. In Europe and North America, this means that many employers assume a Monday-to-Friday work week, leaving the Christian day of worship—Sunday—free. Moreover, states usually have a set of public holidays that match the cultural practices of the majority, with many businesses in Europe and North America shutting down over Christmas and

---

[2] Iris Marion Young, 'Policy and Group Difference: A Critique of the Ideal of Universal Citizenship', *Ethics*, 99 (1989), 250–74.

Easter. These arrangements are convenient for those who observe these holidays, but they can create difficulties for members of minority groups whose religion and traditions expect different patterns of employment. Furthermore, once at work, employees' uniforms commonly cohere with the dress conventions of the majority group, and not with those of minorities. Wearing a police helmet or motorcycle crash helmet is straightforwardly compatible with Christian customs, but in tension with the demands of Sikhism.

In what follows, we elaborate on the moral significance of these facts, and we show how minority exemptions might be part of the appropriate response.

9.2.1 MISRECOGNITION

Individuals suffer misrecognition when 'institutionalized patterns of cultural value constitute some actors as inferior, excluded, wholly other, or simply invisible, hence as less than full partners in social interaction.'[3] What this means is that it's bad for individuals when we organize institutions in a way that excludes them or characterizes them as on the fringes of society. When this occurs, someone may feel confined and demeaned, and they may even develop a sense of self-contempt.[4] This can make it less likely that others will listen to their views, and, as a result, this makes it more difficult for them to influence those around them, including in political decision-making.[5]

Members of minority groups may experience misrecognition when laws and policies place them on the margins of society, such as when an employer expects their workers to conform to a particular working pattern or to comply with a given dress code.[6] If these demands are particularly pervasive in the labour market, then it may be especially difficult for some members of minority groups to find employment at all. Similarly, when dress codes for public spaces such as swimming pools, beaches, or public squares conflict with individuals' religiously motivated standards of dress, these individuals may find themselves effectively unable to participate in social and cultural life. Worse than this, rules such as these may stigmatize members of minority groups, who may be perceived by others as odd, or even deviant. In stark contrast to the vibrant atmosphere surrounding the public holidays shared by the majority, if society fails to recognize the holy days of minority cultures, members of these groups may be effectively barred from participating in social life on a par with others.

The disvalue of misrecognition gives us reason to avoid such outcomes and to favour policies that promote greater acceptance and understanding of a variety of lifestyles. One way to do this is to empower members of minority groups to play a more influential role in political decision-making, company policy-setting, and community

---

[3] Nancy Fraser, 'Social Justice in the Age of Identity Politics: Redistribution, Recognition, and Participation' in Nancy Fraser and Axel Honneth, *Redistribution or Recognition? A Political-Philosophical Exchange* (London: Verso, 2003), 7–109 at 29.

[4] Charles Taylor, 'The Politics of Recognition', *New Contexts of Canadian Criticism*, 98 (1997), 25–73 at 26.

[5] Miranda Fricker, *Epistemic Injustice: Power and the Ethics of Knowing* (Oxford: Oxford University Press, 2007), ch. 1.

[6] Nancy Fraser, 'Recognition without Ethics?', *Theory, Culture, & Society*, 18 (2001), 21–42 at 24–5.

organization.[7] Another possibility is to raise awareness of different lifestyles, such as by pursuing integrative housing and education policies, or to ensure members of minority groups are visible in mainstream culture—being careful to ensure that they aren't represented in a caricatured fashion—with the aim of promoting the social status of these individuals.[8]

A further avenue available to us is to grant minority exemptions, since these exemptions offer a way through which the state can publicly affirm its commitment to the fair treatment of members of diverse cultures.[9] This argument can take the following form:

Recognition moral claim: The state should minimize misrecognition.

Recognition empirical claim: Minority exemptions reduce misrecognition.

Conclusion: The state should grant minority exemptions.

We call this the *argument from recognition*.

One immediate concern with this argument is that, even if we acknowledge the disvalue of misrecognition, it's not obvious how this justifies the use of minority exemptions. Certainly, we've reasons to address injustices that affect members of minority groups, and, as we discuss in Chapter 5, there may be a strong case for using affirmative action to address under-representation in advantaged social positions. However, what's unclear is whether the successful pursuit of these goals warrants exemptions from otherwise universally applicable laws and policies.

The central problem here is the difficulty of verifying the recognition empirical claim. Unlike some other empirical claims that are central to the analysis of public policy, this one is especially difficult to validate. This is for two reasons. First, given its nature, misrecognition is hard to measure—harder than, say, measuring the impact of heroin use on a user's health or perhaps the deterrence effects of prison sentences. Second, it's difficult to isolate the effects of minority exemptions from other changes, including changes in social attitudes, that may accompany the use of these policies. Noting these complexities doesn't establish that the recognition empirical claim is false. However, these remarks suggest that we should be cautious about relying on it to defend minority exemptions.

9.2.2 MINORITY EQUALITY

Another way we might proceed is to focus on the role that exemptions can play in rectifying *inequalities* between minority and majority groups.[10] As we've noted, working patterns and uniforms tend to serve the interests of members of majority groups better

---

[7] Iris Marion Young, *Justice and the Politics of Difference* (Princeton, NJ: Princeton University Press, 1990), ch. 7.

[8] Elizabeth Anderson, *The Imperative of Integration* (Princeton, NJ: Princeton University Press, 2010), ch. 6.

[9] Jonathan Seglow, 'Recognition and Religious Diversity: The Case of Legal Exemptions' in Shane O'Neill and Nicholas Smith (eds), *Recognition Theory as Social Research* (London: Palgrave Macmillan, 2012), 127–46.

[10] Will Kymlicka, *Multicultural Citizenship: A Liberal Theory of Minority Rights* (Oxford: Oxford University Press, 1996), ch. 6; Jonathan Quong, 'Cultural Exemptions, Expensive Tastes, and Equal Opportunities', *Journal of Applied Philosophy*, 23 (2006), 53–71; and Parekh, *Rethinking Multiculturalism*, ch. 8.

than those of minority groups. In some cases, this can effectively foreclose employment opportunities that would otherwise be available. Because of this, there's a meaningful sense in which members of minority groups enjoy fewer opportunities than others. What's appealing about minority exemptions is that they can open up employment opportunities, and so eliminate this disadvantage.

One way to develop this argument starts with the idea that members of minority groups face special burdens in complying with laws and policies that require them to act in ways that are incompatible with their religious commitments. For example, policies that require teachers to observe a Monday-to-Friday work week make it impossible for some Muslims to perform Friday afternoon prayers, as demanded by their religion.[11] We can strengthen this argument by noting that such laws and policies make it difficult or costly for members of minority groups to honour their *deep commitments*.[12] These are commitments that emerge from beliefs that constitute an individual's identity and that are fundamental to them. In many cases, these individuals perceive themselves to have a duty—indeed, a sacred duty—not to renege on these deep commitments.

These facts are important because it's common in other areas of social and political life to treat deep commitments as worthy of special protection. For example, many believe that this is appropriate in the case of a conscientious objector, who demands exemption from the legal requirement to kill in war, because they're a pacifist who perceives themselves to be under a stringent duty not to kill. If we must accommodate their objection to being conscripted, then it seems that we must accommodate the complaints of members of minority groups who face disadvantages in virtue of deep commitments as well.

The bearing of this result on our topic might be obvious. One way in which the state can rectify these disadvantages is to grant members of minority groups exemptions from the laws and policies that conflict with their religious commitments. If Muslims are exempted from having to work for a period on Friday afternoons, then they no longer face the impossible challenge of complying with the rules of both their employer and their religion. It's straightforward to see why this is an appropriate solution to the problem at hand, namely because exemptions directly remove the specific disadvantages that laws and policies attuned to the majority culture create for members of minority groups. This is the *argument from minority equality*, and it takes the following form:

Minority equality moral claim: The state should ensure that no one suffers less valuable opportunities than others in virtue of belonging to a minority group.

Minority equality empirical claim: Minority exemptions reduce inequalities in opportunities that laws and policies attuned to majority cultures create for members of minority groups.

Conclusion: The state should grant minority exemptions.

[11] Bhikhu Parekh, 'Equality in a Multicultural Society', *Citizenship Studies*, 2 (1998), 397–411 at 397–400.
[12] Paul Bou-Habib, 'A Theory of Religious Accommodation', *Journal of Applied Philosophy*, 23 (2006), 109–26.

Throughout this section, we've identified several cases where this argument for minority exemptions is appealing. These go some way towards validating the minority equality empirical claim, and they hint at the plausibility of the minority equality moral claim as well. It's possible to strengthen the latter by appealing to the value of equality of opportunity. We discuss this idea in detail in Chapters 5 and 6. Here it suffices to note that it's widely accepted that no one should suffer less valuable opportunities than others in virtue of their religion or culture. This idea is what supports opposition to a variety of historical practices that privileged the interests of members of majority groups, and it lends further credence to the minority equality moral claim.

Nevertheless, for the argument from minority equality to succeed, we must refine it in numerous ways. To see why, let's turn to some objections.

9.3 THE BADS OF MULTICULTURALISM

The first objection that we consider is one that's often pressed against multiculturalism more generally, but that has implications for minority exemptions in particular. The concern is that some multicultural policies have harmful effects, sometimes on members of minority groups themselves and sometimes on others. This is the *bads of multiculturalism objection*.

Critics of multiculturalism object that, when we empower minority groups by granting their members certain protections and privileges, we risk preserving unjust practices. For example, Susan Moller Okin draws attention to examples of cultural customs that oppress women.[13] Even within legal systems that tightly regulate women's rights, practices like forced marriage, forced marriage of a victim of rape to the perpetrator, forced abortion, polygyny, widow immolation, and female genital mutilation are sustained partly through considerable social protection of cultural groups. Of course, not all support for minorities will have this effect, but there's a range of cases where it will. One reason for this is that sexism is a widespread phenomenon that permeates many cultures. Similar issues arise with respect to cultural practices that involve the oppressive treatment of sexual minorities and those with disabilities.[14] This objection is especially menacing because it directs our attention towards the most vulnerable members of minority groups—minorities within minorities. Moreover, oppression in these contexts might spill over into the rest of society, in turn maintaining wider cultural trends that disadvantage women, individuals who're gay, and those with disabilities.

To illustrate the force of this objection in the case of minority exemptions, let's consider the circumstances of members of various groups, whose interests may be jeopardized by granting particular exemptions. In each of these cases, our earlier arguments

---

[13] Susan Moller Okin, 'Feminism and Multiculturalism: Some Tensions', *Ethics*, 108 (1998), 661–84.

[14] Susan Moller Okin, 'Reply' in Susan Moller Okin et al., *Is Multiculturalism Bad for Women?* (Princeton, NJ: Princeton University Press, 1999), 115–32 at 120.

appear to support an exemption, and yet we've reason to resist these calls on the basis of the likely harm that would result.

Women: Many states prohibit female genital mutilation, forced marriage, and under-age marriage. In doing so, they deny opportunities to members of minority groups whose customs and traditions involve these practices. But granting exemptions to these laws would permit violating the bodily integrity and marital autonomy of women.[15]

Children: Practices such as female genital mutilation and under-age marriage not only harm their victims as women, but also as children. The exemption that gives Amish parents the right to remove their child from education at only thirteen years old may also jeopardize their interests.

Animals: The European Union requires that animals farmed for human consumption are stunned before they're slaughtered. However, it grants an exemption for those animals slaughtered in accordance with kosher and halal rituals, thereby permitting treatment that would otherwise be legally forbidden because of the suffering it causes.[16] Similarly, despite various laws that prohibit the unnecessary or cruel killing of animals, members of the Santeria religion in Florida are permitted to practise an annual sacrifice of nearly 20,000 animals. These animals are raised in a manner that fails to meet standards set out in other laws that regulate the treatment of animals, and their bodies are then left to rot in public locations.[17]

In each of these cases, there's a clear worry about granting an exemption. This remains true even though the absence of exemptions might cause members of some minority groups to bear special burdens in comparison with others. The moral concerns that underlie the worries about these practices explain the need for having a law in the first place. For example, it's because we're concerned about women's rights that it makes sense to prohibit forced marriage. The underlying justification for this law also provides a reason against granting an exemption to it. Martha Nussbaum goes further, writing:

> there are universal obligations to protect human functioning and its dignity, and that the dignity of women is equal to that of men. If that involves assault on many local traditions, both Western and non-Western, so much the better, because any tradition that denies these things is unjust.[18]

We believe the same reasoning applies with respect to exemptions that set back the interests of children. The case of animals is perhaps more complicated, as some will contend that animals aren't entitled to any comparable level of protection. We explore this claim in Chapter 12. For present purposes, it suffices to note that defending minority exemptions to slaughter rules requires showing why treatment of animals that's otherwise unacceptable doesn't give us sufficient justification to ban forms of religious

---

[15] Okin, 'Feminism and Multiculturalism', 669–70 and 680–3.
[16] Paula Casal, 'Is Multiculturalism Bad for Animals?', *Journal of Political Philosophy*, 11 (2003), 1–22 at 4–5.
[17] Casal, 'Is Multiculturalism Bad for Animals?', 6–9.
[18] Martha Nussbaum, *Sex and Social Justice* (Oxford: Oxford University Press, 1999), 30.

slaughter that involve it. But, even setting aside this more complex case, the bads of multiculturalism objection gives us reason to reject a wide range of exemptions that would permit harms to others that we've reason to prohibit.[19]

Nonetheless, this objection doesn't impugn all minority exemptions.[20] In particular, the concerns that motivate it don't arise in several of the cases we've mentioned, such as the exemption that permits turban-wearing Sikhs to ride motorcycles without crash helmets. This is to say that, though the objection is plausible, there are limits to its reach. Accordingly, we can accommodate the relevant concerns by altering our moral claim as follows:

> *Revised minority equality moral claim*: The state should ensure that no one suffers less valuable opportunities than others in virtue of belonging to a minority group, providing that the means of achieving this don't permit harm to others.

In some cases, it'll be difficult to determine whether an exemption satisfies the final clause in this moral claim.[21] Nevertheless, we hope that the rationale for revising the minority equality moral claim in this way is sufficiently clear.

9.4 UNIVERSAL COMPLIANCE

We now turn to a distinct objection to minority exemptions. This objection holds that we should reject exemptions from any justifiable law or policy. Advocates of this objection might reason as follows. In order to be justifiable, a law must be an appropriate tool for achieving a valuable end. Of course, some existing laws don't meet this standard, and it follows that we should revise or discard those laws. But when a law is justifiable, this seems to support the conclusion that what's required is universal compliance with its demands, irrespective of individuals' membership of a minority or majority group.[22]

To illustrate this point, let's consider the exemption for members of the Native American Church from a law that prohibits the use of peyote. On the one hand, it might be that the law is an unjustifiable one that we should overturn. As we argue in Chapter 4, perhaps this is because the state should permit individuals to engage in risky activities, such as taking drugs, even if this might leave them very badly off. If this is the case, then we should reject this law at the outset. Accordingly, we needn't argue for an exemption to this law, since the law shouldn't exist in the first place. On the other hand, perhaps the law is a justifiable one that we should uphold. But, if this is the case, then it might seem that the law should make the same demands on everyone, regardless of their religion or culture. In other words, we've a dilemma: either

---

[19] For critical discussion, see Avishai Margalit and Moshe Halbertal, 'Liberalism and the Right to Culture', *Social Research*, 61 (1994), 491–510 and Chandran Kukathas, 'Are There Any Cultural Rights?', *Political Theory*, 20 (1992), 105–39.   [20] Kymlicka, *Multicultural Citizenship*, 35–44.

[21] For example, see Parekh, *Rethinking Multiculturalism*, 249–54.

[22] Brian Barry, *Culture and Equality: An Egalitarian Critique of Multiculturalism* (Cambridge: Polity Press, 2001), 40–50.

the law is unjustifiable, in which case it should apply to no one, or it's justifiable, in which case it should apply without exception. This is the *objection from universal compliance*.

In considering this issue, we make two points. The first is to emphasize that the objection doesn't supply us with a defence of the legal status quo. This is because, as the first horn of the dilemma states, if the law is unjustifiable, then we should overturn it. We believe this point bears on a variety of relevant cases, including laws that prohibit the use of peyote. This is because a range of arguments support abolishing laws that prohibit the use of such drugs. Here's another example. In the United Kingdom, the Cremation Act 1902 had required an individual's cremation to take place inside a building.[23] This law conflicted with Hindu rituals that require cremation by open-air pyre—a point that was brought to light when Davender Ghai was prosecuted (though not convicted) for holding a funeral of this kind in 2006.[24] One way in which those sympathetic to Ghai's case could've responded is by lobbying for an exemption to the Cremation Act for Hindus. But an alternative response would've been to reform the act so that a cremation needn't take place inside a building. In fact, this is what happened, and we believe this is the better of the two options.

Second, the objection leaves some room for manoeuvre even with respect to justifiable laws.[25] The reason for this is that what's required for a law to achieve its ends can differ between cases. For some laws, it's necessary that *everyone* complies. This is the case with the law against murder, for example. This is because preventing all murders requires that everyone abide by this law. But some laws can function effectively when only a *sufficient* number of individuals comply. For example, laws designed to ease traffic congestion in cities can serve their purpose of easing congestion provided that enough drivers obey them. This means that granting an exemption might not undermine the law's effectiveness. For example, in London, drivers with disabilities are exempted from paying the 'congestion charge' that's levied on others.

This result is important for our purposes because we might reason in a similar way about some minority exemptions. For example, one justification for the law that requires the use of a crash helmet is to ensure that others don't have to cover exorbitant medical costs that might arise from thousands of accidents involving those who ride without one. But perhaps we can achieve this aim without requiring all motorcyclists to wear a crash helmet. If enough riders comply with the requirement, then the medical bills that arise from a few accidents involving those without crash helmets are unlikely to be so high as to worry us.

---

[23] *Cremation Act 1902.*

[24] Sonia Sharma, 'Should Open-Air Funeral Pyres Be Allowed to Take Place in the North East? Davender Ghai Thinks So', *The Chronicle*, 12 January 2018, available at https://www.chroniclelive.co.uk/news/north-east-news/should-open-air-funeral-pyres-14140881.

[25] Jeremy Waldron, 'One Law for All? The Logic of Cultural Accommodation', *Washington and Lee Law Review*, 59 (2002), 3–34.

What these points suggest is that we can accommodate the objection from universal compliance by revising our argument's moral claim in the following way:

> *Final minority equality moral claim*: The state should ensure that no one suffers less valuable opportunities than others in virtue of belonging to a minority group, providing that the means of achieving this (a) don't permit harm to others, and (b) don't prevent a justifiable law or policy from serving its purpose.

Revising the claim in this way isn't to say that we're discarding the objection from universal compliance. In fact, we accept one central component of it, namely that, when justifiable laws require everyone to comply with them, we should oppose exemptions from those laws. Rather, our point is that, when justifiable laws don't require universal compliance, then there's space for minority exemptions. An instructive case is state service dress codes. In many states, so that members of the public can identify them, police officers are required to dress in common uniforms, which include hats. This requirement has a good justification, but this doesn't mean that all police officers need to wear the *same* uniform. This means that we could allow an exemption to this rule for those whose religion governs their choice of headwear. In this way, the objection from universal compliance doesn't rule out minority exemptions of this kind.

Our analysis of the objection from universal compliance sheds important light on a neglected question: why is the proper response to the argument from minority equality to grant exemptions to members of minority groups rather than to overturn the laws that create the disadvantage that they suffer? Our answer is to acknowledge that, when the law is unjustifiable, it's better to reform it rather than grant exemptions. Exemptions can emerge as an appropriate tool only when the law is justifiable.

9.5 EXEMPTION FAIRNESS

Critics of minority exemptions might protest that we've overlooked a crucial part of what underlies the objection from universal compliance. Maybe it's true that we *could* exempt some individuals from the requirement to comply with a justifiable law, but it doesn't follow that we *should*. On the contrary, that a law is justifiable seems to give us some reason to require everyone to operate within its bounds, even if an exemption wouldn't prevent this law from serving its purpose. Advocates of this claim might support it by highlighting the fact that we don't grant exemptions to members of other groups. Even if it were compatible with achieving the aims of crash helmet laws, we don't grant exemptions to those who'd prefer to feel the wind in their hair as they ride.

One way to develop this objection gets at the heart of our case for minority exemptions. The argument from minority equality rests on the idea that we should remove the disadvantages that laws and policies attuned to majority cultures create for members of minority groups. But a critic might deny that there's any such disadvantage, at least of the kind that ought to concern us.[26] This is because, in the absence of any exemptions, members of minority groups enjoy identical opportunities to those enjoyed by others. Sikh men are as free to ride a motorcycle as others, so long as they wear a crash helmet. Others are as constrained as Sikhs in being unable to wear head-gear that doesn't fit under a crash helmet when riding a motorcycle. Laws that require motorcyclists to wear a crash helmet require the same from everyone.

To be sure, these laws might leave some in a better position to pursue their interests than others. Any motorcyclist who wishes to ride without a helmet faces greater difficulty fulfilling their ambitions than those happy to use one. But it's also true that, given our laws, those who wish to assault others have greater difficulty pursuing their goals than those who're less violent. It might seem that the fact that some individuals are able to get more out of the same opportunities that everyone enjoys shouldn't trouble us. This is the *fairness objection* to minority exemptions.

A deeper philosophical basis for this objection appeals to the idea that individuals should bear responsibility for the costs they face in virtue of their commitments, including their beliefs about their religious or cultural duties. Those who're religious endorse these convictions, subject them to scrutiny, and occasionally revise their views accordingly. Because of this, these individuals ordinarily see their religion as something that enhances the value of their life, rather than as some disadvantage which calls for compensation. It's true that, because of religious convictions, an individual might rule out some options, including some occupations. For example, some tee-total Christians refuse to work in pubs for this reason. A similar point applies to individuals with other kinds of deep commitments, including those who hold ethical objections to killing animals who refuse to work in slaughterhouses, and pacifists who refuse to apply for work in the army.

Now, there's some sense in which these individuals may suffer worse prospects than those who don't share their commitments, perhaps because it's harder for someone to find paid employment if they rule out a number of professions. But the same is true of an individual who's devoted to expensive wine over cheap wine. This is because there's the same sense in which they suffer worse prospects than those who don't share their preference for expensive wine, as they'll have less leftover income to spend in other ways. Critics of minority exemptions claim that what matters in both cases is that these worse prospects are a product of the commitments with which individuals identify. So, just as there's no reason to subsidize the lifestyle of the lover of expensive wine, so too it seems there's no reason to grant minority exemptions to members of some groups.

Our response to this objection draws a distinction between two ways in which an individual can suffer worse prospects in virtue of their commitments.[27] On the one hand, there are costs that arise unavoidably, as a direct result of an individual's beliefs. For example, everyone who attends prayer on a Friday must give up their afternoon

---

[26] Barry, *Culture and Equality*, 32–40.
[27] Peter Jones, 'Bearing the Consequences of Belief', *Journal of Political Philosophy*, 2 (1994), 24–43 at 38.

to do this. On the other hand, there are costs that arise as a result of holding a belief in a particular context. For example, it's only if the conventional work week includes Friday afternoons that those who attend prayer at this time will experience a conflict between the demands of their employment and those of their religion. This is significant because, with respect to the latter costs, a member of a minority group can complain that their prospects are worse than those enjoyed by others not solely because of their commitments, but also because of how the prevailing laws and policies affect individuals with those commitments.

We might flesh out the relevance of this in two ways. On one account, there's *always* some reason to worry about laws and policies that make it more costly for individuals with certain commitments to pursue their goals than for those with others. If this is correct, then the fairness objection misses the mark since, even if everyone faces identical opportunities, it neglects the fact that these opportunities will be more valuable to some individuals than others.[28] This is the case with the Monday-to-Friday work week, given that this makes it more costly to follow certain Muslim beliefs than those of some other religions.

The problem with this view is that it seems to yield the implausible result that those who're committed to expensive pastimes, such as drinking fine wine, have a complaint based on how prevailing laws and policies affect individuals with those commitments. After all, it's only because we allow market forces to set a high price for this wine that those with a taste for it have less leftover income than others. With alternative laws and policies that reduce its price, those devoted to it wouldn't be as badly off.

But all isn't lost for advocates of minority exemptions, who might resort to a weaker claim. On this account, there's *sometimes* reason to worry about laws and policies that make it more costly for individuals with certain commitments to pursue their goals than for those with others. In particular, we've cause for concern only if these laws and policies have been designed or applied in a defective manner. Though we're normally unmoved by the case of an individual who's devoted to expensive wine, this isn't always true. For example, what if, for no good reason, the state artificially inflates the price of someone's favourite wine, rendering them less well off than would otherwise be the case? In these circumstances, it seems that they have a complaint based on the fact that the system has been rigged against them. Even advocates of the fairness objection should recognize that it's a mistake to insist that an individual should bear responsibility for the costs they face in virtue of their commitments, when those costs arise in such a way.[29]

At the start of section 9.2, we noted that, even though many states have attempted to eradicate the historical privileges enjoyed by members of majority groups, they sometimes overlook laws and policies that achieve the same effect but in less obvious ways. Moreover, even with the best intentions, policymakers can make the mistake

---

[28] G. A. Cohen, 'Expensive Tastes and Multiculturalism' in Rajeev Bhargava, Amiya Kumar Bagchi, and R. Sudarshan (eds), *Multiculturalism, Liberalism, and Democracy* (Oxford: Oxford University Press, 1999), 80–100.

[29] Kristi Olson, 'Our Choices, Our Wage Gap?', *Philosophical Topics*, 40 (2012), 45–61.

of designing laws and policies with the norms and interests of the majority culture in mind. The significance of these remarks should now be clear. These are ways in which prevailing laws and policies have been designed and applied defectively ways, with the result that the current system is rigged against the interests of members of minority groups. The fairness objection has little appeal in the light of these facts.

The importance of this concern is heightened once we focus on cases in which members of minority groups endure especially serious burdens. Perhaps it wouldn't be as troubling if the only disadvantage suffered by members of minority groups were that they had less disposable income, like someone devoted to expensive wine. But, more often than not, this isn't the case. Instead, the effects of prevailing laws and policies are much more pervasive, with the result that members of some groups are effectively excluded from whole professions or industries. When a job involves a valuable public service, such as being a teacher or a police officer, then the case for minority exemptions is especially strong.[30]

9.6 CONCLUSIONS

Drawing together the various lines of reasoning we've developed throughout the chapter, we can reformulate our argument for minority exemptions as follows:

> *Final minority equality moral claim*: The state should ensure that no one suffers less valuable opportunities than others in virtue of belonging to a minority group, providing that the means of achieving this (a) don't permit harm to others, and (b) don't prevent a justifiable law or policy from serving its purpose.

> *Final minority equality empirical claim*: Some minority exemptions ensure that no one suffers less valuable opportunities than others in virtue of belonging to a minority group, without (a) permitting harm to others, or (b) preventing a justifiable law or policy from serving its purpose.

> *Conclusion*: The state should grant some minority exemptions.

One minority exemption that we believe this argument justifies is from the dress code that requires a police officer to wear a hat as part of the uniform. As we noted in section 9.4, this wouldn't prevent a justifiable policy from achieving its aim, and it'd reduce the disadvantage suffered by members of a minority group, without causing harm to others. The same goes for exemptions from a range of laws and policies, including those that govern work hours and rest days, as well as other dress code requirements.

Though sympathetic to *these* exemptions, we're less persuaded that there's a case for some other minority exemptions that currently exist. More specifically, we should oppose minority exemptions that permit an individual to harm others, notably women, children, and animals, because this violates clause (a) of the final minority

---

[30] Quong, 'Cultural Exemptions, Expensive Tastes, and Equal Opportunities', 61–6.

equality moral claim. Several other minority exemptions violate clause (b), and we should reject them on this basis. For example, let's take the law that requires everyone to wear a hard hat on a construction site. Since the law requires universal compliance to serve its purpose, namely to protect everyone's safety, we ought not to allow an exemption from it.

Finally, it's worth emphasizing that we've been unable to consider the full range of arguments that bear on the justifiability of minority exemptions. In some cases, the practicalities of law are relevant to what we ought to do. We're open to the idea that, if we should expect legal change to take a while, then it might be appropriate to favour a minority exemption as a short-term fix. Nonetheless, we've focused on what we take to be several of the deepest and most important moral issues. If nothing else, this works as a platform for assessing the case for minority exemptions and, to some extent, the case for multiculturalism more generally.

FURTHER READING

To begin exploring the debate around exemptions, it's worth reading the accessible defences of these policies in Will Kymlicka, *Multicultural Citizenship: A Liberal Theory of Minority Rights* (Oxford: Oxford University Press, 1996), esp. ch. 6 and Bhikhu Parekh, 'Equality in Multicultural Society', *Citizenship Studies*, 2 (1998), 397–411. It's then worth reflecting on these arguments in the light of the criticisms advanced in Brian Barry, 'Liberalism and Multiculturalism', *Ethical Perspectives*, 4 (1997), 3–14.

For an overview of debates around multiculturalism, there's Sarah Song, 'Multiculturalism', *The Stanford Encyclopedia of Philosophy* (2017), available at https://plato.stanford.edu/archives/spr2017/entries/multiculturalism. For detailed treatment of the case for exemptions and multiculturalism, it's worth reading the whole of Will Kymlicka, *Multicultural Citizenship* and Iris Marion Young, *Justice and the Politics of Difference* (Princeton, NJ: Princeton University Press, 1990), ch. 6. For extended critical discussion, see Brian Barry, *Culture and Equality: An Egalitarian Critique of Multiculturalism* (Cambridge: Polity Press, 2001).

For detailed exploration of the bads of multiculturalism, important pieces include Paula Casal, 'Is Multiculturalism Bad for Animals?', *Journal of Political Philosophy*, 11 (2003), 1–22; Susan Moller Okin, 'Feminism and Multiculturalism: Some Tensions', *Ethics*, 108 (1998), 661–84; and all of Susan Moller Okin et al., *Is Multiculturalism Bad for Women?* (Princeton, NJ: Princeton University Press, 1999).

 For additional material and resources, including web links and self-test questions, please visit the online resources **www.oup.com/he/walton1e**.

10

JUDICIAL REVIEW
AND DEMOCRACY

SUMMARY

- In this chapter, we argue that the state should use judicial review to constrain democracy.
- We identify several rights that individuals possess, and then defend judicial review as a mechanism for protecting these rights.
- We consider the objection that judicial review is undemocratic because it constrains the laws that an electorate or their representatives might adopt.
- To explore this idea, we distinguish two arguments in defence of democracy. The first holds that democracy is valuable because it produces good outcomes, and the second holds that democracy is valuable because it treats each member of a society equally when they disagree about which outcomes are good.
- While we acknowledge that each of these arguments provides some reason to endorse democracy, we show that neither furnishes us with a strong objection to the use of judicial review.
- We conclude by reflecting on the implications of our argument.

10.1 INTRODUCTION

The Human Rights Act 1998 marked an interesting juncture in the United Kingdom's political system.[1] Traditionally, the United Kingdom has been committed to parliamentary sovereignty, meaning that its politicians can make or unmake any law as they see fit. This contrasts with the practice in many other states where laws passed by parliament can be overruled by *judicial review*. This is a process in which a group of judges, often called a Supreme Court, may strike down legislation that breaches established rules that are normally enumerated in a bill of rights or a constitution. This arrangement exists across the world in countries as varied as Bolivia, Ireland, Kenya, New Zealand, South Korea, and the United States.

In passing the Human Rights Act, the United Kingdom made a small step away from parliamentary sovereignty towards judicial review. It did this by granting courts the

---

[1] *Human Rights Act 1998.*

power to declare legislation incompatible with the European Convention on Human Rights. This is a very small step. Unlike the other states we've mentioned, courts in the United Kingdom are permitted only to declare incompatibility. When they do so, it remains within parliament's remit to respond as it wishes. In this way, parliament retains ultimate power. Yet, even this small step has been met with resistance. Some within the United Kingdom contend that it's imperative to repeal the Human Rights Act and to return to the traditional political system.[2]

At the heart of these debates is a question about the kind of *democracy* that we ought to prefer. On the one hand, those who defend parliamentary sovereignty contend that it's wrong to grant courts the legal power to overrule the decisions of elected politicians. This concern is bolstered when we consider the concrete remit judicial review entails. Over the years, the United States' Supreme Court has appealed to its constitution to strike down legislation that prohibits abortion and gun ownership, as well as to require school desegregation and the legal recognition of same-sex marriages. Many are concerned that unelected judges who're not accountable to the electorate can decide matters of such deep moral significance. On the other hand, champions of judicial review argue that this is an effective means for preventing elected governments from trampling over an individual's rights. Advocates of this policy claim that a democratic system without judicial review leaves too much up for grabs, with the effect that members of minority groups may be left vulnerable to the tyranny of the majority. In short, disputes about judicial review raise a question about the value and remit of democracy. In particular, should we favour a *constrained democracy* in which a judiciary limits the power of elected governments, or an *unconstrained democracy* in which politicians have free rein?

In this chapter, we explore these debates by developing an argument in favour of judicial review. We proceed as follows. In sections 10.2 and 10.3, we argue that an individual possesses rights that warrant protection, and that judicial review is an appropriate means of ensuring this. In section 10.4, we consider the objection that this is inconsistent with the value of democracy. In response, we distinguish two arguments in favour of democracy and, in sections 10.5 and 10.6, we show that neither of these undermines our case for judicial review. In section 10.7, we discuss the implications of our arguments.

10.2 RIGHTS

The idea that an individual has rights is commonplace. But what's a right? Simply put, to say that an individual has a *right* is to say that they're *entitled* to something.[3] This involves identifying the thing to which its holder is entitled. For example, we might claim that an individual has rights that entitle them to vote, to free speech, to trial by a jury of peers, to roam the countryside unimpeded, and to clean drinking water.

---

[2] For example, see The Conservative Party, 'Protecting Human Rights in the UK', (2015), available at https://www.conservatives.com/~/media/files/downloadable%20files/human_rights.pdf.

[3] Peter Jones, *Rights* (London: Macmillan, 1994), ch. 1.

But these claims often have implications for others. This is because having a right can affect how others may act, say, if they're required to respect it. In other words, invoking a right sometimes involves identifying duty-bearers, namely those who're required to perform or refrain from performing certain actions in order to ensure that the rights-holder has the thing to which they're entitled. To see how this works, let's consider the right not to be tortured. When we say that an individual has this right, we mean specifically that others have a duty not to torture them.

It's common to distinguish between different types of rights in the following way.[4] First, there are *liberty rights*. These are the only type of right that don't impose any duty on others. Let's consider an individual's right to freedom of expression, which means that they're entitled to speak freely and do no wrong by doing so. Conceived in this way, the distinctive feature of a liberty right is that it bestows a privilege on its holder to act in a certain way, but it doesn't impose any duties on others.[5] Second, there are *claim rights*, which impose duties on others in a straightforward way. An individual's right not to be assaulted means that others have a duty not to assault them. An employee's right that they're paid means that their employer must pay up. Third, there are *power rights*, which are rights to change the entitlements or duties of others. When an individual invites their neighbours around for dinner, they relieve them of their duty not to enter their house. Fourth, there are *immunity rights*. An individual has an immunity right when others have no moral permission to change their entitlements or duties. If a corporation has an immunity right over an oil rig, this means that others can't change what rights and duties the corporation has with respect to that rig.

In addition to distinguishing between different types, we can also distinguish between different categories of rights based on their content.[6] There are *civil rights*, which concern the legal system within a state. These include the right to a fair trial, as well as the right to freedom from arbitrary arrest. There are *political rights*, which concern the organization of the state. These may include the right to freedom of speech and the right to vote. Finally, there are *socioeconomic rights*, which concern the resources to which an individual is entitled. These include the right to basic sanitation and the right to healthcare.

These classifications were originally designed to enable us to understand similarities and differences between rival legal systems. However, it's important to note that we can think about rights in another sense as well. More specifically, there are *moral rights*. These are the moral entitlements that each individual possesses, regardless of whether they're enforced or recognized by the state or the legal system. Equipped with the distinction between legal rights and moral rights, we can make sense of the judgement that an individual may have a moral right that's not legally recognized or

[4] Wesley Hohfeld, 'Some Fundamental Legal Conceptions as Applied in Judicial Reasoning', *Yale Law Journal*, 23 (1913), 16–59.

[5] The right to freedom of expression may also entail duties, such as a duty not to impede the individual speaking freely or a duty to provide them with a platform to voice their views. But when we add these dimensions, we move from talking about freedom of expression as a liberty right to another type of right.

[6] T. H. Marshall, *Citizenship and Social Class, and Other Essays* (Cambridge: Cambridge University Press, 1950).

protected. For example, one aspect of recent gay rights movements has been to argue that everyone has the moral right to freedom in sexuality, and to campaign for the legal recognition of this right worldwide.

A similar consideration underlies one of the most well-known rights documents: the Universal Declaration of Human Rights.[7] This declaration specifies a set of entitlements that individuals around the world possess regardless of class, ethnicity, gender, nationality, political beliefs, or religion. While it also serves various legal purposes, one of the central functions of this document is to identify some of the moral rights of individuals. These are rights that the state should legally recognize and protect wherever an individual resides.

That there are moral rights should prompt us to ask the following question: what's the basis of these rights? What makes it the case that there's a right to something? It's somewhat easier to grasp the notion of an individual's legal entitlements, but what can we say to justify the idea that, even in the absence of legal recognition and protection, an individual is morally entitled to certain kinds of treatment from others?

There's a range of philosophical answers to this question. Since our central concern in this chapter isn't with the basis of rights, we hope that a brief summary of two prominent views will suffice. On one account, rights are justified by the importance of an individual having power over how others treat them. This account draws force from the idea that it's valuable that an individual is able to exercise control over how others may interact with them and their property. According to this view, each individual should be a 'small-scale sovereign', and rights give expression to this idea.[8] This is the *will theory of rights*. By contrast, there's the *interest theory of rights*, according to which rights are justified by an individual's fundamental interests.[9] This theory is more expansive than the will theory of rights since it includes not only interests in how an individual is treated by others, but also further interests, such as in living free from disease.

But whichever of these views we adopt, there's widespread agreement that an individual has some moral rights, and this piece of the puzzle is sufficient for us to start making our case for judicial review.

10.3 THE ROLE OF COURTS

In three steps, we can move from the idea that an individual has rights to the conclusion that the state should have judicial review.[10]

The first step is to describe the implications of an individual having moral rights. We can do this using terminology that we've already introduced. When we say that an

---

[7] UN General Assembly, 'Universal Declaration of Human Rights' (1948), available at http://www.un.org/en/universal-declaration-human-rights.

[8] H. L. A. Hart, *Essays on Bentham* (Oxford: Clarendon Press, 1982), 183.

[9] Joseph Raz, *The Morality of Freedom* (Oxford: Clarendon, 1986), ch. 7.

[10] Cécile Fabre, 'A Philosophical Argument for a Bill of Rights', *British Journal of Political Science*, 30 (2000), 77–98. See also Aileen Kavanagh, *Constitutional Review Under the UK Human Rights Act* (Cambridge: Cambridge University Press, 2009), ch. 12.

individual holds a claim right to be treated by others in a certain way, we mean that others mustn't treat them in ways that violate this demand. Another way to express this point is to say that others lack a liberty right to act in ways that would transgress the individual's claim right. For example, if someone has a claim right not to be tortured, then others have no liberty right to torture them.

Moreover, others aren't entitled to deprive an individual of the right in question. They can't change the fact that the individual has a right not to be tortured. That is, others have no power right to change the individual's entitlements in this respect, and so they have an immunity right against them doing so. Not only are others under a duty not to torture them, they also lack the permission to strip them of the right not to be tortured.

The second step is to specify membership of the group who're under duties in virtue of the rights that an individual possesses. In the first instance, it's other *individuals* who must treat rights-holders accordingly. Someone's right not to be tortured implies that other individuals mustn't torture them. But it's not only other individuals against whom they have this claim. They possess the same claim against any actor that might torture them, including the state. In other words, rights set limits not merely on how individuals may treat each other, but also on how a state, through the decisions of its politicians, may treat its members. Accordingly, states also lack liberty rights to torture an individual, and they lack a power right to strip them of this protection.

The final step in this argument is to show why it's appropriate to convert some of an individual's moral rights into legal rights. To be sure, we don't want to do this for every right. Even if an individual is entitled to others keeping their promises, various principled and practical considerations suggest that this shouldn't be under the purview of the law. But there are many instances in which the state should grant legal status to a moral right. This is clearly the case with the right not to be tortured and the right to freedom of speech, for example. The state mustn't leave it to the discretion of individuals to respect these rights as they see fit. Any kind of protection this afforded would be nominal, at best. Rather, we recognize that the law can offer an effective route through which to guarantee these rights, granting an individual an effective safeguard against their violation, as well as a means of taking action against those who attempt to treat them in wrongful ways. As Cécile Fabre puts it, we recognize that individuals aren't permitted to act in these ways, and we ensure that they're 'denied the legal power to do [so], on pain of sanction'.[11]

Putting these steps together, we've our case for judicial review. We've claimed that there are strong reasons to turn some moral rights into legal rights. Because the relevant group of those who must respect an individual's rights includes the state, this amounts to the claim that there are some legislative decisions that should be legally unavailable. In other words, there's a case for a bill of rights that constrains the policies

---

[11] Fabre, 'A Philosophical Argument for a Bill of Rights', 87.

that governments may adopt. This is the *rights argument* for judicial review, and we can formulate it as follows:

> *Rights moral claim*: The state should recognize and protect some of an individual's rights.
>
> *Judicial review empirical claim*: Judicial review is a means for the state to recognize and to protect some of an individual's rights.
>
> *Conclusion*: The state should have judicial review.

Before closing this section, it's worth highlighting that there's some dispute over *which* rights should be under the power of judiciaries. For example, what about socioeconomic rights, such as the right to healthcare? Some challenge the idea that an individual can have entitlements to such goods, while others argue that, even if such rights exist, they aren't suitable for inclusion in a constitution.[12] We disagree with both of these claims.[13] But what's important for our purpose isn't which rights should appear in a constitution. Our claim is merely that there should be a constitution in the first place. Having made our case for this, it's now time for us to consider the objections of those who reject even this much.

10.4 DEMOCRACY

The rights argument for judicial review restricts a government's abilities to make and unmake laws by giving judges power over a set of issues. A common objection to this view targets the fact that this places controversial political matters beyond the reach of politicians and those who elect them. Instead, it gives veto power to an unelected legal body. Critics contend that this is undemocratic.[14]

We must be careful to understand this objection properly. As we noted in section 10.1, advocates of judicial review aren't outright critics of democracy. They don't defend dictatorships, oligarchies, or something of that kind. They believe only that the state should constrain the power of elected politicians to some extent. What they oppose isn't democracy, but unconstrained democracy. To clarify this point, let's look more closely at how to define democracy, before then returning to the allegation that judicial review is undemocratic.

10.4.1 DEFINING DEMOCRACY

Though it's well known that democracy means 'rule by the people', beyond this there's considerable disagreement about how best to define the term. One strategy is to proceed comparatively, by identifying features of democratic government that contrast

---

[12] Antonio Carlos Pereira-Menaut, 'Against Positive Rights', *Valparaiso University Law Review*, 22 (1988), 359–84.

[13] Cécile Fabre, 'Constitutionalising Social Rights', *Journal of Political Philosophy*, 6 (1998), 263–84.

[14] Jeremy Waldron, *Law and Disagreement* (Oxford: Oxford University Press, 1999) and Richard Bellamy, *Political Constitutionalism: A Republican Defence of the Constitutionality of Democracy* (Cambridge: Cambridge University Press, 2007).

with those of paradigmatically undemocratic systems of rule, such as dictatorships.[15] Two properties then stand out. First, in democracies, political decisions depend in some way on the views of the population. Second, this population expresses its view through some form of voting system in which individuals enjoy an equal opportunity for influence, or something close to this.

Although this is a broad definition, it allows us to distinguish democracy from a variety of other forms of government. For a start, it classifies dictatorships in which the government pays little attention to public opinion as undemocratic. The same holds for technocracies, in which political decisions are made by experts, as well as so-called vanguard democracies, in which party rulers who're deemed to have better insights than others steer towards certain political arrangements without granting the population a vote on these matters.

Yet this definition leaves many questions unanswered. For example, it doesn't specify which members of a population are entitled to a say. It's compatible with a traditional understanding, whereby only adults can vote, as well as with a much more expansive understanding, such that everyone affected by the political decision has this right, regardless of age or geographical residence.[16] It also leaves open what it means for each individual to enjoy equal opportunity for influence in a voting system.

Accordingly, this broad definition is compatible with a considerable variety of political arrangements.[17] One option is *direct democracy*, where every significant political decision requires approval via a vote. Although Switzerland operates a system with regular referenda of this kind, it's an outlier in the contemporary world. A more common system is *representative democracy*, in which the electorate vote for politicians at periodic intervals. This includes *constitutional democracy*, in which there's a considerable representative aspect, but the remit of the government is limited by a bill of rights.

We might think that a constitutional democracy qualifies as democratic only if its bill of rights was approved through a vote at some point. For example, the definition of a democracy might require that a state's constitution be agreed on by a referendum, or be subject to change through a political process if a majority of the electorate supports this. But, even if this is the case, a system that includes some form of judicial review would still qualify as democratic if its constitution were to depend in some such way on the views of the population.

The crucial point is that the central disagreement about judicial review is best understood as a debate about whether we should prefer a constrained democracy or an unconstrained democracy. We can't settle this dispute by appealing to a definition of democracy alone. Rather, we must explore what reasons we have to favour some political arrangements over others. That is, to address the challenge that comes from those who oppose judicial review on the grounds that it's undemocratic, we must examine whether the practice serves or frustrates whatever reasons we have to embrace democracy.

---

[15] Albert Weale, *Democracy, Second Edition* (London: Palgrave, 2007), ch. 1.
[16] For discussion, see Weale, *Democracy*, ch. 9.   [17] For a taxonomy, see Weale, *Democracy*, ch. 2.

10.4.2 JUDICIAL REVIEW AND DEFENCES OF DEMOCRACY

When critics of judicial review contend that it's undemocratic, they tend to emphasize how it's problematic to grant a judiciary the power to preclude or overrule legislation that has the support of the general public, either directly (in the case of direct democracy) or through the politicians they elect (in the case of representative democracy).

The worry is that restricting governments' powers in this way does a disservice to the reasons we have to endorse democracy. In order to assess this criticism, we must first look at what these reasons are. In what follows, we focus on two ideas. First, there's an *instrumental defence of democracy* that appeals to the likely positive effects of democratic rule. This case turns on the sorts of policies and decisions that this system of government is likely to produce. Second, there's an *intrinsic defence of democracy* that rests on the conviction that there's something morally valuable about the procedures of democratic rule. After clarifying these ideas, we examine whether either can support an objection to the rights argument for judicial review.

10.5 THE INSTRUMENTAL DEFENCE OF DEMOCRACY

We start with the argument that we should value democracy because of the outcomes it produces.

10.5.1 THE INSTRUMENTAL DEFENCE

Perhaps the most familiar argument in favour of democracy is based on the claim that it produces better results—better laws and public policies, for example—than other forms of government.[18] The structure of such an argument is simple: there are better and worse legal, social, and economic arrangements, and democracies tend to produce superior ones than alternative systems of rule. On this view, democracy is the best available instrument to achieve results that are independently valuable. What evidence supports this thesis?

First, democracy establishes an incentive for political rulers to respond sensitively to the interests of everyone who has a say in the democratic process.[19] To see why, let's consider a representative democracy in which candidates compete for political power by presenting a manifesto to the electorate, and in which the candidate who receives the most votes is elected to office. Because voters are more likely to support a politician who credibly commits to advancing the interests of their constituents, or who best

---

[18] Richard Arneson, 'Democracy Is Not Intrinsically Just' in Keith Dowding, Robert Goodin, and Carole Pateman (eds), *Justice as Democracy: Essays for Brian Barry* (Cambridge: Cambridge University Press, 2004), 40–58.

[19] John Stuart Mill, *Considerations on Representative Government* (Buffalo, NY: Prometheus Books, 1991 [1861]), ch. 3.

reflects their personal and political values, this system pressures those standing for office towards policies that reflect these interests and values. Likewise, it incentivizes a politician to make good on their commitments, especially if they plan to seek re-election. Indeed, one of democracy's great virtues lies in the option to 'vote the rascals out' if they prove to be a let-down. Let's call this the *incentive mechanism*.

Second, because those subject to political power play a role in formulating and enacting legislation (even if only indirectly), democracy collects a wider and more diverse range of inputs than other systems of government.[20] As we discuss in Chapter 5, there's evidence that diversity tends to improve decision-making, and it's plausible that this reasoning extends to the democratic process as well. A particularly acute version of this point concerns collecting information about when things are going badly. Because non-democratic systems of government aren't sensitive to public opinion in the same way, they're typically less well equipped to determine when and to what extent parts of their population are experiencing hardships. Thus, even with the best intentions, non-democratic rulers normally lack information about which issues need addressing that is as good as their democratically elected counterparts. Democracy's sensitivity to public input is superior in this respect. Let's call this the *information mechanism*.

Third, we can point to the track record of democracies in delivering better outcomes. An especially powerful example comes from development economics, where systematic empirical work shows that democracies are much less likely to suffer famines.[21] We can broaden this point by referring to some of the rights that we mentioned in section 10.2, using these as a benchmark against which to judge rival forms of government. Although we've refrained from enumerating a complete list of rights, there's ample evidence to show that democracies tend to fare better than alternative systems of government on a number of metrics. For example, democracies more consistently uphold an individual's right to be free from torture and arbitrary arrest.[22] Therefore, we've a reason of *track record* to endorse democracy.

Armed with these three ideas, we've a sketch of the instrumental defence of democracy. Now let's shift our attention to whether this supports an objection to the use of judicial review.

10.5.2 THE INSTRUMENTAL DEFENCE AND JUDICIAL REVIEW

In constructing the rights argument for judicial review, we relied on the following:

> *Judicial review empirical claim*: Judicial review is a means for the state to recognize and to protect some of an individual's rights.

Critics of judicial review might focus on this claim, protesting that, if the state's goal is to protect an individual's rights, then unconstrained democracy is the proper solution.

---

[20] Amartya Sen, 'Democracy as a Universal Value', *Journal of Democracy*, 10 (1999), 3–17.

[21] Jean Dreze and Amartya Sen, *Hunger and Public Action* (Oxford: Oxford University Press, 1989).

[22] Thomas Christiano, 'An Instrumental Argument for a Human Right to Democracy', *Philosophy & Public Affairs*, 39 (2011), 142–76 at 148–54.

According to proponents of this objection, what matters is that democracy without judicial review can achieve this end equally well. Indeed, it may even be that judicial review protects an individual's rights less reliably than unconstrained democracy.

The most threatening version of this objection involves the following:

Unconstrained democracy empirical claim: Unconstrained democracy more reliably recognizes and protects an individual's rights than democracy constrained by judicial review.

If this empirical claim were true, then it'd seriously weaken our case for judicial review. Although this wouldn't establish that judicial review is wholly without merit, it'd show this system of government to be inferior to unconstrained democracy, which would count strongly in favour of the latter.

It's difficult to assess the unconstrained democracy empirical claim, partly because doing so would require us to outline a complete set of rights to use as a benchmark against which to judge rival systems of government. However, it bears noting that there's some evidence that states with constitutions that are upheld through judicial review tend to fare better in terms of protecting several important rights than those without such constitutions.[23] Though we must be careful not to overstate these results, what we tentatively suggest is that, if anything, unconstrained democracies tend to protect an individual's rights less reliably than systems that include judicial review.

We don't find this result surprising. This is because some of the mechanisms that make democracy instrumentally valuable also have downsides. For example, while the incentive effect highlights how public opinion can exert pressure on a politician to act in the interests of their voters, the same mechanism provides them with incentives to promote the interests of electoral majorities ahead of those of minorities. For this reason, we can expect democracies constrained by judicial review to fare better in terms of upholding an individual's rights because they've a mechanism for protecting against the tyranny of the majority.

10.6 THE INTRINSIC DEFENCE OF DEMOCRACY

We turn now to arguments in favour of democracy that don't rely on ideas about its likely effects.

10.6.1 THE INTRINSIC DEFENCE

Let's begin with the circumstances of politics.[24] These are circumstances in which individuals reasonably disagree about matters of public policy, at least partly because they disagree about the values that matter in this arena. That such disagreement exists is hard

[23] Adam Chilton and Mila Versteeg, 'Do Constitutional Rights Make a Difference?', *American Journal of Political Science*, 60 (2016), 575–89.   [24] Waldron, *Law and Disagreement*, 101–3.

to dispute, and this is important because it bears on which political arrangements are defensible.

According to the instrumental defence of democracy, we should select between systems of government by considering which one produces the best outcomes. But if we disagree about what constitutes the best outcome, we seem to be stuck. A system that's the best according to one understanding won't be the best according to another. Given such disagreement, it's difficult to see how we can pick between systems of government by referring to the merits of their outcomes.

In the light of this, one alternative is to focus on *procedures*. There are several possibilities here, one of which runs as follows.[25] In the absence of agreement about the best outcomes by which to judge systems of government, we should select the one that's committed to advancing the interests of all members of the relevant population equally.[26] There are two components to this claim. First, political arrangements should equally advance the interests of a population. Second, they should be seen to do this publicly—that is, there must be a verifiable way that a population can judge its institutions to be serving this end. Of course, individuals will disagree about whether a particular system does advance their interests equally. This is true not only because individuals disagree about what constitutes equal advancement of their interests, but also because they're subject to biases and erroneous reasoning that affects their judgements about such matters. Against this background, democracy emerges as the unique solution. Providing each individual with an equal opportunity to influence political decision-making is a clear way in which to treat their interests equally.

Does this argument present a challenge to judicial review? In answering this question, we mustn't forget that our concern isn't with whether or not to endorse democracy. What's at stake is whether we should favour an unconstrained democracy over one that includes judicial review. Crucially, even if the intrinsic defence of democracy supplies us with a strong reason to oppose non-democratic systems of government, we deny that it generates the same kind of resistance to arrangements that include judicial review.

To clarify this reasoning, it bears noting that a public commitment to the equal advancement of interests requires not only that policies track public opinion, at least to some extent, but also that the state safeguards the appropriate procedures for delivering these outcomes. As Thomas Christiano reminds us, 'disenfranchisement . . . is [also] a public violation of equality'.[27]

Furthermore, disenfranchisement isn't the only means by which the state can fail to safeguard the equal advancement of interests. The same goes whenever a state permits or supports enslavement, racial discrimination, and the violation of some rights, such as an individual's rights to freedom of speech or their freedom from arbitrary arrest.

---

[25] For a rival argument that we lack the space to address, see Carol Gould, *Rethinking Democracy: Freedom and Social Cooperation in Politics, Economics, and Society* (Cambridge: Cambridge University Press, 1988).

[26] Thomas Christiano, 'The Authority of Democracy', *Journal of Political Philosophy*, 12 (2004), 266–90.

[27] Christiano, 'The Authority of Democracy', 288.

In each of these cases, the state would send a public signal that political institutions don't embody the equal advancement of each individual's interests. The implication of this is that, while the appeal of public equality helps us to understand what's intrinsically valuable about democracy, it also explains the moral imperative to prevent decisions that undermine the effective functioning of democratic institutions. This provides a basis on which to defend judicial review, so long as this process is a more effective means than the alternatives at preventing such decisions.

Not everyone who offers an intrinsic defence of democracy locates its value in an appeal to equality. For example, some hold that democracy is intrinsically valuable because it offers a system of political rule that's free from domination. Domination occurs when an individual is in a position to exercise unchecked power over others. This might seem to offer a promising basis on which to oppose judicial review insofar as this process gives judges unchecked power over voters and democratically elected politicians.[28]

But the argument we've been considering cuts against this conclusion too. More specifically, if it's a concern for freedom from domination that explains the intrinsic value of democracy, this suggests not only that each individual should enjoy equal opportunity for political influence, but also that the state should prevent decisions that leave some individuals vulnerable to domination. Again, this provides a basis on which to defend judicial review, so long as this process is a more effective means than the alternatives at preventing decisions that give some unchecked power over others.

The upshot of this is that, if the intrinsic defence of democracy is to challenge the rights argument for judicial review, it must invoke additional considerations. Let's now turn to one such possibility.

10.6.2 REVISITING DISAGREEMENT

The rights argument for judicial review appeals to the following:

> *Rights moral claim*: The state should recognize and protect some of an individual's rights.

In reaching the conclusion that the intrinsic defence of democracy is consistent with, and indeed may even support, constraining democracy with judicial review, we've relied on a particular version of this moral claim. We've advanced the idea that the values that underpin the appeal of democracy commit us to protecting a set of rights.

How might critics of judicial review respond? One possibility is developed by Jeremy Waldron.[29] Though he doesn't dispute the idea that an individual has rights, he emphasizes that various aspects of these rights remain subject to reasonable disagreement. For example, although many believe that there's a right to education, it's hotly disputed whether this supports the public funding of universities. Moreover, even

---

[28] Bellamy, *Political Constitutionalism*, ch. 4.   [29] Waldron, *Law and Disagreement*, part 3.

with respect to the most fundamental rights, such as the right not to be tortured, there may remain disagreements about the extent and limits of this right, and about how the state should act when rights conflict. May the state torture an individual when doing so can save many thousands of lives? In the light of questions like these, Waldron argues that it's a mistake to empower judges to resolve such controversial matters and that, instead, these decisions should be in the hands of the electorate and the politicians that they select.

In reply to this line of reasoning, it's vital that we inspect how these considerations might support an objection to the use of judicial review. One way to read Waldron's argument is as saying that, when there's such dispute, the state should rely on agreed mechanisms for resolving these matters. Interpreted in this way, his argument relies on the claim that there's agreement that unconstrained democracy is the appropriate mechanism for addressing political controversy. But this claim is false. Just as there's disagreement about the nature and extent of an individual's rights, so too there's disagreement about what role, if any, judicial review should play in political decision-making. In fact, a similar set of disputes arise. Individuals disagree about the extent and limits of judicial review, what to do when this process conflicts with other moral concerns, and so forth. For this reason, as Fabre wisely notes, a concern for disagreement is no basis for 'giving pre-eminence to the right to political participation'.[30]

Perhaps there are other ways to interpret Waldron's claims. However, even if this is the case, we believe that he's likely to face a dilemma. On the one hand, it's possible to appeal directly to the fact of disagreement about an individual's rights in order to show that democracy should be free from judicial review. But, if we pursue this route, then we encounter the concern raised in the previous paragraph, namely that it's unclear why unconstrained democracy emerges as the appropriate solution given than it garners no more widespread agreement than the alternatives, including democracy constrained by judicial review. On the other hand, it's possible to maintain that unconstrained democracy is the appropriate solution to disagreements about an individual's rights for a substantive reason. Maybe it arises from a concern for public equality or non-domination, for example. But making this move takes us back to a problem that we've already identified, namely that the value of public equality or non-domination also gives us reason to protect an associated series of rights.

10.7 CONCLUSIONS

The central conclusion of this chapter is that the state should use judicial review to constrain democracy. Our case for this result rests on the value of an individual's rights, and the importance of taking measures to protect these rights. In sections 10.5 and 10.6, we

---

[30] Fabre, 'A Philosophical Argument for a Bill of Rights', 93.

observed that many of the reasons that we have to favour democracy over alternative systems of government also bolster, or at least don't damage, the case for judicial review.

With this in mind, we conclude by making two final points about the kind of judicial review that the state should favour. First, it should exercise extreme caution in designing a constitution. In recent years, we've seen an extension of the list of rights that individuals are thought to possess. However, there's some reason to restrict the contents of a bill of rights to only the most fundamental, such as the rights to vote, to freedom of speech, and to freedom from torture. The chief justification for this relates to the intrinsic defence of democracy. As we acknowledged in section 10.6, it's desirable for a population to influence policy through a voting system, at least whenever matters such as public equality and domination aren't at stake. Thus, we've reasons to limit a bill of rights to leave space for democratic decision-making of this kind.

Second, any constitution should be subject to some form of oversight and adjustment through the mechanism of public opinion expressed through a voting system. Perhaps the state should establish the bill of rights through democratic avenues with the support of majorities or super-majorities. An advantage of this approach is that it means the constitution harbours the values of the democratic process. It's also important to recognize that individuals can make mistakes about which rights are worthy of protection through judicial review. For this reason, the state should ensure that it's possible to rectify such errors.

But neither of these qualifications undermine the central arguments of this chapter. Irrespective of how the state should arrive at it, and whatever it should contain, the case for constraining democracy with a bill of rights that's interpreted and enforced by judicial review remains powerful.

FURTHER READING

A useful entry point to the debate on democracy and judicial review is to read the defence of judicial review in Cécile Fabre, 'A Philosophical Argument for a Bill of Rights', *British Journal of Political Science*, 30 (2000), 77–98 and the criticism of judicial review in Jeremy Waldron, 'A Rights-Based Critique of Constitutional Rights', *Oxford Journal of Legal Studies*, 13 (1993), 18–51 or Jeremy Waldron, 'The Core Case Against Judicial Review', *Yale Law Journal*, 115 (2006), 1346–406.

To explore ideas about the values of democracy, a good overview is Thomas Christiano, 'Democracy', *Stanford Encyclopedia of Philosophy* (2006), available at https://plato.stanford .edu/entries/democracy. For more extended treatment of how these values connect with particular democratic arrangements, an excellent treatment is Albert Weale, *Democracy, Second Edition* (London: Palgrave, 2007).

To deepen knowledge of the democratic case against judicial review, good texts are Jeremy Waldron, *Law and Disagreement* (Oxford: Clarendon, 1999) and Richard Bellamy, *Political Constitutionalism: A Republican Defence of the Constitutionality of Democracy* (Cambridge: Cambridge University Press, 2007).

For a sophisticated defence of judicial review, good texts are Ronald Dworkin, *Sovereign Virtue: The Theory and Practice of Equality* (Cambridge, MA: Harvard University Press, 2000), ch. 4; Cécile Fabre, *Social Rights Under the Constitution* (Oxford: Oxford University Press, 2000), chs 3–5; and Aileen Kavanagh, *Constitutional Review Under the UK Human Rights Act* (Cambridge: Cambridge University Press, 2009), ch. 12.

 For additional material and resources, including web links and self-test questions, please visit the online resources **www.oup.com/he/walton1e**.

11

PRISON SENTENCES AND PUNISHMENT

SUMMARY

- In this chapter, we assess whether the state should shorten the length of prison sentences. We do this by exploring the justification for state punishment.
- We argue in favour of shorter prison sentences, drawing on the idea that an individual who commits a crime has a remedial duty to those they've wronged, and that one way to discharge this duty is by spending time in prison in order to deter future crime.
- We contend that this justification for punishment supports shorter prison sentences because the beneficial effect of longer prison sentences on crime rates is too low to justify the burdens they impose.
- We consider a retributivist objection, which claims that the state should favour longer prison sentences because an individual who commits a crime deserves to suffer. We argue that concerns about retribution are unable to justify the high costs of the prison system and, more fundamentally, that they provide an unattractive justification for all forms of punishment.
- We discuss the appeal and relevance of a communicative account of punishment, according to which the state should punish an individual who commits a crime in order to condemn their actions. While we're sympathetic to this justification for punishment, it doesn't provide the state with grounds for longer prison sentences.
- We conclude by reflecting on the implications of our arguments.

11.1 INTRODUCTION

It was among 2015's most extraordinary political events when, in the United States, the Democratic and Republican parties made a bipartisan push to introduce the Sentencing Reform and Corrections Act. Among other things, this act proposed to reduce the length of prison sentences for various crimes.[1] For the two parties to find any common ground, let alone work together, is so rare that any such occurrence is momentous. But

---

[1] United States Congress, *S.2123—Sentencing Reform and Corrections Act of 2015*.

the development was also striking because it's set against a long-term trend towards *increasing* the length of prison sentences.

In the United Kingdom, a 2013 Ministry of Justice report notes that between 1993 and 2012, the prison population rose by 98 per cent.[2] It attributes a large amount of this rise to two factors: courts sentence more offenders to prison and the average length of these sentences has increased. In the period between 1999 and 2011, the average custodial sentence length given for indictable offences rose by greater than three months, and the average time served increased by six weeks. The increase in the length of prison sentences is particularly clear with respect to a subset of offences, notably for crimes relating to violence, drug offences, and sexual offences. Furthermore, the trend is especially significant in the case of those serving terms of more than four years, as well as those serving indeterminate sentences.

To some extent, this rise in the length of prison sentences sits in tension with a countervailing trend in favour of less cruel forms of state punishment. Long prison sentences have replaced (some) use of chain gangs, torture, and the death penalty. However, even if prison sentences are more humane than other forms of punishment, this isn't sufficient to justify their use. Rather, we must assess whether they offer a morally acceptable form of punishment and, if so, for how long the state may incarcerate someone who commits a crime.

There's disagreement about these matters because there are competing views about the merits of *punishment*. In public debate surrounding the Sentencing Reform and Corrections Act, perhaps the most commonly cited concern relates to how changes in prison sentence length might affect crime rates. In opposition to shorter sentences, Senator Ted Cruz claimed that they 'could result in more violent criminals being let out on the streets, and potentially more lives being lost'.[3] Bernard Kerik, the former police commissioner of New York, responded by claiming that this 'is simply false' and, indeed, that 'the longer anyone sits in prison, their chances for a successful transition back into society diminishes with each passing day'.[4]

This is straightforwardly an empirical matter, which turns on whether longer prison sentences really do reduce crime to a greater extent than shorter ones. As we note later in this chapter, this empirical question is vitally important. But this is only because it relies on an underlying moral claim about the justifiability of state punishment. In particular, it rests on the idea that we should assess punishment, and the length of prison sentences in particular, in terms of how these decisions affect crime rates. This brings us to the deterrence account of punishment, which holds that the state should punish an individual who commits a crime when and because this reduces the likelihood of future criminal conduct.

---

[2] Ministry of Justice, 'Story of Prison Population: 1993–2012 England and Wales', *Ministry of Justice Summary* (2013), available at https://www.gov.uk/government/statistics/story-of-the-prison-population-1993-2012.

[3] The Times Editorial Board, 'Pass the U.S. Sentencing Reform Bill to Rein in Mass Incarceration', *Los Angeles Times*, 17 February 2016, available at http://www.latimes.com/opinion/editorials/la-ed-criminal-justice-20160215-story.html.

[4] Bernard Kerik, 'Cotton Letter Final', *Huffington Post*, 16 February 2016, available at http://big.assets.huffingtonpost.com/Cotton.Letter.Final.pdf.

The deterrence account is a prominent and widely endorsed view. However, it's not the only game in town. For this reason, to evaluate disputes about sentencing reform that rely on it—and, indeed, to assess sentencing reform in general—we need to reflect in further detail on the purpose and limits of state punishment. Although this may sound like a grand enterprise, we expect that the main theories are somewhat familiar. To see this, let's briefly consider various statements regarding the use of the death penalty. In perhaps its most significant ruling on the matter, the United States' Supreme Court decided to uphold the use of this form of punishment on the grounds that it serves three ends.[5] The first relates to deterrence, which, as we've seen, appeals to the importance of reducing crime rates. The second refers to the claim that an individual who commits a crime deserves to suffer for what they've done. In the words of the Supreme Court, the third idea is that 'capital punishment is an expression of society's moral outrage at particularly offensive conduct'.[6]

With this in mind, we can distinguish three justifications for state punishment:

Deterrence moral claim: The state should punish an individual who commits a criminal offence so as to deter wrongdoing.

Retributivist moral claim: The state should punish an individual who commits a criminal offence on the grounds that they deserve to suffer.

Communicative moral claim: The state should punish an individual who commits a criminal offence in order to condemn them publicly for what they've done.

Each of these accounts bears not only on the purpose of state punishment, but also on the appropriate length of prison sentences. We might claim that the state should set the length of sentences to act as an effective deterrent, to reflect the amount an individual deserves to suffer, or to ensure the appropriate level of public condemnation. With these different justifications, we can reach rather different conclusions about what'd be an appropriate time for someone who's committed a crime to spend in prison.

Moreover, various realities of the criminal justice system make a crucial difference to how the state should act. As we discuss below, the suffering endured by those sent to prison bears on our deliberations here. We must also take into account the highly racialized nature of extant policing practices, whereby police disproportionately target black communities. This tendency partly explains why those who're black make up a disproportionate share of the prison population.[7] When considering the appropriate use of incarceration, it's imperative to reflect carefully on how realities such as these should inform any conclusions that we reach.

In this chapter, we explore each of these ideas and issues, and their relevance to the length of prison sentences. In section 11.2, we defend a justification for state punishment that appeals to its role in deterring criminal wrongdoing. In section 11.3, we

---

[5] *Gregg v. Georgia*, 428 U.S. 153 (1976).   [6] *Gregg v. Georgia*, 183.

[7] Nazgol Ghandnoosh, 'Black Lives Matter: Eliminating Racial Inequality in the Criminal Justice System', *The Sentencing Project* (2015), available at https://www.sentencingproject.org/publications/black-lives-matter-eliminating-racial-inequity-in-the-criminal-justice-system.

elaborate on the implications of this for whether the state should shorten prison sentences. We argue that it should. In section 11.4, we consider a retributivist challenge to our view. In section 11.5, we examine the relevance of the idea that the state should punish an individual who commits a crime in order to communicate its condemnation of their actions. We show that neither provides strong support for longer prison sentences. In section 11.6, we return to some of the practical concerns that bear on prison sentencing, including those relating to the problem of racial bias in the criminal justice system.

For two reasons, we can't aim to provide a complete account of sentencing. First, what's an appropriate custodial term is context-specific, meaning that whether current sentences are too long is something that's likely to vary across contexts. After all, it may be preferable to serve a sentence of ten months in decent conditions than to serve a sentence of eight months in conditions that are rather grimmer. Moreover, the appropriate length of a prison sentence is likely to depend on many other features of the criminal justice system, including parole, non-prison sentences (such as community service), and the existence and duration of criminal records.

Second, what's an appropriate custodial term is crime-specific, meaning that whether current sentences are too long is something that's likely to depend on the crime in question. In supporting shorter prison sentences, we don't mean to say that the state should shorten all prison sentences. In fact, we're open to the idea that the state should lengthen prison sentences for some crimes, such as domestic abuse.

Despite these caveats, we believe that it's intelligible to theorize about the appropriate length of prison sentences in a general fashion. And, to mitigate any remaining worries, we'll identify examples where we're confident our arguments have definite application.

11.2 THE IMPORTANCE OF DETERRENCE

We begin with the idea that the purpose of state punishment is to deter criminal wrongdoing. The appeal of this view resides in the fact that, when we think about what would be bad about abolishing the criminal justice system, the central concern is that doing so would increase our chance of becoming victims of crime. Likewise, one argument for making use of prison sentences is that they reduce the likelihood of misconduct.

To flesh out this idea, it's helpful to distinguish three different effects of imprisonment. *Incapacitation effects* are those generated by detaining an individual who'd otherwise commit a crime. This means taking criminals off the street, so to speak. *Recidivism effects* refer to the role that punishment plays in reducing further criminal behaviour by an individual after they've been punished. This can occur through rehabilitation, whereby imprisonment reforms an individual's views such that they become less inclined to commit crimes. Or it can occur because the experience of prison is so unpleasant that they avoid crime in order not to return. Finally, there are *general deterrence effects*, which refer to the disincentives to commit crimes that result from the threat of punishment. These effects arise when an individual chooses not to commit a crime for fear of being sent to prison.

Each of these is an attractive consequence of imprisonment, but do they justify its use? One reason why it's not straightforward to answer this question is that there are serious costs involved. Simply put, sending an individual to prison is among the most brutal things that a state can do. Most immediately, this means depriving them of a huge range of their freedoms, including freedom of association and freedom of movement. In addition to this, prisons are often extremely inhospitable places, where an inmate is at serious risk of physical and psychological harm. Incarceration can also damage an individual's relationships with friends and family.

Moreover, the costs don't fall exclusively on those who're imprisoned. In the first instance, it can be hurtful to see loved ones behind bars. Beyond this, there can be serious social and economic repercussions for those on the outside, who may have to survive without a second parent to share in household work or on only one income. This can affect every aspect of personal life, with hugely damaging implications for education, housing, and family stability. Finally, the prison system is enormously expensive to maintain, using up funds that the state might otherwise devote to financing valuable public services or leave in the pockets of taxpayers. In this respect, it imposes costs on the entire population.

So, while imprisonment promises several beneficial effects, and we shouldn't forget that its use is to prevent innocent individuals falling victim to (potentially very serious) crimes, it's far from obvious that this is worth its associated costs. In the rest of this section, we consider two ways in which to weigh up these competing considerations, before returning to the implications of our analysis for the appropriate length of prison sentences.

11.2.1 OUTCOMES AND DETERRENCE

One approach to this task emerges from the idea that our moral assessment of any institution should be guided solely by what brings about the best outcomes. On this view, the state should punish an individual whenever the deterrence effects of doing so are large enough to outweigh the costs associated with that act of punishment.[8] Accordingly, the various costs to those who're imprisoned, their families, and the taxpayer are justifiable so long as the prison system reduces crime rates to a sufficiently great extent.

There's something attractive about the idea that, if the costs associated with the prison system are to be justifiable, then they must give rise to significant benefits. In fact, we'll shortly argue that such reasoning plays an indispensable role in justifying imprisonment. However, there's a significant problem with the argument as we've

---

[8] Jeremy Bentham, *An Introduction to the Principles of Morals and Legislation* (New York: Prometheus Books, 1988 [1789]).

currently stated it. The concern is that the moral ideas on which it relies might justify punishments that are deeply unjust.[9]

For our purposes, it's useful to identify two instances of this. First, it might justify framing someone who's innocent for a crime they didn't commit. This is because doing so might reinforce the widespread belief that the state will punish criminal conduct, and so serve as an effective general deterrent. Second, it might justify enacting extremely severe, perhaps even inhumane, punishment if doing so would have sufficient deterrent effects. For example, this reasoning would support chopping off the hands of those who steal loaves of bread so long as this deters enough crime. It goes without saying that we should reject justifications for punishment that license these brutal conclusions. We call this the *problem of unjust punishment*.

One way in which to tackle this problem is to maintain that, in practice, it's always unwise to frame the innocent or to enact inhumane punishments. This is because there's always a risk that the former will come to light and, if this were to happen, it could weaken trust in legal structures. Similarly, inhumane treatment at the hands of the state might undermine support for the criminal justice system. For each of these reasons, perhaps it's prudent to avoid unjust punishments.

While there may be some truth to this, it severely mischaracterizes the nature of the problem. Surely, we'd still regard it as gravely unjust to frame someone who's innocent even if we were (unrealistically) to suppose that this would never come to light. The problem is that justifying acts of punishment solely in terms of what brings about the best outcomes fails to account for the fact that it's *unjust* to frame the innocent and to treat those who commit crimes inhumanely. The real issue with these practices isn't simply that they're imprudent. What we're after is a principled explanation of why it's wrong for the state to act in this way. Put more generally, the problem of unjust punishment highlights an especially important moral concern that we neglect if we focus purely on the outcomes of punishment. The emphasis on the ends of punishment overlooks the problems with the means.

11.2.2 DUTIES AND DETERRENCE

A different way to approach this problem is to develop an account of punishment that assigns some role to deterrence, but begins from a rather different basis.[10] To start, let's consider the following simple case:

Crime: Angela grievously assaults Bacchus.

Through her wrongdoing, Angela incurs several duties, including a duty to remedy what she's done to Bacchus. This might take different forms, but one possibility is for

---

[9] H. L. A. Hart, *Punishment and Responsibility* (Oxford: Oxford University Press, 1968), chs 1–2.

[10] Victor Tadros, *The Ends of Harm: The Moral Foundations of Criminal Law* (Oxford: Oxford University Press, 2011).

Angela to protect Bacchus against the future threat of similar crimes.[11] If Angela were to prevent Bacchus from being grievously assaulted a second time, by someone else, then there's an important sense in which she's offset her own wrong. Needless to say, this doesn't justify Angela's initial misconduct, nor is it to say that Angela owes nothing else to Bacchus. Rather, what we're drawing attention to is the fact that this is one way in which Angela can discharge the remedial duty that she owes to her victim.

To be sure, we don't deny that there may be a general duty that falls on everyone to protect others from wrongdoing. What's significant is that Angela owes an especially stringent duty to her victim. This explains why we can demand much more of her to protect Bacchus than we can of other individuals. This result is salient, as it supplies us with a principled reply to one strand of the problem of unjust punishment. More specifically, Angela can have no good complaint against being forced to bear significant burdens in the service of compensating her victim, since she renders herself *liable* to these burdens through her wrongdoing. In this respect, her situation is rather different from those who're innocent. Therefore, we've principled grounds on which to distinguish between punishing the guilty and punishing the innocent.

The account also provides us with a reply to the second strand of the problem of unjust punishment. In saying that Angela renders herself liable to bear significant burdens to remedy the wrongs done to her victim, we aren't saying that she's liable to shoulder unlimited burdens. Rather, the duty she incurs must be *proportionate* to the wrong she's done. In this respect, we've principled grounds not to exact inhumane punishments. Instead, the state must adopt punishments that are proportionate to the crime.

This line of reasoning gives us a lead in thinking about what form of punishment is justifiable. We've suggested that Angela might discharge her duty to Bacchus by protecting him from being grievously assaulted again in the future. In reality, it's likely to be impossible for Angela physically to protect Bacchus in this way. But there's a less direct way in which she can play this role: she could act in a manner that deters others from wronging Bacchus. In at least some cases, serving time in prison might be the best way for an individual to do this. If this is correct, then we'd have a deterrence-based justification for imprisonment—but crucially, one that provides a principled objection to punishing the innocent and to inhumane punishment that imposes disproportionate costs on the offender.

Taking these details seriously requires us to revise the deterrence moral claim in the following way:

> *Revised deterrence moral claim*: The state should punish an individual who commits a criminal offence if this deters wrongdoing and the punishment is proportionate to the offence.

This claim offers a plausible justification for state punishment. But its implications for the use of prisons are still unclear, since we need to know whether and what kinds of sentences deter wrongdoing and are proportionate. Let's now turn to these issues.

---

[11] Tadros, *The Ends of Harm*, 275–9.

11.3 DETERRENCE AND PRISON SENTENCES

In this section, we draw on the revised deterrence moral claim to show that short prison sentences may be justifiable in the light of their deterrence effects, but that we should reject the use of longer sentences.

11.3.1 THE EFFECTS OF PRISON SENTENCES

Determining the effect of prison sentences on crime rates is a difficult task. Many factors affect crime levels, including poverty, economic inequality, unemployment, law enforcement practices, and cultural norms. Despite this, there's ample evidence to show that prison sentences are a useful deterrent.

Two considerations support this claim. First, it's widely accepted that short prison sentences can be effective at reducing levels of recidivism.[12] As an example of the success of these measures, let's consider the Hawaii Opportunity Probation with Enforcement (HOPE) programme, which punished those who violated parole conditions with a short prison sentence, typically of only a few days. Studying the effects of this initiative, researchers found that those subject to the regime were 55 per cent less likely to commit further crimes than comparable individuals on probation.[13]

Second, it's plausible that short prison sentences have general deterrence effects, as the threat of imprisonment disincentivizes an individual from committing a crime.[14] The existence of these sentences contributes to a culture in which an individual is aware that imprisonment is a possible consequence of unlawful behaviour, and this is likely to shape their general outlook. It may also be important for more indirect reasons. For example, the existence of prisons enables parents credibly to warn their child about the serious consequences of acting criminally.

All of this is to suggest that we've reason to believe that prison sentences can act as a useful deterrent. However, it's crucial to emphasize that longer prison sentences aren't significantly more effective in this respect than shorter ones.

Some support for this comes from research into the effect of the three-strikes regime in California.[15] These laws mandate courts to impose longer sentences—and, in some cases, life prison sentences—on a persistent offender, typically defined as an

---

[12] Randi Hjalmarsson, 'Juvenile Jails: A Path to the Straight and Narrow or to Hardened Criminality', *Journal of Law and Economics*, 52 (2009), 779–809.

[13] Angela Hawken and Mark Kleiman, 'Managing Drug Involved Probationers with Swift and Certain Sanctions: Evaluating Hawaii's HOPE', *National Institute of Justice* (2009), available at https://www.ncjrs.gov/pdffiles1/nij/grants/229023.pdf.

[14] For an example of a relevant study, see Jérôme Adda, Brendon McConnell, and Imran Rasul, 'Crime and the Depenalization of Cannabis Possession: Evidence from a Policing Experiment', *Journal of Political Economy*, 122 (2014), 1130–202.

[15] Eric Helland and Alexander Tabarrok, 'Does Three Strikes Deter? A Nonparametric Estimation', *Journal of Human Resources*, 42 (2007), 309–30.

individual who's committed at least three crimes. Though the evidence suggests that utilizing longer prison sentences has some effect on crime rates, this effect is small considering the massively increased prison sentences that these individuals face. In fact, the authors estimate that a doubling of sentence length results in only a 6 per cent decline in crime rates. This finding is consistent with other research in this area.[16]

In sum, what the evidence indicates is that prison sentences of some kind effectively deter crime, but that longer sentences aren't much more effective in this regard than shorter ones. It's partly on this basis that we conclude that short prison sentences offer an appropriate means through which an individual who's committed a crime can fulfil the remedial duty that they owe to their victim.

11.3.2 PROPORTIONALITY

To consider the matter of proportionality, it'll help to introduce some terminology. *Narrow proportionality* refers to the costs that we may impose on an individual who's committed a crime and is therefore liable to punishment. For a prison sentence to be narrowly proportionate, it mustn't impose too large a burden on the individual who'll spend time behind bars. We can contrast this idea with *wide proportionality*, which concerns the costs that we can expect third parties to bear in the pursuit of our aims. For a prison sentence to be widely proportionate, it mustn't impose too large a burden on the friends or family of the inmate or on the taxpayer. Wide proportionality explains why we might oppose criminal justice systems that are very expensive to fund, and so require very high levels of taxation to achieve their desired ends.

What exactly counts as a narrowly disproportionate cost for an individual who's committed a crime to bear is a difficult question to answer at the general level. We acknowledge that a complete theory of punishment must answer this question.[17] However, since our aims are more modest, this isn't necessary for our purposes. This is because we're able to rest our case on intuitive judgements about the demands of narrow proportionality.

For example, let's return to the three-strikes laws that operate in parts of the United States. This practice has produced a number of extraordinary cases, including that of Leandro Andrade, who was handed two life sentences for multiple counts of shoplifting with the equivalent value of around $150.[18] Laws relating to drug possession provide another compelling example. Even assuming that these laws are justifiable (which we contest in Chapter 4), a prison sentence of seven years for the possession of certain class A drugs is surely disproportionate, given the character of the alleged wrongdoing in question.

---

[16] David S. Lee and Justin McCrary, 'The Deterrence Effect of Prison: Dynamic Theory and Evidence' in Matias D. Cattaneo and Juan Carlos Escanciano (eds), *Regression Discontinuity Designs: Theory and Applications* (Bingley: Emerald Publishing Limited, 2017), 73–146 and Hjalmarsson, 'Juvenile Jails'.

[17] For more detailed discussion, see Tadros, *The Ends of Harm*, ch. 15.

[18] For discussion, see Joe Domanick, *Cruel Justice: Three Strikes and the Politics of Crime in America's Golden State* (Berkeley and Los Angeles, CA: University of California Press, 2004).

We also believe that long prison sentences can be widely disproportionate.[19] To see this, let's consider the fact that Andrade's sentence for petty theft would result in his lifelong absence from his family, including from his three children. Meanwhile, his sentence would cost taxpayers thousands of times more each year than the value of what he stole. Again, it's difficult to offer a general account of which sentences are widely proportionate. But our intuitive reaction to this case suggests that we should reject at least some current practices on this basis.

11.3.3 THE CASE FOR SHORTER PRISON SENTENCES

It's useful to bring together the arguments from this section and section 11.2. An implication of the revised deterrence moral claim is that we can justify the state's use of prison sentences by appealing to their deterrence effects, where a concern for this emerges via the remedial duties of those who've committed crimes. Crucially, though, we maintain that this justification for state punishment speaks in favour of shorter prison sentences for two reasons. First, shorter prison sentences are about as effective at deterring crimes as longer ones, and so the state can accrue nearly all of the benefits without extending an offender's term. For this reason, long prison sentences are unnecessary for achieving the state's goals. Second, many long sentences are disproportionate, both narrowly and widely. This means that they impose costs on an offender, their friends and family, and the taxpayer that are excessive in comparison with the benefits that they promise.

It adds to these considerations to reflect on the relationship between them. In particular, even if longer prison sentences are a little more effective than shorter ones at deterring crime, they achieve this by generating *many* more costs. It's difficult to see how the state can justify these enormous additional burdens given that the benefits are so minor. Put in simpler terms, our concern is that, in comparison with shorter prison sentences that are nearly as good in terms of deterrence, longer sentences impose unjustifiable costs on offenders and third parties.

Armed with these ideas, we can now construct the *deterrence argument* for shorter prison sentences:

Revised deterrence moral claim: The state should punish an individual who commits a criminal offence if this deters wrongdoing and the punishment is proportionate to the offence.

Prison sentences empirical claim: Longer prison sentences aren't significantly better at deterring crime than shorter prison sentences, and they're much more likely to be disproportionate.

Conclusion: The state should adopt shorter prison sentences.

Having set out the terms of this argument, we now turn to a variety of objections. We do this by considering how those who defend other justifications for punishment might challenge our claims.

---

[19] Tadros, *The Ends of Harm*, 356–9.

11.4 RETRIBUTIVISM

The core of the retributivist moral claim is most commonly expressed in the phrase 'an eye for an eye'. In essence, it holds that it's intrinsically good or right for an individual who's committed a crime to suffer for this. We might say that, because they've done something morally wrong, they *deserve* to suffer. On this view, whereas an individual's suffering is normally a bad that we've reason to regret and to avoid, in the case of a criminal offender, it's something that we've reason to welcome and to bring about.[20]

We can qualify this idea in various ways. Retributivists tend to emphasize the importance of punishment being proportionate to the offence an individual has committed. It's common to hold that an individual's wrongdoing involves a certain amount of badness and that it's intrinsically good or right for them to suffer an amount that matches this. It's this idea that the 'eye for an eye' phrase captures. Nonetheless, retributivists needn't hold that punishment must be an exact mirror of the crime. They needn't propose that we should torture those who've tortured others, for example. The aim is to achieve a close fit or a proximate punishment.

For a retributivist to challenge our case for shortening prison sentences, it's necessary to show that an individual who commits a criminal offence deserves to suffer more than they would if we designed prison sentences with only deterrence in mind. One complication here is that it's sometimes unclear how to determine what this involves. Unlike approaches that look to the effects of prison sentences on crime rates, it's much harder to work out what should guide calculations about the appropriate amount an individual should suffer.

However, even if we set aside this concern, there are two problems with mobilizing retributivist ideas to oppose the case for shorter sentences. Retributivist accounts of state punishment involve the following moral claim:

> *Retributivist moral claim*: The state should punish an individual who commits a criminal offence on the grounds that they deserve to suffer.

This moral claim has two components. The first is the idea that it's good or right for an individual who commits a criminal offence to suffer. But this alone isn't enough to justify the use of imprisonment. For the retributivist moral claim to be true, it must also be that the state should bring about the suffering that an individual who commits a crime deserves. These two components together constitute the *retributivist objection* to our view. But we believe that neither of them is plausible. Let's address each in turn.

The idea that it's good or right for an individual who commits a criminal offence to suffer is a widely shared conviction. Its proponents allege that this view helps us to

---

[20] Larry Alexander and Kimberley Kessler Ferzan, *Crime and Culpability: A Theory of Criminal Law* (Cambridge: Cambridge University Press, 2009); Michael S. Moore, *Placing Blame: A Theory of Criminal Law* (Oxford: Oxford University Press, 1997), ch. 2; and Jeffrie G. Murphy and Jean Hampton, *Forgiveness and Mercy* (Cambridge: Cambridge University Press, 1988).

make sense of some of our most deep-rooted intuitions, such as why we cheer when the villain needlessly suffers at the end of the film. Despite this, there's something perverse about celebrating others' suffering. This is especially so when we're supposed to assume that there's something morally laudable in an individual's suffering when it serves no other purpose. Here, it's important to put aside the fact that such suffering can generate various benefits to the victim, the wrongdoer, and to other individuals. The retributivist moral claim doesn't rely on any such considerations. It holds that the suffering of an individual who's committed a criminal offence is good or right even when it doesn't produce any other benefits. This idea seems harder to accept. As H. L. A. Hart famously notes, it seems to involve 'a mysterious piece of moral alchemy in which the combination of the two evils of moral wickedness [the crime] and suffering [the imprisonment] are transmuted into good'.[21] To be sure, we needn't deny that the idea of deserved suffering is intuitively appealing. Rather, what we're sceptical of is according this intuition any serious weight within our theorizing about justifications of state punishment.

Even if we accept that it's good or right for an individual who's committed a crime to suffer, there's reason to doubt that the state should play any serious role in bringing this about. This is because it's unlikely that the value of an individual's deserved suffering is sufficient to justify the extensive costs that imprisonment imposes on the taxpayer, as well as on the friends and family of the offender. In other words, we believe that this aspect of retributivism entails consequences that are widely disproportionate.

It's important to remember that there's a vast range of costs that are typically connected with prison sentences, including the immense emotional and psychological damage that can fall on the friends and families of those imprisoned. However, it's difficult to believe that retribution is sufficiently important to justify state punishment even if we consider only the financial burdens of the prison system. In the United Kingdom, the Ministry of Justice conservatively estimates the overall cost per prisoner to be over £42,000 per year.[22] This amounts to a total annual cost of over £4.5 billion. Moreover, these figures don't even take into account a vast array of other costs, such as those relating to trials, which can easily run into the tens of thousands per court case.

Whatever the value of an individual's deserved suffering, it's unclear how this could be sufficiently high as to justify the exorbitant taxation necessary to fund the state inflicting it. That is, given that prisons and their related infrastructure involve such costs, the retributivist moral claim relies on the idea that the state may heavily tax innocent individuals to punish the guilty. But this result should strike us as troubling, especially if the innocent individuals who pay taxes don't consent to this use of their money.

---

[21] Hart, *Punishment and Responsibility*, 234–5. See also Erin Kelly, 'Criminal-Justice Minded: Retribution, Punishment and Authority' in Derrick Darby and Tommie Shelby (eds), *Hip Hop and Philosophy: From Rhyme to Reason* (Chicago, IL: Open Court, 2005), 183–92; Tadros, *The Ends of Harm*, ch. 4; and Victor Tadros, 'Distributing Responsibility', *Philosophy & Public Affairs*, 48 (2020), 223–61.

[22] Ministry of Justice, 'Costs Per Place and Costs Per Prisoner', *Ministry of Justice Information Release* (2019), available at https://assets.publishing.service.gov.uk/government/uploads/system/uploads/attachment_data/file/841948/costs-per-place-costs-per-prisoner-2018-2019.pdf.

It adds to this point to reflect on the fact that there are many better ways to spend this revenue. Rather than use its resources to increase the amount of suffering in the world, the state could invest more heavily in our healthcare or education systems. We could even use the resources simply to ensure that those who're morally praiseworthy prosper. So, even if retributivists were to insist that imposing suffering has great value, and that this is sufficient to make it worth taxing innocent individuals, it's hard to see how they could show that there are no better purposes for this revenue.

Based on this analysis, we should reject the retributivist moral claim. While this view is widely shared, we should resist the idea that the goodness or rightness of an individual's deserved suffering can justify the use of state punishment, especially once we keep a keen eye on its extensive associated costs.

11.5 COMMUNICATING CONDEMNATION

The communicative account holds that the state should punish an individual who commits a criminal offence in order to condemn them publicly for their misconduct. In doing so, the state demonstrates its support for the offence's victim. On this view, state punishment is justifiable because of what it *communicates* about both the conduct of the individual who committed the offence and the moral importance of the victim.[23] This account relies on the following claim:

Communicative moral claim: The state should punish an individual who commits a criminal offence in order to condemn them publicly for what they've done.

To pose a challenge to our case for shortening prison sentences, it must be that longer terms provide a better means of publicly condemning misconduct. In other words, an advocate has to explain why we must imprison an individual in order to condemn them and, furthermore, why longer prison sentences are better at serving this purpose than shorter ones. Thomas Scanlon memorably summarizes the problem as follows: 'insofar as expression is our aim, we could just as well "say it with flowers" or, perhaps more appropriately, with weeds'.[24]

Anthony Duff develops one influential response to this challenge. He claims that punishment is the form of communication that's apt or fitting in these cases.[25] His defence of this conviction appeals to the idea that, when the state condemns an individual, its aim should be for them to recognize that they've acted wrongly and to apologize accordingly. Imprisonment can serve this morally educative function.[26] Just as

[23] Anthony Duff, *Punishment, Communication, and Community* (Oxford: Oxford University Press, 2001).
[24] Thomas Scanlon, 'The Significance of Choice' in Sterling McMurrin (ed.), *The Tanner Lectures on Human Values* (Salt Lake City, UT: University of Utah Press, 1986), 214.
[25] Duff, *Punishment, Communication, and Community*, ch. 3.
[26] Jeffrey Howard, 'Punishment as Moral Fortification', *Law and Philosophy*, 36 (2017), 45–75. For further discussion, see Areti Theofilopoulou, 'Punishment and Moral Fortification and Non-Consensual Neurointerventions', *Law and Philosophy*, 38 (2019), 149–67.

we may tell a naughty child to go to their room and spend some time thinking about what they've done, we may imprison someone so that they have the time to reflect on the seriousness of their wrongdoing. Meanwhile, serving this sentence can act as a medium through which an individual who's committed a crime can apologize to their victim and to society more generally. In a sense, accepting this burden is a means of acknowledging the wrongness of their actions.

It's worth noting that Duff expresses some reservations about the use of imprisonment. Given his concern to encourage an individual who commits a criminal offence to understand the wrongfulness of their actions and to change their views and behaviour, he expresses support for greater use of victim–offender mediation initiatives, probation, education programmes, and community service.[27] Nevertheless, Duff maintains that the use of imprisonment is justifiable when it's the best means by which the state can induce an individual to recognize their misconduct and to reform their behaviour accordingly. Along the same lines, we might think that long prison sentences are necessary to ensure that an individual takes the appropriate time to appreciate the seriousness of their wrongdoing.

There are two problems with this view. First, we might question whether imprisonment is really conducive to education and reform, such that it increases the likelihood of an individual recognizing that they've acted wrongly.[28] One reason to doubt that it'll have this effect is that prison is often such a horrid experience that the pains drown out the space for an inmate to engage in much careful reflection. Instead, the experience may be more likely to generate hostility. This scepticism is further supported by the fact that evidence suggests that longer prison sentences can increase (rather than decrease) the chances of an individual committing further crimes after their release. We can explain this result by appeal to the *learning effect*, whereby increased exposure to other offenders makes it easier for an individual to learn new criminal skills;[29] and the *outside option effect*, whereby longer prison sentences both decrease an individual's chance of employment once released and contribute to the loss of or distancing from friends and family members.[30] These explanations are important because they imply that we should be sceptical of the morally educative role of long prison sentences. Accordingly, the link between public condemnation and these sentences remains unestablished.

The second problem relates to the costliness of state punishment. Even if we've good reasons to punish an individual in order to condemn them publicly for what they've done, we need to enquire into whether these reasons are sufficient to justify the associated costs to friends, family, and taxpayers. For many, even the value of publicly

---

[27] Duff, *Punishment, Communication, and Community*, 53–8.

[28] Alasdair Cochrane, 'Prison on Appeal: The Idea of Communicative Incarceration', *Criminal Law and Philosophy*, 11 (2017), 295–312.

[29] For discussion, see Patrick Bayer, Randi Hjalmarsson, and David Pozen, 'Building Capital Behind Bars: Peer Effects in Juvenile Corrections', *The Quarterly Journal of Economics*, 124 (2009), 105–47.

[30] For discussion, see Michael Mueller-Smith, 'The Criminal and Labor Market Impacts of Incarceration', Working Paper (2015), available at http://cep.lse.ac.uk/conference_papers/01_10_2015/smith.pdf.

condemning those who commit crimes will not seem worth it. Again, it looks plausible to us to conclude that long prison sentences are widely disproportionate in relation to the aims of the communicative moral claim.

11.6 CONCLUSIONS

Our argument in this chapter consists of two claims. The first is that we should accord a concern for deterrence a central role in justifying state punishment. The second is that, if we accept this, then we should shorten prison sentences. To defend this result, we've looked at the purpose of state punishment, as well as several empirical findings regarding the effects of prison sentences, including the claim that longer prison sentences aren't much more effective at deterring crime than shorter ones.

Needless to say, public policy in this area is more complex than these claims may suggest. As we've indicated, what's an appropriate length of a prison sentence depends somewhat on the criminal justice system of which it forms a part. In our world, there are several problems with these systems, of which we'll mention three. First, many prisons are barely fit for purpose. They employ practices that are inhumane, such as solitary confinement, and, given their levels of violence, they place inmates in severe physical and mental danger. Nothing we say in this chapter justifies these forms of treatment.[31]

Second, it's widely recognized that the criminal justice system, including the use of prisons, exhibits a strong racial bias.[32] Police officers tend to be more heavily concentrated in particular neighbourhoods, and those who're black are subject to police questioning at rates that are much higher than those who're white. Furthermore, once arrested, an individual's likelihood of being prosecuted depends partly on their race, as does their likelihood of being convicted by a jury of their peers, if they stand trial. The use of algorithms to determine sentences, including whether an inmate is eligible for early release, may even exacerbate racial disparities in the criminal justice system.

Third, we must take seriously the fact that an individual's propensity to commit a crime will depend at least partly on their circumstances. For example, it's well known that those with few opportunities for employment are more likely to turn to crime than high earners. Of course, this needn't exonerate the guilty who, if our arguments are correct, incur remedial duties to their victims. But still, we should be troubled by the fact that states enact social and economic policies that make it more likely that some individuals, such as those who grow up in deprived neighbourhoods, will commit crimes.[33] Given the highly racialized distribution of income and wealth in many

---

[31] For discussion of one aspect of this, see Kimberley Brownlee, 'A Human Right Against Social Deprivation', *Philosophical Quarterly*, 63 (2013), 199–222.

[32] For discussion, see Angela Y. Davis, *Are Prisons Obsolete?* (New York: Seven Stories Press, 2003).

[33] For discussion, see Christopher Lewis, 'Inequality, Incentives, Criminality, and Blame', *Legal Theory*, 22 (2016), 153–80 and Tadros, 'Distributing Responsibility'.

states, this is a racist injustice in itself, above and beyond those that exist *in* the criminal justice system.

For these reasons, our conclusions must be read with a word of caution. They aren't a defence of current criminal justice systems. Indeed, we think it's important to close this chapter by stressing that the contemporary practice of state punishment is an area riddled with deep and pervasive injustice, and that many features of it require reform urgently. All we've aimed to show is that shortening prison sentences is a vital step in the right direction.

FURTHER READING

An excellent overview of the philosophical literature on the purpose of state punishment is Anthony Duff and Zachary Hoskins, 'Legal Punishment', *Stanford Encyclopedia of Philosophy* (2017), available at https://plato.stanford.edu/entries/legal-punishment.

Deterrence-based theories of punishment come in many varieties. For a consequentialist version, there's Jeremy Bentham, *An Introduction to the Principles of Morals and Legislation* (Oxford: Oxford University Press, 1996 [1789]). For a non-consequentialist version, there's Victor Tadros, *The Ends of Harm: The Moral Foundations of Criminal Law* (Oxford: Oxford University Press, 2011).

For discussion of retribution and its relevance to state punishment, influential texts include Michael Moore, *Placing Blame: A Theory of Criminal Law* (Oxford: Oxford University Press, 1997) and Jeffrie Murphy and Jean Hampton, *Forgiveness and Mercy* (Cambridge: Cambridge University Press, 1988). For discussion of the communicative justification, there's Anthony Duff, *Punishment, Communication, and Community* (Oxford: Oxford University Press, 2001).

For discussion of the effects of prison, there's Patrick Bayer, Randi Hjalmarsson, and David Pozen, 'Building Capital Behind Bars: Peer Effects in Juvenile Corrections', *The Quarterly Journal of Economics*, 124 (2009), 105–47 and Alisdair Cochrane, 'Prison on Appeal: The Idea of Communicative Incarceration', *Criminal Law and Philosophy*, 11 (2017), 295–312. And, for discussion of the deterrence effects of prison in particular, there's Francesco Drago, Roberto Galbiati, and Pietro Vertova, 'The Deterrent Effects of Prison: Evidence from a Natural Experiment', *Journal of Political Economy*, 117 (2009), 257–80 and Randi Hjalmarsson, 'Juvenile Jails: A Path to the Straight and Narrow or to Hardened Criminality', *Journal of Law and Economics*, 52 (2009), 779–809.

 For additional material and resources, including web links and self-test questions, please visit the online resources **www.oup.com/he/walton1e.**

12

INTENSIVE ANIMAL FARMING AND MORAL STATUS

SUMMARY

- In this chapter, we consider which principles should govern the state's regulation of the treatment of non-human animals raised for human consumption.
- We defend the claim that it's wrong to inflict pain on or to kill animals, and that the state should prohibit intensive animal farming on these bases.
- We consider the objection that there's no moral duty to act in this way because animals aren't part of the relevant community of moral concern. We respond by demonstrating that it's unappealing to restrict the scope of moral duties in this way.
- We explore the claim that it'd be wrong for the state to enforce compliance with these duties, but we contend that limiting the state's role in this way leads to various implausible conclusions regarding how it should regulate the treatment of both animals and humans.
- We conclude by reflecting on the implications of our analysis for other kinds of farming.

12.1 INTRODUCTION

According to some estimates, humans kill and consume in excess of 100 billion farmed animals every year.[1] Many of these animals live their entire lives in highly confined spaces, experiencing various kinds of discomfort, and subject to both physical and chemical alterations to their bodies. These conditions are particularly extreme in the case of *intensive animal farming*, sometimes known as 'factory farming', which refers to the practice of rearing livestock for human consumption using methods designed to yield large quantities of meat at the lowest costs. This practice is commonly subject to regulations, which set limits on how farmers may treat these animals. But opinion is divided on whether existing legislation is adequate. In 2019,

---

[1] FishCount, 'Fish Count Estimates', available at http://fishcount.org.uk/fish-count-estimates and Animal Equality, 'Food', available at https://www.animalequality.net/food.

an initiative in Switzerland gained enough popular support to trigger a referendum on banning intensive animal farming altogether.[2] Yet, in the same year, the European Parliament voted to continue subsidizing even those farms that fail to meet minimal animal welfare standards.[3]

One issue that underlies disputes about how the state should regulate intensive animal farming is disagreement about the *moral status* of animals. Here, there are debates about two important questions. First, in what ways is it morally wrong to treat animals? Second, is it justifiable for the state to coerce an individual to treat animals in accordance with these demands? This second question is important since it may be that, even if intensive animal farming is wrong, it's not the kind of wrong that the state should legally forbid. For example, many think that, though it's wrong to lie, to break promises, or to cheat on a spouse, it's beyond the state's remit to interfere in these personal matters. For this reason, when examining the regulation of farming, it's essential that we address both questions, and not only the first.

In this chapter, we explore these matters by developing an argument for prohibiting the intensive farming of animals. This conclusion flows from a defence of the claim that the moral standards that should govern the farming of animals are highly demanding, and that the state may coerce an individual to uphold these standards. Using this claim, we show that the overwhelming majority of current commercial animal farming methods are seriously wrongful, and that the state should outlaw them accordingly. Moreover, our arguments indicate that it'll be very difficult to defend any farming of animals for human consumption, such that the burden of proof lies squarely with those who wish to do so.

Our argument proceeds as follows. In section 12.2, we identify two concerns that impose moral limits on how we may treat animals. In section 12.3, we show how intensive animal farming runs afoul of these. In section 12.4, we consider but reject defences of these practices that stem from the idea that animals have a lower moral status than humans. In section 12.5, we respond to those who argue that it'd be wrong for the state to coerce an individual to comply with their moral duties towards animals. We conclude in section 12.6.

Before moving on, a note is in order. There are many moral concerns that relate to intensive animal farming. For example, there's a compelling case for prohibiting this practice because it contributes significantly to climate change.[4] For the most part, we set such arguments aside in this chapter. We do this in order to focus on farming's most direct victims.

---

[2] Sven Kaestner, 'Swiss to Vote on Banning Factory Farming', *SwissInfo*, 17 September 2019, available at https://www.swissinfo.ch/eng/politics/animal-rights_swiss-to-vote-on-banning-factory-farming/45233958.

[3] The Brussels Times, 'EU Parliament Divided on Animal Welfare in Agricultural Policy', *The Brussels Times*, 14 April 2019, available at https://www.brusselstimes.com/all-news/eu-affairs/55473/eu-parliament-divided-on-animal-welfare-in-agricultural-policy.

[4] Christopher Schlottmann and Jeff Sebo, *Foods, Animals, and the Environment: An Ethical Approach* (Oxford: Routledge, 2019), chs 5–6.

12.2 THE TREATMENT OF ANIMALS

Let's begin by considering the following case:

> *Fred's Club*: Disturbed by the sounds emanating from Fred's basement, the police
> arrive to find fifty small wire cages, each containing a puppy. Many of the pup-
> pies show signs of bodily alteration, wounding, starvation, and disease. The cages
> are covered in urine and faeces. When questioned, Fred explains that he and his
> friends breed puppies and subject them to gruelling physical treatment in prepa-
> ration for an annual tournament, during which the puppies fight with each other,
> before being slaughtered and served at a feast. Fred keenly stresses how much
> enjoyment he and his friends get from this practice.[5]

We doubt that anyone will find Fred's conduct morally acceptable. What explains this
judgement? Let's consider two possibilities.

12.2.1 SUFFERING AND KILLING

One reason to think that Fred's conduct is morally wrong is that he inflicts suffering on
an animal without good reason. The central concern here relates to the undesirability
of pain. Though it can differ in character, intensity, and duration, one thing common
to all forms of pain is that it's experienced as something negative, such that we're generally better off without it. We react with concern when we see a child touch something
very hot or when we see a footballer break their leg. Even in the case of a boxing match,
where the pain is part and parcel of what's been agreed to, we grimace when one boxer
lands a blow on another. These reactions make sense because these beings have interests in the avoidance of pain.

The nature of our reasons to avoid inflicting pain is complex. We might disagree
about how much weight to give the pain of different animals in our moral reasoning,
how to make choices when we can relieve the pain of only some, and how to trade
off less intense or short-term pain for greater or longer-term gains. But, again, what's
not in doubt is that this pain warrants some kind of response from us. As Christine
Korsgaard puts it, 'when you pity a suffering animal, it is because you are perceiving a
reason . . . to change its condition'.[6] With this in mind, we suggest the following:

> *Suffering moral claim*: It's wrong to inflict pain on an animal.

A claim along these lines is widely supported in moral and political philosophy. One
of the earliest and foremost advocates of improving our treatment of animals is Peter
Singer, who contends that all of our moral duties derive from the imperative to minimize

---

[5] Alistair Norcross, 'Puppies, Pigs, and People: Eating Meat and Marginal Cases', *Philosophical Perspectives*,
18 (2004), 229–45 at 229–30.

[6] Christine Korsgaard, *The Sources of Normativity* (Cambridge: Cambridge University Press, 1996), 153.

suffering and to maximize pleasure.[7] However, it's not essential to adopt this outlook to see the moral importance of pain. Indeed, the suffering moral claim is a staple feature of almost all moral frameworks.[8] To maintain that we've *no* duties to minimize suffering is to hold that it's morally permissible to inflict pain on an animal without any good reason, which strikes us as deeply implausible.

Despite its widespread appeal and obvious bearing on the treatment of animals, we might think that even the suffering moral claim overlooks what's most problematic about *Fred's Club*, namely that the puppies are butchered for human consumption. To establish what's wrong with this aspect of Fred's conduct isn't as simple as it may sound. After all, it's almost universally accepted that we may euthanize a pet to prevent them from suffering. Partly because of this complication, it's important to reflect on when and why it's wrong to kill.

One influential account holds that, just as it's wrong to inflict pain, so too it's wrong to deprive an animal of pleasure. Advocates of this argument maintain that these are two sides of the same coin. On this view, part of what makes Fred's conduct objectionable is that he truncates the puppies' lives, and so deprives them of any future pleasure that they could've experienced. Or, at any rate, in shortening the animals' lives, he denies them the opportunity to have pleasurable experiences in the future.[9]

These considerations suggest the following:

Killing moral claim: It's wrong to kill an animal.

12.2.2 PAIN AND PLEASURE IN ANIMALS

At this point, it's crucial to discuss a subtlety in our moral claims. We've suggested that it's wrong to kill an animal because doing so deprives them of future pleasure. But perhaps it's not obvious that killing an animal has this effect. Whether this is true depends on which capacities the animal possesses. On reflection, the same question arises in relation to the suffering moral claim. It's time that we consider these issues.

For it to be wrong to inflict suffering on an animal, it must be the case that animals can experience pain. Three reasons support the verdict that they can. First, we can sometimes *observe* pain in animals, who may wince, recoil, and shriek in much the same way that humans do when they're in pain.[10] It's true that we sometimes rely on an adult to tell us if they feel pain, but we don't rely on this method of communication in the case of infants who're unable to speak. There's no reason to think that our observations support different conclusions in the case of animals.

---

[7] Peter Singer, *Practical Ethics, Second Edition* (Cambridge: Cambridge University Press, 1993), chs 2–3.

[8] Lori Gruen, *Entangled Empathy: An Alternative Ethic for Our Relationships with Animals* (New York: Lantern Books, 2015); Christine Korsgaard, *Fellow Creatures: Our Obligations to the Other Animals* (Oxford: Oxford University Press, 2018); Jeff McMahan, 'Animals' in R. G. Frey and Christopher Wellman (eds), *A Companion to Applied Ethics* (Oxford: Blackwell, 2003), 525–36; and Martha Nussbaum, *Frontiers of Justice: Disability, Nationality, Species Membership* (Cambridge, MA: Harvard University Press, 2007), ch. 6.

[9] Singer, *Practical Ethics*, chs 4–5.   [10] Singer, *Practical Ethics*, 69.

Second, there's the *physiological* fact that many animals share with humans the anatomy for experiencing pain. Humans feel pain via nociceptors around the body that are sensitive to noxious stimuli and that generate impulses that are carried along our nervous pathways to receptors in the brain.[11] This is true for animals that share the same basic anatomy.

Third, there's an *evolutionary* basis for animals being able to feel pain.[12] The leading explanation for human sensitivity to pain is its role in assisting survival, namely that, without adverse reactions of these kinds, humans would be less likely to avoid threats to their health and lives. Subsequently, humans would have lower prospects of passing on their genes. The very same reasoning applies to the evolution of animals. Indeed, if the physiological systems don't exist for the same reason, it's difficult to see why they'd exist at all.

For these reasons, it's simple to see the relevance of the suffering moral claim to the treatment of animals. The relevance of the killing moral claim is more complicated. This is because, for it to be wrong to kill an animal because doing so deprives them of future pleasure, two conditions must be satisfied. First, animals must be capable of experiencing pleasure. Without this capacity, shortening their lives wouldn't cause any loss of pleasure. Second, animals must have some psychological continuity between their past, present, and future.[13] For example, they must be able to form and act on a plan, or to remember doing so. This is important because it gives meaning to the idea that an animal persists over time, and this is necessary to explain why we should care about *this* animal experiencing future pleasure. Without such psychological continuity, there's no more connection between this animal and their future than there's between this animal and another. An implication of this is that we'd have no more reason to preserve its life than to bring into existence some other animal equally capable of having positive experiences. For it to be wrong to deprive an animal of future pleasure, there must be some connection between the future pleasure and *this* animal. This is possible only if there's psychological continuity.

It's plausible to believe that the first of these conditions is satisfied for the same reasons that we believe animals suffer. Just as we can sometimes observe pain in animals, so too we can sometimes observe their pleasure. This occurs when they engage in certain activities, such as eating, playing, and interacting with others. Moreover, many animals share with humans the physiological anatomy for experiencing pleasure, something that makes evolutionary sense as well.[14]

---

[11] G. John Benson, 'Pain in Farm Animals: Nature, Recognition, and Management' in G. John Benson and Bernard E. Rollin (eds), *The Well-Being of Farm Animals: Challenges and Solutions* (Oxford: Blackwell, 2004), 61–84 at 65–8.

[12] Bernard E. Rollin, 'Animal Pain' in Susan J. Armstrong and Richard G. Botzler (eds), *The Animal Ethics Reader, Third Edition* (London: Routledge, 2017), 111–15 at 111–12.

[13] Jeff McMahan, *The Ethics of Killing: Problems at the Margin of Life* (Oxford: Oxford University Press, 2002), 232–40.

[14] Jonathan Balcombe, 'Animal Pleasure and Its Moral Significance', *Applied Animal Behaviour Science*, 118 (2009), 208–16.

Similar considerations give us reason to believe that the second condition is satisfied as well. There's a wealth of evidence that animals remember past events and make plans that project into the future. Simple examples of this involve animals finding their way home and making predictive assumptions about the behaviour of others. Again, there's a reasonable evolutionary explanation of this, as 'anticipation is useful for getting a jump on predictable events and selecting behaviours accordingly'.[15]

We recognize that these claims might not be true for *all* animals. For example, there remains dispute about whether prawns, shrimps, and certain other crustaceans can feel pain.[16] If they don't, then it'd be an obvious mistake to appeal to the suffering moral claim in order to condemn the ways in which they're treated. Similarly, if certain animals don't experience pleasure, then it'd be an error to appeal to the killing moral claim to object to their demise. There may also be animals for which psychosocial continuity is tenuous or non-existent. Again, this could be the case for some crustaceans given their limited cognitive capacities and, if so, the killing moral claim can't pertain to their treatment. But even if this is the case, let's not forget that there's no such doubts about the fact that the overwhelming majority of farmed animals experience pain, pleasure, and psychological continuity.

Accordingly, we now have all of the building blocks in place to condemn practices that mistreat animals. This brings us nicely to the central focus of this chapter.

12.3 INTENSIVE ANIMAL FARMING

Our aim in this section is to establish the wrongness of intensive animal farming by showing that, without good reason, this practice involves the suffering and killing of animals. We begin with one part of this:

> *Intensive animal farming empirical claim*: Intensive animal farming involves inflicting pain on and killing animals.

While a complete defence of this claim would require us to document the full range of experiences of all intensively farmed animals, and acknowledge how practices vary under different authorities, it suffices for our purposes to describe the *usual* experiences of some commonly farmed animals.[17]

---

[15] David DeGrazia, 'Self-Awareness in Animals' in Armstrong and Botzler, *The Animal Ethics Reader*, 149–59 at 152.

[16] Stuart Barr et al., 'Nociception or Pain in a Decapod Crustacean?', *Animal Behaviour*, 75 (2008), 745–51 and Brian Key, 'Fish Do Not Feel Pain and Its Implications for Understanding Phenomenal Consciousness', *Biology & Philosophy*, 30 (2015), 149–65.

[17] We draw this summary of intensive animal farming from several accounts, but we acknowledge particular debts to Mary Finelli and Jim Mason, 'Brave New Farm?' in Peter Singer (ed.), *In Defense of Animals: The Second Wave* (Oxford: Blackwell, 2006), 104–22; David DeGrazia, 'Meat Eating' in Armstrong and Botzler, *The Animal Ethics Reader*, 245–50; and Benson, 'Pain in Farm Animals'.

The farming of chickens used for egg production starts at a hatchery, where they're bred to produce more chicks for poultry and egg production. At this stage, around half the chicks (the males) are killed because they'll not lay eggs. They're crushed or suffocated in plastic bags, asphyxiated, or ground up live through a machine. The chicks that are spared this fate are caged without sufficient space to stretch their wings and they lack the environment to allow for their usual nest-building and feeding behaviour. When their egg productivity drops, they're put through 'forced molting', which accelerates a new egg cycle by reducing their access to light and depriving them of food for two weeks. Following this, the procedure is repeated or they're ground up, gassed, electrocuted, or killed by having their necks broken.

The scenario for chickens raised for meat consumption is comparable. Usually they're kept in sheds in vast numbers, with their room for manoeuvre severely limited. The shed floors are covered in urine and faeces and their close vicinity to each other leads to inbreeding, which produces crippled and unhealthy offspring, and regular aggression (including cannibalism) between birds. A traditional means of combating the latter is 'debeaking', where the chickens' beaks are burned off with a blowtorch or cut off by machine.

Female pigs used for breeding are typically kept for four months in a gestation crate in which there's not enough room to turn around, and there's neither space nor the environment for the normal practices of nest-building and foraging. To prevent weight gain that'd make them unable to reproduce, they're kept hungry throughout, often being fed only every couple of days. Following this, they're moved to a farrowing crate, where they're held in position to eat, drink, and keep their teats available to piglets. Two to four weeks after birth, mothers will move back to their breeding locations. Throughout each of these stages, evidence demonstrates unusually high levels of cortisol, which is the body's stress hormone.[18]

Piglets have their teeth clipped and their tails cut off, and they're castrated (if male). When mothers return to breeding areas, the piglets are moved to pens for around sixteen weeks until they reach slaughter weight. These pens have no straw for bedding, no sources of amusement, and no possibility of social interaction. Essentially, they're nothing other than a space to stand, lie, eat, and sleep. When ready for slaughter, they'll be moved to an overcrowded truck, which often leads to fighting between pigs, for a two-day journey without food, water, or protection from high temperatures.

Calves raised for human consumption face similar prospects. They're taken from their mothers on their day of birth, castrated (if male) and dehorned, placed in narrow stalls that are barely larger than their own bodies, and tied at the neck. They're fed on a liquid mixture of dried milk, additives, and antibiotics that's intentionally deficient in iron in order to induce anaemia that'll ensure their meat is sufficiently white to attract a good market price. Likewise, beef cattle are branded, kept in crowded facilities with limited access to natural light, and given an unnatural diet that shapes their meat for sale.

---

[18] David Fraser and Daniel M. Weary, 'Quality of Life for Farm Animals: Linking Science, Ethics, and Animal Welfare' in Benson and Rollin, *The Well-Being of Farm Animals*, 39–60 at 45.

Farmed fish are subject to overcrowding that causes them to suffer from parasitic infections, diseases, and debilitating injuries. Up to a quarter of farmed fish have stunted growth and also exhibit behaviours and brain chemistry characteristic of what we find in humans suffering extreme stress and depression.[19] Perhaps because there are no laws requiring farmed or wild fish to be humanely slaughtered, many are completely conscious while the gills are removed, and they're often left to bleed to death. Though there's dispute about whether all fish can feel pain, it's very likely that a sizeable number do. Moreover, we must bear in mind that, where we're uncertain, this means that there's a risk that these farming practices inflict considerable suffering.

We could elaborate on this harrowing description by linking it specifically to biological accounts of pain and pleasure or to other accounts of animal behaviour. But these further details merely add to what the reader can infer from what we've already described, specifically that 'factory farming routinely causes animals massive harm in the form of suffering, confinement, and [premature] death'.[20]

We're now in a position to present the *mistreatment argument* against intensive animal farming:

Mistreatment moral claim: It's wrong to inflict pain on or to kill an animal.

Intensive animal farming empirical claim: Intensive animal farming involves inflicting pain on and killing animals.

Conclusion: It's wrong to practise intensive animal farming.

This argument succeeds only if our reasons not to inflict pain on or to kill an animal aren't defeated by other reasons. This qualifier is important since we must be responsive to the possibility that intensive animal farming might be morally justifiable in some emergency scenario, such as in a historical or fictitious situation in which this practice is absolutely necessary to sustain someone's life.

An advocate of intensive animal farming might exploit this condition by maintaining that the case against this practice is defeated by the fact that some humans enjoy consuming these animals. Perhaps the pleasure that humans derive from eating the carcasses of dead animals justifies the suffering and killing that's involved in farming.

We've no time for this response to our argument. To see why, let's return to the example with which we began, *Fred's Club*. If Fred's appeal to the joy he gets from pitting puppies in fights with one another and then feasting on them fails to outweigh the horrific suffering and death that he causes, then similar appeals shouldn't outweigh the equally horrific suffering and killing that's involved in intensive animal farming.

Moreover, what exactly would it mean for a human's enjoyment of meat to outweigh these concerns? What matters isn't the absolute enjoyment that humans derive, but the *marginal* difference between a consumer's enjoyment in eating meat and their

---

[19] Marco Vindas, 'Brain Serotonergic Activation in Growth-Stunted Farmed Salmon: Adaption Versus Pathology', *Royal Society of Open Science*, 3 (2016), 1–8.   [20] DeGrazia, 'Meat Eating', 247.

enjoyment in eating some non-meat alternative.[21] We think that it verges on insulting to insist that these small benefits can justify the pain and deprivation of pleasure that animals endure in intensive animal farming.

12.4 THE MORAL COMMUNITY

The mistreatment argument relies on the claim that, unless defeated by other considerations, it's wrong to inflict pain on or kill animals. But this claim may be more complicated than it initially appears. Some critics hold that there are limits to the kinds of beings to whom we owe moral duties. One version of this view maintains that we've moral duties only to those who're members of our moral community—that is, individuals who can offer and understand reasons for treating each other in accordance with moral principles. We call this the *moral community objection.*

The most influential version of this objection focuses on the capacity of humans to *reason*.[22] On this view, only those who're capable of reasoning are morally entitled to certain kinds of treatment. These beings possess a capacity that others ought to respect, because it enables them to experience more complex thought and possess more serious interests, in virtue of which they're able to understand and obey the moral rules that regulate conduct. Proponents of this view might suggest that it's the capacity to reason that underlies our objections to mistreatment, such that moral restrictions on our conduct apply with much less force in relation to those who don't possess this capacity.

One reason that this line of argument is appealing is that it appears to make sense of the common conviction that humans enjoy a higher moral status than animals. In turn, this'd enable us to make sense of a range of judgements, including the fact that, other things being equal, we should prioritize saving a human's life over that of an animal.

In order to assess the bearing of the moral community objection on intensive animal farming, we must distinguish two possible claims that its advocates might mean to assert. One is the idea suggested in the final sentence of the previous paragraph, namely that we've stronger reasons to value the lives of humans than the lives of animals, and that we owe humans certain kinds of treatment that we don't owe animals. We might motivate this point by appealing to variations of the claims we've already introduced. For example, some hold that, because humans typically experience more complex pleasures than animals, or because they possess a capacity that animals don't (the ability to reason), we tend to do more harm when we kill a human than when we kill an animal.[23]

---

[21] Jeff McMahan, 'Vegetarianism', Interview with Nigel Warburton for *Philosophy Bites* (2010), available at http://philosophybites.com/2010/06/jeff-mcmahan-on-vegetarianism.html.

[22] Michael Allen Fox, 'The Moral Community' in Hugh LaFollette (ed.), *Ethics in Practice: An Anthology, Third Edition* (Oxford: Blackwell, 2007), 181–91 and Mary Anne Warren, *Moral Status: Obligations to Persons and to Other Living Things* (Oxford: Oxford University Press, 1997), ch. 10.

[23] McMahan, *The Ethics of Killing*, 198.

Whatever the merits of this position, it's consistent with the mistreatment moral claim. As some of its proponents readily acknowledge, holding that there's value to a human's life above and beyond the value of an animal's life is compatible with holding that it's wrong to inflict pain on or to kill an animal. We can accept that, since animals lack the capacity to reason, respect for this capacity can't explain why it's wrong to mistreat them. But still it remains wrong to inflict pain on or kill animals for other reasons. Put another way, even those who believe that humans enjoy a higher moral status than animals should accept that we've some moral duties to animals, and this is all that we need to oppose intensive animal farming.

The only way in which the moral community objection challenges our view is if it holds that we do *nothing* wrong when we inflict pain on or kill animals that lack the capacity to reason. An advocate might propose the following claim:

> *Moral community moral claim*: It's wrong to inflict pain on or to kill a being only if it possesses the capacity to reason.

One difficulty with this claim is that it implies that Fred doesn't act wrongly in our opening example. Indeed, it implies that there's nothing wrong with brutalizing puppies for fun, raising gamecocks to pit them in death matches against each other, hunting foxes or dolphins for sport, or executing rhinos and elephants to decorate one's home with trophies. We find this deeply counterintuitive. But perhaps some will be willing to accept these conclusions. For this reason, we turn to an alternative response to the moral community objection.

12.4.1 FRED'S EXPERIMENT

Let's consider the following example:

> *Fred's Experiment*: Over a series of years, Fred conducts medical experiments on a group of children who're radically cognitively limited, meaning that they possess psychological capacities that are equivalent to or lower than those of some animals. In order to test a cure for liver disease, he feeds the children a live virus whose symptoms include vomiting, acute pain, and a 10 per cent chance of death. Fred's experiment advances research into this disease.[24]

Before we proceed, we want to make one point very clear. In this example, we use the term 'radically cognitively limited'.[25] This term doesn't refer generally to individuals who have a disability. It refers specifically to those who meet the definition that we've given, namely someone who possesses psychological capacities that are equivalent to or lower than those of some animals. Children born with anencephaly fall into this

---

[24] This example draws on a real-life case that has some similarities, which is discussed in Tom Regan, 'Empty Cages: Animal Rights and Vivisection' in Andrew I. Cohen and Christopher Heath Wellman (eds), *Contemporary Debates in Applied Ethics, Second Edition* (Oxford: Blackwell, 2014), 95–108 at 99–100.

[25] We take this term from Jeff McMahan, 'Radical Cognitive Limitation' in Kimberley Brownlee and Adam Cureton (eds), *Disability and Disadvantage* (Oxford: Oxford University Press, 2011), 240–59.

category, and there may be others too. But we emphasize that we aren't referring to anyone other than those who meet this exact criterion.

We take it that *Fred's Experiment* should provoke moral outrage. However, defenders of the moral community objection may find it difficult to justify this reaction. The reason for this is that what outrages us in this case is that a group of vulnerable children are intentionally subjected to serious pain and a chance of death. Medical experiments of this kind may be justifiable when an individual agrees to participate in them. But in *Fred's Experiment*, the subjects don't consent and the treatment isn't administered to serve their own long-term interests. In this case, we should be morally concerned about every child who suffers and who's put at risk by Fred's actions.

The difficulty arises because the children in *Fred's Experiment* lack, and we can assume they'll never develop, the capacity to reason. Therefore, according to the moral community moral claim, our duties not to inflict pain on or to kill other beings don't apply to them. Even worse, an advocate of this objection may even be committed to giving a positive endorsement of Fred's conduct because of the advances in scientific knowledge that the experiments generate. This is a deeply implausible conclusion, and probably even an offensive one. For this reason, we believe that we should firmly reject the moral community moral claim.

12.4.2 RECONSIDERING THE MORAL COMMUNITY

There are various ways in which proponents of the moral community objection might respond to this challenge.[26] One option is to appeal to the negative effects of the experiments on the parents or other concerned family members of the children subject to them.[27] Pursuing this avenue might allow advocates of the moral community objection to condemn the events in *Fred's Experiment*.

The obvious problem with this response is that it both mischaracterizes the nature of the wrong in question and misidentifies its primary victim. According to the response we're considering, Fred's conduct is morally deplorable only because of how it affects the parents and families of those subjected to experimentation. But this misses the point. These effects might aggravate the seriousness of the wrong, but it's a mistake to see the primary victims as the parents rather than the children on whom the testing takes place. Partly for this reason, we must resist this attempt to salvage the moral community objection.

There's an alternative response available to those who wish simultaneously to condemn Fred's conduct and to approve of intensive animal farming. It's to claim that what justifies our outrage in the first case is that it involves inflicting pain on and killing *humans*. On this view, the suffering and killing of a human is wrong because

---

[26] Eva Feder Kittay offers a sophisticated response in her 'At the Margins of Moral Personhood', *Ethics*, 116 (2005), 100–31. We set this argument aside since it'd take us too far from the central philosophical matters of this chapter to discuss her view in proper depth.   [27] Fox, 'The Moral Community', 188–9.

they're a homo sapien. This reply has the advantage of recognizing that the events in *Fred's Experiment* wrong the children involved.

However, the problem is that it identifies members of one species as being morally entitled to better protection than members of other species without offering any justification for this. Without some reason to explain this difference, this response is arbitrary. It's unclear how this differs from claiming that we should privilege the interests of some humans over others because of morally arbitrary differences between them, such as their ethnicity or gender. We rightly condemn such prejudice, and label it as racism and sexism. In a similar way, we can refer to the view that we should privilege a human over an animal merely because they're human as *speciesism*.[28] The challenge for defenders of the moral community objection is to explain why it isn't arbitrary to give special moral weight to humans.[29]

12.5 ENFORCING BETTER TREATMENT

Until this point, the main issues we've explored are those surrounding the mistreatment argument against intensive animal farming. This reflects the philosophical research on animals, which focuses on the moral duties that we owe to animals. But this isn't the only issue relevant to debates about intensive animal farming. In particular, someone might accept the mistreatment argument, but deny that the state has any role to play in the enforcement of the moral duties to which it refers. If this were correct, then the argument that we've presented would be inadequate to establish the justifiability of legislation whose purpose is to prohibit intensive animal farming. Let's call this the *objection to coercive prohibition*.

One version of this objection begins in the same way as the moral community objection, by emphasizing that we've distinctive duties that we owe only to those who're members of our moral community: those who possess the capacity to reason. However, unlike the moral community objection, advocates of this view don't claim that we may exclude beings without this capacity from our moral consideration. Rather, they claim that those with the capacity to reason are owed *special justification* whenever their own judgements about how to act are constrained or usurped by the state.[30]

According to this view, we can give special justification in one of two ways. The first is if the state's use of coercion has democratic approval. The second is if the state's use of coercion is to protect a significant interest of all members of the moral community. Defenders of the objection to coercive prohibition can accept that animals are morally entitled to a certain kind of treatment, and perhaps even a form of treatment violated

---

[28] Singer, *Practical Ethics*, 53–70.

[29] For attempts, see Rahul Kumar, 'Permissible Killing and the Irrelevance of Being Human', *The Journal of Ethics*, 12 (2008), 57–80 and Mary Midgley, *Animals and Why They Matter* (Athens, GA: University of Georgia Press, 1998), ch. 9.

[30] John Basl and Gina Schouten, 'Can We Use Social Policy to Enhance Compliance with Moral Obligations to Animals?', *Ethical Theory and Moral Practice*, 21 (2018), 629–47.

by intensive farming. But they maintain that it's justifiable for the state to coerce an individual to live up to this moral standard only if this legislation is the upshot of a democratic decision *or* if it serves a significant interest of all members of the moral community. Regrettable as it may be, intensive animal farming hasn't been rejected through democratic decision, and perhaps it doesn't jeopardize a significant interest of the moral community. For this reason, proponents of this objection conclude that it's wrong to use the state's coercive powers to prohibit intensive animal farming.

In reply to this argument, it's worth reiterating a point that we made in section 12.1, namely that intensive animal farming contributes significantly to climate change. For this reason, this practice does jeopardize a significant interest of the moral community, and so the state has a special justification for using coercion to prohibit it. But we needn't press this point, since there are two more fundamental problems with the objection to coercive prohibition.

First, it bears emphasizing that, in their role as a democratic citizen, an individual should still support legislation that outlaws intensive animal farming. This is because defenders of the objection to coercive prohibition should recognize that this is what morality requires and, if the legislation receives sufficient democratic support, that it'd be justifiable for the state to use coercion in the service of this goal. In this way, this objection isn't at odds with the idea that democratic citizens should lobby for the state to use its powers to prohibit intensive animal farming. Given that we can understand all philosophical arguments about public policy as providing guidance about which policies an individual should democratically support, there's nothing distinctive here.

A second response starts by drawing attention to the implications of this objection. States have legislation that prevents the abuse of children, including those with radical cognitive limitations. But unless we can justify these laws by appeal to a significant interest of all members of the moral community, defenders of the objection to coercive prohibition must invoke the fact that the legal protection afforded to children with radical cognitive limitations results from a democratic process. This makes its justifiability contingent on continued democratic support. If this were overturned, then these protections could no longer be legally enforced by the state, with the consequence that an individual would be legally free to undertake activities such as those that occur in *Fred's Experiment*. Proper consideration of this implication brings into serious doubt the plausibility of the objection.

12.6 CONCLUSIONS

The case against intensive animal farming rests on the ideas that it's wrong to inflict pain on or to kill an animal, and that the state should ensure compliance with these moral duties. But our arguments support even more radical conclusions. One possibility is that we can appeal to the same moral considerations to condemn all farming practices, or at least the overwhelming majority of farming practices that we find in the real world, including those that are much more humane. A similar line of reasoning might support opposition to the killing of wild animals, including game and non-farmed fish. This is because, even if these practices don't involve inflicting pain (something that's dubious in the case of more humane methods of farming), they still involve slaughter.[31] If correct, this would mean that, in addition to prohibiting intensive animal farming, we should also outlaw related activities, including those involving free-range, organic, and traditional farming methods.

Someone might attempt to defend more humane practices by pointing out that they can be *beneficial* to the animals involved.[32] This view draws on the idea that it's better for an animal to enjoy a decent quality of life for, say, five years and then be humanely slaughtered than it is for the animal not to exist at all. One significant feature of this view is that it provides morally salient grounds for distinguishing humane farming practices from intensive animal farming, where the majority of animals endure so much pain that their lives are not worth living.

However, this view isn't obviously attractive. In particular, its advocates must explain why the same reasoning doesn't apply in the case of having a child. After all, it might also be better for a child to enjoy a decent quality of life for some specified amount of time and then be humanely slaughtered than it is for the child not to exist at all. This morally repugnant conclusion means that the defender of this approach must distinguish between the cases or drop their defence of humane farming.

We lack the space to explore in detail whether it's possible to respond to this challenge. As we indicated in section 12.1, this means we must stop short of claiming that we've shown that we should prohibit all animal farming. However, we end this chapter with the challenge we pose to advocates of more humane practice ringing loud and clear. As we've argued throughout, there are very strong reasons to think that inflicting pain on and killing an animal is highly objectionable, and this puts a significant burden of proof on someone who wishes to defend *any* form of farming animals for human consumption.

FURTHER READING

A great introduction to what we owe to animals is given in Peter Singer, *Practical Ethics, Second Edition* (Cambridge: Cambridge University Press, 1993), ch. 5. Meanwhile, an excellent overview of the literature on animal ethics is Lori Gruen, 'The Moral Status of Animals', *Stanford Encyclopedia of Philosophy* (2017), available at https://plato.stanford.edu/entries/moral-animal.

An accessible argument against intensive animal farming is Alistair Norcross, 'Puppies, Pigs, and People: Eating Meat and Marginal Cases', *Philosophical Perspectives*, 18 (2004), 229–45 and detailed discussions of the wrongness of mistreating animals are Christine Korsgaard, *Fellow Creatures: Our Obligations to the Other Animals* (Oxford: Oxford University Press, 2018)

---

[31] DeGrazia, 'Meat Eating', 248–9.

[32] For discussion, see Jeff McMahan, 'Causing Animals to Exist in Order to Eat Them' (unpublished manuscript).

and Jeff McMahan, *The Ethics of Killing: Problems at the Margin of Life* (Oxford: Oxford University Press, 2002), ch. 1, esp. 39–66.

Clear defences of the moral community objection are Michael Allen Fox, 'The Moral Community' in Hugh LaFollette (ed.), *Ethics in Practice: An Anthology, Third Edition* (Oxford: Blackwell, 2007), 181–91 and Mary Anne Warren, *Moral Status: Obligations to Persons and to Other Living Things* (Oxford: Oxford University Press, 1997), ch. 10. Responses to this objection are offered in the works by Singer and Norcross that we've mentioned.

For a detailed discussion of coercively enforcing ethical treatment of animals, there's John Basl and Gina Schouten, 'Can We Use Social Policy to Enhance Compliance with Moral Obligations to Animals?', *Ethical Theory and Moral Practice*, 21 (2018), 629–47.

For broader discussions of animal ethics, good reads include Susan J. Armstrong and Richard G. Botzler (eds), *The Animal Ethics Reader, Third Edition* (London: Routledge, 2017); Clare Palmer, *Animal Ethics in Context* (New York: Columbia University Press, 2010); and Peter Singer (ed.), *In Defense of Animals: The Second Wave* (Oxford: Blackwell, 2006).

 For additional material and resources, including web links and self-test questions, please visit the online resources **www.oup.com/he/walton1e**.

13

ENVIRONMENTAL TAXES AND INTERGENERATIONAL JUSTICE

SUMMARY

- In this chapter, we defend environmental taxes as part of a set of policies to address the threats that climate change poses.
- These taxes increase the price of activities that are environmentally harmful. In doing so, they discourage such behaviour and raise revenue that the state can use to redress its effects.
- We embed these considerations in an account of intergenerational justice, arguing that the current generation has a duty to provide future generations with prospects at least equal to its own.
- We examine the objection that the proposed approach allows historical emitters off of the moral hook. We respond by showing that the state can adjust environmental taxes to take account of this.
- We explore how to amend these taxes so that they're not regressive and they don't present undue barriers to particularly valuable activities.
- We conclude by reflecting on the implications of our argument, as well as the more general context in which climate change is taking place.

13.1 INTRODUCTION

According to the Intergovernmental Panel on Climate Change (IPCC), the global average temperature rose by 0.85°C from 1880 to 2012, and it's likely that the period from 1983 to 2012 was the hottest thirty-year period of the last 1,400 years in the northern hemisphere. Moreover, it's almost certain that more than half of the observed increase in global average temperature was caused by human activity, specifically emissions of greenhouse gases.[1] If the current rate of global warming continues, the temperature rise is likely to reach 1.5°C in the next couple of decades.[2]

---

[1] United Nations IPCC, 'Climate Change 2014: Synthesis Report' (Geneva: IPCC, 2015), available at http://www.ipcc.ch/report/ar5/syr.

[2] United Nations IPCC, 'Global Warming of 1.5°C' (Geneva: IPCC, 2018), available at https://report.ipcc.ch/sr15/pdf/sr15_spm_final.pdf.

There are a variety of policy tools at our disposal to respond to climate change.[3] Some of these measures, such as cap and trade regimes, limit the quantity of greenhouse gas emissions produced, while others change the cost of these emissions. It's likely that tackling climate change requires the use of many such instruments. Rather than survey these options, our aim in this chapter is to consider and defend one version of the second strategy, namely the use of *environmental taxes*. This is the proposal that the state should levy taxes on goods and services that predictably exacerbate climate change and therefore increase the associated risks. One example of this is a carbon tax, which increases the price of carbon-emitting activities, such as driving and flying. Other examples include taxes on goods and services that emit methane, nitrous oxide, sulphur oxide, and fluorinated gases.

But why do anything about climate change at all? One answer to this question is that we're already feeling its effects. According to some estimates, climate change kills at least 300,000 individuals each year and it causes annual economic losses exceeding $125 billion.[4] It jeopardizes access to food because of increased desertification and crop failure; it threatens health because of an increase in the spread of infectious diseases; and it destroys homes, livelihoods, and infrastructure.[5]

However, it's future generations who'll suffer the most serious effects. This is because they're fated to inherit a much less hospitable ecosystem, unless the current generation takes action urgently. Indeed, the IPCC predicts that an increase in global temperature of any more than 1.5°C would pose severe risks to food security, health, and general quality of life globally.[6] In this respect, climate change requires us to confront difficult questions about *intergenerational justice*—that is, about what the current generation owes to those who'll exist in the future. What constitutes an appropriate response to climate change depends heavily on how we answer this question. Defending environmental taxes requires that we explore this terrain.

Our analysis proceeds as follows. In sections 13.2 and 13.3, we develop our case for environmental taxes, connecting this to an account of intergenerational justice. In section 13.4, we respond to the concern that environmental taxes let historical emitters off of the moral hook. In section 13.5, we address the worry that such taxes pose a threat to living standards. In section 13.6, we conclude by reflecting on the context and implications of our arguments.

---

[3] Andrea Baranzini et al., 'Carbon Pricing in Climate Policy: Seven Reasons, Complementary Instruments, and Political Economy Considerations', *WIREs Climate Change*, 8 (2017), 1–17.

[4] Global Humanitarian Forum, 'Human Impact Report: Climate Change, the Anatomy of a Silent Crisis' (Geneva, 2009), available at http://www.eird.org/publicaciones/humanimpactreport.pdf.

[5] Nick Watts et al., 'The 2018 Report of the Lancet Countdown on Health and Climate Change', *The Lancet*, 392 (2018), 2479–514.   [6] IPCC, 'Global Warming of 1.5°C'.

13.2 ENVIRONMENTAL TAXES

Let's begin by considering the following case:

> *Pollution*: Evi sets up a factory that releases pollutants into a nearby stream, and so contaminates the local water supply. As a result, the yield of Kapo's crops decreases markedly.

One response to this scenario is for the state to require Evi to cease polluting, closing her factory if necessary. After all, Evi's conduct seems to wrong Kapo by reducing the yield of his crops.

However, an alternative response is available. The state could tax Evi's conduct at a rate that reflects the costs it imposes, and use the revenue to compensate Kapo. There are two major benefits of doing this. First, this tax burden may incentivize Evi to close her factory (or not set it up in the first place) or find other ways to operate that don't pollute. This is the *disincentive effect*. Second, if Evi maintains business as usual, the tax will swell the funds available to assist those who're harmed by her actions, such as Kapo. This is the *revenue-raising effect*.

These beneficial effects don't establish that it's better for the state to tax rather than to prohibit Evi's conduct. Other factors bear on what's the right course of action. For example, the state can't and shouldn't redress some kinds of wrongs by compensation. It'd still be wrong for Evi to steal Kapo's crops even if she fully compensated him afterwards. But there are instances in which taxes can be appropriate. This might be the case if Kapo consents to Evi setting up her factory on the condition that she internalizes the costs, or perhaps if a population democratically agrees that certain harmful actions are justifiable when properly compensated.

Similarly, it may be justifiable for the state to use taxes when relevant individuals *would* have agreed to this if given the choice. To see this, let's consider a case in which it's impossible or impractical to ascertain consent. In *Pollution*, perhaps Kapo lives very far away, such that Evi can't communicate with him. Were this true, the state might allow her to operate the factory if there's evidence that Kapo would be happy to receive a tax rebate instead of what his crops would otherwise yield. In this case, the tax may be justifiable because the state can assume Kapo's *hypothetical consent*.

Our analysis of this case is important because it has obvious parallels to that of climate change. Like Evi, those who emit greenhouse gases act in ways that contaminate the planet. Like Kapo, future generations will suffer as a result and, since these individuals don't yet exist, the state must appeal to their hypothetical consent to establish how they may be treated. In the light of this, one response is for the state to introduce environmental taxes—that is, to tax emitters at a rate that reflects the expected costs to others—and to use the revenue to redress the predicted damage.[7]

---

[7] Simon Caney, *On Cosmopolitanism: Equality, Ecology, and Resistance* (Oxford: Oxford University Press, forthcoming), ch. 6 and Paula Casal, 'Progressive Environmental Taxes', *Political Studies*, 60 (2012), 419–33.

Again, this'll have two desirable effects. It'll *discourage* an individual from engaging in activities that emit greenhouse gases, and it'll *raise revenue* from those who continue to emit, thereby swelling the funds available to assist those who'll suffer from these activities.

In practical terms, enacting this policy involves taxing goods and services that produce greenhouse gas emissions. One example here is fossil fuels. Because using these fuels emits greenhouse gases, they'd be subject to this tax, and activities that rely on them would cost more as a result. In turn, this'll have a knock-on effect for the costs of travel, food, and other consumer goods, and so it'll increase the general cost of living.

There are several other activities that we might tax on account of their contribution to the production of greenhouse gases. These include not recycling and not using energy-efficient household lightbulbs. These contribute 0.2 tonnes of CO_2 (0.2 tCO_2) per year and 0.1 tCO_2 per year, respectively.[8] However, these figures pale into insignificance in comparison with the following four, which are the worst offenders in terms of increasing greenhouse gas emissions. Eating a plant-based diet saves 0.8 tCO_2 per year compared to average non-vegan diets. Avoiding transatlantic flying saves 1.6 tCO_2 per roundtrip. Living car-free saves 2.4 tCO_2 per year. And having one fewer child saves 58.6 tCO_2 per year.[9] There might be important differences between these activities that bear on whether and how the state should tax them. We'll return to these later. For the moment, it suffices to note that there are a set of obvious candidates to which environmental taxes might apply, and we expect that at least some of these will seem like attractive options for raising revenues in response to climate change.

The state might use this revenue in three distinct ways. First, it can *mitigate* the effects of climate change, which means reducing or offsetting emissions by developing cleaner energy and creating greenhouse gas sinks. Second, it can *adapt* to the effects of climate change by designing its structures so that future generations are able to cope with climate-related threats. This might involve building sea walls and cooler homes, for example. Third, it can make *loss and damage payments* that compensate for the effects of climate change by giving future generations additional resources to use as they see fit.

How to choose between or combine these strategies is a complex question. One consideration is the efficiency of rival policies. As an empirical fact, sometimes the best use of funds is to invest in solar energy (mitigation), sometimes it's to build more

---

[8] Seth Wynes and Kimberley Nicholas, 'The Climate Mitigation Map: Education and Government Recommendations Miss the Most Effective Individual Actions', *Environmental Research Letters*, 12 (2017), 1–9.

[9] There are disagreements about how to calculate and distribute the emissions involved in having a child. For example, which emissions are the responsibility of the parents, and which are the responsibility of the child? Should everyone or only those who have a child shoulder the extra environmental costs? We can set these questions aside. For our purposes, it's sufficient to note that an extra child generates significant emissions and at least some of these are the responsibility of the parents.

reliable forms of irrigation (adaptation), and sometimes it's to make cash transfers to those suffering the harmful effects of climate change (loss and damage). Another consideration relates to a specific aspect of climate change. As we've noted, there are some wrongs that the state should prevent, rather than compensate. Plausibly, there are some features of climate change where this is true.[10] If nothing can compensate for the loss of a healthy environment or bio-diversity, then the state might have reason to favour mitigation over adaptation or damage payments even if the costs are higher. Whatever the right combination of policies, the point that matters for our purposes is that there are multiple ways in which to spend the revenue raised from environmental taxes to redress climate change and its effects.

But even working in this way, an important aspect of the case for environmental taxes is missing. To see this, let's draw our thoughts together into the following *intergenerational justice argument* for environmental taxes:

> *Intergenerational moral claim*: The state should ensure that the current generation avoids wronging future generations.
>
> *Environmental taxes empirical claim*: Environmental taxes work to ensure that the current generation avoids wronging future generations.
>
> *Conclusion*: The state should adopt environmental taxes.

So far, we've focused mostly on explaining the empirical claim of this argument, showing how environmental taxes discourage particular kinds of behaviour and raise revenue that the state can use to mitigate, adapt, or provide loss and damage payments for the effects of climate change. We've also given some defence of the moral claim by considering the case of *Pollution*.

However, there's an important way in which the intergenerational moral claim requires more development. In *Pollution*, part of what explains why it's so objectionable for Evi to release pollutants without compensating Kapo is that she deprives him of a good to which he's *morally entitled*, namely the healthy water supply that generates a certain crop yield. To clarify this point, let's suppose that, rather than polluting the water, Evi merely offers an exciting new food product, and Kapo's profit falls because customers purchase goods from her instead. In this case, we see no reason to tax Evi's activity even though it makes Kapo worse off. The intuitive difference is that, unlike in the case in which Evi pollutes the water, Kapo loses only his customer base and market share, which aren't things to which he's entitled.

For this reason, to make more precise the intergenerational justice argument, we must offer an account of the entitlements of future generations. In other words, our defence of environmental taxes requires analysis of what the current generation owes to posterity.

---

[10] Danielle Zwarthoed, 'Should Future Generations Be Content with Plastic Trees and Singing Electronic Birds?', *Journal of Agricultural and Environmental Ethics*, 29 (2016), 219–36.

13.3 INTERGENERATIONAL DUTIES

To identify the moral entitlements of other generations, we evaluate two prominent accounts. We conclude that what the current generation owes to future generations are prospects that are at least of equal value to its own. Our aim is to defend this view against those who argue that these duties are more limited.[11] We begin by considering one such account.

13.3.1 INTERGENERATIONAL SUFFICIENCY

In 1987, the United Nations' Brundtland Report defined sustainable development as 'development that meets the needs of the present without compromising the ability of future generations to meet their own needs'.[12] This definition suggests the following:

> *Intergenerational sufficiency moral claim*: Each generation has a duty to ensure that future generations enjoy sufficiently valuable prospects.

This claim requires that each generation bequeath to future generations the goods necessary for them to enjoy lives of a quality that exceeds some specified threshold.[13] To put it another way, the account forbids leaving the environment in such a terrible state that future generations can't have decent lives.

A problem with the intergenerational sufficiency moral claim is that, since it requires only that future generations enjoy prospects that surpass some level, adherence to it is consistent with enormous inequalities between generations. This is because the claim grants to each generation considerable latitude when deciding what to pass on to future generations, with the predictable result that, whereas some will inherit only the bare minimum, others will inherit much more.

This is morally troubling because it means that some individuals will enjoy much worse prospects than others simply because of their date of birth. This is something for which we can't hold them responsible and that shouldn't affect their prospects so greatly. In other words, inequalities that arise from birth dates alone seem objectionably arbitrary, much like when an individual suffers worse prospects than others in virtue of their race, gender, or family background. Just as we deem these arbitrary inequalities unfair, we should also worry about the unfairness of inequalities of prospects that would persist over time under adherence to the intergenerational sufficiency moral claim.

---

[11] With this emphasis on the *extent* of the current generation's duties, we use the term 'prospects' to remain neutral in debates about *what* it owes them—whether this should be an equal quality of life, equal resources, or something else. For discussion, see Edward Page, 'Intergenerational Justice of What: Welfare, Resources, or Capabilities?', *Environmental Politics*, 16 (2007), 453–69.

[12] Report of the World Commission on Environment and Development: *Our Common Future* (New York: Oxford University Press, 1987), 43.

[13] Lukas Meyer and Dominic Roser, 'Enough for the Future' in Axel Gosseries and Lukas Meyer (eds), *Intergenerational Justice* (Oxford: Oxford University Press, 2009), 219–48.

13.3.2 INTERGENERATIONAL EQUALITY

Given these arguments, the following emerges as a possible alternative:

> *Intergenerational equality moral claim*: Each generation has a duty to ensure that future generations enjoy prospects that are at least of equal value to its own.

This claim implies that it'd be unjust for the current generation to leave future generations with less valuable prospects than it inherited. It may leave them better off than this, but may not leave them worse off. Part of what's intuitively appealing about this claim is that it gives voice to the idea that 'those alive at any time are custodians rather than owners of the planet, and ought to pass it on in at least no worse shape than they found it in'.[14] Moreover, unlike the previous contender, the intergenerational equality moral claim guarantees that posterity won't be consigned to worse prospects merely on account of birth dates. In this way, it's not hostage to the objection that we pressed against the intergenerational sufficiency moral claim.

A critic might argue that this line of reasoning encounters a similar problem, though. If it's unjust to leave posterity with less valuable prospects because of birth dates, isn't it also unjust to leave them at least as well off as the current generation, since this effectively consigns *past generations* to less valuable prospects than future generations merely on account of their date of birth?

Simon Caney replies to this concern as follows:

> there is a morally significant difference between the two cases, namely that whilst it is not possible to improve the condition of past generations, it is possible to leave those who live in the future at a higher standard of living. So whilst it is true that this view will permit people to be worse off than others through no fault of their own, it sanctions lower levels to some *only because it is not possible to increase them*.[15]

Given the availability of this reply and the intuitive plausibility of the intergenerational equality moral claim, we think this view provides an attractive account of what the current generation owes to posterity.

This moral claim is a highly demanding one, especially given current standards of living in affluent states and the sizeable risks associated with climate change. Because of this, the claim requires the current generation to make considerable sacrifices, and it's reasonable to expect the level of environmental taxation justified on these grounds to be very high. However, this merely reflects the damage that's been done to the environment and the gravity of discharging the duties to change course and to provide proper compensation.

---

[14] Brian Barry, 'Justice Between Generations' in *Liberty and Justice: Essays in Political Theory Volume 2* (Oxford: Clarendon Press, 1991), 258. See also Caney, *On Cosmopolitanism*, ch. 6.

[15] Caney, *On Cosmopolitanism*, ch. 6 (emphasis in original).

13.3.3 THE NON-IDENTITY PROBLEM

To reiterate, we've proposed the following:

> *Intergenerational equality moral claim*: Each generation has a duty to ensure that future generations enjoy prospects that are at least of equal value to its own.

This claim articulates more precisely the notion outlined in section 13.2 that no generation may deprive other generations of their moral entitlements. It gives concrete meaning to the idea that, if the current generation fails to redress climate change and its effects, it *wrongs* posterity.

But an important objection emerges here. The problem is that the world will turn out very differently depending on how existing individuals act. In particular, we've good reason to think that, when the current generation changes its behaviour, this will lead to different individuals being born. For example, if someone travels less frequently, this will alter their network of acquaintances. In turn, this is likely to affect who they choose as their spouse, and their child will be a different person, composed of a different sperm and egg, to the one that'd be born in the alternative world in which they travel more frequently.

For this reason, if the current generation takes action to avert the threats of climate change, the particular individuals who'd have been born in a world where business continues as normal will never exist. It's different future individuals who'll enjoy the more hospitable world created by its environmental efforts. As a result, there are no *particular individuals* who're made worse off by either choice. Even if the current generation continues to emit greenhouse gases, the future individuals who'll inhabit the resulting inhospitable world aren't worse off than they'd be otherwise. This is because, for them, it's this existence or no existence. This is the *non-identity problem*.[16]

The non-identity problem poses a distinct challenge to theories of intergenerational justice that assess environmental policies in terms of the complaints from particular future individuals that the current generation has wrongfully *harmed* them. Even if the current generation leaves posterity less valuable prospects than it enjoyed, and than it could've made available, we can respond to the complaints of those who'll exist in the future by pointing out that these actions haven't made *them* worse off than they'd be otherwise. This is because, if it weren't for the current generation continuing to emit, these individuals wouldn't have existed at all. The current generation might ask: how could actions that don't make any particular individuals worse off be thought to harm them?

There are different ways in which a defender of intergenerational duties might reply to this problem. One option is to abandon the idea of assessing environmental policies in terms of possible complaints of harm from future generations. For example, perhaps the current generation's decision to damage the environment is wrong because it produces worse consequences—say, a lower level of average well-being—even though

---

[16] Derek Parfit, *Reasons and Persons* (Oxford: Clarendon Press, 1984), ch. 16.

no particular individual is made worse off by this action.[17] The downside of this move is that we lose from our moral toolkit the idea that the current generation *wrongs* posterity by bequeathing to them a less hospitable planet.

An alternative response that doesn't incur this cost is to accept the implications of the non-identity problem, and thus to conclude that intergenerational duties are very limited. Since the current generation can't harm those who'll exist in the future, perhaps all it owes to them is that they enjoy lives worth living. This might still require some response to the threats of climate change, but, given that an individual can have a worthwhile life even in pretty hostile circumstances, it suggests that the current generation owes posterity very little. On this view, it wouldn't need to make much adjustment to its environmental policies. This position isn't without its supporters.[18] But we find the idea of such limited intergenerational duties intuitively implausible.

This motivates a third response, which neither loses the appeal to wronging future generations nor limits intergenerational duties so much. It holds that we can talk meaningfully about harm in the context of climate change despite the difficulty presented by the non-identity problem.[19] One reason for this is that some individuals who'll be deprived of their entitlements by prevailing environmental policies already exist. As we've noted, their effects are already a reality for many around the world, and they'll be severe by the time today's children reach adulthood, let alone by the time they retire. So, whatever the bearing of the non-identity problem on those who're yet to be born, it remains plausible that the current generation would wrong younger individuals by leaving them with less valuable prospects than it inherited.

Furthermore, we can challenge the notion of harm assumed by the non-identity problem. In our characterization of it, we noted that those who'll exist if the current generation continues to emit greenhouse gases couldn't complain that they've been made worse off since, without these actions, they'd not have existed at all. This line of reasoning assumes a *counterfactual* notion of harm, in determining whether harm occurs by comparing an individual's circumstances to how things *would* have been with a different course of events. This is often a plausible measure of harm. However, there are other plausible measures. One of these is *subjunctive*, which determines whether harm occurs by comparing an individual's circumstances to how they *should* have been.

We often deploy the subjunctive measure when considering duties that others have failed to fulfil. Let's consider the following example:

Theft: Reema prevents an arson attack on Arjun's house but, for her mere enjoyment, she steals his family's heirloom as she departs.

---

[17] Rahul Kumar, 'Future Generations' in Serena Olsaretti (ed.), *The Oxford Handbook of Distributive Justice* (Oxford: Oxford University Press, 2018), 689–710 and Derek Parfit, 'Future People, the Non-Identity Problem, and Person-Affecting Principles', *Philosophy & Public Affairs*, 45 (2017), 118–57.

[18] David Boonin, *The Non-Identity Problem and the Ethics of Future People* (Oxford: Oxford University Press, 2014).

[19] Derek Bell, 'Does Anthropogenic Climate Change Violate Human Rights?', *Critical Review of International and Political Philosophy*, 14 (2011), 99–124 at 104 and 109.

While Arjun isn't worse off as a result of Reema's overall intervention, since he'd be homeless without it, Reema still wrongfully harms Arjun in needlessly stealing his property. He can sensibly complain that he's not as well off as should be the case. Likewise, future generations may complain that they've been harmed by a failure to fulfil a duty to bequeath equal prospects to whomever exists, because these individuals will be less well off than should be the case.

It bears noting that the non-identity problem is among the trickiest philosophical puzzles, and so we can't expect to answer it in this chapter. But we think there's enough promise to these remarks that we'll leave the matter here, and turn our attention to other challenges to environmental taxes.

13.4 HISTORICAL EMISSIONS

Although environmental taxes could ensure the price of current and future emissions reflects their damaging effects, one concern is that they overlook a further morally relevant factor, namely historical emissions.[20] This insensitivity suggests that such taxes ignore the contributions to climate change of those who emitted vast amounts of greenhouse gases in the past. We call this the *historical emissions objection*.

To elaborate the concern, let's consider a variation on a case we've already discussed:

Historical Pollution: Evi and Akna each own a factory that releases pollutants into a nearby stream, and so contaminate the local water supply. As a result, the yield of Kapo's crops decreases markedly. Whereas Evi's factory was set up only recently, Akna's factory has been operating for decades, and so it's made a much greater overall contribution to the water contamination.

In sections 13.2 and 13.3, we showed why it's justifiable to tax Evi's conduct at a rate that reflects the costs her current and future pollution imposes on Kapo. If we apply the same reasoning to *Historical Pollution*, we might conclude that the state should tax Akna's pollution likewise. But it seems morally problematic to tax them both at the same rate, given that Akna has contributed much more than Evi to the water contamination. To make this concern even more acute, let's imagine that Akna uses some of her earlier profits to purchase expensive green technology so that her factory no longer releases pollutants. Because of this, Akna avoids having to pay any tax, and Evi is left to pick up the tab. This result strikes us as unfair.

The same problem arises in the case of climate change. As an example, let's note that the bulk of industrialization has taken place in urban areas, rather than in rural areas, and it occurred to a greater extent and longer ago in some states than in others. Applying environmental taxes uniformly throughout these regions neglects the greater contribution to climate change made in urban areas and early industrializing states.

---

[20] For discussion, see Megan Blomfield, *Global Justice, Natural Resources, and Climate Change* (Oxford: Oxford University Press, 2019), ch. 9.

Moreover, if those in these places use the wealth generated by this process to invest in greener technology, those in rural areas and in states that industrialized later will end up shouldering a larger share of the burden to fix a problem they contributed less to creating. Again, this result looks unfair.

These judgements underpin a contributor-pays principle, according to which those who play a greater role in generating the threats associated with climate change should shoulder more of the costs to redress them.[21] This idea has considerable intuitive appeal, resting on the familiar conviction that an individual should make amends for having wronged others.

One limitation of this reasoning relates to how to deal with the emissions of past generations. Because many of the individuals who emitted these greenhouse gases are dead, they can't bear the burdens involved in redressing their contributions to climate change. Given that this includes most of those alive between 1800 and 1950, when annual emissions rose from 8 million metric tons to 1,630 million metric tons, this greatly restricts the relevance of contribution on current responses to climate change.[22]

However, our defence of environmental taxes shouldn't ignore the importance of contribution altogether. This is because, even though many past emitters are dead, some are still alive. Carbon emissions increased more than five-fold from 1950 to 2006, with half of the carbon in the atmosphere having been emitted since the 1970s.[23] The living individuals who generated these emissions—mainly those in industrialized states, such as the United Kingdom and the United States and, to a lesser extent, those in newly advanced economies, such as Brazil, Russia, India, and China—stand in the same relation to others as Akna does to Evi and Kapo. They can and should bear extra burdens for redressing a problem that's caused disproportionately by their conduct.

Moreover, even though many historical emitters are dead, the beneficiaries of their actions survive. In some cases, this relationship has moral implications. To see this, let's imagine that Akna's daughter benefits from her mother's history of pollution by receiving a large inheritance. Plausibly, the daughter should bear extra costs to compensate Kapo because her inheritance was made possible by wrongful conduct that occurred at his expense. Like inheriting a stolen heirloom, this is a form of ill-gotten gains that she should return. Generalizing this, we arrive at the beneficiary-pays principle, according to which those who benefit from wrongful conduct that produces climate-related threats should shoulder extra burdens to resolve them.[24] For this

---

[21] Henry Shue, 'Global Environment and International Inequality', *International Affairs*, 75 (1999), 531–45 at 533–7.

[22] Simon Caney, 'Climate Change and the Duties of the Advantaged', *Critical Review of International and Social Political Philosophy*, 13 (2010), 203–28 at 211.

[23] Caney, 'Climate Change and the Duties of the Advantages', 211.

[24] Edward Page, 'Give It Up for Climate Change: A Defence of the Beneficiary Pays Principle', *International Theory*, 4 (2012), 300–30 and Avia Pasternak, 'Benefiting from Wrongdoing' in Kasper Lippert-Rasmussen, Kimberley Brownlee, and David Coady (eds), *A Companion to Applied Philosophy* (Oxford: Wiley, 2016), 411–23.

reason as well, we should demand more of those alive today in states that profited from rapid industrialization, including much of Europe and North America.

Equipped with both of these ideas, an advocate of the historical emissions objection might complain that environmental taxes, applied uniformly to current and future generations, don't distribute costs in a way that's appropriately sensitive to the past.

This objection isn't fatal to our argument. To see this, let's consider how a case for rejecting environmental taxes on this basis might work:

> *Historical emissions moral claim*: A historical emitter and the beneficiaries of this injustice should bear a greater share of the costs of redressing climate change.

> *Uniform taxes empirical claim*: Uniform environmental taxes on current and future emissions don't impose greater costs on a historical emitter or the beneficiaries of this injustice.

> *Conclusion*: The state shouldn't adopt environmental taxes.

The problem with this line of reasoning is that the proposed conclusion doesn't follow from the two claims. First, there's a subtle difference in the wording of the empirical claim and the conclusion. The former notes that *uniform* environmental taxes don't impose greater costs on a historical emitter or the beneficiaries of this injustice. An implication of this might be that the state shouldn't adopt uniform environmental taxes. But we can't conclude from it that the state should give up on our proposal. This is because there are alternatives to uniformity. In particular, the state might adopt discriminatory environmental taxes. For example, it might levy higher rates in particular places, such as in urban areas, or throughout the entire state if it has a history of excessive emissions. Because these taxes would impose greater costs on those who've contributed more to climate change or benefited from the relevant injustices, the historical emissions moral claim gives us no reason to reject them. It follows that, amended to support these specific environmental taxes, our argument survives the historical emissions objection.

Second, we've the option of supplementing environmental taxes with additional policies that address the concern for historical emissions. For example, states that industrialized early could raise general taxation and use the additional funds to redress the effects of the extra contributions they've made to climate change. Thus, we might accept that the historical emissions objection establishes that the state shouldn't adopt *only* uniform environmental taxes, but we can retain the verdict that such taxes are justifiable if the state adopts other policies to take account of the additional costs that historical emitters and their beneficiaries should bear.

Ultimately, we suspect that justifiable environmental policy requires some combination of environmental taxation alongside other measures. But the crucial point for the intergenerational justice argument is, because the state can be appropriately sensitive to the significance of historical emissions in various ways, concerns along these lines provide no reason to reject *some* use of environmental taxes.

13.5 THE IMPACT OF ENVIRONMENTAL TAXES

Another worry about our proposal relates to the way in which it might affect an individual's opportunities to perform certain activities, particularly if they're poor. One version of this concern draws on the fact that environmental taxes would raise living costs significantly. A general increase in day-to-day expenses will affect those who're poor the most since they'll have to forgo a larger proportion of their income than those who're wealthier. In turn, this'll exacerbate existing economic inequalities and it may impoverish some low earners.[25] In Chapter 7, we discuss various accounts of distributive justice that'd condemn this result, and it's intuitive that the state shouldn't impose disproportionate burdens on the worst off in response to climate-related threats. This is the *regressiveness objection*.

A related concern is that environmental taxes will make some particularly valuable pursuits unaffordable, at least to those who aren't wealthy. To elaborate this point, let's imagine that the following two activities have the same environmental impact: (i) heating a home during winter, and (ii) taking a transatlantic holiday. If the state taxes emissions at the same rate, the increase in cost of these two activities will be the same. But this will strike many as objectionable. This is because, whereas heating a home is something that many individuals *need* to do, transatlantic holidays are a *luxury*. This seems to give us reason to treat them differently.[26] This concern might be especially significant with respect to one activity we mentioned that contributes significantly to greenhouse gas emissions, namely having a child. The idea that the state may use tax policy in ways that limit an individual's opportunities to have a family may strike some readers as deeply implausible.[27] This is the *cherished goods objection*.

It strengthens this point further to note, again, that taxes are likely to affect those on low incomes the most. We've some reason to object to any society in which only the affluent can afford to keep a car or take a holiday abroad, but we've even greater reason to object to a society in which only the rich can have children or survive a cold winter in old age. These taxes may mean that those who're poor face horrendous choices, such as between purchasing nutritious food and having adequate warmth.

---

[25] Mette Wier et al., 'Are CO2 Taxes Regressive? Evidence from the Danish Experience', *Ecological Economics*, 52 (2005), 239–52.

[26] Henry Shue, 'Subsistence Emissions and Luxury Emissions', *Law & Policy*, 15 (1993), 39–60. See also Derek Bell and Joanne Swaffield, 'To Fly or Not to Fly? Climate Change, Air Travel, and Moral Responsibility' (unpublished manuscript).

[27] For discussion, see Elizabeth Cripps, 'Climate Change, Population, and Justice: Hard Choices to Avoid Tragic Choices', *Global Justice: Theory, Practice, Rhetoric*, 8 (2015), 1–22; Elizabeth Cripps, 'Population and Environment: The Impossible, The Impermissible, and the Imperative' in Stephen Gardiner and Allen Thompson (eds), *The Oxford Handbook of Environmental Ethics* (Oxford: Oxford University Press, 2016), 380–90; and Sarah Conly, *One Child: Do We Have a Right to More?* (Oxford: Oxford University Press, 2016).

Our response to these two objections is to insist that they aren't fatal to the case for environmental taxes. To see this, let's consider the following formulation of the regressiveness objection:

> *Regressiveness moral claim*: The state shouldn't adopt regressive policies.
>
> *Taxes empirical claim*: Environmental taxes that increase the cost of activities according to their level of environmental damage are regressive.
>
> *Conclusion*: The state shouldn't adopt environmental taxes.

Again, the difficulty with this argument lies in the specifics of the empirical claim and the conclusion. First, while it might be true that environmental taxes that increase the cost of activities according to their level of environmental damage are regressive, this won't be true of other possible options.[28] The state could adopt progressive environmental taxes, which levy higher rates on luxury items purchased disproportionately by the wealthy, such as second homes, fast cars, and private jets. Alternatively, the state could apply environmental taxes exponentially, such that their rates increase in accordance with an individual's level of spending on activities that emit greenhouse gases.

Second, the state could accompany environmental taxes with supplementary policies, such as tax rebates for low-earning individuals. Better yet, it might favour a more comprehensive system of progressive redistribution. Because these approaches work to shift the burdens onto higher earners, the state can mitigate or even reverse the potentially regressive effects of environmental taxes.

Though this may not be immediately obvious, we can make similar points in relation to the cherished goods objection. Let's consider the case of winter heating. The worry here is that environmental taxes may result in an individual being unable to afford to heat their home. But one response is for the state to provide everyone with an environmental allowance, such that the tax would be levied on an individual only once their emissions surpass some threshold. The state could set the level of this allowance to enable an individual to purchase necessities, such as winter heating. Alternatively, it could invest in public programmes to finance home insulation and to subsidize greener electricity. Again, policies of this kind would ease the concern that someone with less means at their disposal would be cut off from cherished goods.

Although this reply might allay some concerns, perhaps it'll not suffice with respect to all. A good example is the case of having a child. On the proposed response, the state might allow an individual to have one or two children without incurring any tax burden, but require those with larger families to pay additional costs. While this'd ensure that those on any income could have children, many will find it problematic that those who're poor will suffer much worse opportunities to have large families.

We might deny that these results are as concerning as they initially seem. Being unable to afford to have a large family is morally different from being priced out of having a family altogether. It's far less bad to be deprived of the option to have *more*

---

[28] Casal, 'Progressive Environmental Taxes', 423–5.

children than the option to have *any* children. Moreover, even if we recognize that losing the opportunity to have a larger family represents a significant cost, desperate times may call for desperate measures. Perhaps averting the threats of climate change requires some significant sacrifices.

Yet we don't need to bite the bullet on this. This is because an alternative is available that follows in the same spirit as our response to the other objections we've considered. More specifically, we can concede that the state shouldn't apply taxes to *all* activities according to the level of environmental damage they cause. But we can retain the idea that the state should apply taxes *selectively*, to some activities. In particular, the state might exempt goods that an individual needs, but tax luxury goods, such as transatlantic flying, at a much greater rate. Meanwhile, even if the state doesn't use taxes to discourage an individual from pursuing cherished goods, it might adopt other policies that have a similar effect. For example, it might attempt to lower birth rates by improving education or access to contraceptives. In short, because the cherished goods objection applies to only some goods, it doesn't give us reason to reject the use of environmental taxes in any wholesale way.

13.6 CONCLUSIONS

In this chapter, we've defended the use of environmental taxes, so as to disincentivize activities that emit greenhouse gases and to raise funds to redress their contribution to climate change. In response to several objections, we've refined this view. We've endorsed making such taxes discriminatory, so that the state can ensure that historical emitters and their beneficiaries bear greater burdens for addressing the threats of climate change. We've endorsed adjusting them to avoid overburdening individuals who're poor and exacerbating economic inequality. And we've endorsed applying them selectively, perhaps lessening or avoiding taxation on certain activities that are especially valuable. However, we insist that these revisions leave untouched a compelling case for the state to adopt environmental taxes as a means of fulfilling the current generation's duty to provide posterity with prospects that are at least as valuable as those it inherited.

For all that we've said on this matter, we've barely scratched the surface of the vast literature examining the causes of climate change, the nature of its threats, and the various policies that the state might adopt in response. One important debate concerns how to deal with uncertainty. We've written about climate change as if we're in possession of the full range of empirical facts. But this is far from the case. Though we can be sure that human activities affect the environment, we're less sure on many issues, such as how easily existing infrastructure can handle climate change and the technological capacity of future generations to respond to it. This raises significant philosophical questions, such as who should bear the burdens associated with this uncertainty.[29] Exploring these

---

[29] For discussion, see Catriona McKinnon, *Climate Change and Future Justice: Precaution, Compensation, and Triage* (London: Routledge, 2012).

questions is a task for another occasion, as are many other matters we've left unsettled, such as determining the right balance of mitigation, adaptation, and loss and damage payments. But with so much at stake, and with the arguments we've offered, we're confident that environmental taxes must be high on the political agenda.

FURTHER READING

For an accessible and thoroughly argued defence of environmental taxes, a good place to begin is Paula Casal, 'Progressive Environmental Taxes', *Political Studies*, 60 (2012), 419–33. Another good read on this is Simon Caney, *On Cosmopolitanism: Equality, Ecology, and Resistance* (Oxford: Oxford University Press, forthcoming), ch. 6.

Arguments that speak against environmental taxes often focus on particular areas or aspects that this strategy shares with various other mechanisms for redressing climate change. An excellent read on strategies targeting population control (such as birth rates) is Elizabeth Cripps, 'Climate Change, Population, and Justice: Hard Choices to Avoid Tragic Choices', *Global Justice: Theory, Practice, Rhetoric*, 8 (2015), 1–22. Meanwhile, a good discussion of the claim that environmental taxes are regressive is Mette Wier et al., 'Are CO2 Taxes Regressive? Evidence from the Danish Experience', *Ecological Economics*, 52 (2005), 239–51.

For an overview of positions on what we owe to future generations, see Lukas Meyer, 'Intergenerational Justice', *Stanford Encyclopedia of Philosophy* (2015), available at https://plato.stanford.edu/entries/justice-intergenerational. For statements of principles of intergenerational justice and arguments among them, see the collection of chapters on 'Global Justice and Future Generations' in Stephen Gardiner et al. (eds), *Climate Ethics: Essential Readings* (Oxford: Oxford University Press, 2010).

For additional material and resources, including web links and self-test questions, please visit the online resources
www.oup.com/he/walton1e.

14

IMMIGRATION AND THE POLITICAL COMMUNITY

SUMMARY

- In this chapter, we argue against policies that restrict immigration. We contend that states should have open borders that allow an individual to move between political communities.
- We begin by defending a presumption in favour of open borders that appeals to the value of freedom of movement.
- We respond to those who deny that freedom of movement is sufficiently important to generate such a presumption, as well as to those who insist that states enjoy a prerogative over whether or not to grant an individual the opportunity to migrate.
- We outline an objection to open borders that refers to their potentially harmful effects on those in developing states. We reply by pointing out that the existence of these effects is controversial and that, even if they do exist, it's better to respond in ways other than closing borders.
- We consider a range of objections that emphasize how open borders can jeopardize the security, economy, and culture of receiving states. We show that a proper concern for these values is consistent with borders that are largely (even if not fully) open.
- Finally, we reflect on the implications of our argument.

14.1 INTRODUCTION

Few issues dominate headlines more than immigration. We regularly see pictures and videos of large numbers of individuals making treacherous journeys across land and sea to start new lives in more prosperous places. Few of us are entirely unmoved by this, and some take it as clear evidence of the injustice of existing immigration policies. Yet, others oppose this idea very strongly. Indeed, much of the electorate in affluent states believe that current rates of immigration are too high. In response, many states are making their border policies even more restrictive.[1]

---

[1] Melissa Edey, 'Austria Could Be the Next E.U. Country to Tighten Its Borders', *New York Times*, 3 July 2018, available at https://www.nytimes.com/2018/07/03/world/europe/austria-borders-migrants-kurz.html.

One reason that immigration causes such controversy is that multiple factors bear on this hotly contested topic. Among other things, disputes about immigration raise issues relating to migrant poverty, the protection of security and national culture, freedom of movement, and economic development and sustainability. But the bearing of each of these issues ultimately turns on different views about who's entitled to membership of a *political community*. For example, those who advocate for open borders on grounds of promoting freedom of movement stress the importance of granting an individual the opportunity to join new political communities. By contrast, those who favour restrictive immigration policies emphasize the need to protect existing political communities by allowing them to limit their membership.

In this chapter, we explore these matters by arguing for the position that states have few reasons to restrict immigration and, therefore, that they should have largely open borders. This means that we reject both the view that states should have closed borders, and the view that they should enjoy the capacity to exclude migrants at will, for any reason they like. Our conclusion is a radical one that involves a serious departure from the prevailing immigration policies in many parts of the world.

To limit the scope of our investigation, we focus on what we call *opportunity migrants*— that is, those who seek better educational or employment prospects, association with friends or family members, or a more pleasant political or cultural environment.[2] For the most part, we set aside the case of refugees—that is, those fleeing from persecution, persistent violations of their human rights, environmental devastation, and so forth—as well as those who visit other states only temporarily, such as tourists. However, as will become apparent, our arguments have implications for these groups too.

We proceed as follows. In section 14.2, we offer an argument for open borders that appeals to the moral importance of freedom of movement. In section 14.3, we respond to objections from those who deny that this interest is sufficiently valuable to justify this conclusion. In section 14.4, we consider and respond to an argument for closed borders that's grounded in our duties to address global poverty. In section 14.5, we analyse a range of further reasons that are often cited as part of the case against open borders. These concern security, the economy, and culture. We argue that, while some of these reasons are important, they can support only a modest amendment to our proposal. We conclude in section 14.6.

14.2 THE CASE FOR OPEN BORDERS

Migration restrictions prevent a would-be opportunity migrant from settling in a state's territory and becoming a member of its political community. The most familiar way in which this occurs is through immigration policies, which restrict the entry of a would-be migrant into a particular state. However, it's also possible to prevent a would-be migrant from crossing borders through emigration policies, which restrict exit from

---

[2] Anna Stilz, *Territorial Sovereignty: A Philosophical Exploration* (Oxford: Oxford University Press, 2019), 187.

the territory in which they currently reside. In both cases, these migration restrictions limit an individual's freedom to cross borders in order to settle in other states. This point is important because it helps to explain one attractive feature of open borders, namely that they enhance an individual's freedom by providing them with the option of becoming a member of another political community.

In Chapters 2–4, we discuss the value and limits of different freedoms. Here, we focus on the ways in which the freedom to migrate is especially morally valuable. One argument starts by noting that this freedom is necessary in order for an individual to enjoy *freedom of movement*, which is commonly held to be one of the most significant liberties.[3] To give this point some intuitive force, let's consider the fact that it's very difficult to justify detaining an individual, placing them under house arrest, or confining them to one part of the country. We might think that, even without exploring the reasons that underlie this verdict, it's safe to assume that our general support for freedom of movement indicates that it'll be very difficult to justify restricting an individual's freedom to migrate.

To be sure, there may be instances in which other concerns outweigh this value. For example, states sometimes put individuals in prison or limit their movement through the use of electronic tags to reduce the risk of harm to others. But these activities are controversial and, if they're justifiable at all, it's because there are very serious competing interests at stake. To restrict an individual's freedom of movement in the absence of such a justification rightly provokes outrage. Arguably, we should feel similar outrage about restrictions on migration.

This argument makes use of the idea that whatever reasons support freedom of movement in several cases with which we're familiar in the domestic context seem likely to support freedom of movement beyond this context too. This line of reasoning suggests that we don't need to know the content of these reasons in order to advance the claim that we should treat the two similarly. However, we think this is too quick. For example, as we discuss in Chapter 3, just because there are reasons to permit some kinds of offensive speech, it doesn't follow that we should permit hate speech. In order to work out whether this is the case, we must examine the value and limits of freedom of expression. The same goes for freedom of movement.[4]

With this in mind, let's turn our attention to the content of our reasons to value *domestic* freedom of movement. Most obviously, this is important because of the central role it plays in many individuals' lives. It enables someone to relocate to other areas of their state in order to enjoy better prospects for education or employment, to reunify with friends or family members, and to reside in places with their favoured political or cultural environment. Even many of those who don't relocate value the option of being able to do so. In these ways, freedom of movement serves a range of significant goods, including an individual's educational and economic prospects, their freedom of association (including their freedom of intimate association), and their political and cultural concerns.

---

[3] Joseph Carens, *The Ethics of Immigration* (Oxford: Oxford University Press, 2013), ch. 11.

[4] Stilz, *Territorial Sovereignty*, 203.

This analysis is instructive because all of these interests also supply us with reasons to protect freedom of movement across international borders. After all, individuals often settle in another state's territory for the very same reasons, namely to enjoy better prospects for education or employment, to reunify with friends or family members, or to reside in places that they prefer politically or culturally.[5] So, on this closer inspection, it seems reasonable to infer that the same concerns that support domestic freedom of movement offer a presumptive case for open borders.

It adds to this to consider the fact that it isn't only an individual who crosses borders who has interests in the opportunity to do so.[6] To take an obvious example, when Amir is able to move to a new political community to reunite with his partner, Oliana, it not only serves Amir's interests in freedom of association, but Oliana's too. The general point is that we mustn't overlook the significant ways in which border controls affect the interests of the would-be friends, family, and employers of those looking to migrate.

Together, these considerations explain the importance of the freedom to migrate. In virtue of the interests that this freedom serves, we've a presumption in favour of open borders. This places the burden of proof on defenders of migration restrictions. We call this the *argument from freedom of movement*, and we can state it as follows:

Freedom of movement moral claim: The state should protect an individual's freedom of movement.

Open borders empirical claim: Whereas open borders protect an individual's freedom of movement, migration restrictions don't.

Conclusion: The state should have open borders.

The conclusion of this argument isn't absolute. As we've noted, there are other moral concerns that bear on when the state should allow or restrict freedom of movement. Accordingly, the appropriate conclusion to draw from our argument is a conditional one: the state should have open borders, *unless* there are countervailing considerations that defeat this presumption. This clause is sensible because it's appropriate sometimes to restrict freedoms when there are competing interests at stake. And it's this possibility that an opponent of open borders may seize on to defend their view. Let's now consider some objections along these lines.

14.3 IS MIGRATION A LUXURY?

Some critics of the argument from freedom of movement contest the presumption in favour of open borders. Proponents of this challenge tend not to dispute the claim that freedom of movement is valuable or that restrictions on migration can set back

---

[5] Chandran Kukathas, 'The Case for Open Immigration' in Andrew I. Cohen and Christopher Heath Wellman (eds), *Contemporary Debates in Applied Ethics, Second Edition* (Oxford: Wiley Blackwell, 2014), 376–88 at 380.
[6] Joseph Carens, 'Aliens and Citizens: The Case for Open Borders', *Review of Politics*, 49 (1987), 251–73 at 253.

this value. Rather, they maintain that the freedom to cross borders isn't the kind of freedom that states *must* protect. Instead, they argue that it's the kind of freedom that states can choose whether or not to protect. If correct, the implication of this is that states should enjoy a permission to exclude migrants at will.

In order to mobilize this response, it helps to draw a distinction between two kinds of freedom.[7] On the one hand, there are *basic* freedoms that are part of a minimum entitlement that's owed to everyone. On the other hand, there are *wider* freedoms that go beyond this minimum entitlement. For example, whereas everyone is entitled to avoid starvation, the opportunity to drive around in a luxury sports car is something that'd be nice to enjoy but that isn't owed to anyone. This distinction is important because, though the state has a duty to protect basic freedoms, it has a prerogative over whether or not to protect wider freedoms. Therefore, if the freedom to migrate were merely a wider freedom and not a basic freedom, then we'd have no presumption in favour of its protection. What would follow is that states should enjoy discretionary control over their migration policies, and they could have restricted borders if they wish. We call this the *wider freedoms objection*.

In support of this objection, let's review some of section 14.2's discussions. It's beyond doubt that detaining someone who's innocent violates their freedom of movement. However, we can curtail freedom of movement in many other ways that are much more trivial.[8] For example, trespass laws forbid an individual from entering others' property or land without permission, and traffic laws prohibit someone from driving on the wrong side of the road or from parking in an unauthorized area. Though these regulations set back an individual's freedom of movement, we find them morally acceptable. This is partly because they set back only wider freedoms, and because they leave an individual's basic freedoms intact.

It can be tricky to work out which freedoms we should class as basic and which we should class as wider. One possibility is that a freedom is basic if it's essential for an individual to live a decent life, where this requires only an *adequate* range of options from which to select, rather than the *fullest* range of options. This test can explain why we judge avoiding starvation very differently to the opportunity to drive a luxury sports car. In particular, while the former is essential to any adequate range of options, the latter is only among the class of a fuller range of options.

The wider freedoms objection implies that we should treat differently the following two categories of migrants. On the one hand, there are refugees. Historically, refugees are defined as those fleeing persecution. Some argue that this definition is too narrow, and that we should expand it to include any individual whose basic freedoms (or other basic interests) aren't protected in their state. On this definition, an individual who migrates to avoid economic deprivation or environmental devastation may qualify

---

[7] David Miller, *Strangers in Our Midst: The Political Philosophy of Immigration* (Cambridge, MA: Harvard University Press, 2016), ch. 3.

[8] David Miller, 'Immigration: The Case for Limits' in Cohen and Wellman (eds), *Contemporary Debates in Applied Ethics*, 363–75 at 365.

as a refugee.[9] Proponents of the present objection recognize that the state has a duty to ensure that everyone's basic freedoms are protected, and that this will sometimes require opening borders to refugees.

On the other hand, there are opportunity migrants who seek better educational or employment prospects, association with friends or family members, or a more pleasant political or cultural environment, but whose basic freedoms aren't in danger. Those who press the wider freedoms objection concede that open borders might enhance the wider freedoms of these individuals, but they maintain that, since states have no duty to deliver this, migration policy is something that falls within their discretion.

We might bolster this view by pointing out that, even if we acknowledge that migration restrictions can set back an individual's basic freedom, the argument from freedom of movement seems to support only *sufficiently* open borders. This requires only that each individual has a range of states to which they can emigrate, rather than access to all other states. As David Miller puts it:

> Contingently, of course, it may be true that moving to another country is the only way for an individual to escape persecution, to find work, to obtain necessary medical care, and so forth. In these circumstances the person concerned may have the right to move, not to any state that she chooses, but to *some* state where these interests can be protected.[10]

Moreover, we can ask the same question of wider freedoms. In other words, even when migration policies set back only the wider freedoms of opportunity migrants, why does this count in favour of open borders rather than sufficiently open borders? In practice, what this suggests is that we might guarantee an individual's freedom to migrate within a particular area, such as within the European Union, but then leave it to each state to decide their migration policies beyond this.

We've two responses to the wider freedoms objection. First, it's unclear why we should think that the freedom to move within a state is a basic freedom, but the freedom to migrate is a wider freedom. We might reasonably ask: why would it be wrong to confine an individual to a particular region (or perhaps a handful of regions) within the United States, but not wrong to confine them to a particular country (or perhaps a handful of countries) in South East Asia? This response is particularly forceful when the opportunities to emigrate from the latter are at least as valuable as the opportunities to emigrate from the former, as may be true in this example.

Second, an implication of the wider freedoms objection is that states should enjoy discretionary control over their migration policies, and so they're morally permitted to close their borders if they wish, even when immigration has no harmful effects, either on their local inhabitants or those abroad.[11] But it's difficult to see what could justify this view. Since it'd serve a would-be migrant's freedom to be able to relocate,

---

[9] Michelle Foster, *International Refugee Law and Socio-Economic Rights: Refuge from Deprivation* (Cambridge: Cambridge University Press, 2007).

[10] Miller, 'Immigration', 365.   [11] Stilz, *Territorial Sovereignty*, 207.

it's plausible that states have a duty to allow this when their movement isn't harmful to anyone else.

Proponents of more restrictive immigration practices may be critical of these two suggestions, maintaining that there are special reasons that explain why states should control who may enter their political community, and where this means that they should enjoy a prerogative to exclude migrants at will. Some defences of this claim appeal to the idea that it's either intrinsically or instrumentally valuable for members of a state to enjoy a shared culture.[12] Others emphasize the threat of institutional takeover from outsiders.[13] But if these arguments are persuasive, then it's because we've reasons that defeat the presumption in favour of open borders, and *not* because there's no presumption at all. Accordingly, it pays for us to examine more closely the value of these reasons. In section 14.4, we look at an argument that appeals to the interests of those in states that migrants leave behind. After that, we turn our attention to several arguments that highlight the interests of those in receiving states.

14.4 BRAIN DRAIN

As we note in Chapter 15, hundreds of millions of individuals around the world lack access to many of life's essentials, including adequate food, shelter, sanitation, clothing, and healthcare. Few contest that this is a morally terrible state of affairs, that it'd be better if no one lived in poverty, and that these facts make various demands on how we should act.

These issues bear on the design of migration policies in several ways. We mentioned one of these when developing the argument from freedom of movement, namely that a valuable thing about the freedom to migrate is the opportunities it provides to those seeking to avoid deprivation. We now turn our attention to an argument that runs in the opposite direction. This stems from the concern that, if we protect an individual's opportunities to migrate, then this may worsen the prospects of those they leave behind, who continue to reside in their state of origin. This threat arises from the fact that the highly skilled are more likely to emigrate. The departure of these individuals means that the origin state loses productive workers and many of those who can make valuable contributions to reducing poverty. We call this the *brain drain objection* to open borders.

To illustrate the force of this objection, let's consider the case of healthcare.[14] Lacking access to this good is one aspect of poverty. But since individuals in affluent states also get ill, there's demand for healthcare workers in those parts of the world as well. In fact, many affluent states offer generous incentives to medical professionals to migrate in order to enhance the level of healthcare that their members enjoy.

---

[12] David Miller, *Citizenship and National Identity* (Cambridge: Polity Press, 2000).

[13] Christopher Heath Wellman, 'Immigration and Freedom of Association', *Ethics*, 119 (2008), 109–41.

[14] Gillian Brock, *Global Justice: A Cosmopolitan Account* (Oxford: Oxford University Press, 1999), 198–204.

This can be attractive for an individual wanting to improve their economic prospects or looking to relocate for other reasons. But one likely consequence is that there'll be fewer individuals with medical qualifications to meet the healthcare needs of those in the state from which individuals emigrate. Moving from Ghana to the United States might benefit the doctor and their new patients, but it's likely to harm those in need of their medical expertise in Ghana. In this way, open borders might exacerbate the healthcare problems faced by members of poorer states. Moreover, this worry isn't merely speculative. Some evidence indicates a pattern along these lines. For example, data suggests that there's a positive correlation between physician emigration from sub-Saharan Africa and adult HIV-related deaths.[15]

Healthcare is merely one arena among many in which open borders might worsen the prospects of members of political communities from which highly skilled individuals would emigrate. The same phenomenon arises in the case of education and the civil service, as well as in industries in which high rates of productivity attract greater international investments. The more general point is that open borders enable highly skilled workers, who've the potential to assist in the economic development of their state, to leave for more attractive opportunities elsewhere.

What're the implications of these considerations? One possibility is that duties to respond to poverty are sufficiently weighty that an affluent state should close its borders to would-be migrants from poorer states for the sake of those who'd be harmed by the emigration of highly skilled workers. This wouldn't justify shutting the doors completely. But an advocate might hold that it justifies *selectively* closed borders, whereby an affluent state should restrict entry to anyone who's likely to contribute to poverty-relief by remaining in their origin state.[16] The brain drain objection therefore identifies an important consideration to which defenders of open borders must be sensitive. We can state its case as follows:

Poverty moral claim: The state should adopt policies that reduce global poverty.

Brain drain empirical claim: Whereas borders of affluent states that are open to highly skilled migrants exacerbate global poverty, closed borders don't.

Conclusion: An affluent state should close its borders to highly skilled migrants.

In reply to this argument, we make four points. First, there's much criticism of the brain drain empirical claim. In response to the supportive findings that we've already noted, critics point to the numerous ways in which members of states *benefit* from the emigration of highly skilled workers. For example, open borders increase an individual's incentives to invest in their education, as the potential reward is greater than it'd be otherwise. While some individuals who engage in additional training will then emigrate, not all of them will do so, and even fewer of them will emigrate as soon as

---

[15] Alok Bhargava and Frédéric Docquier, 'HIV Pandemic, Medical Brain Drain, and Economic Development in Sub-Saharan Africa', *World Bank Economic Review*, 22 (2008), 345–66.

[16] Brock, *Global Justice*, 208–10.

they're qualified. Additionally, large flows of remittances from skilled emigrants can more than offset the costs of their departures.[17] Furthermore, there's substantial evidence that the departure of highly skilled workers can lead to increased investment in the states they leave, as some emigrants return home after a period abroad.[18] In short, whether open borders lead to a *brain drain* or a *brain gain* is a complicated empirical issue that varies across contexts. This doesn't mean we've sufficient evidence to reject the brain drain empirical claim. But it does indicate that we should be cautious when advancing arguments that rely on it.

Second, even if open borders produce a brain drain, a state might eliminate this effect by accompanying open borders with additional policies that compensate for it.[19] An affluent state might continue to recruit highly skilled immigrants from poorer countries, but only on the condition that these migrants agree to make remittance payments. Alternatively, an affluent state might make direct payments to the state that migrants leave. Therefore, even if the brain drain empirical claim is true, the conclusion of the argument above doesn't follow, because we can adopt other institutional arrangements to combat global poverty without closing borders.

Third, we might think that states not only *could* respond to the brain drain in different ways, but that they *should* opt for these alternatives. The brain drain objection appeals to the duties of an affluent state to address global poverty in order to justify migration restrictions. But it's plausible that an affluent state should discharge its duties to reduce global poverty via other avenues.[20] As we argue in Chapter 15, we think that affluent states should commit substantial funds to poverty-relief, as well as lobby to reform international institutions to serve this goal. One reason to prefer these strategies is that they're likely to be more effective at reducing poverty because they address one of the main structural causes from which the problem stems. Meanwhile, they combat poverty without restricting migration, and so they avoid setting back anyone's freedom of movement.

Finally, the brain drain objection challenges the justifiability of open borders by identifying a countervailing consideration that purports to defeat the value of freedom of movement. This reason relates to the importance of addressing poverty. But it's not obvious that we should be willing to sacrifice freedom of movement in order to protect against whatever negative consequences are associated with brain drain. To see this, it helps to note that, even within states in which some regions are comparatively deprived, we rarely think that it's justifiable to restrict the freedom of movement

[17] William Easterly and Yaw Nyarko, 'Is Brain Drain Good for Africa?' in Jagdish Bhagwati and Gordon Hanson (eds), *Skilled Immigration Today: Prospects, Problems, and Policies* (Oxford: Oxford University Press, 2009), 316–61.

[18] William Kerr, 'Ethnic Scientific Communities and International Technology Diffusion', *Review of Economics and Statistics*, 90 (2008), 518–37 and AnnaLee Saxenian, 'Brain Circulation: How High-Skill Immigration Makes Everyone Better Off', *Brookings Review*, 20 (2002), 28–31.

[19] Jagdish Bhagwati, 'The United States in the Nixon Era: The End of Innocence,' *Daedalus*, 101 (1972), 25–47 and Anna Stilz, 'Is There an Unqualified Right to Leave?' in Sarah Fine and Lea Ypi (eds), *Migration in Political Theory* (Oxford: Oxford University Press, 2016), 57–79.

[20] Kieran Oberman, 'Can Brain Drain Justify Immigration Restrictions?', *Ethics*, 123 (2013), 427–55.

of highly skilled workers in order to improve the prospects of those in that area. At the very least, proponents of this objection again face the task of explaining why we should treat domestic and international freedom of movement so differently.

14.5 THE HARMFUL EFFECTS OF IMMIGRATION

Let's now examine arguments against open borders that appeal to the interests of those in states that receive migrants. Advocates of these views worry that open borders are detrimental to a range of morally valuable goods. These fall into three groups: those relating to security, to the economy, and to culture. Arguments of this kind are politically popular, and we agree that they sometimes contain a kernel of truth. However, these considerations can't justify extensive restrictions on migration. Critics cite these factors in support of the conclusion that states should have closed borders, or that they should enjoy the capacity to exclude migrants at will. We argue that, at most, these reasons can justify only very minor restrictions on immigration.

One purpose of the state is to serve an individual's interest in being a member of a political community.[21] This is relevant because several conditions are necessary for political communities to function well. One of these is security, without which it can be impossible to maintain fair and effective institutions that persist over time. Another is the economy. In order to deliver benefits to its members, a state must be able to protect their economic opportunities and use its resources to provide public goods, such as infrastructure, education, and healthcare. Finally, we've the state's culture—or, more precisely, its members' culture. Arguably, without a stable set of shared commitments, members lack a valuable sense of community and can't rely on each other to act in ways that sustain their common institutions. Critics of open borders often point to one or more of these goods in order to justify restricting migration, claiming that unlimited flows of new members into the political community are likely to disrupt the state's functioning. This is the *community goods objection*.

It's consistent with this objection that there's a presumption in favour of open borders. The central claim that its advocates invoke is that the reasons that support this presumption are defeated by the harmful effects of immigration.[22] Pressing this objection involves the following claims:

Community goods moral claim: The state may set back an individual's freedom to migrate in order to protect its political community's security, economy, and culture.

Community goods empirical claim: Open borders are more harmful to security, the economy, and culture than closed borders.

Conclusion: The state should have closed borders.

---

[21] Stilz, *Territorial Sovereignty*, ch. 1. For further discussion of a value of political community, see Anna Stilz, 'Decolonization and Self-Determination', *Social Philosophy and Policy*, 32 (2015), 1–24.

[22] For one version of this argument, see Miller, 'Immigration: The Case for Limits' and Miller, *Strangers in Our Midst*, ch. 6.

We'll examine the plausibility of this objection with respect to each of the community goods that we've mentioned. Casting doubt on each of the claims, we conclude that the most they can justify is that borders should be largely open rather than fully open.[23]

14.5.1 SECURITY

The idea that open borders might jeopardize a state's security has considerable traction in much of the public debate about immigration. Newspapers are replete with stories of immigrants allegedly involved in illegal activities, including terrorism. We agree that states have reasons for closing their borders to those known to be involved in terrorist activities, as well as in response to other genuine threats to their security, such as invading armies. However, in practice, the kinds of restrictions that these concerns justify are *much* more minimal than is suggested by media coverage of these issues. This is for two reasons.[24]

First, the relationship between a state's border policies and its security is a complex one. For example, screening for terrorists doesn't guarantee security. One reason for this is that some of the relevant threats, especially those associated with cyber-terrorism, can be carried out from abroad. Additionally, some of those who're desperate to cross borders to engage in activities that threaten security will enter on tourist visas, or illegally if necessary. This isn't to deny that effective border controls can reduce threats to security to some extent. Our point is that other factors, such as vigilant domestic law enforcement, may have a much larger bearing on these issues.

Second, border security screening can be hugely costly. Let's pause for a moment to consider what this involves. If states enact more exacting conditions for entering their political community, border officials will have to interrogate an individual's travel arrangements, as well as their residential, employment, and travel history. When this scrutiny affects someone who poses a threat to security, these costs may be justifiable. But we shouldn't look at these costs in isolation from the fact that the overwhelming majority of those subject to these vetting processes are wholly innocent. Meanwhile, if states attempt to ensure their security by fully restricting immigration, they'll have to pay for a patrol force to watch and protect every inch of the border. Simply put, even if occasionally effective, there are some border control policies that must be ruled out either because of their enormous financial expense or because their level of intrusion in individuals' lives is too great.

Altogether, it's far from clear that the community goods empirical claim is plausible with respect to security. While it may be true that some regime other than fully open borders is optimal, only a very minimal departure from this can be justifiable in the light of security-based concerns. As we've suggested, the most that this can justify is that a state can restrict immigration to only a very minor extent.

---

[23] Much of the analysis in the remainder of this section draws on Stilz, *Territorial Sovereignty*, ch. 7.

[24] Kukathas, 'The Case for Open Immigration', 386–7.

14.5.2 THE ECONOMY

There are two dimensions to the concern that open borders might have harmful economic effects. First, some oppose open borders on the grounds that, because immigration increases the supply of labour within a state, they lower employees' wages or increase the rate of unemployment.[25] This concern is especially serious when it's the least advantaged who suffer most. Second, others oppose open borders on the grounds that, because immigration increases the number of those reliant on public services, they increase the strain on these services. In support of this concern, commentators might point to the fact that the comparative generosity of the welfare system in most affluent states may attract those seeking to live off of public benefits and that some immigrants, especially from poorer states, are unlikely to have the skills to integrate without considerable social support.

The majority of the literature finds little or no impact of immigration on the rate of unemployment.[26] Evidence of the effect on wages is more mixed.[27] But even where it's alleged to suppress the wages of the lowest earners, typically when rates of immigration are very high, the effect is small. This is because native-born workers tend not to compete directly with immigrants, whose communication skills and smaller pool of contacts mean that they seek other kinds of jobs. Moreover, this trend is normally accompanied by an increase in average wages, some of which the state could tax in order to eliminate the harmful effects of immigration on the wages of the worst off.[28] Regarding public services, comprehensive summaries of research indicate that immigration is a financial benefit to receiving states and, therefore, that it's a mistake to worry about welfare systems being pushed to breaking point.[29]

We must be careful to avoid overconfidence here. We recognize that high rates of immigration may disrupt public services in the short and medium term as they adjust to higher numbers of users. Even if immigrants contribute more than they receive, it still takes time to expand a hospital or to build a new school. More generally, it's important to bear in mind that the evidence we've detailed is based on current levels of migration, which are restricted in several ways. For this reason, it's difficult to extrapolate from these findings to what might happen if borders between states were fully open.

---

[25] Stephen Macedo, 'The Moral Dilemma of US Immigration Policy: Open Borders versus Social Justice?' in Carol Swain (ed.), *Debating Immigration* (New York: Cambridge University Press, 2007), 63–81.

[26] Raquel Carrasco, Juan Jimeno, and A. Carolina Ortega, 'The Effect of Immigration on the Labour Market Performance of Native-Born Workers: Some Evidence for Spain', *Journal of Population Economics*, 21 (2008), 627–48; Paolo Lucchino, Chiara Rosazza-Bondibene, and Jonathan Portes, 'Examining the Relationship Between Immigration and Unemployment Using National Insurance Number Registration Data', *NIESR Discussion Paper*, No. 386 (2012); and The National Academies of Sciences, Engineering, and Medicine, *The Economic and Fiscal Consequences of Immigration* (Washington, DC: The National Academies Press, 2016).

[27] For example, see David Card, 'Is the New Immigration Really So Bad?', *Economic Journal*, 115 (2005), 300–23 and George J. Borjas, 'The Labor Demand Curve Is Downward Sloping: Reexamining the Impact of Immigration on the Labor Market', *Quarterly Journal of Economics*, 118 (2003), 1335–74.

[28] David Card, 'Immigration Inflows, Native Outflows, and the Local Labor Market Impacts of Higher Immigration', *Journal of Labour Economics*, 19 (2001), 22–64.

[29] Francine D. Blau and Christopher Mackie (eds), *The Economic and Fiscal Consequences of Immigration* (Washington, DC: The National Academies Press, 2017).

Nonetheless, it's significant that analyses of the economic impact of current rates of immigration are generally positive. This means that this lends little support to the community goods empirical claim in relation to economic concerns. Though we don't rule out the force of an argument relying on this claim, the available evidence places the burden of proof squarely on the shoulders of critics of open borders.

14.5.3 CULTURE

Miller opposes open borders on the grounds that some say over the membership of a political community is vital for maintaining its culture, including its shared language, practices, and public and religious institutions.[30] The worry with open borders is that an influx of immigrants arriving with their own languages, religions, and cultural norms will reduce the ability of the existing population to continue their culture. This harm may be particularly serious in the case of indigenous communities, whose traditional ways of life wouldn't survive in the face of this.[31]

However, we should be cautious in advancing this line of reasoning. This is because local inhabitants are sometimes hostile towards immigrants who they perceive as a threat to their culture. These inhabitants may be unwilling to associate with them because of prejudice. For example, those who value living in an all-white community might complain about the migration of blacks into the area. Even advocates of this objection note that these concerns don't supply us with a valid basis on which to restrict migration.[32] This is because we should exclude complaints that are grounded in the unreasonable judgement that certain groups of individuals are morally inferior to others. We do no wrong to fascists, racists, and imperialists when we deny them the opportunity to continue their culture of prejudice. The upshot of this is that we can have reasons to restrict migration only when it poses harms to social practices that aren't unjust or a product of prejudice.

In cases where there's such a threat, we agree that this may occasionally justify limiting the rate of immigration. But we believe that it can't justify anything approximating closed borders. This is for two reasons. First, it's a mistake to think that high levels of immigration necessarily disrupt the prevailing culture within a state. In most cases, a significant proportion of migrants will adopt (some of) the cultural commitments of the political community to which they move, especially when they're welcomed hospitably. And even when this isn't the case, the state might limit cultural harms by enacting legislation to protect established social practices against the threats that immigration might otherwise pose. Examples of this include the use of cultural subsidies or citizenship tests. For this reason, it's doubtful that the community goods empirical claim is plausible with respect to concerns about culture.

---

[30] Miller, 'Immigration: The Case for Limits', 369–70 and Miller, *Strangers in Our Midst*, ch. 6.
[31] Stilz, *Territorial Sovereignty*, 200.   [32] Miller, *Strangers in Our Midst*, 105.

Second, even where immigration restrictions are the only way in which to guard against cultural harms, it's doubtful that the community goods moral claim is attractive in this case. Let's recall that this claim holds that the state may set back an individual's freedom to migrate in order to protect its culture. But it's unclear that shared social practices are sufficiently important to justify these restrictions.[33] Making this case is particularly difficult given that, although the effects of many waves of immigration have been viewed with suspicion at the time, many individuals reflect positively on those changes after the event.

One way to approach this challenge is to focus on the relationship between immigration and social trust. Some scholars express concern that the increased cultural diversity that open borders enables erodes social trust. In turn, this reduces individuals' willingness to maintain fair terms of cooperation between members, jeopardizing the stability of institutions such as the welfare state. On this view, one instrumental reason for prioritizing existing culture is that it extends the life-expectancy of the social structures of a political community.

These claims are controversial, as critics argue that social trust depends to a greater extent on a state's institutional arrangements than on the characteristics of its population.[34] Moreover, it's significant that, where cultural diversity does undermine social trust, this is only because of attitudes towards those who're perceived as different. As Anna Stilz explains, this is important for the following reason:

> People's attitudes are not a brute sociological fact: they are subject to rational control, and where those attitudes are intrinsically morally objectionable, we should try to alter them. Public policy may foster increased social interaction in diverse contexts, or institute civic education programs to combat prejudice against migrants.[35]

If this is correct, the implication of these concerns about culture isn't that the state should restrict immigration. It's that the state should adopt policies that allow its political institutions to flourish in the face of cultural diversity.

14.6 CONCLUSIONS

The most immediate upshot of our arguments in this chapter is that states should have borders that are largely or entirely open. The main reason for this is that doing so enhances an individual's freedom of movement and that states have few reasons to restrict membership of their political community.

---

[33] Samuel Scheffler, 'Immigration and the Significance of Culture', *Philosophy & Public Affairs*, 35 (2007), 93–125.

[34] Will Kymlicka and Keith Banting, 'Immigration, Multiculturalism, and the Welfare State', *Ethics and International Affairs*, 20 (2006), 281–304.   [35] Stilz, *Territorial Sovereignty*, 196.

We've considered the idea that it may be justifiable for states to adopt measures whose purpose is to ensure that immigration occurs without damaging their security, economy, or culture. But it bears emphasizing that the burden of proof here lies with those who advocate these policies. To make such a case, they must do two things. First, they must show that immigration produces certain effects. This involves empirical analysis. Second, they must show that these effects are sufficiently bad so as to justify restricting freedom of movement. This involves moral analysis. On the basis of our discussion, we're open to the possibility that there might be some persuasive arguments of this kind, but we maintain that any migration restrictions that they justify will be minor.

FURTHER READING

A good overview of writing on immigration is Christopher Heath Wellman, 'Immigration', *Stanford Encyclopedia of Philosophy* (2019), available at https://plato.stanford.edu/entries/immigration.

For arguments in favour of open borders or largely open borders, good places to begin are Joseph Carens, 'Aliens and Citizens: The Case for Open Borders', *Review of Politics*, 49 (1987), 251–73. A sophisticated variation of this argument is developed in Anna Stilz, *Territorial Sovereignty: A Philosophical Exploration* (Oxford: Oxford University Press, 2019), esp. in ch. 7. For an alternative argument in defence of a similar conclusion, there's David Owen, 'Migration, Structural Injustice and Domination: On "Race", Mobility and Transnational Positional Difference', *Journal of Ethnic and Migration Studies*, 46 (2020), 2585–601.

Opposing arguments often focus on particular goods that would be set back by the requirement for states to have open borders. Accessible and influential arguments of this kind are developed by David Miller in his *Strangers in Our Midst: The Political Philosophy of Immigration* (Cambridge, MA: Harvard University Press, 2016), ch. 3 and his 'Immigration: The Case for Limits' in Andrew I. Cohen and Christopher Heath Wellman (eds), *Contemporary Debates in Applied Ethics, Second Edition* (Oxford: Wiley Blackwell, 2014), 363–75. A related argument is discussed in Christopher Heath Wellman, 'Immigration and Freedom of Association', *Ethics*, 119 (2008), 109–41, with an interesting reply coming in Sarah Fine, 'Freedom of Association Is Not the Answer', *Ethics*, 120 (2010), 338–56.

For excellent discussion of the brain drain and its bearing on the justifiability of migration restrictions, there's Gillian Brock, 'Part I' in Gillian Brock and Michael Blake, *Debating Brain Drain: May Governments Restrict Emigration?* (Oxford: Oxford University Press, 2015), 11–110 and Kieran Oberman, 'Can Brain Drain Justify Immigration Restrictions?', *Ethics*, 123 (2013), 427–55.

 For additional material and resources, including web links and self-test questions, please visit the online resources **www.oup.com/he/walton1e**.

15

DEVELOPMENT AID
AND GLOBAL JUSTICE

SUMMARY

- In this chapter, we consider whether affluent states should commit significant funds to alleviate poverty abroad. We argue not only that they should, but also that their duties to those who live in poverty go far beyond this.
- We formulate an argument in favour of development aid that's based on the idea that an individual has a duty to prevent something very bad from happening when they can do so at little cost to themselves.
- We engage with those who contend that poverty is caused solely by the policies of the state in which it exists. In response, we point out that the global order plays a significant role in the persistence of global poverty, and we explain how this supports the case for development aid.
- We consider the claim that states should prioritize meeting the claims of their own members ahead of the claims of those who live abroad. We show that, even if this is true, it doesn't undermine the case for committing significant funds to alleviate global poverty.
- We explore two criticisms relating to the appropriateness of aid, but we show that these concerns are unfounded.
- We conclude by reflecting on the wider implications of our argument, focusing on the importance of reforming the global order.

15.1 INTRODUCTION

Many affluent states sign up to give at least 0.7 per cent of their national income to *development aid*, and some states make good on this commitment. However, most G7 states get less than halfway to this target, and public opinion is deeply divided on whether this is a good or bad thing. When the United Kingdom pledged to meet this figure in 2015, many charities, politicians, and high-profile figures rallied around the hashtag #ProudOfAid. These individuals emphasize the moral imperative of ending global poverty.[1] Yet, others worry that it's a mistake to send funds abroad when there are so many at home with unmet needs. Moreover, spending on development aid might be wasteful or, worse still, it might mean giving funds to corrupt governments.[2]

One reason for this disagreement stems from the fact that members of the opposing camps tend to hold very different views about how states should balance the interests of their own populations against those of more distant others. A range of considerations bear on this issue, including the urgency of an individual's claims to support, who's responsible for the unmet needs, and the likely effectiveness of the various responses. However, at the heart of this matter is a tricky philosophical question about whether there's anything morally special about the claims of someone's compatriots in comparison with the claims of those who live abroad. Simply put, how do states' duties to their members relate to the demands of *global justice*?

In this chapter, we explore this matter by arguing in support of the claim that affluent states should devote significant funds to development aid. We do this as follows. In section 15.2, we formulate a case for development aid that draws on the idea that an individual has a duty to prevent something very bad from happening when they can do so without sacrificing anything of comparable moral importance. In section 15.3, we reply to those who suggest that affluent states don't have duties to alleviate poverty abroad since they didn't cause it. In section 15.4, we consider and respond to the claim that states should prioritize the needs of their own populations over those of others because there's something morally special about the relationship between compatriots. In section 15.5, we examine the appropriateness of aid as a response to poverty. In section 15.6, we reflect on the wider implications of our arguments.

15.2 DUTIES OF AID

The contemporary world is characterized by disfiguring poverty.[3] In 2015, 10 per cent of the global population lived on the equivalent of $1.90/day. This means that greater than 700 million individuals lived each day consuming less than what $1.90 would purchase in the

---

[1] Ben Jackson, 'It's Not Just Bono and Bill Gates Who Are #ProudOfAid', *The Guardian*, 14 May 2016, available at https://www.theguardian.com/global-development-professionals-network/2016/may/14/its-not-just-bono-and-bill-gates-who-are-proudofaid. While many supported the general commitment, they remained critical of the government for directing aid on the basis of strategic economic and political interests rather than alleviating global poverty. See Karen McVeigh, 'UK Under Fire as New Figures Show Aid Spending by Broad Range of Ministries', *The Guardian*, 16 November 2017, available at https://www.theguardian.com/global-development/2017/nov/16/uk-under-fire-as-new-figures-show-aid-spending-by-broad-range-of-ministries.

[2] Telegraph Reporters, 'Britain Spends £1.3bn on Foreign Aid for Most Corrupt Countries', *The Telegraph*, 22 December 2016, available at https://www.telegraph.co.uk/news/2016/12/22/britain-spends-13billionon-foreign-aid-corrupt-countries.

[3] The following analysis draws on United Nations, *The Sustainable Development Goals Report 2019* (New York: United Nations, 2019).

United States. Let's take a moment to consider that. $1.90 is little more than the cost of a cup of coffee. But these individuals have to stretch this amount to cover food, clothing, shelter, heating, sanitation, health, security, and everything else. It's also important to bear in mind that this figure is based on consumption and not spending. This means that it includes even what someone has grown, made, or found, and not merely what they could purchase. The bottom line is that a huge number of individuals worldwide live on only the barest of essentials. Around 800 million individuals lack access to basic drinking water, a similar number are undernourished, and approximately 3 billion lack access to decent sanitation facilities. In short, extreme poverty afflicts a significant proportion of those alive today.

It's easy to assess the moral significance of these facts. Irrespective of the justifiability of development aid, it's difficult to imagine someone who sincerely believes that the widespread existence of extreme poverty isn't cause for concern. It's tragic so many individuals suffer these hardships, and things would obviously be much better if this weren't the case. This judgement provides the background for an influential argument in defence of a moral duty to assist those in poverty, which begins with the following well-known example:

> *Pond*: Irina's passing through a park when she sees a child struggling to stay afloat in a pond. The water isn't deep and she realizes that she could easily wade in and pull the child to safety. However, this would muddy her clothes, and it'd cost her money to clean or replace them.

Despite the costs involved, it's hard to deny that Irina has a moral duty to wade in and rescue the child. Peter Singer claims that this supports the following principle: 'If it is in our power to prevent something very bad from happening, without thereby sacrificing anything of comparable moral importance, we ought, morally, to do it'.[4]

Accepting such a duty implies that someone who's affluent is morally required to provide aid to those in extreme poverty. After all, though a couple of hundred dollars makes some difference to the life of an average American or European, it can go a long way towards saving the life of someone in dire poverty. The argument runs as follows:

> *Aid moral claim*: If an individual can prevent something very bad from happening, without sacrificing anything of comparable moral importance, then they're morally required to do so.

> *Aid empirical claim*: Without sacrificing anything of comparable moral importance, an affluent individual can prevent something very bad from happening by devoting money to development aid.

> *Conclusion*: An affluent individual is morally required to devote money to development aid.

Since this reasoning centres on the positive steps that an individual can take to bring about a better world, we call it the *positive duties argument* for development aid.

So far, we've discussed only the aid moral claim, drawing on *Pond* to provide powerful intuitive support for it. But for the positive duties argument to succeed,

---

[4] Peter Singer, 'Famine, Affluence, and Morality', *Philosophy & Public Affairs*, 1 (1972), 229–43 at 231.

it must also be true that suffering extreme poverty is something very bad and that, for someone who's affluent, having less disposable income as a result of devoting money to aid isn't of comparable moral importance. Though we haven't defended these ideas, we take them to be self-evident. There are further complexities with the aid empirical claim, discussion of which we defer until section 15.5. For now, we can accept the more modest conclusion that, *if* this empirical claim is true, then it must follow that an affluent individual is morally required to devote money to development aid.

The positive duties argument focuses on what an individual is morally required to do. In *Pond*, we're concerned with whether Irina has a duty to wade into the water to save the child's life. In order to reach implications about the justifiability of competing policies, we must assume that states may enforce compliance with this duty by taxing their members to fund development aid. We think that it's fine for states to do this. To see why, let's return to *Pond*. But now, let's focus on whether it'd be justifiable for the state to require Irina to pay tax to establish a service that rescues children in cases like this. Again, it's powerfully intuitive that the state is permitted to act in this way. Moreover, by doing so, the state can ensure that the revenue that's raised is spent wisely, and it can guarantee that the policy's burdens are distributed fairly. These points provide further support for the idea that an affluent state may use public funds to alleviate global poverty.

15.3 THE CAUSES OF POVERTY

One criticism of the positive duties argument for development aid focuses on who's *causally responsible* for the existence and persistence of extreme poverty—that is to say, on whose actions brought it about. Some argue that many states with extreme poverty have corrupt or incompetent governments, and that poverty in these states is the causal responsibility of such regimes, rather than something that affluent states have a duty to resolve. This is the *responsibility objection* to development aid.

There are two versions of this objection. The first focuses on the claim that poor states are causally responsible for their own poverty and that, because of this, it's up to those states to resolve it. The second focuses not on who *is* responsible for poverty, but instead on who *isn't*. It claims that affluent states aren't responsible for poverty elsewhere, and that they've no duty to resolve a problem they didn't create. We consider each of these objections in turn.

15.3.1 THE RESPONSIBILITY OF THE POOR?

Outlining the first version of the responsibility objection, David Miller argues that the economic policies that poor states adopt have a significant effect on the extent to which their members continue to live in poverty.[5] To see this, let's contrast the fate of Malaysia with that of Ghana. These states had similar levels of poverty in the 1950s, when each

---

[5] David Miller, *National Responsibility and Global Justice* (Oxford: Oxford University Press, 2007), 244–7.

gained independence from the United Kingdom. But now the average income in Malaysia is about ten times greater than the average income in Ghana. Miller claims that this difference is attributable to Malaysia's use of effective economic development policies, and Ghana's failure to do likewise. If this is correct, then there's a crucial sense in which the cause of continued poverty in Ghana is its government's policy decisions.

Miller maintains that this fact makes a moral difference to what affluent states owe to those in Ghana. More specifically, advocates of this responsibility objection contend that *Pond* is misleading. This is because it clouds our judgements that the individual in need is a *child*, who can't be responsible for their dire situation. The example would be somewhat different if Irina were required to come to the assistance of an adult who's at fault for their peril.

Reasoning along these lines, some may be tempted to revise the aid moral claim and to formulate the following version of the responsibility objection:

> *Responsibility-sensitive aid moral claim*: If an individual can prevent something very bad from happening, without sacrificing anything of comparable moral importance, then they're morally required to do so, unless those in need are causally responsible for their plight.

> *Responsibility empirical claim*: Poor states are causally responsible for their own poverty.

> *Conclusion*: An affluent individual isn't morally required to devote money to development aid.

It's possible to qualify this objection in various ways, perhaps by noting that not all poor states are responsible for their poverty. Advocates of this view might then assert that these concerns apply only in the case of some states. But even when weakened in this way, this objection still poses some threat to the positive duties argument.

We've two responses. The first targets the plausibility of the responsibility-sensitive aid moral claim—that is, the claim that duties to prevent very bad things from happening apply only to those not causally responsible for their plight. A simple revision to *Pond* illustrates the issue:

> *Undercurrent*: Irina's passing a river when she sees an adult struggling to stay afloat in the water, having recklessly ignored signs about its dangerous undercurrent. She realizes that she can pull him to safety by rolling up her hardy scarf, throwing him one end, and dragging him to shore. However, this would ruin her scarf, and it'd cost her money to replace it.

This case is similar to *Pond* in that it involves bearing a small cost to save someone's life. The crucial difference is that the individual drowning is an adult who's responsible for his own plight. Despite this, it'd still be abhorrent to allow the man to drown. Even if he put himself in danger, surely Irina's required to rescue him rather than to abandon him.

Perhaps, if he persistently ignores safety warnings—say, on a daily basis—we might eventually become weary of his endless claims for assistance, which interfere with

Irina's plans and absorb her resources. But even in this case, there's significant disagreement regarding the exact role that responsibility should play in weakening an individual's claims to assistance. For example, it's not clear at what point Irina can rightfully
lose patience with someone who persistently ignores safety warnings. After the fifth
time? The hundredth time? When the costs become exorbitant? It's difficult to address
this issue in a chapter of this length. But it'll suffice for our purposes to say that the
responsibility-sensitive aid moral claim is deeply controversial, and so too are the implications alleged by proponents of this version of the responsibility objection.

A second reply targets the responsibility empirical claim—that is, the claim that poor
states are causally responsible for their own poverty. Even if it's true that *states* are causally responsible for their own poverty, very often it isn't the responsibility of the *individuals*
who suffer it. Many of them are children, who bear no responsibility for either the economic policies of their state or the quality of its institutions. Moreover, some states suffering poverty are undemocratic and, given this, we can't plausibly assign any responsibility
for their policies or institutions to the general population. Indeed, even in democratic
states, it's unclear whether we should regard members as responsible for this, particularly
those who're opposed to the government in power.[6] For these reasons, this version of the
responsibility objection fails to show that affluent states may withhold development aid
from those with poor-quality institutions and a record of bad economic governance.

15.3.2 THE RESPONSIBILITY OF THE AFFLUENT?

Given these difficulties, opponents of development aid may take a different approach to
the relevance of responsibility. Rather than holding that states are causally responsible
for their own poverty, critics may argue that those in affluent states are *not* responsible
for it, and that this is sufficient to deny that they've a duty to alleviate global poverty.

This objection utilizes the claim that affluent states and their members don't have
positive duties to assist those who live elsewhere. On this view, all that's owed to those
abroad are *negative* duties not to harm others.[7] Accordingly, the only way in which an
individual can incur duties to address the needs of others is if they caused their plight.
This version of the responsibility objection takes the following form:

Negative duties moral claim: An individual is morally required to assist those in
poverty only if they're causally responsible for that poverty.

Non-responsibility empirical claim: An affluent individual isn't causally responsible
for poverty abroad.

Conclusion: An affluent individual isn't morally required to devote money to
development aid.

---

[6] For discussion, see Avia Pasternak, 'The Collective Responsibility of Democratic Publics', *Canadian
Journal of Philosophy*, 41 (2011), 99–123 and Holly Lawford-Smith, *Not in Their Name: Are Citizens Culpable
for Their States' Actions?* (Oxford: Oxford University Press, 2019).

[7] Jan Narveson, 'We Don't Owe Them A Thing! A Tough-Minded but Soft-Hearted View of Aid to the
Faraway Needy', *The Monist*, 86 (2003), 419–33.

We reject both claims in this argument.

One reason to doubt the negative duties moral claim is that it leads to the result that the state isn't permitted legally to require an individual to come to the rescue of a drowning child, as in *Pond*. This strikes us as deeply counterintuitive, and we reject the claim for this reason alone.

It adds to this that we can identify many grounds other than causal responsibility that plausibly give rise to duties to alleviate poverty. One possibility is that an individual can incur a duty to alleviate poverty abroad when they *benefit from injustices* inflicted on those individuals. For instance, let's consider duties of aid owed to formerly colonized states. Colonialism involved some states taking over territories abroad, imposing a governance regime on those territories, and extracting their wealth. Plausibly, modern-day beneficiaries of colonialism, such as those who live in states whose rapid industrialization was funded by resources extracted under colonial conditions, have a duty to relinquish the fruits of this injustice in the form of development aid.[8]

There are further reasons to doubt the non-responsibility empirical claim. Again, colonialism is a useful example here. Many states had empires, and many more helped to uphold the system by recognizing colonial relations rather than by challenging them.[9] Colonialism inflicts various kinds of injustices on colonies and this has lasting effects on their capacity to develop. In this way, former colonial states and their sympathizers played a vital role in the persistence of poverty. Therefore, even if we were to accept the negative duties moral claim, many affluent states owe development aid as part of the reparation for this historical injustice.[10]

Additionally, we mustn't overlook the role that the current global order plays in sustaining extreme poverty.[11] We can support this claim by identifying ways in which the global order produces the poor-quality institutions that are causally responsible for poverty. Examples of this include international borrowing rights and international resource privileges. These two rules of international relations mean that any government, no matter how it came to power, can borrow money on behalf of its population and determine who owns the natural resources within its territory. This enables actors within a state to seize political control by whatever means necessary, to line their own pockets by borrowing and selling resources, and to use this wealth to keep power by subduing a population. This point is important because it reveals how, even if poor governance is a cause of poverty, it's a mistake to attribute responsibility for this solely to the populations of states suffering it. Rather, we should assign causal responsibility for poor governance, and the poverty it creates, at least partly

---

[8] Avia Pasternak, 'Benefiting from Wrongdoing' in Kasper Lippert-Rasmussen, Kimberley Brownlee, and David Coady (eds), *A Companion to Applied Philosophy* (Oxford: Wiley, 2016), 411–23.

[9] Catherine Lu, 'Colonialism as Structural Injustice: Historical Responsibility and Contemporary Redress', *Journal of Political Philosophy*, 19 (2011), 261–81.

[10] Kok-Chor Tan, 'Colonialism, Reparations, and Global Justice' in Jon Miller and Rahul Kumar (eds), *Reparations: Interdisciplinary Inquires* (Oxford: Oxford University Press, 2007), 280–306.

[11] Thomas Pogge, *World Poverty and Human Rights: Cosmopolitan Responsibilities and Reforms* (Cambridge: Polity Press, 2008). See also Iris Marion Young, *Responsibility for Justice* (Oxford: Oxford University Press, 2011).

to the global order and, more specifically, to the states that orchestrate this system. Accordingly, even if duties to reduce poverty arise only when an individual is causally responsible for that poverty, this still generates a duty for those who're affluent to give development aid in the world in which we live. This is the *negative duties argument* for development aid.

We now have two arguments for a duty to alleviate global poverty. There's the positive duties argument, which we've defended against the responsibility objection. In addition, we've identified a further basis on which to support development aid, which flows from the negative duties moral claim. This is the negative duties argument. Together, these make a compelling case for states to adopt a generous aid policy.

15.4 DOES CHARITY START AT HOME?

Another common objection to development aid is that affluent states and their members should focus on responding to the claims of compatriots, rather than address the needs of distant strangers. We call this the *statist objection*.

An extreme version of this view holds that there are no moral duties at all to those in other states. On this account, the *scope* of all moral duties is bounded by national borders. But this is wildly implausible. It'd imply that states can treat those who don't belong to their populations in any way they choose without moral transgression. This would permit capturing foreigners and harvesting their organs for profit!

A more attractive version of the statist objection accepts that there are some moral duties to distant strangers, but maintains that duties to compatriots should take priority. Most straightforwardly, this argument relies on the following claim:

> *Statist priority moral claim*: The moral duties that an individual owes to their compatriots take precedence over their duties to those in other states.

One way in which to motivate this is to appeal to a claim about the relationship in which fellow members of a state stand to each other. This is a fairly familiar idea. For example, it's common to believe that the distinctive nature of a family means that its members have special duties to one another. The parallel thought is as follows:

> *Statist special duties moral claim*: Because of the particular relationship in which they stand to each other, an individual owes special duties to their compatriots that they don't owe to those in other states.

To examine the statist objection, we'll explore a set of arguments from the philosophical literature that are designed to support the statist special duties moral claim. It bears mentioning at the outset that those who advance these arguments don't do so with the aim of supporting the statist priority moral claim. Nonetheless, these arguments can illuminate how we might motivate that claim, and so they're a useful means of exploring the philosophical terrain. As we'll show, it's more difficult than is often thought to defend the idea that compatriots have special duties to each other, let alone that this can justify the conclusion that the moral duties that an individual owes to their compatriots take precedence over their duties to those in other states.

15.4.1 RECIPROCITY AND POLITICAL POWER

An initial argument in favour of special duties between compatriots focuses on their involvement, as both contributors and beneficiaries, in a particular kind of shared enterprise.[12] To elaborate this idea, let's consider the fact that one way in which we can reason about the duty of an individual to care for their relatives when they're in need is by drawing attention to the fact that these relatives care for them when they're in need. This draws on the moral idea that, when we're in a reciprocal relationship of care with others, we've a duty to honour that relationship by contributing appropriately in turn. Some advocates of special duties to compatriots extend this line of reasoning to relationships between fellow members of a state.

Compatriots may not directly provide each other with personal care, as members of a family often do. But they typically provide each other with public goods and services through their state, such as a functioning legal system, healthcare, education, and unemployment benefits. Perhaps it's a matter of reciprocity that, as an individual benefits from the contributions of others, they incur a duty to contribute in return. This is a duty to support and maintain institutions that attend to others' needs. On this view, it's this relationship of reciprocity that grounds special duties to compatriots. This is the *argument from reciprocity*.

A second argument holds that compatriots have special duties to each other because they're joint subjects of the same political regime. What matters on this view is that the state exercises political power over these individuals together, by making and enforcing laws upon them. This is the *argument from political power*.

One version of this argument emphasizes the fact that the relationship between members of a state is special because it involves *mutual coercion*.[13] According to this approach, when the state uses the police and court system to enforce laws, contracts, and taxation regimes, it exercises a near monopoly of violence and, in doing so, it becomes responsible for the social conditions within which its population live. Because this use of power is justifiable only if it serves the needs and interests of those over whom it's exercised, those subject to it incur special duties to each other. An alternative version of the argument holds that the relationship between compatriots is distinctive because it involves an exercise of *authority*.[14] According to this approach, by establishing a state and setting laws, individuals make a moral claim to rule jointly over each other—a claim to set the legal and social framework in which their lives unfold. We might think that this exercise of political power generates special duties to those subject to it.

---

[12] Andrea Sangiovanni, 'Global Justice, Reciprocity, and the State', *Philosophy & Public Affairs*, 35 (2007), 3–39.

[13] Michael Blake, 'Distributive Justice, State Coercion, and Autonomy', *Philosophy & Public Affairs*, 30 (2001), 257–96.

[14] Thomas Nagel, 'The Problem of Global Justice', *Philosophy & Public Affairs*, 33 (2005), 113–47.

15.4.2 SPECIAL DUTIES AND PRIORITY

There are two problems with appealing to these arguments in order to support a statist objection to development aid. The first concerns whether they're even sufficient to support the central claim they aim at defending, namely that an individual has special duties to their compatriots that they lack to those in other states.

For one thing, some deny that concerns for reciprocity and political power have the special significance that proponents of these views attribute to them, concluding that the duties an individual owes to their compatriots are no different to those they owe to others elsewhere in the world.[15] Defenders of this reply appeal to the idea that it's unfair for an individual's entitlements to differ in virtue of where they were born or the nationality of their parents. However, it bears noting that we can also reach the same conclusion without denying that the relationships described above can generate special moral duties. This is because believing that an individual has special duties to their compatriots as a matter of reciprocity or in virtue of their joint subjection to political power is compatible with believing that they owe the same duties to noncompatriots as a matter of common humanity.[16] After all, there can be more than one moral reason to respond to another's claims.

A related problem is that, even if we accept the ideas that underlie the arguments from reciprocity and political power, we can deny that these relations exist only within and not beyond borders. For example, while it's true that a state coerces its members, it coerces others as well. One instance of this concerns those who attempt to cross state borders.[17] These individuals are made to comply with the state's immigration policy or repelled by the use of walls, detention, and weapons. In this respect, it's not only members of a state who're subject to its coercive power, but anyone affected by its border controls. In effect, this means everyone. Furthermore, states engage in many coercive acts in international warfare, and they exercise coercion and authority in the framework and rules set by global institutions, such as the World Trade Organization.[18] Similar remarks apply in the case of relationships of reciprocity, given the way in which world trade, global communications, and environmental agreements operate.[19] If an individual owes special duties to those with whom they stand in these kinds of relationships, then they must owe such duties to individuals around the world, and not only to their compatriots.

For each of these reasons, we doubt that the claims we've outlined regarding special relationships vindicate the statist special duties moral claim. But it's important to

---

[15] Simon Caney, *Justice Beyond Borders: A Global Political Theory* (Oxford: Oxford University Press, 2005), 111–16.

[16] Simon Caney, *On Cosmopolitanism: Equality, Ecology, and Resistance* (Oxford: Oxford University Press, forthcoming), ch. 3.

[17] Arash Abizadeh, 'Cooperation, Pervasive Impact, and Coercion: On the Scope (Not Site) of Distributive Justice', *Philosophy & Public Affairs*, 35 (2007), 318–58.

[18] Andrew Walton, 'Justice, Authority, and the World Order', *Journal of Global Ethics*, 5 (2009), 215–30.

[19] Pietro Maffettone, 'Reciprocity, Equality, and International Justice', *Global Policy*, 5 (2014), 181–90.

remember that this was only one step in supporting the statist objection to develop-ment aid. In particular, the purpose of discussing these ideas here is to consider how advocates might defend the statist priority moral claim and, more specifically, the idea that compatriots' duties to each other take precedence over their duties to relieve the poverty of distant strangers. Whether or not the statist special duties claim is plau-sible, we think that it doesn't vindicate this further move.

The problem is that neither the argument from reciprocity nor the argument from political power gives us any reason to think that affluent states should entirely ignore the claims of those in extreme poverty abroad. In fact, these arguments aren't even attempts to defend the extreme view that there are no moral duties at all to those in other states. As advocates of these arguments acknowledge, they're entirely consistent with believing that an individual has very weighty duties to those in need abroad.[20] It follows that a defender of the statist objection to development aid can't simply appeal to the idea of special relationships between compatriots. The point is that an individ-ual in an affluent state should fulfil both their duties to compatriots *and* their duties to those in poverty abroad.

For this reason, to bring the statist priority moral claim into focus, we must consider a scenario in which it's infeasible to discharge both sets of duties. In this case, a propo-nent of the statist objection might maintain that an individual's special duties to their compatriots must take precedence.[21] A concrete way to press this point is to claim that, when there's a shortage of public funds, attending to the claims of compatriots should have priority over discharging duties of aid to those abroad.

We can formulate this *limited funds objection* as follows:

Statist priority moral claim: The moral duties that an individual owes to their com-patriots take precedence over their duties to those in other states.

Limited funds empirical claim: An affluent individual has enough funds to dis-charge only one set of duties.

Conclusion: An affluent individual isn't morally required to devote money to development aid.

There are two problems with this objection. First, just as there's no reason to think that the special relationships that exist between compatriots are incompatible with duties to those elsewhere, there's no reason to think that the existence of special duties should take precedence over duties to those with whom an individual doesn't share a special relationship. By way of illustration, let's notice that, even if parents have more extensive duties to their own child, this doesn't imply that they can always prioritize these duties over those owed to other children. A father can't sensibly defend his decision to buy his child an ice-cream rather than to save another child from drowning by pointing out that he has more extensive duties to his own child. In similar vein, an affluent state can't

[20] For example, see Nagel, 'The Problem of Global Justice', 126–7.
[21] David Miller, *On Nationality* (Oxford: Oxford University Press, 1995), ch. 3.

defend its decision not to provide development aid to those in poverty abroad on the basis that it has special duties to deliver public goods and services to its own population. At the very least, some further argument is necessary to justify the statist priority moral claim.

Second, we've good reason to reject the limited funds empirical claim. Of course, it may be true that the current budgets of affluent states are insufficient to meet the claims of both compatriots and non-compatriots. The response to this problem is to increase the state's budget, perhaps by raising taxes. Because of this, the objection could be persuasive only if the empirical claim is interpreted to mean that there's no way to make the state's budget large enough to discharge all of the relevant duties. But this is very hard to believe when we consider the gross national income of affluent states and the exorbitant fortunes of some individuals living within them. Plausibly, the possible budgets of these states could extend way beyond what's required to support domestic public goods and services *and* to devote a considerable amount to development aid. Simply put, we don't see much reason for charity to *start* at home, but, even if this is the case, there's certainly no reason for charity to *end* there.

15.5 IS AID APPROPRIATE?

The positive duties argument for development aid involves the following:

> *Aid empirical claim*: Without sacrificing anything of comparable moral importance, an affluent individual can prevent something very bad from happening by devoting money to development aid.

Although we didn't state this claim explicitly in the negative duties argument, it occurs there as well. However, some critics object to the use of development aid to alleviate poverty. There are two common forms of this complaint. We'll call them the *domination objection* and the *effectiveness objection*.

The domination objection runs as follows. Recipients of aid may become reliant on providers who possess arbitrary power to deprive them of essential goods and services, with no mechanism by which to hold the provider accountable. This constitutes a problematic relationship of domination.[22] Moreover, the concern with domination doesn't disappear once we're confident that the provider will not exercise their power in this way. What matters is merely the possession of the capacity to do so. A classic case that demonstrates this point is that of a benevolent dictator, who protects their subjects' interests, but who can remove this protection whenever they wish. Even though they treat their subjects appropriately, it's clearly wrong for the dictator to possess this kind of power.

The most direct implication of the domination objection is that affluent states have reason to work towards global institutional reform and, in particular, to establish

---

[22] Frank Lovett, 'Republican Global Distributive Justice', *Diacritica*, 24 (2010), 13–31.

accountable mechanisms to alleviate global poverty. We agree with the importance of this agenda, and we recognize that this may justify devoting funds and other resources towards reform. However, it's consistent with this conclusion that, in addition to lobbying for global reform, affluent states are morally required to devote significant funds to development aid.

The only way in which this objection challenges our arguments is for its advocates to assert that relations of domination are sufficiently problematic that it's better not to give development aid in order to avoid establishing them. But stated in this way, the domination objection has strongly counterintuitive implications. It suggests that it's better to leave those in desperate need to suffer than to exercise arbitrary power over them to lessen their plight. We can't see what argument could justify this conclusion.

Let's now turn to the effectiveness objection, which centres on whether development aid works. Some doubt the efficiency of such aid in current circumstances, where a lack of knowledge, skills, and infrastructure prevents success. As Angus Deaton puts it, 'without effective states working with active and involved citizens, there is little chance for the growth that is needed to abolish global poverty' and 'unfortunately the world's rich countries currently are making things worse' because 'foreign aid also undermines the development of local state capacity'.[23] Others might go further, emphasizing the current levels of corruption in many developing states.

It's common to defend this objection by considering the relationship between development aid and economic growth, which provides the resources to alleviate poverty. Not all studies find a robust relationship between these two phenomena.[24] Some suggest that development aid simply increases the size of governments, with no or few beneficial consequences for those who live under them.[25] Nonetheless, this pessimistic outlook remains a minority view. For example, a summary of recent findings concludes that a 'sustained inflow of foreign aid equivalent to 10 percent of GDP is roughly expected to raise growth rates per capita by one percentage point on average'.[26]

Moreover, there's compelling evidence that particular avenues for transferring resources to those in poverty can improve their circumstances.[27] Accordingly, there are ways to design development aid that would ensure it serves its purposes.[28] This makes it difficult to sustain the effectiveness objection.

---

[23] Angus Deaton, 'Weak States, Poor Countries', *Project Syndicate*, 12 October 2015, available at https://www.project-syndicate.org/commentary/economic-development-requires-effective-governments-by-angus-deaton.

[24] Axel Draher and Sarah Langlotz, 'Aid and Growth: New Evidence Using an Excludable Instrument', *CESifo Working Paper Series 5515*, CESifo Group Munich (2015).

[25] Peter Boone, 'Politics and the Effectiveness of Foreign Aid', *European Economic Review*, 40 (1996), 289–329.

[26] Channing Arndt, Sam Jones, and Finn Tarp, 'What Is the Aggregate Economic Rate of Return to Foreign Aid?', *The World Bank Economic Review*, 30 (2016), 446–74 at 469.

[27] Francesca Bastagli et al., 'Cash Transfers: What Does the Evidence Say? A Rigorous Review of Programme Impact and of the Role of Design and Implementation Features', *ODI Report* (2016), available at https://www.odi.org/sites/odi.org.uk/files/resource-documents/10749.pdf.

[28] For discussion, see Raghuram Rajan and Arvind Subramanian, 'Aid and Growth: What Does the Cross-Country Evidence Really Show?', *The Review of Economics and Statistics*, 90 (2008), 643–65.

15.6 CONCLUSIONS

The main policy implication of our arguments is that affluent states should dedicate a significant portion of public funds to effective forms of development aid that alleviate global poverty. At the outset of this chapter, we identified 0.7 per cent of national income as the internationally recommended target. Although it's hard to specify a precise amount that our arguments support, we believe that they demand this much at the very minimum. Most likely, they require a figure that's considerably larger.

Additionally, our arguments indicate that affluent states should do more than give development aid. The negative duties argument suggests that they should look to reform the global order. Concerns about domination point in the same direction. In line with this, current debates about global justice have largely moved beyond discussion of aid. Disputes now focus on special and differential treatment for developing states within global economic rules,[29] how we should distribute the gains of trade,[30] regulating international arms sales,[31] ensuring that supply chains aren't exploitative,[32] upholding international labour standards,[33] reparations for historical injustice,[34] and so forth. Discussing these issues is a task for another occasion. But the arguments in this chapter are sufficient to show that not only must affluent states' commitment to development aid be firm and substantial, but also that they must pursue more widespread reform to meet their duties to those elsewhere.

FURTHER READING

A useful place to begin reading on duties to relieve poverty is Peter Singer, 'Famine, Affluence, and Morality', *Philosophy & Public Affairs*, 1 (1972), 229–43. This is a readily accessible article and provides a good entry point to the debate. This can be supplemented by reading Singer's later publications with similar arguments, such as Peter Singer, *The Life You Can Save: How to Play Your Part in Ending World Poverty* (London: Random House, 2009).

A highly influential account of the negative duties argument is Thomas Pogge, *World Poverty and Human Rights: Cosmopolitan Responsibilities and Reforms* (Cambridge: Polity Press, 2008), and

[29] Gillian Brock, *Global Justice: A Cosmopolitan Account* (Oxford: Oxford University Press, 2009), ch. 9.
[30] Andrew Walton, 'Trade Justice: An Argument for Integrationist, Not Internal, Principles', *Journal of Political Philosophy*, 28 (2020), 51–72.
[31] James Christensen, 'Weapons, Security, and Oppression: A Normative Study of International Arms Transfers', *Journal of Political Philosophy*, 23 (2015), 23–39.
[32] Sarah Goff, 'Fair Trade: Global Problems and Individual Responsibilities', *Critical Review of International Social and Political Philosophy*, 21 (2018), 521–43.
[33] Christian Barry and Sanjay Reddy, *International Trade and Labour Standards: A Proposal for Linkage* (New York: Columbia University Press, 2008) and Lisa Herzog and Andrew Walton, 'Qualified Market Access and Interdisciplinarity', *Ethics and Global Politics*, 7 (2014), 83–94.
[34] Sara Amighetti and Alasia Nuti, 'Towards a Shared Redress: Achieving Historical Justice through Democratic Deliberation', *Journal of Political Philosophy*, 23 (2015), 385–405 and Sara Amighetti and Alasia Nuti, 'David Miller's Theory of Redress and the Complexity of Colonial Injustice', *Ethics & Global Politics*, 8 (2015), 1–13.

it's worth exploring the discussion his work has generated, such as the symposium in *Ethics & International Affairs*, 19 (2005).

An excellent overview of the wider literature on duties to address poverty is Katherine Smits, *Applying Political Theory: Issues and Debates* (Basingstoke: Palgrave Macmillan, 2009), ch. 10. Meanwhile, a thorough examination of both positive and negative duties with regards to poverty is Christian Barry and Gerhard Øverland, *Responding to Global Poverty* (Cambridge: Cambridge University Press, 2016). On positive and negative duties and the effectiveness objection see Elizabeth Ashford, 'Severe Poverty as an Unjust Emergency' in Paul Woodruff (ed.), *The Ethics of Giving* (Oxford: Oxford University Press, 2018), 103–48.

Within the literature on the scope of duties of justice, an influential statist view is David Miller, *National Responsibility and Global Justice* (Oxford: Oxford University Press, 2007). For contrasting views, good reads are Gillian Brock, *Global Justice: A Cosmopolitan Account* (Oxford: Oxford University Press, 2009); Simon Caney, *Justice Beyond Borders: A Global Political Theory* (Oxford: Oxford University Press, 2005); and Laura Valentini, *Justice in a Globalized World: A Normative Framework* (Oxford: Oxford University Press, 2011).

For additional material and resources, including web links and self-test questions, please visit the online resources **www.oup.com/he/walton1e**.

16

HUMANITARIAN INTERVENTION AND POLITICAL SELF-DETERMINATION

SUMMARY

- In this chapter, we argue that there's a just cause to intervene militarily in a state that systematically violates the human rights of its members.
- We reject the views of those who contend that there's no justification for humanitarian intervention because there are no universal moral values.
- We accept that the value of political self-determination can explain what's wrong with humanitarian intervention in some cases. But we argue that appeals to this value are decisive less often than many critics of intervention suppose.
- One concern with adopting a permissive attitude towards humanitarian intervention is that this might be open to misuse. We articulate a role for international law in authorizing intervention to minimize this risk.
- We respond to a final objection from those who oppose humanitarian intervention on the grounds that it too often fails to achieve its ends.
- We conclude by clarifying how our arguments fit within a wider set of considerations pertinent to the justifiability of humanitarian intervention.

16.1 INTRODUCTION

It's widely accepted that military intervention can be justifiable in cases of supreme humanitarian emergency—that is, in response to 'extraordinary acts of killing and brutality that belong to the category of "crimes against humanity"'.[1] In addition to genocide and massacre, enslavement and mass expulsion also come into this category, along

---

[1] Nicholas J. Wheeler, *Saving Strangers: Humanitarian Intervention in International Society* (Oxford: Oxford University Press, 2000), 34.

with other morally equivalent acts. As an example, we can consider the Cambodian genocide carried out by the Khmer Rouge regime from 1975 to 1979, in which nearly 2 million individuals were killed, or the Rwandan genocide in 1994, where the death toll is estimated to be near to a million. In these circumstances, domestic populations are morally permitted, perhaps even morally required, to use violence to rebel against the ruling powers. Moreover, it's plausible that other states have strong reason to intervene militarily to assist those in peril.

But can humanitarian intervention be justifiable when the threat to the domestic population falls short of supreme humanitarian emergency? To make this question more concrete, let's consider the idea that all individuals have a set of human rights. We discuss the notion of rights in detail in Chapter 10. Here, it suffices to note that there's widespread allegiance to the idea that there are some forms of treatment to which each individual is entitled. Everyone has a right not to be tortured, not to be imprisoned without charge or fair trial, and not to be subject to systematic persecution on grounds of their race or religion. But, of course, some states violate these human rights. At the turn of 2020, there's no shortage of places where this occurs. Syria and Afghanistan are obvious examples, but we could easily provide a lengthy list. The question is: does the systematic violation of human rights constitute a just cause for *humanitarian intervention*?

Unlike the case of supreme humanitarian emergency, there's considerable disagreement about the answer to this question. This isn't because human rights violations aren't a clear and important injustice. Indeed, the United Nations' Responsibility to Protect policy both stresses the significance of these rights and holds that it's the duty of all states to protect them worldwide, including by military intervention if necessary. But some critics hold that the systematic violation of human rights doesn't justify intervening in the affairs of other states. This is because it violates their *political self-determination*. It's partly because it aligns with this value that many think that domestic populations may still be justified in using violence to rebel against their oppressive governments. But it's much more controversial whether other states may also be justified in intervening militarily.

In this chapter, we explore these issues by arguing that systematic human rights violations provide a just cause for humanitarian intervention. We develop this argument in a slightly unusual order, allowing our view to emerge through criticisms of contrasting positions. In section 16.2, we reject the idea that there are no universal moral values, thereby defending the claim that there are some standards to which we should hold states to account. In section 16.3, we consider the view that there's a moral duty not to intervene in the affairs of other states out of respect for their political self-determination. While we accept the significance of this value, we argue that it can't support the results its proponents allege. Instead, we show that there can be a just cause for intervention even in cases that fall short of supreme humanitarian emergency. In section 16.4, we consider an objection to our position that emphasizes the risks associated with allowing states to engage in humanitarian intervention. In responding, we reflect on the objection's consequences for how we should conceive of the role of international law in this domain. In section 16.5, we consider and respond to one final objection relating to intervention's likelihood of success. We conclude in section 16.6 by commenting on the implications of our arguments.

Before we begin, it's important to clarify the scope of our investigation in two ways. First, we're interested in the justifiability of *military intervention* for *humanitarian purposes*. In other words, we restrict our focus to cases in which one or more states use violence to effect or to prevent changes in the policies or practices of another state for the sake of those subject to oppression by that state's government or ruling powers.[2] We can distinguish humanitarian intervention from other kinds of interventions, such as wars of aggression and those waged in self-defence, as well as from non-violent humanitarian efforts carried out for the sake of those subject to an oppressive regime, such as the use of economic sanctions or the provision of conditional aid.[3]

Second, we focus our attention primarily on disputes over when there's a *just cause* for humanitarian intervention. Satisfying this condition is necessary but far from sufficient to justify the kind of conduct in which we're interested. That is, in addition to having a just cause, there are further conditions that must be satisfied if military intervention is to be justifiable. The conditions that specify when it's justifiable to engage in war are referred to as principles of *jus ad bellum* (Latin for 'right to war'). Precisely what conditions are on this list is a hotly disputed issue. Traditionally, scholars have thought that wars must also be fought by entities that have legitimate authority, that these entities must have the right intentions, that there must be reasonable prospects of success, that the intervention must be proportionate in the sense that the benefits justify the costs, and that they must be waged only as a last resort.[4] There are also distinct sets of principles pertaining to just conduct *in* warfare (*jus in bello*) and to conduct in the aftermath of war (*jus post bellum*). Although we'll touch on some of the other conditions, we can't discuss them all comprehensively in a chapter of this length. Here, we concentrate on the specific case of whether human rights violations constitute a just cause to intervene militarily in another state.

16.2 UNIVERSAL VALUES

Let's begin by considering an objection to humanitarian intervention that focuses on the universality of moral value. Moral values are universal if they're valid across the entire world, such that they apply to everyone, irrespective of whether or not their culture recognizes this fact.

---

[2] Jeff McMahan, 'Intervention and Collective Self-Determination', *Ethics and International Affairs*, 10 (1996), 1–24 at 3–4.

[3] For discussion, see Cécile Fabre, *Economic Statecraft: Human Rights, Sanctions, and Conditionality* (Cambridge, MA: Harvard University Press, 2018).

[4] For an overview of these principles, see Seth Lazar, 'War', *Stanford Encyclopedia of Philosophy* (2016), available at https://plato.stanford.edu/entries/war. See also Helen Frowe, 'War and Intervention' in Catriona McKinnon (ed.), *Issues in Political Theory, Third Edition* (Oxford: Oxford University Press, 2015), 213–35.

When we introduced the question of whether humanitarian intervention is justifi-able, we relied on a concern for human rights. The core idea is that each individual has a weighty moral claim to be treated in certain ways. They have a right not to be impris-oned without charge or trial, a right to freedom of speech, a right not to be assaulted, and so forth. Each individual is morally entitled to these regardless of where they live, and whether or not their state or fellow members of their political community endorse this idea. In this respect, the claim is that these are *universal* human rights.

But some critics of humanitarian intervention doubt the validity of this idea, insist-ing that there are no universal moral values. If this is the case, then there can't be universal human rights. Accordingly, we can't condemn another state's actions as immoral for violating its members' human rights, and interventions whose purpose is to prevent a state from treating its members in this way would be off the table. We call this the *anti-universalism objection*.

There are two ways in which to support this view. One option is to deny that there are any moral values whatsoever. This is called *moral scepticism*. Another possibility is to acknowledge that moral values exist, but to maintain that the content of these values varies across cultures, depending on the social customs, practices, and conven-tions that their members accept. On this view, the demands of morality are like the demands of etiquette: they're specific to particular cultures, rather than universal in character. This is called *cultural relativism*.[5]

There are several problems with these ideas.[6] First, to deny universal moral values is to deny that there's any universal standard by which to assess acts, practices, and institutions. If moral scepticism is true, this is because there's no standard by which to judge conduct as wrongful. If cultural relativism is true, this is because conduct is wrongful only if the society in question disapproves of it. But this is difficult to accept. It means giving up on the judgement that the practice of slavery in the United States in the seventeenth century was deeply unjust. This is because defending this judgement requires some moral benchmark against which to make the claim. And, since this practice enjoyed popular support at the time, this benchmark must be more than pre-vailing opinion. As cases such as this demonstrate, those who embrace either moral scepticism or cultural relativism lack the philosophical resources with which to judge communities that are historically or geographically distinct from their own.

Worse still, this approach threatens our ability to assess the justifiability of our own institutions. This is because, even within a state, there are distinct communities whose members accept different social customs, practices, and conventions. If moral values are relative to particular cultures, then this should be true for each of the cultures within a single state, such that there are no moral values that apply to everyone within that territory, irrespective of whether or not their specific culture recognizes this. For

[5] Philippa Foot, *Moral Dilemmas and Other Topics in Moral Philosophy* (Oxford: Clarendon Press, 2002), ch. 2.
[6] Simon Caney, *Justice Beyond Borders: A Global Political Theory* (Oxford: Oxford University Press, 2005), ch. 2.

example, in the current context in the United Kingdom, it'd follow that there are no grounds for criticizing sub-communities that perform female genital mutilation if, as its practitioners claim, it's accepted in their culture. We find this deeply counterintuitive.

Second, critics of universal moral values have a hard time explaining why we should treat cases of supreme humanitarian emergency differently from cases of other human rights violations. If there are no moral values at all (as believed by moral sceptics), then genocide and massacre can be morally no worse than less severe abuses of human rights. And, if moral values are only ever specific to particular cultures (as believed by cultural relativists), then we must accept that genocide and massacre would be morally acceptable, perhaps even morally required, by any communities that possess a favourable attitude towards them. It'd follow that, rather than cases in which the international community should've acted to save those who're massacred, the genocides in Cambodia and Rwanda (along with many others) weren't morally wrong. These conclusions are extreme, and verge on being offensive.

Finally, none of the ideas that we've considered so far provides a firm basis on which to oppose humanitarian intervention. This is because, if moral scepticism is true, then humanitarian intervention couldn't be morally wrong, since nothing could be morally wrong.[7] And, if cultural relativism is true, then humanitarian intervention couldn't be wrong for those cultures support actions of this kind. Indeed, for those whose culture is colonialist and imperialist, cultural relativism implies that they may be required, as a matter of morality, to intervene in the affairs of other states. In this respect, despite how these views are often presented, both moral scepticism and cultural relativism actually involve a universal moral claim along the following lines:

Anti-universalism moral claim: No conduct is morally wrong, at least so long as it's supported by those who practise it.

That moral scepticism and cultural relativism involve a claim of this kind threatens to render the views self-defeating. The reason for this is that their opposition to universal moral values seems to rest on one such value. But what's important for our purposes is to note that, because they rely on such a claim, neither view is capable of delivering the verdict that it can be wrong for a state to intervene in the affairs of another. To justify this position, we need a universal moral claim that licenses it.

16.3 POLITICAL SELF-DETERMINATION

Given these remarks, it's sensible to believe that there are some universal moral values and that human rights correspond to one such set of values. If this is correct, then we've a standard of treatment that's owed to each individual, and it's justifiable to hold a state to account when it violates these rights.

---

[7] Ronald Dworkin, 'Objectivity and Truth: You'd Better Believe It', *Philosophy & Public Affairs*, 25 (1996), 87–139.

But the implications of this fact for humanitarian intervention aren't obvious. This is because accepting the existence of one set of universal moral values opens the door to the possibility that there are others, as well as to the possibility that these values may conflict. This bring us neatly to a second objection to humanitarian intervention, which appeals to the (universal moral) idea that each state has a claim to political self-determination. In this section, we outline the details of this objection before defending our view against it.

16.3.1 THE POLITICAL SELF-DETERMINATION OBJECTION

Political self-determination is a process through which a community governs itself independently. This requires not only that its institutions reflect its members' values and priorities, but also that this process takes place in a way that's free from outside interference.[8] The importance of this ideal can help to explain what's wrong with a range of phenomena, including colonialism.[9] It's not merely that colonial powers fail to treat their subjects justly (although this is nearly always the case). Additionally, colonialism deprives communities of the ability to govern themselves independently. It violates individuals' claims to political self-determination.

It's on this basis that Michael Walzer concludes that 'the state is presumptively . . . the arena within which self-determination is worked out and from which, therefore, foreign armies have to be excluded'.[10] As the members of a state form a political community, there's value in its governance, institutions, laws, and practices following their preferences. This is true even when its decisions involve various kinds of injustice. An alleged implication of this is that humanitarian intervention is unjustifiable, at least in the case of human rights violations short of supreme emergency. These are the kinds of injustices that must be left in the hands of the members of a state to address as they see fit. According to the *political self-determination objection*, this is the price we must pay for having a world that protects each community's claims to political self-determination.

To strengthen this line of reasoning, it may help to consider the parallel between families and states. It's often thought that families have some claim to govern themselves independently, which means not only that the family's structure and activities reflect its members' values and priorities, but also that decisions about these matters should be made in a way that's free from outside interference. This notion of familial self-determination can help to explain what's problematic about government policies that attempt to regulate the intimate aspects of family life. But, it bears noting, an inevitable consequence of protecting familial self-determination is that some injustices will

---

[8] Anna Stilz, 'The Value of Self-Determination', *Oxford Studies in Political Philosophy Volume 2* (Oxford: Oxford University Press, 2016), ch. 4.

[9] Anna Stilz, 'Decolonization and Self-Determination', *Social Philosophy and Policy*, 32 (2015), 1–24. For further discussion, see Lea Ypi, 'What's Wrong with Colonialism?', *Philosophy & Public Affairs*, 41 (2013), 158–91.

[10] Michael Walzer, 'The Moral Standing of States: A Response to Four Critics', *Philosophy & Public Affairs*, 9 (1980), 209–29 at 210. See also Michael Walzer, *Just and Unjust Wars* (New York: Basic Books, 1977), ch. 6.

go unaddressed. This is the price that must be paid if families are permitted to govern themselves independently.

Proponents of the political self-determination objection maintain that we should extend these claims about families to the case of the state. Various aspects of current practices confirm this idea. For example, the Chinese state has long restricted the political and civil rights of its members, but it's rarely suggested that other states may intervene militarily to establish a new government. Indeed, even North Korea's documented history of oppression prompts little call for such action. Of course, many argue that the international community should encourage and pressure these states to change. But they retain the conviction that it's important for any change to happen via domestic processes, upholding the value of the political community to change (or not to change) in accordance with its collective commitments.

It's compatible with this to hold that a community's claim to political self-determination has moral limits.[11] In particular, while this value protects a plurality of ways in which to organize society, it doesn't protect all ways. Again, the analogy with the family is powerful here. Even though the state should grant parents some discretion over how they raise their child, we rightly think that it's justifiable for the state to step in if things go beyond the pale, such as in cases of abuse or neglect. Something similar is true in the case of supreme humanitarian emergency.

We can flesh out this idea in two distinct ways. One option is to say that states engaging in genocide, massacre, or other morally equivalent acts retain a claim to political self-determination, but this claim is *overridden* by our reasons to assist its victims. Another possibility is to hold that a community's claim to political self-determination is *conditional*, such that other states have reasons to respect its decisions only if they meet some minimal moral threshold. This view delivers the result that there's no reason to respect political self-determination in the case of supreme humanitarian emergency. Though we believe that the second option more accurately reflects the moral landscape, little turns on this for the purposes of assessing the justifiability of humanitarian intervention. The crucial point is that, unlike with moral scepticism and cultural relativism, defenders of the political self-determination objection can acknowledge the case for humanitarian intervention in supreme emergency, but retain opposition to this practice in cases short of this.

We can construct the political self-determination objection formally in the following way:

Political self-determination moral claim: States should respect each other's political self-determination, so long as any human rights violations they commit fall short of supreme humanitarian emergency.

Intervention empirical claim: Humanitarian intervention doesn't respect states' political self-determination.

Conclusion: States shouldn't engage in humanitarian intervention in cases of human rights violations short of supreme humanitarian emergency.

---

[11] Walzer, 'The Moral Standing of States', 217–18.

16.3.2 THE LIMITS OF POLITICAL SELF-DETERMINATION

Our aim in this section is to challenge the political self-determination objection, and to establish that a state can have a just cause for intervention in cases of human rights violations that fall short of supreme humanitarian emergency. As will become apparent, we don't reject the value of political self-determination altogether, nor do we oppose the claim that it can provide a strong reason against intervention. Instead, we claim only that this reason is less decisive than many critics of humanitarian intervention suppose.

To establish this position, we make three points. First, let's note that political self-determination is an ideal that comes in degrees, such that some states realize it better than others. This fact influences the strength of other states' duties not to intervene.[12] More specifically, the value of political self-determination is strongest when the community in question is unified in certain ways, such as when its members share a culture and the views of all subjects are represented in political decision-making. Perhaps democratic states tend to fare especially (though maybe not uniquely) well in this respect.

However, things are more complicated in the case of states that realize the ideal of political self-determination less well, as is typically the case in highly authoritarian states and in states where there are multiple groups vying for control of the territory. For example, let's consider the later years of the Federal Republic of Yugoslavia, when the country was run with the systematic exclusion and persecution of Kosovans, or the late 2010s in the Democratic Republic of Congo and Libya, where many regions were controlled by armed groups that operated with no regard for the putative authority of the government. In these cases, it's a mistake to insist that intervention compromises political self-determination in a manner similar to how it'd compromise the value in states that realize this ideal more perfectly. Indeed, when some groups are denied any kind of political and social involvement in how a state is run, it's unclear that the value is realized to any compelling extent, and this case against intervention collapses.

Second, even if we accept that political self-determination possesses moral value in such divided states, to conclude from this that other states shouldn't intervene would exhibit a status quo basis that unfairly advantages ruling governments and various powerful groups. This is because, if other states are forbidden from intervening to support the oppressed population, the injustices inflicted on these individuals are likely to continue. In this respect, the political self-determination objection is somewhat misleading, because it suggests that existing injustices are collective problems that'll be resolved in a collective manner, reflecting members' values and priorities. However, given the advantages that ruling governments and other powerful groups have over other members of the state, this is rarely the case. In situations like these, intervention might serve (rather than frustrate) political self-determination by levelling the playing field.[13]

[12] McMahan, 'Intervention and Collective Self-Determination', 23.
[13] Allen Buchanan, 'The Ethics of Revolution and Its Implications for the Ethics of Intervention', *Philosophy & Public Affairs*, 41 (2013), 291–323.

To support this analysis, we can look at the war in Bosnia that took place between 1992 and 1995.[14] During this conflict, the Serbs inherited a stock of weapons much larger than those possessed by other groups and, as a result, they enjoyed a degree of power that was disproportionate to their numbers. One worry about this case is that this state lacked the degree of unity necessary for considerations relating to political self-determination to arise at all, as we've suggested. But, even setting this complication aside, there's the further matter of whether it'd have served or frustrated political self-determination for another state to equalize the distribution of power, either by stripping the Serbs of their weapons or by providing weapons to the other factions. In order for the political self-determination objection to justify non-interference, it must be that levelling the playing field frustrates political self-determination, but it's difficult to see how this is true in the war in Bosnia.

Third, the political self-determination objection disregards or overlooks the extent to which this value should be constrained by human rights.[15] To see this point, it's useful to reflect on the fact that an individual can't appeal to the value of *personal* self-determination to justify the decision to torture someone they dislike, and they could have no complaint if a third party intervened to prevent them from executing this plan. Others' rights constrain how an individual may live their life. The same applies to *political* self-determination. This simple point explains why there's a just cause for humanitarian intervention in most cases of human rights violations, including those short of supreme humanitarian emergency.

In response, a critic of humanitarian intervention might maintain that it makes a moral difference that the individuals subject to oppression belong to the state responsible for this treatment.[16] This is important because an alleged consequence of this fact is that we should think about the state's actions as self-regarding. On this view, a state that violates the human rights of some of its members is analogous to an individual who harms some part of their *own* body, and not someone who inflicts harm on others. While self-regarding harms may be imprudent, we don't normally think of them as morally wrong such that others are permitted to intervene in response. If the same were true for human rights violations, perhaps there'd be a reply to our criticisms of the political self-determination objection.

We find this unpersuasive. This is for reasons described by Jeff McMahan, who writes,

> This . . . is to take the fiction of a collective self too literally. When the government wrongly harms certain citizens of the state it controls, it is absurd to suppose that this can be described as a single self-determining unit harming itself. It is obviously possible for the members of a subgroup within a single political community seriously to wrong or harm the members of another subgroup, and there is no reason to suppose that such action is protected by a right of self-determination possessed collectively by the members of both groups . . . There may be

---

[14] Discussed in McMahan, 'Intervention and Collective Self-Determination', 16–17.

[15] Caney, *Justice Beyond Borders*, ch. 7; David Luban, 'Just War and Human Rights', *Philosophy & Public Affairs*, 9 (1980), 160–81; and McMahan, 'Intervention and Collective Self-Determination'.

[16] Christian Wolff, *Jus Gentium Methodo Scientifica Pertractatum* (Oxford: Clarendon, 1934 [1749]).

good reasons why others outside the community ought not to intervene, but the claim that intervention would violate a single right of self-determination possessed by the agents and their victims alike is not among them.[17]

The implication of these remarks is that appeals to the value of political self-determination can play at most a role that's much more limited than critics of humanitarian intervention often suppose. This is because, even if political self-determination has value, and even if its value supports non-interference, this reason is decisive in a much narrower range of cases than we might otherwise assume. A concern for human rights must take priority.

In our original statement of it, we suggested that the political self-determination objection involved the following:

> *Political self-determination moral claim*: States should respect each other's political self-determination, so long as any human rights violations they commit fall short of supreme humanitarian emergency.

Our arguments suggest an important amendment:

> *Revised political self-determination moral claim*: States should respect each other's political self-determination, so long as any injustices they commit aren't human rights violations.

According to this moral claim, there's no just cause for humanitarian intervention in a range of cases, namely when a state acts within the limits set by human rights.

However, the political self-determination objection also made use of the following:

> *Intervention empirical claim*: Humanitarian intervention doesn't respect states' political self-determination.

Given what we've argued in this section, this claim is no longer sustainable. This is because there are at least some cases of humanitarian intervention, even cases that involve human rights violations short of supreme emergency, where political self-determination is non-existent, partial, or misused, and where humanitarian intervention works not to frustrate but to serve this value.

16.3.3 A RADICAL CONCLUSION?

Some critics of the political self-determination objection might be tempted by the radical conclusion that a state can have a just cause for humanitarian intervention whenever there are any injustices, whether human rights violations or otherwise. On this view, a state can have a just cause for intervention whenever there are any rights violations, and there's no threshold of seriousness that must be surpassed to satisfy this condition. In support of this conclusion, Fernando Tesón invites us to consider the following example:

> *Green Button Experiment*: A state is violating the rights of its subjects. A foreigner owns a fabulous machine that, if activated by pressing a green button, would instantly discontinue all rights violations. The green button will have no effects, other than to block the rights violations.[18]

---

[17] McMahan, 'Intervention and Collective Self-Determination', 23.

[18] Fernando Tesón and Bas van der Vossen, *Debating Humanitarian Intervention: Should We Try to Save Strangers?* (Oxford: Oxford University Press, 2017), 45–9.

Tesón concludes not only that it's justifiable to press the button, but he adds: 'I cannot imagine reasons why anyone should not press the button'.[19] Of course, he recognizes that a state may have other reasons to refrain from intervening—say, because its bad consequences will be disproportionate to its good ones. But these reasons are distinct from concerns about whether the cause for intervention is a just one.

We believe that Tesón's view is too extreme. We agree that it'd be justifiable to press the green button in order to prevent human rights violations, such as those occurring in Syria and Afghanistan in the early 2020s. But we deny that it's justifiable to press the green button when the violations of rights are much less serious. To make this more concrete, let's suppose that social justice requires doing away with compulsory retirement, and that pressing the green button would achieve this. In this case, we believe that it'd be wrong to press the button.

What explains this? Unsurprisingly, our answer centres on the value of political self-determination. More specifically, the reason that it'd be wrong to press the green button in this case is because doing so would effectively deprive members of the state of the capacity to govern it independently. In this respect, pressing the button is in one important respect similar to preventing voters from turning up at their polling stations.

It's true that a state's capacity to govern itself independently may not be a very valuable one when it's used to subjugate or disregard certain individuals or to violate human rights. But things are different when the state perpetrates much less serious injustices, as in the case we've described. The upshot of this is that there's a class of injustices that, because they're relatively minor, the international community should tolerate in the name of political self-determination. In practice, this condition will rarely come into play, since humanitarian intervention is normally considered only in response to more serious rights violations. Nonetheless, the existence of this condition helps us to understand the limited role that appeals to political self-determination can play in evaluating whether a state can have a just cause for humanitarian intervention.

16.4 THE ROLE OF INTERNATIONAL LAW

We now shift attention to a different objection to humanitarian intervention, which comes from those who're concerned that a permissive attitude towards this practice may leave it open to misuse. More specifically, the worry is that a state may be able to intervene elsewhere in ways that serve its own economic and ideological interests under the pretext of humanitarian causes. This concern is especially serious when one state intervenes in the affairs of multiple other states, and so assumes a hegemonic international position. This is the *objection from misuse*.

We may be worried about a system that admits of this possibility even if states don't abuse their power. Akin to the fear that a benign dictator can revoke their subjects' legal rights at whim, it's cause for concern that a state could intervene for self-interested

---

[19] Tesón and van der Vossen, *Debating Humanitarian Intervention*, 46.

reasons, even if it doesn't choose to act in this way. Many such concerns have been voiced in recent years, including in 2003 when it was feared that the United States' intervention in Iraq was pretext for action designed to secure oil contracts and geo-strategic power in the Middle East.

One version of the objection is that there's something problematic whenever a state uses military force to interfere in the affairs of other states, irrespective of the moral credentials of the particular intervention. We might think that, even if it were to do so in ways that satisfy all of the principles of *jus ad bellum*, including having a just cause, there's something troublesome about a state doing so.

However, there's good reason to be sceptical of this critique. Surely, if the relevant moral principles really are satisfied, it'd be wrong to criticize the intervention. To see why, let's consider the case of the 2003 invasion of Iraq. If it had been the case that the United States' deployment of military personnel really was an effective and necessary means to end the systematic abuse of human rights taking place, it's difficult to see on what basis anyone can justifiably oppose the intervention merely because it was the United States that was involved. What justification could be given to those who'd suffer as a result of the refusal to come to their assistance if all the grounds for justifying humanitarian intervention are in fact satisfied?

Nonetheless, we recognize that encouraging states to intervene for humanitarian purposes, or at least not condemning them for doing so, leaves an opening for misuse. A similar concern arises in domestic law enforcement. While crimes should be prosecuted, we don't leave it open to individuals to undertake these tasks themselves. One reason for this is that we fear that individuals may be biased in addressing the situation.[20] Furthermore, we may worry that they don't have the relevant authority to act on such matters. Similar concerns arise when some states are permitted to address human rights violations elsewhere.

But, akin to the case of domestic law enforcement, the appropriate response to this problem isn't to abandon the practice of preventing and prosecuting wrongs. It's to create appropriate legal structures with checks and balances that reduce the relevant risks. We can do this by establishing a legally binding international institution to authorize the use of military force for humanitarian purposes.[21] For this organization to play its role effectively, it'd need to be suitably impartial, well funded, and able to sanction those who violate its commands. How to achieve each of these things is a tough task. But it's clear that institutional authorization of some kind would help to combat the possibility of misuse.

One criticism of this response is that there'd be significant costs to such an arrangement, because many lives could be lost and many human rights could be violated in

[20] For an influential defence of this view, see John Locke, *Two Treatises of Government* (Cambridge: Cambridge University Press, 1988 [1689]), book 2, ch. 9.

[21] Gillian Brock, 'Humanitarian Intervention: Closing the Gap Between Theory and Practice', *Journal of Applied Philosophy*, 23 (2006), 277–91. See also Cécile Fabre, *Cosmopolitan War* (Oxford: Oxford University Press, 2012), ch. 5.

the time it'd take for a state to acquire legal permission.[22] To support this concern, we might consider the existing global institution charged with considering cases of humanitarian intervention: the United Nations Security Council. According to chapter VI of The Charter of the United Nations, the Security Council may 'investigate any dispute, or any situation which might lead to international friction or give rise to a dispute' (Article 34) and, when it determines that international peace is at risk, it may 'recommend appropriate procedures or methods of adjustment' (Article 36). In the course of discharging these duties, the Security Council may give or withhold their approval on proposals for humanitarian intervention.

There are several difficulties with the Security Council, but chief among these are that its membership comes from only fifteen countries at any one time, and its five permanent members enjoy veto power, meaning that a single vote can overturn a decision that has the overwhelming support of everyone else.[23] Because of this, the Security Council lacks the degree of impartiality necessary for it to apply effective checks and balances on the use of intervention, and there are several cases, including the 1994 genocide in Rwanda, where it failed to act even in response to supreme emergencies.

While we share scepticism about whether the Security Council is fit for purpose, we don't think that these points defeat the case for requiring institutional approval for intervention.[24] One reason for this is that we must be sensitive not only to injustices that can occur while a state seeks institutional approval, but also to the injustices that can occur when it acts without authorization. Self-interested interventions conducted under the pretext of humanitarianism can cause losses in life and rights violations. Additionally, such unilateral action can lead to unease about humanitarian intervention, and thus a lack of support for a practice that could provide vital protection for those suffering oppression. To be sure, it can be frustrating—indeed, tragic—when institutions fail to fulfil their role properly. But the best response to this isn't to devolve matters to individual actors. It's to build better institutions.

16.5 THE OBJECTION FROM LIKELY FAILURE

Some critics maintain that the most serious obstacle to the justifiability of humanitarian intervention lies elsewhere. The major problem isn't to do with whether it can have a just cause. It's that interventions of this kind too often fail to meet their own objectives. In support of this concern, its defenders can point to countless examples of failed efforts, such as in Somalia from 1993 to 1995, as well as to evidence revealing that peacemaking activities are often unsuccessful.[25] We call this the *objection from likely failure*.

Several factors are relevant to this. One is *information*. Even where there are human rights violations, external parties are unlikely to know the ins and outs of the situation,

[22] Darrel Moellendorf, *Cosmopolitan Justice* (Boulder, CO: Westview Press, 2002), 118–22.
[23] Brock, 'Humanitarian Intervention', 289.   [24] Caney, *Justice Beyond Borders*, 251–3.
[25] Paul Diehl, Jennifer Reifschneider, and Paul Hensel, 'United Nations Interventions and Recurring Conflict', *International Organization*, 50 (1996), 683–700.

or what's needed to correct for it. Interventions in Somalia and Cambodia in the 1990s have been criticized along these lines.[26] Another consideration relates to *motivations*. States often have mixed or ulterior interests in conducting interventions, and this can cloud their ability to do the job in a way that best benefits the oppressed population. A further concern is raised by John Stuart Mill, who focuses on the likelihood of *local support*.[27] Mill feared that, if those within the state didn't lead the change, they'd lack the commitment or allegiance necessary to maintain the new order in the long run.

It bears emphasizing that, even if the objection from likely failure hits the mark, it doesn't cast doubt on our arguments. To hold that we should oppose humanitarian intervention because it's likely to fail isn't to hold that we should oppose humanitarian intervention because there's no just cause. These views rely on different claims and, for this reason, they require distinct arguments in their defence. In particular, the objection from likely failure relies on the following:

> *Likelihood of success moral claim*: For humanitarian intervention to be justifiable, it must be reasonably likely to succeed.

> *Likely failure empirical claim*: Humanitarian interventions aren't reasonably likely to succeed.

> *Conclusion*: States shouldn't engage in humanitarian intervention.

The moral claim in this objection has some appeal, and proponents are correct to point out that humanitarian intervention doesn't have a perfect track record. Indeed, there are numerous cases where intervention not only failed to succeed, but made things worse.

However, this doesn't support the supposed conclusion of the objection. This is for two reasons. First, when assessing the case for humanitarian intervention, we mustn't forget that there are also cases in which victims endure serious injustices because of other states' unwillingness to intervene.[28] That is, we mustn't overlook the fact that doing nothing also brings costs, specifically to those suffering from ongoing oppression at the hands of an unjust regime. One of the clearest examples of this kind of failure is provided by the Rwandan genocide in 1994, in which states refused to intervene in order to stop violence that killed nearly a million individuals. We must weigh these considerations in the balance when deciding how to act. When not intervening means greater losses of life and human rights violations, even a botched intervention might be the better outcome.

Second, the likely failure empirical claim makes a generalization about humanitarian interventions that ignores crucial differences that affect the chances of success. It's notable that the alleged issues with information and motivations don't hold in every case. This is because appropriately designed international institutions can quell

---

[26] For discussion, see Ioan Lewis and James Mayall, 'Somalia' in James Mayall (ed.), *The New Interventionism 1991–1994* (Cambridge: Cambridge University Press, 1996), 94–124 and Mats Berdal and Michael Leifer, 'Cambodia' in Mayall, *The New Interventionism 1991–1994*, 25–58.

[27] John Stuart Mill, 'A Few Words on Non-Intervention' in John Robson (ed.), *Essays on Equality, Law, and Education: Collective Works of John Stuart Mill Volume XXI* (Toronto: Toronto University Press, 1984 [1859]), 111–24.   [28] Caney, *Justice Beyond Borders*, 245–6.

these problems significantly. Moreover, Mill's emphasis on local support seems misguided, since a population might be dedicated to revolution and the resulting political order, but lack the resources to bring it about. Empirical research supports this analysis, suggesting that there can be a reasonable likelihood of success with carefully designed and well-organized interventions.[29] The general point is that, rather than treat humanitarian invention in such a blanket way, it'd be better to identify the conditions under which it's most likely to succeed, as well as to explore what states can do to increase these chances further.[30]

Crucially, we mustn't be overly confident that intervention will succeed, nor should we naively believe that it's sure to do more good than non-intervention. But, just as we must avoid excessive optimism, so too we should avoid excessive pessimism. Instead, it's important to approach this issue in a way that takes into account the costs of refusing to intervene, and that's appropriately sensitive to the empirical research regarding the factors that affect the likelihood of success.

16.6 CONCLUSIONS

Our main aim in this chapter has been to show that intervention may be justifiable in response to instances of human rights violations that fall short of supreme humanitarian emergency. We achieved this by showing that, though the ideal of political self-determination gives some reason not to interfere in the affairs of other states, this reason loses force against a concern for the fate of those subject to an oppressive regime.

Throughout, we've been keen to stress that whether there's a just cause for humanitarian intervention is only one necessary condition among many. Other principles of *jus ad bellum* explain why so many humanitarian interventions are seriously unjust, for reasons unrelated to the issues we address in this chapter. We mustn't forget that our conclusions here are only one part of a much larger picture. It adds to this point to emphasize how the philosophical analysis takes us only so far. In any given case, it can be a tricky business to determine whether the conditions of a just war are satisfied. Disputes about humanitarian intervention are as often about its empirical details as they're about the moral principles that should guide states' decision-making. For this reason, when evaluating the case of humanitarian intervention, it's essential that we complement philosophical analysis with empirical investigation. As a result, it's difficult to conclude this chapter with very specific policy recommendations. However, it remains that our arguments about what constitutes a just cause are an important part of the puzzle.

---

[29] Gerardo Munck and Chetan Kumar, 'Civil Conflicts and the Conditions of Successful International Intervention: A Comparative Study of Cambodia and El Salvador', *Review of International Studies*, 21 (1995), 159–81 at 163–4.   [30] Caney, *Justice Beyond Borders*, 246.

FURTHER READING

A seminal discussion of humanitarian intervention is Michael Walzer, *Just and Unjust Wars* (New York: Basic Books, 1977), ch. 6. Influential replies are Jeff McMahan, 'Intervention and Collective Self-Determination', *Ethics and International Affairs*, 10 (1996), 1–24 and Simon Caney, *Justice Beyond Borders: A Global Political Theory* (Oxford: Oxford University Press, 2005), ch. 7. There's also a comprehensive overview of the moral principles that arise in the context of war in Seth Lazar, 'War', *Stanford Encyclopedia of Philosophy*, available at https://plato.stanford.edu/entries/war.

For further reading on political self-determination, a good place to begin is with Anna Stilz, 'The Value of Self-Determination', *Oxford Studies in Political Philosophy Volume 2* (Oxford: Oxford University Press, 2016), ch. 4 and Anna Stilz, 'Decolonization and Self-Determination', *Social Philosophy and Policy*, 32 (2015), 1–24.

For further reading that seeks to criticize the idea that political self-determination can justify non-interference, an influential text is David Luban, 'Just War and Human Rights', *Philosophy & Public Affairs*, 9 (1980), 160–81. For more sustained analysis of this line of reasoning, there's Fernando Tesón and Bas van der Vossen, *Debating Humanitarian Intervention: Should We Try to Save Strangers?* (Oxford: Oxford University Press, 2017), part 1. For responses to this line of reasoning, see part 2 of the same book.

Finally, for discussion of worries relating to risk of misuse, there's an excellent discussion of the role of institutions in Gillian Brock, 'Humanitarian Intervention: Closing the Gap Between Theory and Practice', *Journal of Applied Philosophy*, 23 (2006), 277–91.

 For additional material and resources, including web links and self-test questions, please visit the online resources **www.oup.com/he/walton1e**.

REFERENCES

ABIZADEH, Arash, 'Cooperation, Pervasive Impact, and Coercion: On the Scope (Not Site) of Distributive Justice', *Philosophy & Public Affairs*, 35 (2007), 318–58.

ADAMS, Richard, 'Abolish Eton: Labour Groups Aim to Strip Elite Schools of Privilege', *The Guardian*, 9 July 2019, available at https://www.theguardian.com/education/2019/jul/09/abolish-eton-labour-groups-aim-to-strip-elite-private-schools-of-privileges.

ADDA, Jérôme, Brendon McConnell, and Imran Rasul, 'Crime and the Depenalization of Cannabis Possession: Evidence from a Policing Experiment', *Journal of Political Economy*, 122 (2014), 1130–202.

ADEMA, Willem, Chris Clarke, and Valérie Frey, 'Paid Parental Leave: Lessons from OECD Countries and Selected US States', *OECD Social, Employment, and Migration Working Papers*, No. 172 (2015), available at http://dx.doi.org/10.1787/5jrqgvqqb4vb-en.

ALEXANDER, Larry and Kimberley Kessler Ferzan, *Crime and Culpability: A Theory of Criminal Law* (Cambridge: Cambridge University Press, 2009).

ALTMAN, Andrew, 'Discrimination', *Stanford Encyclopedia of Philosophy* (2015), available at https://plato.stanford.edu/entries/discrimination.

ALWAKEEL, Ramzy, 'Assisted Dying Bill: MPs Vote Down Controversial Legislation as Protest Pages Outside Parliament', *Evening Standard*, 11 September 2015, available at http://www.standard.co.uk/news/uk/assisted-dying-bill-mps-vote-down-controversial-legislation-as-protest-rages-outside-parliament-a2945541.html.

AMIGHETTI, Sara and Alasia Nuti, 'David Miller's Theory of Redress and the Complexity of Colonial Injustice', *Ethics & Global Politics*, 8 (2015), 1–13.

AMIGHETTI, Sara and Alasia Nuti, 'Towards a Shared Redress: Achieving Historical Justice through Democratic Deliberation', *Journal of Political Philosophy*, 23 (2015), 385–405.

ANDERSON, Elizabeth, 'What Is the Point of Equality?', *Ethics*, 109 (1999), 287–337.

ANDERSON, Elizabeth, 'Rethinking Equality of Opportunity: Comment on Adam Swift's How Not to Be a Hypocrite', *Theory and Research in Education*, 2 (2004), 99–110.

ANDERSON, Elizabeth, 'Fair Opportunity in Education: A Democratic Equality Perspective', *Ethics*, 117 (2007), 595–622.

ANDERSON, Elizabeth, *The Imperative of Integration* (Princeton, NJ: Princeton University Press, 2010).

ARMSTRONG, Susan J. and Richard G. Botzler (eds), *The Animal Ethics Reader, Third Edition* (London: Routledge, 2017).

ARNDT, Channing, Sam Jones, and Finn Tarp, 'What Is the Aggregate Economic Rate of Return to Foreign Aid?', *The World Bank Economic Review*, 30 (2016), 446–74.

ARNESON, Richard, 'What Sort of Sexual Equality Should Feminists Seek?', *Journal of Contemporary Legal Issues*, 9 (1998), 21–36.

ARNESON, Richard, 'Democracy Is Not Intrinsically Just' in Keith Dowding, Robert Goodin, and Carole Pateman (eds), *Justice as Democracy: Essays for Brian Barry* (Cambridge: Cambridge University Press, 2004), 40–58.

ARNESON, Richard, 'Equality of Opportunity', *Stanford Encyclopedia of Philosophy* (2015), available at https://plato.stanford.edu/entries/equal-opportunity.

ASHFORD, Elizabeth, 'Severe Poverty as an Unjust Emergency' in Paul Woodruff (ed.), *The Ethics of Giving* (Oxford: Oxford University Press, 2018), 103–48.

BALCOMBE, Jonathan, 'Animal Pleasure and Its Moral Significance', *Applied Animal Behaviour Science*, 118 (2009), 208–16.

BARANZINI, Andrea et al., 'Carbon Pricing in Climate Policy: Seven Reasons, Complementary Instruments, and Political Economy Considerations', *WIREs Climate Change*, 8 (2017), 1–17.

BARCLAY, Linda, 'Liberal Daddy Quotas: Why Men Should Take Care of the Children, and How Liberals Can Get Them to Do It', *Hypatia*, 28 (2013), 163–78.

BARR, Stuart et al., 'Nociception or Pain in a Decapod Crustacean?', *Animal Behaviour*, 75 (2008), 745–51.

BARRY, Brian, *Liberty and Justice: Essays in Political Theory Volume 2* (Oxford: Clarendon Press, 1991).

BARRY, Brian, 'Liberalism and Multiculturalism', *Ethical Perspectives*, 4 (1997), 3–14.

BARRY, Brian, *Culture and Equality: An Egalitarian Critique of Multiculturalism* (Cambridge: Polity Press, 2001).

BARRY, Brian, *Why Social Justice Matters* (Cambridge: Polity, 2005).

BARRY, Christian and Sanjay Reddy, *International Trade and Labour Standards: A Proposal for Linkage* (New York: Columbia University Press, 2008).

BARRY, Christian and Gerhard Øverland, *Responding to Global Poverty* (Cambridge: Cambridge University Press, 2016).

BASL, John and Gina Schouten, 'Can We Use Social Policy to Enhance Compliance with Moral Obligations to Animals?', *Ethical Theory and Moral Practice*, 21 (2018), 629–47.

BASTAGLI, Francesca et al., 'Cash Transfers: What Does the Evidence Say? A Rigorous Review of Programme Impact and of the Role of Design and Implementation Features', *ODI Report* (2016), available at https://www.odi.org/sites/odi.org.uk/files/resource-documents/10749.pdf.

BATTIN, Margaret, 'Voluntary Euthanasia and the Risks of Abuse: Can We Learn Anything from the Netherlands?', *Law, Medicine and Health Care*, 20 (1992), 133–43.

BAYER, Patrick, Randi Hjalmarsson, and David Pozen, 'Building Capital Behind Bars: Peer Effects in Juvenile Corrections', *The Quarterly Journal of Economics*, 124 (2009), 105–47.

BBC News, 'Election 2019: Britain's Most Diverse Parliament', 17 December 2019, available at https://www.bbc.co.uk/news/election-2019-50808536.

BEAUCHAMP, Tom, 'Justifying Physician-Assisted Deaths' in Hugh LaFollette (ed.), *Ethics in Practice: An Anthology, Fourth Edition* (Oxford: Wiley Blackwell, 2014), 85–91.

BEGON, Jessica, 'Paternalism', *Analysis*, 76 (2016), 355–73.

BEHUNIAK, Susan, 'Death with "Dignity": The Wedge That Divides the Disability Rights Movement from the Right to Die Movement', *Politics and the Life Sciences*, 30 (2011), 17–32.

BELFIELD, Chris, Claire Crawford, and Luke Sibieta, *Long-Run Comparisons of Spending Per Pupil Across Different Stages of Education* (London: Institute for Fiscal Studies, 2017).

BELL, Derek, 'Does Anthropogenic Climate Change Violate Human Rights?', *Critical Review of International and Political Philosophy*, 14 (2011), 99–124.

BELL, Derek and Joanne Swaffield, 'To Fly or Not to Fly? Climate Change, Air Travel, and Moral Responsibility' (unpublished manuscript).

BELLAMY, Richard, *Political Constitutionalism: A Republican Defence of the Constitutionality of Democracy* (Cambridge: Cambridge University Press, 2007).

BENSON, G. John, 'Pain in Farm Animals: Nature, Recognition, and Management' in G. John Benson and Bernard E. Rollin (eds), *The Well-Being of Farm Animals: Challenges and Solutions* (Oxford: Blackwell, 2004), 61–84.

BENTHAM, Jeremy, *An Introduction to the Principles of Morals and Legislation* (New York: Prometheus Books, 1988 [1789]).

BERDAL, Mats and Michael Leifer, 'Cambodia' in James Mayall (ed.), *The New Interventionism 1991–1994* (Cambridge: Cambridge University Press, 1996), 25–58.

BERGMANN, Barbara, *In Defence of Affirmative Action* (New York: Basic Books, 1996).

BERGMANN, Barbara, 'Long Leaves, Child Well-Being, and Gender Equality', *Politics and Society*, 36 (2008), 350–9.

BHAGWATI, Jagdish, 'The United States in the Nixon Era: The End of Innocence'. *Daedalus*, 101 (1972), 25–47.

BHARGAVA, Alok and Frédéric Docquier, 'HIV Pandemic, Medical Brain Drain, and Economic Development in Sub-Saharan Africa', *World Bank Economic Review*, 22 (2008), 345–66.

BIDADANURE, Juliana Uhuru, 'The Political Theory of Universal Basic Income', *Annual Review of Political Science*, 22 (2019), 481–501.

BIRNBAUM, Simon, 'Radical Liberalism, Rawls and the Welfare State: Justifying the Politics of Basic Income', *Critical Review of International Social and Political Philosophy*, 12 (2010), 495–516.

BLAKE, Michael, 'Distributive Justice, State Coercion, and Autonomy', *Philosophy & Public Affairs*, 30 (2001), 257–96.

BLANC, Sandrine and Tim Meijers, 'Firms and Parental Justice: Should Firms Contribute to the Cost of Parenthood and Procreation?', *Economics & Philosophy*, 36 (2020), 1–27.

BLAU, Adrian (ed.), *Methods in Analytical Political Theory* (Cambridge: Cambridge University Press, 2017).

BLAU, Francine D. and Christopher Mackie (eds), *The Economic and Fiscal Consequences of Immigration* (Washington, DC: The National Academies Press, 2017).

BLOMFIELD, Megan, *Global Justice, Natural Resources, and Climate Change* (Oxford: Oxford University Press, 2019).

BOGGS, Squire Patton, 'Height Requirements, Police Officers and Discrimination: A Short Story', *Employment Law Worldwide*, 13 December 2017, available at https://www.employmentlawworldview.com/height-requirements-police-officers-and-discrimination-a-short-story.

BOONE, Peter, 'Politics and the Effectiveness of Foreign Aid', *European Economic Review*, 40 (1996), 289–329.

BOONIN, David, *The Non-Identity Problem and the Ethics of Future People* (Oxford: Oxford University Press, 2014).

BORJAS, George J., 'The Labor Demand Curve Is Downward Sloping: Reexamining the Impact of Immigration on the Labor Market', *The Quarterly Journal of Economics*, 118 (2003), 1335–74.

BOU-HABIB, Paul, 'A Theory of Religious Accommodation', *Journal of Applied Philosophy*, 23 (2006), 109–26.

BOU-HABIB, Paul and Serena Olsaretti, 'Liberal Egalitarianism and Workfare', *Journal of Applied Philosophy*, 21 (2004), 257–70.

BRIGHOUSE, Harry and Adam Swift, 'Equality, Priority, and Positional Goods', *Ethics*, 116 (2006), 471–97.

BRIGHOUSE, Harry and Adam Swift, 'Educational Equality versus Educational Adequacy: A Critique of Anderson and Swift', *Journal of Applied Philosophy*, 26 (2009), 117–28.

BRIGHOUSE, Harry and Adam Swift, 'Legitimate Parental Partiality', *Philosophy & Public Affairs*, 37 (2009), 43–80.

BRIGHOUSE, Harry and Adam Swift, *Family Values: The Ethics of Parent-Child Relationships* (Princeton, NJ: Princeton University Press, 2014).

BRIGHOUSE, Harry and Erik Olin Wright, 'Strong Gender Egalitarianism', *Politics & Society*, 36 (2008), 360–72.

BRISON, Susan, 'The Autonomy Defence of Free Speech', *Ethics*, 108 (1998), 312–39.

BROCK, Gillian, 'Humanitarian Intervention: Closing the Gap Between Theory and Practice', *Journal of Applied Philosophy*, 23 (2006), 277–91.

BROCK, Gillian, *Global Justice: A Cosmopolitan Account* (Oxford: Oxford University Press, 2009).

BROCK, Gillian and Michael Blake, *Debating Brain Drain: May Governments Restrict Emigration?* (Oxford: Oxford University Press, 2015).

BRODKIN, Evelyn Z. and Flemming Larsen, 'Changing Boundaries: The Policies of Workfare in the U.S. and Europe', *Poverty & Public Policy*, 5 (2013), 37–47.

BROWN, Alexander, 'The Racial and Religious Hatred Act 2006: A Millian Response', *Critical Review of International Social and Political Philosophy*, 11 (2008), 1–24.

BROWNLEE, Kimberley, 'A Human Right Against Social Deprivation', *Philosophical Quarterly*, 63 (2013), 199–222.

BROWNLEE, Kimberley and Zofia Stemplowska, 'Thought Experiments' in Adrian Blau (ed.), *Methods in Analytical Political Theory* (Cambridge: Cambridge University Press, 2017), 21–45.

The Brussels Times, 'EU Parliament Divided on Animal Welfare in Agricultural Policy', *The Brussels Times*, 14 April 2019, available at https://www.brusselstimes.com/all-news/eu-affairs/55473/eu-parliament-divided-on-animal-welfare-in-agricultural-policy.

BUCHANAN, Allen, 'The Ethics of Revolution and Its Implications for the Ethics of Intervention', *Philosophy & Public Affairs*, 41 (2013), 291–323.

CANEY, Simon, *Justice Beyond Borders: A Global Political Theory* (Oxford: Oxford University Press, 2005).

CANEY, Simon, 'Climate Change and the Duties of the Advantaged', *Critical Review of International and Social Political Philosophy*, 13 (2010), 203–28.

CANEY, Simon, *On Cosmopolitanism: Equality, Ecology, and Resistance* (Oxford: Oxford University Press, forthcoming).

CARD, David, 'Immigration Inflows, Native Outflows, and the Local Labor Market Impacts of Higher Immigration', *Journal of Labour Economics*, 19 (2001), 22–64.

CARD, David, 'Is the New Immigration Really So Bad?', *Economic Journal*, 115 (2005), 300–23.

CARENS, Joseph, 'Aliens and Citizens: The Case for Open Borders', *Review of Politics*, 49 (1987), 251–73.

CARENS, Joseph, *The Ethics of Immigration* (Oxford: Oxford University Press, 2013).

CARRASCO, Raquel, Juan Jimeno, and A. Carolina Ortega, 'The Effect of Immigration on the Labour Market Performance of Native-Born Workers: Some Evidence for Spain', *Journal of Population Economics*, 21 (2008), 627–48.

CASAL, Paula, 'Is Multiculturalism Bad for Animals?', *Journal of Political Philosophy*, 11 (2003), 1–22.

CASAL, Paula, 'Progressive Environmental Taxes', *Political Studies*, 60 (2012), 419–33.

CASAL, Paula and Andrew Williams, 'Rights, Equality, and Procreation', *Analyse & Kritik*, 17 (1995), 93–116.

CHAMBERS, Clare, 'Are Breast Implants Better Than Female Genital Mutilation? Autonomy, Gender Equality and Nussbaum's Political Liberalism', *Critical Review of International Social and Political Philosophy*, 7 (2004), 1–33.

CHAMBERS, Clare, *Sex, Culture, and the Limits of Choice* (University Park, PA: Penn State University Press, 2008).

CHAMBERS, Clare, 'Gender' in Catriona McKinnon (ed.), *Issues in Political Theory: Third Edition* (Oxford: Oxford University Press, 2015), 265–88.

CHILTON, Adam and Mila Versteeg, 'Do Constitutional Rights Make a Difference?', *American Journal of Political Science*, 60 (2016), 575–89.

CHRISTENSEN, James, 'Weapons, Security, and Oppression: A Normative Study of International Arms Transfers', *Journal of Political Philosophy*, 23 (2015), 23–39.

CHRISTIANO, Thomas, 'The Authority of Democracy', *Journal of Political Philosophy*, 12 (2004), 266–90.

CHRISTIANO, Thomas, 'Democracy', *Stanford Encyclopedia of Philosophy* (2006), available at https://plato.stanford.edu/entries/democracy.

CHRISTIANO, Thomas, 'An Instrumental Argument for a Human Right to Democracy', *Philosophy & Public Affairs*, 39 (2011), 142–76.

Citizen's Income Trust, 'Citizen's Income: A Brief Introduction' (2013), available at http://citizensincome.org/wp-content/uploads/2016/03/Booklet-2013.pdf.

COCHRANE, Alasdair, 'Prison on Appeal: The Idea of Communicative Incarceration', *Criminal Law and Philosophy*, 11 (2017), 295–312.

COHEN, Carl, 'Who Are Equals?' in Steven Cahn (ed.), *The Affirmative Action Debate, Second Edition* (London: Routledge, 2002), 95–102.

COHEN, Carl, 'Why Race Preference Is Wrong and Bad' in Carl Cohen and James Sterba, *Affirmative Action and Racial Preference* (Oxford: Oxford University Press, 2003).

COHEN, G. A., *Self-Ownership, Freedom and Equality* (Cambridge: Cambridge University Press, 1995).

COHEN, G. A., 'Expensive Tastes and Multiculturalism' in Rajeev Bhargava, Amiya Kumar Bagchi, and R. Sudarshan (eds), *Multiculturalism, Liberalism, and Democracy* (Oxford: Oxford University Press, 1999), 80–100.

COHEN, G. A., *On the Currency of Egalitarian Justice, and Other Essays in Political Philosophy* (Princeton, NJ: Princeton University Press, 2011).

COHEN, Joshua, 'Freedom of Expression', *Philosophy & Public Affairs*, 22 (1993), 207–63.

CONLY, Sarah, *Against Autonomy: Justifying Coercive Paternalism* (Cambridge: Cambridge University Press, 2012).

CONLY, Sarah, *One Child: Do We Have a Right to More?* (Oxford: Oxford University Press, 2016).

The Conservative Party, 'Protecting Human Rights in the UK' (2015), available at https://www.conservatives.com/~/media/files/downloadable%20files/human_rights.pdf.

CRAWFORD, Claire and Anna Vignoles, 'Heterogeneity in Graduate Earnings by Socio-Economic Background', *Institute for Fiscal Studies Working Paper* W14/30

(2014), available at https://www.ifs.org.uk/uploads/publications/wps/WP201430.pdf.

CRIPPS, Elizabeth, 'Climate Change, Population, and Justice: Hard Choices to Avoid Tragic Choices', *Global Justice: Theory, Practice, Rhetoric*, 8 (2015), 1–22.

CRIPPS, Elizabeth, 'Population and Environment: The Impossible, the Impermissible, and the Imperative' in Stephen Gardiner and Allen Thompson (eds), *The Oxford Handbook of Environmental Ethics* (Oxford: Oxford University Press, 2016), 380–90.

DAHLERUP, Drude and Lenita Freidenvall, 'Electoral Gender Quotas and Their Implementation in Europe', *Study for the European Parliament* (2013), available at http://www.europarl.europa.eu/RegData/etudes/note/join/2013/493011/IPOL-FEMM_NT(2013)493011_EN.pdf.

DANIELS, Norman (ed.), *Reading Rawls: Critical Studies on Rawls' 'A Theory of Justice'* (Stanford, CA: Stanford University Press, 1975).

DANIELS, Norman, 'Merit and Meritocracy', *Philosophy & Public Affairs*, 7 (1978), 206–23.

DARDÉ, Véronique Munoz, 'Is the Family to Be Abolished Then?', *Proceedings of the Aristotelian Society*, 99 (1999), 37–56.

DAVIS, Angela Y., *Are Prisons Obsolete?* (New York: Seven Stories Press, 2003).

de MARNEFFE, Peter, 'Avoiding Paternalism', *Philosophy & Public Affairs*, 34 (2006), 68–94.

de MARNEFFE, Peter, 'Against the Legalization of Drugs' in Andrew I. Cohen and Christopher Heath Wellman (eds), *Contemporary Debates in Applied Ethics, Second Edition* (Chichester: Wiley Blackwell, 2014), 346–57.

DEATON, Angus, 'Weak States, Poor Countries', *Project Syndicate*, 12 October 2015, available at https://www.project-syndicate.org/commentary/

economic-development-requires-effective-governments-by-angus-deaton.

DEGRAZIA, David, 'Meat Eating' in Susan J. Armstrong and Richard G. Botzler (eds), *The Animal Ethics Reader, Third Edition* (London: Routledge, 2017), 245–50.

DEGRAZIA, David, 'Self-Awareness in Animals' in Susan J. Armstrong and Richard G. Botzler (eds), *The Animal Ethics Reader, Third Edition* (London: Routledge, 2017), 149–59.

Department for Business, Innovation, and Skills, 'Explanatory Memorandum to the Shared Parental Leave Regulations' (2014), available at https://www.legislation.gov.uk/uksi/2014/3050/pdfs/uksiem_20143050_en.pdf.

Department for Education, *Widening Participation in Higher Education, England, 2013/2014 Age Cohort* (2016).

DIEHL, Paul, Jennifer Reifschneider, and Paul Hensel, 'United Nations Interventions and Recurring Conflict', *International Organization*, 50 (1996), 683–700.

DOMANICK, Joe, *Cruel Justice: Three Strikes and the Politics of Crime in America's Golden State* (Berkeley and Los Angeles, CA: University of California Press, 2004).

DRAGO, Francesco, Roberto Galbiati, and Pietro Vertova, 'The Deterrent Effects of Prison: Evidence from a Natural Experiment', *Journal of Political Economy*, 117 (2009), 257–80.

DRAHER, Axel and Sarah Langlotz, 'Aid and Growth: New Evidence Using an Excludable Instrument', *CESifo Working Paper* Series 5515, CESifo Group Munich (2015).

DREZE, Jean and Amartya Sen, *Hunger and Public Action* (Oxford: Oxford University Press, 1989).

Drug Policy Alliance, 'About the Drug Policy Alliance', available at http://www

.drugpolicy.org/about-us/about-drug-policy-alliance.

Duff, Anthony, *Punishment, Communication, and Community* (Oxford: Oxford University Press, 2001).

Duff, Anthony and Zachary Hoskins, 'Legal Punishment', *Stanford Encyclopedia of Philosophy* (2017), available at https://plato.stanford.edu/entries/legal-punishment.

Dworkin, Andrea, *Pornography: Men Possessing Women* (London: Women's Press, 1981).

Dworkin, Ronald, *Life's Dominion* (London: Vintage Books, 1990).

Dworkin, Ronald, 'Objectivity and Truth: You'd Better Believe It', *Philosophy & Public Affairs*, 25 (1996), 87–139.

Dworkin, Ronald, *Sovereign Virtue: The Theory and Practice of Equality* (Cambridge, MA: Harvard University Press, 2000).

Dworkin, Ronald, 'The Rights of Allan Bakke' in Hugh LaFollette (ed.), *Ethics in Practice: An Anthology, Fourth Edition* (Oxford: Wiley Blackwell, 2014), 443–8.

Dworkin, Ronald et al., 'Assisted Suicide: The Philosophers' Brief', *New York Review of Books*, 44 (1997), 41–7.

Easterly, William and Yaw Nyarko, 'Is Brain Drain Good for Africa?' in Jagdish Bhagwati and Gordon Hanson (eds), *Skilled Immigration Today: Prospects, Problems, and Policies* (Oxford: Oxford University Press, 2009), 316–61.

Edey, Melissa, 'Austria Could Be the Next E.U. Country to Tighten Its Borders', *New York Times*, 3 July 2018, available at https://www.nytimes.com/2018/07/03/world/europe/austria-borders-migrants-kurz.html.

Ellison, Sara Fisher and Wallace Mullin, 'Diversity, Social Goods Provision, and Performance in the Firm', *Journal of Economics & Management Strategy*, 23 (2014), 465–81.

Fabre, Cécile, 'Constitutionalising Social Rights', *Journal of Political Philosophy*, 6 (1998), 263–84.

Fabre, Cécile, 'A Philosophical Argument for a Bill of Rights', *British Journal of Political Science*, 30 (2000), 77–98.

Fabre, Cécile, *Social Rights Under the Constitution* (Oxford: Oxford University Press, 2000).

Fabre, Cécile, *Cosmopolitan War* (Oxford: Oxford University Press, 2012).

Fabre, Cécile, *Economic Statecraft: Human Rights, Sanctions, and Conditionality* (Cambridge, MA: Harvard University Press, 2018).

Feinberg, Joel, *The Moral Limits of the Criminal Law, Volume 2: Offense to Others* (Oxford: Oxford University Press, 1985).

Feinberg, Joel, *The Moral Limits of the Criminal Law, Volume 3: Harm to Self* (Oxford: Oxford University Press, 1986).

FishCount, 'Fish Count Estimates', available at http://fishcount.org.uk/fish-count-estimates and Animal Equality, 'Food', available at https://www.animalequality.net/food.

Fine, Sarah, 'Freedom of Association Is Not the Answer', *Ethics*, 120 (2010), 338–56.

Finelli, Mary and Jim Mason, 'Brave New Farm?' in Peter Singer (ed.), *In Defense of Animals: The Second Wave* (Oxford: Blackwell, 2006), 104–22.

Foot, Philippa, *Moral Dilemmas and Other Topics in Moral Philosophy* (Oxford: Clarendon Press, 2002).

Foster, Michelle, *International Refugee Law and Socio-Economic Rights: Refuge from Deprivation* (Cambridge: Cambridge University Press, 2007).

Fox, Michael Allen, 'The Moral Community' in Hugh LaFollette (ed.), *Ethics in Practice: An Anthology, Third Edition* (Oxford: Blackwell, 2007), 181–91.

FRANKFURT, Harry, 'Freedom of the Will and the Concept of a Person', *Journal of Philosophy*, 68 (1971), 5–20.

FRANKFURT, Harry, 'Equality as a Moral Ideal', *Ethics*, 98 (1987), 21–43.

FRASER, David and Daniel M. Weary, 'Quality of Life for Farm Animals: Linking Science, Ethics, and Animal Welfare' in G. John Benson and Bernard E. Rollin (eds), *The Well-Being of Farm Animals: Challenges and Solutions* (Oxford: Blackwell, 2004), 39–60.

FRASER, Nancy, 'After the Family Wage: Gender Equality and the Welfare State', *Political Theory*, 22 (1994), 591–618.

FRASER, Nancy, 'Recognition without Ethics?', *Theory, Culture, & Society*, 18 (2001), 21–42.

FRASER, Nancy, 'Social Justice in the Age of Identity Politics: Redistribution, Recognition, and Participation' in Nancy Fraser and Axel Honneth, *Redistribution or Recognition? A Political-Philosophical Exchange* (London: Verso, 2003), 7–109.

FRICKER, Miranda, *Epistemic Injustice: Power and the Ethics of Knowing* (Oxford: Oxford University Press, 2007).

FRIEDLAENDER, Christina, 'On Microaggressions: Cumulative Harm and Individual Responsibility', *Hypatia*, 33 (2018), 5–21.

FROWE, Helen, 'War and Intervention' in Catriona McKinnon (ed.), *Issues in Political Theory, Third Edition* (Oxford: Oxford University Press, 2015), 213–35.

FULLINWIDER, Robert, 'Affirmative Action', *Stanford Encyclopedia of Philosophy* (2017), https://plato.stanford.edu/entries/affirmative-action.

GARDINER, Stephen et al. (eds), *Climate Ethics: Essential Readings* (Oxford: Oxford University Press, 2010).

GERVER, Mollie, 'Denying Services to Prevent Regret', *Journal of Applied Philosophy*, 36 (2019), 471–90.

GHANDNOOSH, Nazgol, 'Black Lives Matter: Eliminating Racial Inequality in the Criminal Justice System', *The Sentencing Project* (2015), available at https://www.sentencingproject.org/publications/black-lives-matter-eliminating-racial-inequity-in-the-criminal-justice-system.

GHEAUS, Anca, 'Basic Income, Gender Justice, and the Costs of Gender-Symmetrical Lifestyles', *Basic Incomes Studies*, 3 (2008), 1–8.

GHEAUS, Anca, 'Gender Justice', *Journal of Ethics & Social Philosophy*, 6 (2012), 1–24.

GHEAUS, Anca, 'Gender and Distributive Justice' in Serena Olsaretti (ed.), *Oxford Handbook of Distributive Justice* (Oxford: Oxford University Press, 2018).

GHEAUS, Anca, 'Childrearing with Minimal Domination: A Republican Account', *Political Studies* (forthcoming).

GHEAUS, Anca and Ingrid Robeyns, 'Equality-Promoting Parental Leave', *Journal of Social Philosophy*, 42 (2011), 173–91.

Global Humanitarian Forum, 'Human Impact Report: Climate Change, the Anatomy of a Silent Crisis' (Geneva, 2009), available at http://www.eird.org/publica-ciones/humanimpactreport.pdf.

GLOVER, Jonathan, *Causing Death and Saving Lives* (London: Penguin Books, 1990).

GOFF, Sarah, 'Fair Trade: Global Problems and Individual Responsibilities', *Critical Review of International Social and Political Philosophy*, 21 (2018), 521–43.

GOODIN, Robert, 'Permissible Paternalism: Saving Smokers From Themselves' in Hugh LaFollette (ed.), *Ethics in Practice: An Anthology, Second Edition* (Oxford: Blackwell Publishing, 2002), 307–12.

GORNICK, Janet and Marcia Meyers, 'Creating Gender Egalitarian Societies: An Agenda for Reform', *Politics and Society*, 36 (2008), 313–49.

GOULD, Carol, *Rethinking Democracy: Freedom and Social Cooperation in Politics, Economics, and Society* (Cambridge: Cambridge University Press, 1988).

GREENWALD, Anthony G. and Linda Hamilton Krieger, 'Implicit Bias: Scientific Foundations', *California Law Review*, 94 (2006), 945–67.

GRUEN, Lori, *Entangled Empathy: An Alternative Ethic for Our Relationships with Animals* (New York: Lantern Books, 2015).

GRUEN, Lori, 'The Moral Status of Animals', *Stanford Encyclopedia of Philosophy* (2017), available at https://plato.stanford.edu/entries/moral-animal.

GUNTER, Joel, 'A Reckoning in Charlottesville', *BBC News*, 13 August 2017, available at https://www.bbc.co.uk/news/world-us-canada-40914748.

HALLIDAY, Samantha, 'Comparative Reflections upon the Assisted Dying Bill 2013: A Plea for a More European Approach', *Medical Law International*, 13 (2013), 135–67.

HARRIS, Luke Charles and Uma Narayan, 'Affirmative Action as Equalizing Opportunity: Challenging the Myth of "Preferential Treatment"' in Hugh LaFollette (ed.), *Ethics in Practice: An Anthology, Fourth Edition* (Oxford: Wiley Blackwell, 2014), 449–59.

HART, H. L. A., *Punishment and Responsibility* (Oxford: Oxford University Press, 1968).

HART, H. L. A., *Essays on Bentham* (Oxford: Clarendon Press, 1982).

HASLANGER, Sally et al., 'Topics in Feminism', *Stanford Encyclopedia of Philosophy* (2012), available at https://plato.stanford.edu/archives/sum2018/entries/feminism-topics.

HAWKEN, Angela and Mark Kleiman, 'Managing Drug Involved Probationers with Swift and Certain Sanctions: Evaluating Hawaii's HOPE', *National Institute of Justice* (2009), available at https://www.ncjrs.gov/pdffiles1/nij/grants/229023.pdf.

HAWKINS, Alan and Tomi-Anne Roberts, 'Designing a Primary Intervention to Help Dual-Earner Couples Share Housework and Child Care', *Family Relations*, 41 (1992), 169–77.

HEILMAN, Madeline, Caryn Block, and Peter Stathatos, 'The Affirmative Action Stigma of Incompetence: Effects of Performance Information Ambiguity', *Academy of Management Journal*, 40 (1997), 603–25.

HELLAND, Eric and Alexander Tabarrok, 'Does Three Strikes Deter? A Nonparametric Estimation', *Journal of Human Resources*, 42 (2007), 309–30.

HELLMAN, Deborah, *When Is Discrimination Wrong?* (Cambridge, MA: Harvard University Press, 2011).

HERZOG, Lisa and Andrew Walton, 'Qualified Market Access and Interdisciplinarity', *Ethics and Global Politics*, 7 (2014), 83–94.

HJALMARSSON, Randi, 'Juvenile Jails: A Path to the Straight and Narrow or to Hardened Criminality?', *Journal of Law and Economics*, 52 (2009), 779–809.

HM Government, '2017 Drug Strategy', available at https://assets.publishing.service.gov.uk/government/uploads/system/uploads/attachment_data/file/628148/Drug_strategy_2017.pdf.

HOHFELD, Wesley, 'Some Fundamental Legal Conceptions as Applied in Judicial Reasoning', *Yale Law Journal*, 23 (1913), 16–59.

HOLZER, Harry and David Neumark, 'What Does Affirmative Action Do?', *Industrial and Labour Relations Review*, 53 (2000), 240–71.

HORN, Gabriel et al., 'Brain Science, Addiction, and Drugs', *The Academy of Medical Sciences* (2008), available at https://acmedsci.ac.uk/file-download/34265-524414fc8746a.pdf.

HOWARD, Jeffrey, 'Punishment as Moral Fortification', *Law and Philosophy*, 36 (2017), 45–75.

HUME, David, *Treatise of Human Nature* (Oxford: Oxford University Press, 2000 [1739]).

HUSAK, Douglas, *Drugs and Rights* (Cambridge: Cambridge University Press, 1992).

HUSAK, Douglas, 'In Favor of Drug Decriminalization' in Andrew I. Cohen and Christopher Heath Wellman (eds), *Contemporary Debates in Applied Ethics, Second Edition* (Chichester: Wiley Blackwell, 2014), 335–45.

HUSAK, Douglas and Peter de Marneffe, *The Legalization of Drugs: For and Against* (Cambridge: Cambridge University Press, 2005).

JACKSON, Ben, 'It's Not Just Bono and Bill Gates Who Are #ProudOfAid', *The Guardian*, 14 May 2016, available at https://www.theguardian.com/global-development-professionals-network/2016/may/14/its-not-just-bono-and-bill-gates-who-are-proudofaid.

JOHNSON, Eric and Daniel Goldstein, 'Do Defaults Save Lives?', *Science*, 302 (2003), 1338–9.

JONES, Peter, 'Bearing the Consequences of Belief', *Journal of Political Philosophy*, 2 (1994), 24–43.

JONES, Peter, *Rights* (London: Macmillan, 1994).

JONES, Peter, 'Religious Belief and Freedom of Expression: Is Offensiveness Really the Issue?', *Res Publica*, 17 (2011), 75–90.

JOUROVÁ, Věra, 'Gender Balance on Corporate Boards: Europe Is Cracking the Glass Ceiling', *European Commission* (Brussels: European Commission, 2016).

KAESTNER, Sven, 'Swiss to Vote on Banning Factory Farming', *SwissInfo*, 17 September 2019, available at https://www.swissinfo.ch/eng/politics/animal-rights_swiss-to-vote-on-banning-factory-farming/45233958.

KAGAN, Shelly, *The Limits of Morality* (Oxford: Clarendon Press, 1989).

KAMM, Frances, 'Physician-Assisted Suicide, the Doctrine of Double Effect, and the Ground of Value', *Ethics*, 109 (1999), 586–605.

KAMM, Frances, *Bioethical Prescriptions: To Create, End, Choose, and Improve Lives* (Oxford: Oxford University Press, 2013).

KAVANAGH, Aileen, *Constitutional Review Under the UK Human Rights Act* (Cambridge: Cambridge University Press, 2009).

KELLY, Erin, 'Criminal-Justice Minded: Retribution, Punishment and Authority' in Derrick Darby and Tommie Shelby (eds), *Hip Hop and Philosophy: From Rhyme to Reason* (Chicago, IL: Open Court, 2005), 183–92.

KEOWN, John, 'Euthanasia in the Netherlands: Sliding Down the Slippery Slope?', *Notre Dame Journal of Law, Ethics & Public Policy*, 9 (1995), 407–48.

KEOWN, John, 'Against Decriminalising Euthanasia: For Improving Care' in Emily Jackson and John Keown (eds), *Debating Euthanasia* (Oxford: Hart Publishing, 2012), 87–101.

KERIK, Bernard, 'Cotton Letter Final', *Huffington Post*, 16 February 2016, available at http://big.assets.huffingtonpost.com/Cotton.Letter.Final.pdf.

KERR, William, 'Ethnic Scientific Communities and International Technology Diffusion', *Review of Economics and Statistics*, 90 (2008), 518–37.

KEY, Brian, 'Fish Do Not Feel Pain and Its Implications for Understanding Phenomenal Consciousness', *Biology & Philosophy*, 30 (2015), 149–65.

KHAITAN, Tarunabh, 'Indirect Discrimination' in Kasper Lippert-Rasmussen (ed.), *The Routledge Handbook to the Ethics of Discrimination* (London: Routledge, 2017), 30–41.

KING, Jr., Martin Luther, *Where Do We Go from Here: Chaos or Community* (Boston, MA: Beacon, 2010 [1967]).

KIRBY, Philip, 'Leading People 2016', *The Sutton Trust* (2016), available at https://www.suttontrust.com/research-paper/leading-people-2016.

KITTAY, Eva Feder, *Love's Labour: Essays on Women, Equality, and Dependency* (New York: Routledge, 1999).

KITTAY, Eva Feder, 'At the Margins of Moral Personhood', *Ethics*, 116 (2005), 100–31.

KLEVEN, Henrik, Camille Landais, and Jakob Egholt Søgaard, 'Children and Gender Inequality: Evidence from Denmark', *American Economic Journal: Applied Economics*, 11 (2019), 181–209.

KLEVEN, Henrik, Camille Landais, Johanna Posch, Andreas Steinhauer, and Josef Zweimüller, 'Child Penalties Across Countries: Evidence and Explanations', *AEA Papers and Proceedings*, 109 (2019), 122–6.

KOFOED, Michael and Elizabeth McGovney, 'The Effect of Same-Gender and Same-Race Role Models on Occupational Choice: Evidence from Randomly Assigned Mentors at West Point', *Journal of Human Resources*, 54 (2019), 430–67.

KORSGAARD, Christine, *The Sources of Normativity* (Cambridge: Cambridge University Press, 1996).

KORSGAARD, Christine, *Fellow Creatures: Our Obligations to the Other Animals* (Oxford: Oxford University Press, 2018).

KUKATHAS, Chandran, 'Are There Any Cultural Rights?', *Political Theory*, 20 (1992), 105–39.

KUKATHAS, Chandran, 'The Case for Open Immigration' in Andrew I. Cohen and Christopher Heath Wellman (eds), *Contemporary Debates in Applied Ethics, Second Edition* (Oxford: Wiley Blackwell, 2014), 376–88.

KUMAR, Rahul, 'Permissible Killing and the Irrelevance of Being Human', *The Journal of Ethics*, 12 (2008), 57–80.

KUMAR, Rahul, 'Future Generations' in Serena Olsaretti (ed.), *The Oxford Handbook of Distributive Justice* (Oxford: Oxford University Press, 2018), 689–710.

KYMLICKA, Will, *Multicultural Citizenship: A Liberal Theory of Minority Rights* (Oxford: Oxford University Press, 1996).

KYMLICKA, Will, *Contemporary Political Philosophy: An Introduction, Second Edition* (Oxford: Oxford University Press, 2002).

KYMLICKA, Will and Keith Banting, 'Immigration, Multiculturalism, and the Welfare State', *Ethics and International Affairs*, 20 (2006), 281–304.

LAMONT, Julian and Christi Favor, 'Distributive Justice', *Stanford Encyclopedia of Philosophy* (2017), available at https://plato.stanford.edu/entries/justice-distributive.

LANGTON, Rae, 'Speech Acts and Unspeakable Acts', *Philosophy & Public Affairs*, 22 (1993), 293–330.

LAREAU, Annette, *Unequal Childhoods* (Berkeley, CA: University of California Press, 2003).

LAWFORD-SMITH, Holly, *Not in Their Name: Are Citizens Culpable for Their States' Actions?* (Oxford: Oxford University Press, 2019).

LAZAR, Seth, 'War', *Stanford Encyclopedia of Philosophy* (2016), available at https://plato.stanford.edu/entries/war.

LEE, David S. and Justin McCrary, 'The Deterrence Effect of Prison: Dynamic Theory and Evidence' in Matias D. Cattaneo and Juan Carlos Escanciano (eds), *Regression Discontinuity Designs: Theory and Applications* (Bingley: Emerald Publishing Limited, 2017), 73–146.

LENON, Barnaby, 'Abolishing Private Schools Would Not Improve Education', *The Times*, 18 July 2019, available at https://www .thetimes.co.uk/article/abolishing-private- schools-would-not-improve-education- ww2rhdzj8.

LEWIS, Christopher, 'Inequality, Incentives, Criminality, and Blame', *Legal Theory*, 22 (2016), 153–80.

LEWIS, Ioan and James Mayall, 'Somalia' in James Mayall (ed.), *The New Interventionism 1991–1994* (Cambridge: Cambridge University Press, 1996), 94–124.

LEWIS, Penney, 'The Empirical Slippery Slope from Voluntary to Non-Voluntary Euthanasia', *Journal of Law, Medicine, and Ethics*, 35 (2007), 197–210.

LIPPERT-RASMUSSEN, Kasper, *Born Free and Equal?* (Oxford: Oxford University Press, 2013).

LIPPERT-RASMUSSEN, Kasper, 'Affirmative Action, Historical Injustice, and the Concept of Beneficiaries', *Journal of Political Philosophy*, 25 (2017), 72–90.

LIPPERT-RASMUSSEN, Kasper, 'The Ethics of Anti-Discrimination Policies' in Annabelle Lever and Andrei Poama (eds), *The Routledge Handbook of Ethics and Public Policy* (London: Routledge, 2018), 267–80.

LIPPERT-RASMUSSEN, Kasper, *Making Sense of Affirmative Action* (Oxford: Oxford University Press, 2020).

LIST, Christian and Laura Valentini, 'The Methodology of Political Theory' in Herman Cappelen, Tamar Azabó Gendler, and John Hawthorne (eds), *The Oxford Handbook of Philosophical Methodology* (Oxford: Oxford University Press, 2016), 525–53.

LOCKE, John, *Two Treatises of Government* (Cambridge: Cambridge University Press, 1988 [1689]).

LOVETT, Frank, 'Republican Global Distributive Justice', *Diacritica*, 24 (2010), 13–31.

LU, Catherine, 'Colonialism as Structural Injustice: Historical Responsibility and Contemporary Redress', *Journal of Political Philosophy*, 19 (2011), 261–81.

LUBAN, David, 'Just War and Human Rights', *Philosophy & Public Affairs*, 9 (1980), 160–81.

LUCCHINO, Paolo, Chiara Rosazza-Bondibene, and Jonathan Portes, 'Examining the Relationship Between Immigration and Unemployment Using National Insurance Number Registration Data', *NIESR Discussion Paper*, No. 386 (2012).

LYONS, Kate, 'Racist Incidents Feared to Be Linked to Brexit Result', *The Guardian*, 26 June 2016, available at https://www .theguardian.com/politics/2016/jun/26/ racist-incidents-feared-to-be-linked-to-brexit- result-reported-in-england-and-wales.

MACCALLUM, Gerald, 'Negative and Positive Freedom', *The Philosophical Review*, 76 (1967), 312–34.

MACEDO, Stephen, 'The Moral Dilemma of US Immigration Policy: Open Borders versus Social Justice?' in Carol Swain (ed.), *Debating Immigration* (New York: Cambridge University Press, 2007), 63–81.

MACKINNON, Catherine A., *Feminism Unmodified: Discourses on Life and Law* (Cambridge, MA: Harvard University Press, 1987).

MACKINNON, Catherine A., *Only Words* (Cambridge, MA: Harvard University Press, 1996).

MacMillan, Lindsey, Claire Tyler, and Anna Vignoles, 'Who Gets the Top Jobs? The Role of Family Background and Networks in Recent Graduates' Access to High-Status Professions', *Journal of Social Policy*, 44 (2015), 487–515.

Madan, Richard, 'Anti-Gay Flyers Violated Hate Law, Supreme Court Rules', *CTV News*, 27 February 2013, available at https://www.ctvnews.ca/canada/anti-gay-flyers-violated-hate-law-supreme-court-rules-1.1173807.

Maffettone, Pietro, 'Reciprocity, Equality, and International Justice', *Global Policy*, 5 (2014), 181–90.

Margalit, Avishai and Moshe Halbertal, 'Liberalism and the Right to Culture', *Social Research*, 61 (1994), 491–510.

Marshall, T. H., *Citizenship and Social Class, and Other Essays* (Cambridge: Cambridge University Press, 1950).

Mason, Andrew, 'Equality, Personal Responsibility, and Gender Socialisation', *Proceedings of the Aristotelian Society*, 100 (2000), 227–46.

Matsuda, Mari J., 'Public Response to Racist Speech: Considering the Victim's Story', *Michigan Law Review*, 87 (1989), 2320–81.

McKinnon, Catriona, *Climate Change and Future Justice: Precaution, Compensation, and Triage* (London: Routledge, 2012).

McMahan, Jeff, 'Intervention and Collective Self-Determination', *Ethics and International Affairs*, 1996 (10), 1–24.

McMahan, Jeff, *The Ethics of Killing: Problems at the Margin of Life* (Oxford: Oxford University Press, 2002).

McMahan, Jeff, 'Animals' in R. G. Frey and Christopher Wellman (eds), *A Companion to Applied Ethics* (Oxford: Blackwell, 2003), 525–36.

McMahan, Jeff, 'Vegetarianism', Interview with Nigel Warburton for *Philosophy Bites* (2010), available at http://philosophybites.com/2010/06/jeff-mcmahan-on-vegetarianism.html.

McMahan, Jeff, 'Radical Cognitive Limitation' in Kimberley Brownlee and Adam Cureton (eds), *Disability and Disadvantage* (Oxford: Oxford University Press, 2011), 240–59.

McMahan, Jeff, 'Human Dignity, Suicide, and Assisting Others to Die' in Sebastian Muders (ed.), *Human Dignity and Assisted Death* (Oxford: Oxford University Press, 2017), 13–29.

McMahan, Jeff, 'Causing Animals to Exist in Order to Eat Them' (unpublished manuscript).

McVeigh, Karen, 'UK Under Fire as New Figures Show Aid Spending by Broad Range of Ministries', *The Guardian*, 16 November 2017, available at https://www.theguardian.com/global-development/2017/nov/16/uk-under-fire-as-new-figures-show-aid-spending-by-broad-range-of-ministries.

Meyer, Lukas, 'Intergenerational Justice', *Stanford Encyclopedia of Philosophy* (2015), available at https://plato.stanford.edu/entries/justice-intergenerational.

Meyer, Lukas and Dominic Roser, 'Enough for the Future' in Axel Gosseries and Lukas Meyer (eds), *Intergenerational Justice* (Oxford: Oxford University Press, 2009), 219–48.

Midgley, Mary, *Animals and Why They Matter* (Athens, GA: University of Georgia Press, 1998).

Mill, John Stuart, 'A Few Words on Non-Intervention' in John Robson (ed.), *Essays on Equality, Law, and Education: Collective Works of John Stuart Mill Volume XXI* (Toronto: Toronto University Press, 1984 [1859]), 111–24.

Mill, John Stuart, *Considerations on Representative Government* (Buffalo, NY: Prometheus Books, 1991 [1861]).

MILL, John Stuart, 'On Liberty' in John Gray (ed.), *John Stuart Mill: On Liberty and Other Essays* (Oxford: Oxford University Press, 1991 [1859]).

MILLER, David, *On Nationality* (Oxford: Oxford University Press, 1995).

MILLER, David, *Principles of Social Justice* (Cambridge, MA: Harvard University Press, 1999).

MILLER, David, *Citizenship and National Identity* (Cambridge: Polity Press, 2000).

MILLER, David, *National Responsibility and Global Justice* (Oxford: Oxford University Press, 2007).

MILLER, David, 'Immigration: The Case for Limits' in Andrew I. Cohen and Christopher Heath Wellman (eds), *Contemporary Debates in Applied Ethics, Second Edition* (Chichester: Wiley Blackwell, 2014), 363–75.

MILLER, David, *Strangers in Our Midst: The Political Philosophy of Immigration* (Cambridge, MA: Harvard University Press, 2016).

MILLS, Charles W., '"Ideal Theory" as Ideology', *Hypatia*, 20 (2005), 165–84.

Ministry of Justice, 'Story of Prison Population: 1993–2012 England and Wales', *Ministry of Justice Summary* (2013), available at https://www.gov.uk/government/statistics/story-of-the-prison-population-1993-2012.

Ministry of Justice, 'Costs Per Place and Costs Per Prisoner', *Ministry of Justice Information Release* (2019), available at https://assets.publishing.service.gov.uk/government/uploads/system/uploads/attachment_data/file/841948/costs-per-place-costs-per-prisoner-2018-2019.pdf.

MITCHELL, Daniel, 'Why Parental Leave Is None of the Government's Business', *Foundation for Economic Education*, 30 March 2019, available at https://fee.org/articles/why-parental-leave-is-none-of-the-government-s-business.

MOELLENDORF, Darrel, *Cosmopolitan Justice* (Boulder, CO: Westview Press, 2002).

MOLES, Andres, 'Autonomy, Free Speech and Automatic Behaviour', *Res Publica*, 13 (2007), 53–75.

MOLES, Andres, 'Expressive Interest and the Integrity of Hate Speakers', *Politics in Central Europe*, 6 (2010), 18–38.

MOLES, Andres and Tom Parr, 'Distributions and Relations: A Hybrid Account', *Political Studies*, 67 (2019), 132–48.

MOORE, Michael S., *Placing Blame: A Theory of Criminal Law* (Oxford: Oxford University Press, 1997).

MOREAU, Sophia, *Faces of Inequality: A Theory of Wrongful Discrimination* (Oxford: Oxford University Press, 2020).

MUELLER-SMITH, Michael, 'The Criminal and Labor Market Impacts of Incarceration', *Working Paper* (2015), available at http://cep.lse.ac.uk/conference_papers/01_10_2015/smith.pdf.

MUNCK, Gerardo and Chetan Kumar, 'Civil Conflicts and the Conditions of Successful International Intervention: A Comparative Study of Cambodia and El Salvador', *Review of International Studies*, 21 (1995), 159–81.

MURPHY, Jeffrie G. and Jean Hampton, *Forgiveness and Mercy* (Cambridge: Cambridge University Press, 1988).

My Family Care, 'Shared Parental Leave: Where Are We Now?' (2016), available at https://www.myfamilycare.co.uk/resources/white-papers/shared-parental-leave-where-are-we-now.

NAGEL, Thomas, 'The Problem of Global Justice', *Philosophy & Public Affairs*, 33 (2005), 113–47.

NARVESON, Jan, 'We Don't Owe Them a Thing! A Tough-Minded but Soft-Hearted View of Aid to the Faraway Needy', *The Monist*, 86 (2003), 419–33.

The National Academies of Sciences, Engineering, and Medicine, *The Economic and Fiscal Consequences of Immigration* (Washington, DC: The National Academies Press, 2016).

National Health Service, 'Addiction: What Is It?' (2015), available at https://www.nhs.uk/live-well/healthy-body/addiction-what-is-it.

NEUMARK, David, 'Experimental Research on Labor Market Discrimination', *Journal of Economic Literature*, 56 (2018), 799–866.

NORCROSS, Alistair, 'Puppies, Pigs, and People: Eating Meat and Marginal Cases', *Philosophical Perspectives*, 18 (2004), 229–45.

NOSEK, Brian A. et al., 'Pervasiveness and Correlates of Implicit Attitudes and Stereotypes', *European Review of Social Psychology*, 18 (2007), 36–88.

Not Dead Yet UK, 'Resources', available at http://notdeadyetuk.org/resources.

NOZICK, Robert, *Anarchy, State, and Utopia* (New York: Basic Books, 1974).

NUSSBAUM, Martha, *Sex and Social Justice* (Oxford: Oxford University Press, 1999).

NUSSBAUM, Martha, *Women and Human Development: The Capabilities Approach* (Cambridge: Cambridge University Press, 2000).

NUSSBAUM, Martha, *Frontiers of Justice: Disability, Nationality, Species Membership* (Cambridge, MA: Harvard University Press, 2007).

NUTT, David, Leslie King, and Lawrence Philips, 'Drug Harms in the UK: A Multicriteria Decision Analysis', *The Lancet*, 376 (2010), 1558–65.

OBERMAN, Kieran, 'Can Brain Drain Justify Immigration Restrictions?', *Ethics*, 123 (2013), 427–55.

OECD, 'Gender Brief' (2010), available at http://www.oecd.org/els/family/44720649.pdf.

OECD, 'Parental Leave: Where Are the Fathers?' (March 2016), available at https://www.oecd.org/policy-briefs/parental-leave-where-are-the-fathers.pdf.

OECD, 'Time Spent in Paid and Unpaid Work, by Sex' (2018), available at https://stats.oecd.org/index.aspx?queryid=54757.

OECD, 'Gender Wage Gap' (2020), available at https://data.oecd.org/earnwage/gender-wage-gap.htm.

Office of National Statistics, 'Report: Deaths Related to Drug Poisoning—England and Wales, 1993–2005', *Health Statistics Quarterly*, 33 (2007).

OKIN, Susan Moller, *Gender, Justice, and the Family* (New York: Basic Books, 1989).

OKIN, Susan Moller, 'Feminism and Multiculturalism: Some Tensions', *Ethics*, 108 (1998), 661–84.

OKIN, Susan Moller, 'Reply' in Susan Moller Okin et al., *Is Multiculturalism Bad for Women?* (Princeton, NJ: Princeton University Press, 1999), 115–32.

OKIN, Susan Moller et al., *Is Multiculturalism Bad for Women?* (Princeton, NJ: Princeton University Press, 1999).

OLSARETTI, Serena, 'Children as Public Goods?', *Philosophy & Public Affairs*, 41 (2013), 226–58.

OLSON, Kristi, 'Our Choices, Our Wage Gap?', *Philosophical Topics*, 40 (2012), 45–61.

O'NEILL, Onora, 'Abstraction, Idealization, and Ideology in Ethics' in J. D. G. Evans (ed.), *Moral Philosophy and Contemporary Problems* (Cambridge: Cambridge University Press, 1987), 55–69.

ONWUACHI-WILLIG, Angela, Emily Houh, and Mary Campbell, 'Cracking the Egg: Which Came First—Stigma or Affirmative Action?', *California Law Review*, 96 (2008), 1299–352.

ONWUTEAKA-PHILIPSEN, Bregje et al., 'Trends in End-of-Life Practices Before and After the Enactment of the Euthanasia Law in the Netherlands from 1990 to 2010: A Repeated Cross-Sectional Survey', *The Lancet*, 380 (2012), 908–15.

OWEN, David, 'Migration, Structural Injustice and Domination: On "Race", Mobility and Transnational Positional Difference', *Journal of Ethnic and Migration Studies*, 46 (2020), 2585–601.

PAGE, Edward, 'Intergenerational Justice of What: Welfare, Resources, or Capabilities?', *Environmental Politics*, 16 (2007), 453–69.

PAGE, Edward, 'Give It Up for Climate Change: A Defence of the Beneficiary Pays Principle', *International Theory*, 4 (2012), 300–30.

PALMER, Clare, *Animal Ethics in Context* (New York: Columbia University Press, 2010).

PAREKH, Bhikhu, 'Equality in a Multicultural Society', *Citizenship Studies*, 2 (1998), 397–411.

PAREKH, Bhikhu, 'Hate Speech: Is There a Case for Banning?', *Public Policy Research*, 12 (2006), 213–23.

PAREKH, Bhikhu, *Rethinking Multiculturalism: Cultural Diversity and Political Theory* (Basingstoke: Palgrave Macmillan, 2006).

PARFIT, Derek, *Reasons and Persons* (Oxford: Clarendon Press, 1984).

PARFIT, Derek, 'Future People, the Non-Identity Problem, and Person-Affecting Principles', *Philosophy & Public Affairs*, 45 (2017), 118–57.

PASTERNAK, Avia, 'The Collective Responsibility of Democratic Publics', *Canadian Journal of Philosophy*, 41 (2011), 99–123.

PASTERNAK, Avia, 'Benefiting from Wrongdoing' in Kasper Lippert-Rasmussen, Kimberley Brownlee, and David Coady (eds) *A Companion to Applied Philosophy* (Oxford: Wiley, 2016), 411–23.

PEREIRA-MENAUT, Antonio Carlos, 'Against Positive Rights', *Valparaiso University Law Review*, 22 (1988), 359–84.

PETTIT, Philip, *Republicanism: A Theory of Freedom and Government* (Oxford: Clarendon Press, 1997).

PHILLIPS, Anne, 'Defending Equality of Outcome', *Journal of Political Philosophy*, 12 (2004), 1–19.

POGGE, Thomas, *World Poverty and Human Rights: Cosmopolitan Responsibilities and Reforms* (Cambridge: Polity Press, 2008).

POJMAN, Louis, 'The Case Against Affirmative Action' in Hugh LaFollette (ed.), *Ethics in Practice: An Anthology, Fourth Edition* (Oxford: Wiley Blackwell, 2014), 433–42.

QUONG, Jonathan, 'Cultural Exemptions, Expensive Tastes, and Equal Opportunities', *Journal of Applied Philosophy*, 23 (2006), 53–71.

QUONG, Jonathan, *Liberalism without Perfection* (Oxford: Oxford University Press, 2010).

RACHELS, James, *The End of Life: Euthanasia and Morality* (Oxford: Oxford University Press, 1986).

RADCLIFFE RICHARDS, Janet, 'Equality of Opportunity', *Ratio*, 10 (1997), 253–79.

RAJAN, Raghuram and Arvind Subramanian, 'Aid and Growth: What Does the Cross-Country Evidence Really Show?', *The Review of Economics and Statistics*, 90 (2008), 643–65.

RANDALL, Fiona and Robin Downie, 'Assisted Suicide and Voluntary Euthanasia: Role Contradictions for Physicians', *Clinical Medicine*, 10 (2010), 323–5.

RASMUSSEN, Kipling et al., 'Increasing Husbands' Involvement in Domestic Labor: Issues for Therapists', *Contemporary Family Therapy*, 18 (1996), 209–23.

RawLINSON, Kevin, 'Terminally Ill Man
Loses High Court Fight to End His
Life', *The Guardian*, 5 October 2017,
available at https://www.theguardian.com/
society/2017/oct/05/entombed-man-noel-
conway-loses-high-court-fight-end-life.

RawLS, John, *Political Liberalism* (New York:
Columbia University Press, 1996).

RawLS, John, *A Theory of Justice, Revised
Edition* (Cambridge, MA: Harvard
University Press, 1999).

RawLS, John, *Collected Papers* (Cambridge,
MA: Harvard University Press, 1999).

RawLS, John, *Justice as Fairness: A
Restatement* (Cambridge, MA: Harvard
University Press, 2001).

Raz, Joseph, *The Morality of Freedom*
(Oxford: Clarendon Press, 1986).

Reform Section 5, 'Victory', available at
http://reformsection5.org.uk.

REGAN, Tom, 'Empty Cages: Animal Rights
and Vivisection' in Andrew I. Cohen
and Christopher Heath Wellman (eds),
*Contemporary Debates in Applied Ethics,
Second Edition* (Oxford: Blackwell, 2014),
95–108.

ROBEYNS, Ingrid, 'When Will Society Be
Gender Just?' in Jude Brown (ed.), *The
Future of Gender* (Cambridge: Cambridge
University Press, 2007), 54–74.

ROE, Stephen and Louise Man, 'Drug Misuse
Declared: Findings from the 2005/6 British
Crime Survey, England and Wales', *Home
Office Statistical Bulletin* (2006), available at
http://webarchive.nationalarchives.gov
.uk/20110220105210/rds.homeoffice.gov.uk/
rds/pdfs06/hosb1506.pdf.

ROLLIN, Bernard E., 'Animal Pain' in Susan J.
Armstrong and Richard G. Botzler (eds),
The Animal Ethics Reader, Third Edition
(London: Routledge, 2017), 111–15.

ROTHSTEIN, Jesse and Albert Yoon,
'Affirmative Action in Law School

Admissions', *University of Chicago Law
Review*, 75 (2008), 649–714.

SANDER, Richard H., 'Class in American
Legal Education', *Denver University Law
Review*, 88 (2011), 631–82.

SANGIOVANNI, Andrea, 'Global Justice,
Reciprocity, and the State', *Philosophy &
Public Affairs*, 35 (2007), 3–39.

SATZ, Debra, 'Equality, Adequacy and
Education for Citizenship', *Ethics*, 117
(2007), 623–48.

SAXENIAN, AnnaLee, 'Brain Circulation:
How High-Skill Immigration Makes
Everyone Better Off', *Brookings Review*, 20
(2002), 28–31.

SCANLON, Thomas, 'A Theory of Freedom of
Expression', *Philosophy & Public Affairs*, 1
(1972), 204–26.

SCANLON, Thomas, 'Freedom of Expression
and Categories of Expression', *University of
Pittsburgh Law Review*, 40 (1978), 519–50.

SCANLON, Thomas, 'The Significance of
Choice' in Sterling McMurrin (ed.), *The
Tanner Lectures on Human Values* (Salt Lake
City, UT: University of Utah Press, 1986).

SCHEFFLER, Samuel, 'Natural Rights,
Equality, and the Minimal State' in Jeffrey
Paul (ed.), *Reading Nozick* (London: Wiley
Blackwell, 1982), 148–68.

SCHEFFLER, Samuel, 'Immigration and the
Significance of Culture', *Philosophy &
Public Affairs*, 35 (2007), 93–125.

SCHLOTTMANN, Christopher and Jeff Sebo,
*Foods, Animals, and the Environment:
An Ethical Approach* (Oxford: Routledge,
2019).

SCHOUTEN, Gina, 'Restricting Justice:
Political Interventions in the Home and in
the Market', *Philosophy & Public Affairs*, 41
(2013), 357–88.

SCHOUTEN, Gina, 'Citizenship, Reciprocity,
and the Gendered Division of Labor: A
Stability Argument for Gender Egalitarian

Political Interventions', *Politics, Philosophy, and Economics*, 16 (2017), 174–209.

SCHOUTEN, Gina, *Liberalism, Neutrality, and the Gendered Division of Labor* (Oxford: Oxford University Press, 2019).

SEGLOW, Jonathan, 'Recognition and Religious Diversity: The Case of Legal Exemptions' in Shane O'Neill and Nicholas Smith (eds), *Recognition Theory as Social Research* (London: Palgrave Macmillan, 2012), 127–46.

SEN, Amartya, 'Equality of What?' in *The Tanner Lecture on Human Values* (Cambridge: Cambridge University Press, 1980), 197–220.

SEN, Amartya, 'Democracy as a Universal Value', *Journal of Democracy*, 10 (1999), 3–17.

SERRANO, Christina Castellanos and David Drabble, 'Shared Parental Leave to Have Minimal Impact on Gender Equality', *The Tavistock Institute*, May 2014, available at https://www.tavinstitute.org/news/shared-parental-leave-minimal-impact-gender-equality.

SHARMA, Sonia, 'Should Open-Air Funeral Pyres Be Allowed to Take Place in the North East? Davender Ghai Thinks So', *The Chronicle*, 12 January 2018, available at https://www.chroniclelive.co.uk/news/north-east-news/should-open-air-funeral-pyres-14140881.

SHELBY, Tommie, 'Justice, Work, and the Ghetto Poor', *The Law & Ethics of Human Rights*, 6 (2012), 71–96.

SHER, George, 'Justifying Reverse Discrimination in Employment', *Philosophy & Public Affairs*, 4 (1975), 159–70.

SHIELDS, Liam, Anne Newman, and Debra Satz, 'Equality of Educational Opportunity', *Stanford Encyclopedia of Philosophy* (2017), available at https://plato.stanford.edu/entries/equal-ed-opportunity.

SHIFFRIN, Seana, 'Paternalism, Unconscionability Doctrine, and Accommodation', *Philosophy & Public Affairs*, 29 (2000), 205–50.

SHIFFRIN, Seana, 'Race and Ethnicity, Race, Labor, and the Fair Equality of Opportunity Principle', *Fordham Law Review*, 72 (2004), 1643–75.

SHIFFRIN, Seana, *Speech Matters: On Lying, Morality, and the Law* (Princeton, NJ: Princeton University Press, 2014).

SHUE, Henry, 'Subsistence Emissions and Luxury Emissions', *Law & Policy*, 15 (1993), 39–60.

SHUE, Henry, 'Global Environment and International Inequality', *International Affairs*, 75 (1999), 531–45.

SIMPSON, Robert Mark, 'Dignity, Harm, and Hate Speech', *Law and Philosophy*, 32 (2013), 701–28.

SINGER, Peter, 'Famine, Affluence, and Morality', *Philosophy & Public Affairs*, 1 (1972), 229–43.

SINGER, Peter, *Practical Ethics, Second Edition* (Cambridge: Cambridge University Press, 1993).

SINGER, Peter, 'Making Our Own Decisions about Death', *Free Inquiry*, 25 (2005), 36–8.

SINGER, Peter (ed.), *In Defense of Animals: The Second Wave* (Oxford: Blackwell, 2006).

SINGER, Peter, *The Life You Can Save: How to Play Your Part in Ending World Poverty* (London: Random House, 2009).

SINGLETON, Nicola, Rosemary Murray, and Louise Tinsley (eds), 'Measuring Different Aspects of Problem Drug Use: Methodological Developments', *Home Office Online Report* (2016), available at http://webarchive.nationalarchives.gov.uk/20110218135832/rds.homeoffice.gov.uk/rds/pdfs06/rdsolr1606.pdf.

SMITS, Katherine, *Applying Political Theory: Issues and Debates* (London: Palgrave, 2009).

SONG, Sarah, 'Multiculturalism', *The Stanford Encyclopedia of Philosophy* (2017), available at https://plato.stanford.edu/archives/spr2017/entries/multiculturalism.

STILZ, Anna, 'Decolonization and Self-Determination', *Social Philosophy and Policy*, 32 (2015), 1–24.

STILZ, Anna, 'Is There an Unqualified Right to Leave?' in Sarah Fine and Lea Ypi (eds), *Migration in Political Theory* (Oxford: Oxford University Press, 2016), 57–79.

STILZ, Anna, 'The Value of Self-Determination', *Oxford Studies in Political Philosophy Volume 2* (Oxford: Oxford University Press, 2016).

STILZ, Anna, *Territorial Sovereignty: A Philosophical Exploration* (Oxford: Oxford University Press, 2019).

STOCK, Anke, 'Affirmative Action: A German Perspective on the Promotion of Women's Rights with Regard to Employment', *Journal of Law and Society*, 33 (2006), 59–73.

SUMNER, L. W., 'Positive Sexism', *Social Philosophy & Policy*, 5 (1987), 204–22.

SWIFT, Adam, *Political Philosophy: A Beginners' Guide for Students and Politicians* (Cambridge: Polity, 2001).

SWIFT, Adam, *How Not to Be a Hypocrite: School Choice for the Morally Perplexed Parent* (London: Routledge, 2003).

TADROS, Victor, *The Ends of Harm: The Moral Foundations of Criminal Law* (Oxford: Oxford University Press, 2011).

TADROS, Victor, 'Distributing Responsibility', *Philosophy & Public Affairs*, 48 (2020), 223–61.

TAN, Kok-Chor, 'Colonialism, Reparations, and Global Justice' in Jon Miller and Rahul Kumar (eds), *Reparations: Interdisciplinary Inquires* (Oxford: Oxford University Press, 2007), 280–306.

TAYLOR, Charles, 'The Politics of Recognition', *New Contexts of Canadian Criticism*, 98 (1997), 25–73.

Telegraph Reporters, 'Britain Spends £1.3bn on Foreign Aid for Most Corrupt Countries', *The Telegraph*, 22 December 2016, available at https://www.telegraph.co.uk/news/2016/12/22/britain-spends-13billionon-foreign-aid-corrupt-countries.

TESÓN, Fernando and Bas van der Vossen, *Debating Humanitarian Intervention: Should We Try to Save Strangers?* (Oxford: Oxford University Press, 2017).

THALER, Richard and Cass Sunstein, *Nudge: Improving Decisions about Health, Wealth and Happiness* (New Haven, CT: Yale University Press, 2008).

THEOFILOPOULOU, Areti, 'Punishment and Moral Fortification and Non-Consensual Neurointerventions', *Law and Philosophy*, 38 (2019), 149–67.

THOMSON, Judith Jarvis, 'Preferential Hiring', *Philosophy & Public Affairs*, 2 (1973), 364–84.

THOMSON, Judith Jarvis, 'Physician-Assisted Suicide: Two Moral Arguments', *Ethics*, 109 (1999), 497–518.

The Times Editorial Board, 'Pass the U.S. Sentencing Reform Bill to Rein in Mass Incarceration', *Los Angeles Times*, 17 February 2016, available at http://www.latimes.com/opinion/editorials/la-ed-criminal-justice-20160215-story.html.

United Nations, *Report of the World Commission on Environment and Development: Our Common Future* (New York: Oxford University Press, 1987).

United Nations, *The Sustainable Development Goals Report 2019* (New York: United Nations, 2019).

United Nations General Assembly, 'Universal Declaration of Human Rights' (1948), available at http://www.un.org/en/universal-declaration-human-rights.

United Nations IPCC, 'Climate Change 2014: Synthesis Report' (Geneva: IPCC, 2015), available at http://www.ipcc.ch/report/ar5/syr.

United Nations IPCC, 'Global Warming of 1.5°C' (Geneva: IPCC, 2018), available at https://report.ipcc.ch/sr15/pdf/sr15_spm_final.pdf.

VALENTINI, Laura, 'On the Apparent Paradox of Ideal Theory', *Journal of Applied Philosophy*, 17 (2009), 332–55.

VALENTINI, Laura, *Justice in a Globalized World: A Normative Framework* (Oxford: Oxford University Press, 2011).

VAN PARIJS, Philippe, 'Why Surfers Should Be Fed: The Liberal Case for an Unconditional Basic Income', *Philosophy & Public Affairs*, 20 (1991), 101–31.

VAN PARIJS, Philippe, *Real Freedom for All: What (If Anything) Can Justify Capitalism?* (Oxford: Oxford University Press, 1995).

VAN PARIJS, Philippe, 'Reciprocity and the Justification for Basic Income: Reply to Stuart White', *Political Studies*, 45 (1997), 327–30.

VAN PARIJS, Philippe, 'A Basic Income for All' in Philippe Van Parijs, Joshua Cohen, and Joel Rogers (eds), *What's Wrong with a Free Lunch?* (Boston, MA: Beacon Press, 2001).

VAN PARIJS, Philippe, 'Basic Income: A Simple and Powerful Idea for the Twenty-First Century', *Politics & Society*, 32 (2004), 7–39.

VAN PARIJS, Philippe and Yannick Vanderborght, *Basic Income: A Radical Proposal for a Free Society and Sane Economy* (Cambridge, MA: Harvard University Press, 2017).

VELLEMAN, J. David, 'A Right of Self-Termination?', *Ethics*, 109 (1999), 606–28.

VELLEMAN, J. David, 'Against the Right to Die' in Hugh LaFollette (ed.), *Ethics in Practice: An Anthology, Fourth Edition* (Oxford: Wiley Blackwell, 2014), 92–100.

VINDAS, Marco, 'Brain Serotonergic Activation in Growth-Stunted Farmed Salmon: Adaption Versus Pathology', *Royal Society of Open Science*, 3 (2016), 1–8.

WALDRON, Jeremy, 'A Rights-Based Critique of Constitutional Rights', *Oxford Journal of Legal Studies*, 13 (1993), 18–51.

WALDRON, Jeremy, *Law and Disagreement* (Oxford: Oxford University Press, 1999).

WALDRON, Jeremy, 'One Law for All? The Logic of Cultural Accommodation', *Washington and Lee Law Review*, 59 (2002), 3–34.

WALDRON, Jeremy, 'The Core Case Against Judicial Review', *Yale Law Journal*, 115 (2006), 1346–406.

WALDRON, Jeremy, *The Harm of Hate Speech* (Cambridge, MA: Harvard University Press, 2012).

WALTON, Andrew, 'Justice, Authority, and the World Order', *Journal of Global Ethics*, 5 (2009), 215–30.

WALTON, Andrew, 'Trade Justice: An Argument for Integrationist, Not Internal, Principles', *Journal of Political Philosophy*, 28 (2020), 51–72.

WALZER, Michael, *Just and Unjust Wars* (New York: Basic Books, 1977).

WALZER, Michael, 'The Moral Standing of States: A Response to Four Critics', *Philosophy & Public Affairs*, 9 (1980), 209–29.

WARREN, Mary Anne, *Moral Status: Obligations to Persons and to Other Living Things* (Oxford: Oxford University Press, 1997).

WATT, Nicholas, 'Danish Paper Sorry for Muhammad Cartoons', *The Guardian*, 31 January 2006, available at https://www.theguardian.com/media/2006/jan/31/religion.saudiarabia.

WATTS, Nick et al., 'The 2018 Report of the Lancet Countdown on Health and Climate Change', *The Lancet*, 392 (2018), 2479–514.

WEALE, Albert, *Democracy, Second Edition* (London: Palgrave, 2007).

WELLMAN, Christopher Heath, 'A Defence of Stiffer Penalties for Hate Crimes', *Hypatia*, 21 (2006), 62–80.

WELLMAN, Christopher Heath, 'Immigration and Freedom of Association', *Ethics*, 119 (2008), 109–41.

WELLMAN, Christopher Heath, 'Immigration', *Stanford Encyclopedia of Philosophy* (2019), available at https://plato .stanford.edu/entries/immigration.

WHEELER, Nicholas J., *Saving Strangers: Humanitarian Intervention in International Society* (Oxford: Oxford University Press, 2000).

WHITE, Stuart, 'Liberal Equality, Exploitation, and the Case for an Unconditional Basic Income', *Political Studies*, 45 (1997), 312–26.

WHITE, Stuart, 'What's Wrong with Workfare?', *Journal of Applied Philosophy*, 21 (2004), 271–84.

WHITE, Stuart, 'Reconsidering the Exploitation Objection to Basic Income', *Basic Income Studies*, 1 (2006), 1–17.

WIER, Mette et al., 'Are CO2 Taxes Regressive? Evidence from the Danish Experience', *Ecological Economics*, 52 (2005), 239–52.

WOLFF, Christian, *Jus Gentium Methodo Scientifica Pertractatum* (Oxford: Clarendon, 1934 [1749]).

WOLFF, Jonathan, 'Harm and Hypocrisy: Have We Got It Wrong about Drugs?', *Public Policy Research*, 14 (2007), 126–35.

WOOLLARD, Fiona, 'Doing vs. Allowing Harm', *Stanford Encyclopedia of Philosophy* (2016), available at https://plato.stanford .edu/entries/doing-allowing.

WYLIE, Alison, 'Why Standpoint Matters' in Robert Rigueroa and Sandra Haring (eds), *Science and Other Cultures: Issues in Philosophies of Science and Technology* (London: Routledge, 2003), 26–48.

WYNES, Seth and Kimberley Nicholas, 'The Climate Mitigation Map: Education and Government Recommendations Miss the Most Effective Individual Actions', *Environmental Research Letters*, 12 (2017), 1–9.

YANAGIZAWA-DROTT, David, 'Propaganda and Conflict: Evidence from the Rwandan Genocide', *The Quarterly Journal of Economics*, 129 (2014), 1947–94.

YONG, Caleb, 'Does Freedom of Speech Include Hate Speech?', *Res Publica*, 17 (2011), 385–403.

YOUNG, Iris Marion, 'Policy and Group Difference: A Critique of the Ideal of Universal Citizenship', *Ethics*, 99 (1989), 250–74.

YOUNG, Iris Marion, *Justice and the Politics of Difference* (Princeton, NJ: Princeton University Press, 1990).

YOUNG, Iris Marion, *Responsibility for Justice* (Oxford: Oxford University Press, 2011).

YOUNG, Robert, 'Voluntary Euthanasia', *Stanford Encyclopedia of Philosophy* (2019), available at http://plato.stanford.edu/ entries/euthanasia-voluntary.

YPI, Lea, *Global Justice and Avant-Garde Political Agency* (Oxford: Oxford University Press, 2011).

YPI, Lea, 'What's Wrong with Colonialism?', *Philosophy & Public Affairs*, 41 (2013), 158–91.

ZWARTHOED, Danielle, 'Should Future Generations Be Content with Plastic Trees and Singing Electronic Birds?', *Journal of Agricultural and Environmental Ethics*, 29 (2016), 219–36.

INDEX

Academy of Medical Science 57
affirmative action 6–7, 62–77, 130
  as compensation for discrimination 66–7, 68, 72, 76
  discrimination argument for 68, 72
  diversity and integration argument for 68–70, 76
  equal treatment objection 73–4
  meritocracy objection 71–3
  off–target objection 74–5
  and prevention of discrimination 67–8, 72, 76
  quotas 63, 74, 76
  reverse discrimination objection 7–8, 70–4
  stigma objection 75–6
  tie-breakers 76
Afghanistan 234, 243
Albania 13
Amish 127
analysis in political philosophy 6–10
  argument structure 6–7
  examples and thought experiments 6, 9–10
Anderson, Elizabeth 69, 85, 97, 100–2
Andrade, Leandro 164–5
animals, treatment of 133–4, 139, 174–7
  and lack of reasoning capacity 180–1
  and moral status 173, 180–1, 183
  pain and pleasure 174, 175–6, 177, 184–5
  suffering and killing 174–5, 176, 184–5
  see also humane farming practices; intensive animal farming
anti-discrimination policies 63
anti-paternalism 48–50
  autonomy argument 48–9, 50, 54, 56–7

better judge argument 49–50, 54
  disrespect argument 49, 50, 54
Assisted Dying Bill, UK 13, 22
autonomy 16–17
  anti-paternalist argument for 48–9, 50, 51, 54, 56–7
  and freedom of expression 34–5

Bakke, Allan 70–1, 72, 74
basic freedoms 207, 208
basic income 93–108
  and difference principle 98–100
  and distributive justice 97–102, 103, 105
    democratic equality 97, 100–2
    justice as fairness 97–100
  economic sustainability 107–8
  entitlement objection 105–7
  exit option effect 95–6, 98
  and freedom 95
  income effect 95, 96, 99–100, 102
  and non-contributors, problem of 102–5
  progressive policy design 95, 99
  reciprocity objection 103–5
  redistributive policy design 95, 99
  and taxation problem 105–7
    intuitive problem 105–6
    theoretical problem 106–7
  unconditional nature of 94, 96
  unemployment trap effect 96
  universal nature of 94
Belgium 14
better judge argument, anti-paternalism 49–50, 51, 54
bill of rights 145–6, 147, 154
black and minority ethnic (BME) people 63, 67, 69

see also race/racial discrimination
Book of Mormon, The (musical comedy) 40–1
borders
  control policies 213, 227
  see also open borders
Bosnia 241
brain drain 209–12
Brighouse, Harry 82, 88, 89
Brundtland Report 192

California, three-strikes regime 163–4
Cambodian genocide 234, 237
Caney, Simon 193
cannabis use 45, 57, 58, 59
capabilities 101
carbon tax 188
care work, unpaid 110, 124
childcare 110, 123, 124
children 133, 139
  and environmental taxes 200–1
  with radical cognitive limitations 181–2, 194
China 239
Christiano, Thomas 151
Citizen's Income Trust 107
civil rights 143
claim rights 143, 145
climate change 187–8, 189–90, 195, 196–7
  adaptation to 190, 191
  beneficiary-pays principle 197–8
  contributor-pays principle 197
  loss and damage payments compensating for 190, 191
  mitigation of 190, 191
  policy tools responding to 188
  and uncertainty 201–2
  see also environmental taxes; intergenerational justice
climate of hate 32–3, 42, 43
cocaine use 47, 53, 54, 55, 56, 57, 58, 59

Cohen, G. A. 10–11
Colombia 13
colonialism 238
  and poverty 224
common good 128
communicative account of
  punishment 158, 168–70
community goods 212–13,
  215–16
compatriots, special duties
  between 225–9
  argument from political
    power 226, 227, 228
  argument from reciprocity
    226, 227, 228
compensation 66–7, 68, 72, 76
conscientious objectors 131
consent, and euthanasia 14, 15
constitutional democracy 147
Conway, Noel 19
Cremation Act (1902), UK 135
crime rates, and length of prison
  sentences 157, 163, 164
crimes against humanity 233
criminal justice system
  racial bias in 158, 159, 170–1
  see also prison sentences;
    punishment
Cruz, Ted 157
cultural diversity 216
cultural relativism 236–7
culture, and immigration 204,
  212, 215–16, 217

Danish Mohammed cartoons
  28, 37, 39, 40
death penalty 158
deaths, recreational drug use 56,
  57, 58, 59
Deaton, Angus 230
democracy 146–8
  constitutional 147
  constrained 142, 147, 154
  defining 146–7
  direct 147, 148
  incentive mechanism 149, 150
  information mechanism 149
  instrumental defence of
    148–9, 151
    and judicial review 148,
      149–50
  intrinsic defence of 148,
    150–3
    and judicial review 151–2,
      154

procedures of 148, 151
  representative 147, 148–9
  unconstrained 142, 147,
    149–50, 151, 153
democratic equality 97,
  100–102
Democratic Republic of
  Congo 240
deterrence account of punishment see under punishment
development aid 218–32
  domination objection 229–30
  duties of 219–21
    negative duties argu-
      ment 223–5, 231
    positive duties argu-
      ment 220–1, 225, 229
  and economic growth 230
  effectiveness objection 229,
    230
  limited funds
    objection 228–9
  responsibility objection
    221–4, 225
  statist objection 225–9
  and taxation 221
dictatorships 147
difference principle 98–100, 101
dignity 41–3, 133
direct cognitive
  discrimination 64–5
direct democracy 147, 148
direct non-cognitive
  discrimination 65
disabled people 63, 64, 132, 135
discrimination
  affirmative action as compen-
    sation for 66–7, 68, 72, 76
  affirmative action and preven-
    tion of 67–8, 72, 76
  anti-discrimination
    policies 63
  and equality 73–4
  and implicit biases 65
  and merit 71–3
  see also wrongful
    discrimination
disrespect argument, anti-
  paternalism 49, 50, 51, 54
distributive justice
  and basic income 97–102,
    103, 105
  democratic equality 97,
    100–102
  justice as fairness 97–100

diversity
  and affirmative action 68–70,
    76
  cultural 216
Do Not Resuscitate (DNR)
  requests 14
domination
  freedom from 152, 153
  relations of 100, 152
dress codes 129, 136, 139
driving licences 8, 73
Drug Policy Alliance 46
drugs
  safety ratio 57–8
  toxicity 57
  see also recreational drugs
Duff, Anthony 168–9
Duke Power 65
Dworkin, Ronald 23, 72

economic growth, and development aid 230
economy, and immigration 204,
  212, 214–15, 217
education 78
  and open borders 210
  as a positional good 82
  see also elite private schools
educational adequacy 80, 83–5
efficiency, and meritocratic
  equality of opportunity 84, 85
elite private schools, prohibition
  of 78, 79
  equality of opportunity
    argument 79, 82–3, 90–1
    and bedtime stories
      defence 85–6, 88–9
    educational adequacy
      objection 80, 83–5
    ineffectiveness
      objection 89–90
emigration 204–5, 208
  and brain drain 209–12
empirical claims 2, 3, 4
employment opportunities, and
  minority exemptions 131
employment rents 104
environmental taxes 188,
  189–91, 193, 201–2
  cherished goods
    objection 199–201
  discriminatory 198, 201
  disincentive effect 189, 190
  historical emissions
    objection 196–8

environmental taxes (*cont.*)
  impact of 199–201
  intergenerational justice
    argument for 191
  progressive 200
  regressiveness objection 199,
    200
  revenue
    and adaptation to climate
      change 190, 191
    loss and damage payments
      from 190, 191
    and mitigation of climate
      change 190, 191
  revenue-raising effect 189,
    190
  selective 201
  uniform 198
equality 151–2, 153, 154
  democratic 97, 100–102
  and discrimination 73–4
  gender *see* parental leave and
    gender equality
  intergenerational 193, 194
  minority 130–2, 134, 136,
    139–40
equality of opportunity 132
  fair 84, 98, 99, 115
  and gendered division of
    labour 113
  meritocratic 84–5
  see also elite private schools;
    inequality of opportunity
equality of outcome 112
ethnicity 63, 64, 69
  see also black and minority
    ethnic (BME) people
European Convention on
  Human Rights 142
euthanasia 13–27
  active interventions 14, 22
  assist interventions 14, 22
  and consent 14, 15
  involuntary 14, 24, 25, 26
  non-voluntary 14, 24, 25, 26
  passive interventions 13–14,
    21, 22, 23, 24
  physician-assisted suicide
    2–3, 13, 14–15, 16, 17–26
  voluntary interventions 14
    active 14–15, 16, 17–26
    passive 21, 22, 23, 24
euthanasia and freedom 15–20
  defining freedom 15–16
  doing, enabling, and
    allowing 22–4

fleeting preferences 18, 19
  retrospective endorsement
    18, 19
  and sanctity of life 2, 15, 20–1
  slippery slope objection 24–6
  stability qualification 17–20,
    24, 26
  termination objection 20–2
  value of freedom 16–17
examples, use of to test moral
  claims 6, 9–10
exploitative relations 100
external stigma 75, 76

Fabre, Cécile 145, 153
fair equality of opportunity 84,
  98, 99
fairness
  justice as 97–100
  and minority
    exemptions 136–9
fallibility, and regulation of
  freedom of expression 38,
  39, 41
familial relationship goods
  88–9
familial
  self-determination 238–9
family life
  and gendered division of
    labour 114–15
  parental leave and freedom
    in 120–2
Family and Medical Leave Act,
  US 123
Feinberg, Joel 39–40
female genital mutilation 132,
  133, 237
forced marriage 132
Fraser, Nancy 122–3, 123–4
free-riding 103
freedom of association 98, 160,
  205, 206
freedom of conscience 41, 97
freedom of expression 29, 143
  and autonomy 34–5
  content-based policies
    restricting 31, 40
  means-based policies restrict-
    ing 31, 40
  obstacles to 30
  problems with state
    regulation 37–9
    abuse of power 38, 39, 41
    fallibility 38, 39, 41
    regulatory chill 38, 39, 41

and speaker, audience, and
  thinker interests 36–7,
  40–1
freedom of movement 97, 160,
  206–7
  domestic 205
  and open borders 204–6, 208,
    211–12
freedom of occupational
  choice 97, 98
freedom to choose 48
  value in 48–9
  see also euthanasia and
    freedom
freedom(s)
  basic 207, 208
  and basic income 95
  wider 207–9
  see also liberty

gender 63, 64, 65, 69
  restructuring of institution
    of 123–4
gender equality *see* parental
  leave and gender equality
gender pay gap 110, 117
gendered division of
  labour 109–10, 111–15, 120,
    123, 124
  equality of opportunity
    objection 113
  equality of outcome
    objection 112
  and equality-enabling
    leave 115–16
  and equality-impeding
    parental leave 115
  and equality-promoting
    parental leave 116, 117, 118
  harmful effects
    objection 114–5
generalizations 5
genocide 233, 234, 237, 239, 245
Germany 13
Ghana 221–2
Gheaus, Anca 121
global justice 219, 231
global order, and poverty 224–5
global warming 187, 188
  see also climate change
Greece, police force height
  requirement 65
greenhouse gas emissions 187,
  188, 189–90, 197
  historical 196–8
group libel 42

harm
  allowing, enabling and
    doing 23
  counterfactual notion of 195
  of gendered division of
    labour 114–15
  and hate speech 31–4, 35, 37,
    42, 43
  and immigration 212–16
  of inequality of opportunity
    81, 82–3, 86
  and non–identity problem
    194, 195–6
  and offensive speech 39
  and parental licence 87–8
  and recreational drug use
    45–6, 60
Hart, H. L. A. 167
hate speech
  and enhancement of implicit
    biases 33, 35, 38–9
  defining 30
hate speech, regulation of
  28–44
  argument from dignity 41–3
  argument from offence 39–41
  harm argument 31–4, 35, 37,
    42, 43
    climate of hate 32–3, 42, 43
    incitement 31–2
    threat of harm 31–2, 42
  problems with state regulation
    abuse of power 38, 39, 41
    fallibility 38, 39, 41
    regulatory chill 38, 39, 41
Hawaii Opportunity Probation
  with Enforcement (HOPE)
  programme 163
healthcare 209–10
heroin use 54, 55, 56, 57, 58, 59
Hindu cremation rituals 135
Holloway, Wanda 87, 89
household work 110, 122
human rights
  universal 236
  violation of, and humanitarian
    intervention 9, 234, 236,
    237, 238, 240–3
Human Rights Act (1998), UK
  141–2
humane farming
  practices 184–5
humanitarian intervention 9,
  233–48
  anti-universalism
    objection 235–7

  and human rights viola-
    tions 9, 234, 236, 237, 238,
    240–3
  information issues 245–6,
    246–7
  institutional authorization
    of 244–5
  and international law 243–5
  just cause for 235
  local support for 246, 247
  motivations 246–7
  objection from likely
    failure 245–7
  objection from misuse 243–5
  political self-determination
    objection 234, 237–43, 247
    challenges to 240–3
humans
  capacity to reason 180–1, 183
  suffering and killing of 182–3
Hume, David 3

immigration 203–4, 227
  and culture 204, 212, 215–16,
    217
  and the economy 204, 212,
    214–15, 217
  harmful effects of 212–16
  and public services 214
  and security 204, 212, 213,
    217
  and social trust 216
  and unemployment 214
  and wages 214
immunity rights 143, 145
implicit biases
  and discrimination 65
  hate speech and enhancement
    of 33, 35, 38–9
imprisonment
  costs of 160, 165, 167–8,
    169–70
  financial burden of 167–8
  general deterrence effects
    of 160
  incapacitation effects of 159
  recidivism effects 159, 163
  see also prison sentences
incitement, and hate
  speech 31–2
indirect discrimination 65, 68
inequality of opportunity, unfairness and harm of 81, 82–3,
  85–6
instrumental defence of democracy 148–9, 151

  and judicial review 148,
    149–50
integration, and affirmative
  action 68–70, 76
intensive animal farming
  172–3, 177–80
  mistreatment argument
    against 179–80, 181, 183
  moral community objection
    and 180–1, 182–3
  moral status of animals
    and 173, 180–1, 183
  objection to coercive prohibi-
    tion 173, 183–4
interest theory of rights 144
intergenerational duties 192–6,
  202
  intergenerational equal-
    ity 193, 194
  intergenerational
    sufficiency 192
  non-identity problem 194–6
intergenerational justice 188,
  191, 194, 198
Intergovernmental Panel on
  Climate Change (IPCC) 187,
  188
internal stigma 75, 76
intrinsic defence of democracy 148, 150–3
  and judicial review 151–2, 154
involuntary euthanasia 14, 24,
  25, 26
Iraq, invasion of (2003) 9, 244

Japan 13
  parental leave 119
Jews 126, 127
judicial review 141–2
  and defences of
    democracy 148
    instrumental defence 148,
      149–50
    intrinsic defence 151–2,
      154
  rights argument for 144–6,
    149–50, 152–4
jus ad bellum 235, 244, 247
jus in bello 235
jus post bellum 235
justice
  as fairness 97–100
  global 219, 231
  social 97
  see also distributive justice;
    intergenerational justice

Kerik, Bernard 157
Khmer Rouge 234
killing
    of animals 174, 176, 184–5
    of humans 182–3
Kittay, Eva Feder 123
Korsgaard, Christine 174
Kosovans 240

Labour Party, UK 79
legal rights 143–4, 145–6
LGBT people see sexual
    minorities
libel 41, 42
    group 42
liberty
    basic 98
    see also freedom(s)
liberty rights 143, 145
Libya 240
life
    freedom to choose how to
        live 16–17
    sanctity of 2, 15, 20–1
logic 4
Luxembourg 14

Malaysia 221–2
marriage
    forced 132, 133
    under-age 133
massacre 233, 237, 239
McMahan, Jeff 241–2
means-tested benefits 93, 96
meritocracy 71–3
meritocratic equality of
    opportunity 84–5
    efficiency-based rationale
        of 84, 85
migrants
    opportunity 204, 208
    poverty 204
migration see emigration;
    freedom of movement;
    immigration
Mill, John Stuart 31, 37, 49,
    246, 247
Miller, David 208, 215, 221–2
minority equality 130–2, 134,
    136, 139–40
minority exemptions 126–40
    argument from minority
        equality 130–2, 134, 136,
        139–40
    argument from
        recognition 130

bads of multiculturalism
    objection 132–4
fairness objection 136–9
objection from universal
    compliance 134–6
misrecognition 129–30
moral claims 3–4
    analysis of
        argument structure 6–7
        examples and thought
            experiments 6, 9–10
        refining moral claims 8
        underlying moral
            claims 8–9
moral community 180–3,
    183–4
moral philosophy 4
moral rights 143–6
moral scepticism 236, 237
moral status, of animals 173,
    180–1, 183
moral values, universality
    of 235–7
multiculturalism 127, 132–4
Muslims 126, 127

narrow proportionality 164
Native American Church 127,
    134
negative duties argument for
    development aid 223–5, 231
Netherlands, euthanasia 14, 25
non-identity problem 194–6
non-sequiturs 7
non-voluntary euthanasia 14,
    24, 25, 26
North Korea 239
Nozick, Robert 105–7
Nussbaum, Martha 101, 133

occupational choice, freedom
    of 97, 98
offensive speech 39–41
Okin, Susan Moller 132
open borders 204
    brain drain objection 209–12
    community goods objec-
        tion 212–13, 215–16
    and culture 212, 215–16
    and the economy 212, 214–15
    and freedom of move-
        ment 204–6, 208, 211–12
    and security 212, 213
    sufficiently 208
    wider freedoms
        objection 207–9

opportunity migrants 204,
    208
opposing views, consideration
    of 10–11
Organisation for Economic
    Co-operation and
    Development 109–10
original position 97–8, 99

pain, animal 174, 175–6, 177,
    184–5
parental leave, and freedom in
    family life 120–2
parental leave and gender
    equality 110–11
    equality-enabling
        schemes 115–16
    equality-impeding
        schemes 115
    equality-promoting schemes,
        conditional leave 116,
        117–18
    default leave 116, 118, 119
    mandatory leave 111, 116,
        117, 120, 121–2, 123
    use it or lose it leave 116,
        118–19
    objection from misplaced
        focus 122–4
parental licence, restricted versus
    unrestricted 87–8
parliamentary sovereignty 141,
    142
paternalism see anti–paternalism;
    recreational drugs and
    paternalism
physician-assisted suicide 2–3,
    13, 14–15, 16, 17–26
pleasure, animal 176–7
Pojman, Louis 71
political community,
    membership of 204, 205,
    209, 212, 213, 215, 216
political philosophy 1–12
    analysis in 6–10
    main aims of 2–4
political power 226, 227, 228
political rights 143
political science 4
political self-determination, and
    humanitarian intervention
    234, 237–43, 247
positional goods 82
positive duties argument for
    development aid 220–1, 225,
    229

poverty 209, 210, 211, 219–20
  causes of 221–5
  and colonialism 224
  duties to alleviate *see* development aid
  and global order 224–5
  migrant 204
Powell, Justice Lewis 71
power, abuse of, and regulation of freedom of expression 38, 39, 41
power rights 143, 145
prison sentences, length of 156–9, 157, 158–9
  case for shorter sentences 163–5, 170
  and communicative account of punishment 158, 168–70
  context-specificity of 159
  and crime rates 157, 163, 164
  crime-specificity of 159
  and deterrence account of punishment 158, 163–5, 170
  increase in length 157
  learning effect 169
  outside option effect 169
  and retributivist account of punishment 158, 166–8
  and three-strikes laws 163–4
  see also imprisonment
proportionality, punishment 164–5, 166
#ProudOfAid 218–19
public holidays 128–9
Public Order Act (1986), UK 29, 43
public services, and immigration 214
punishment 157, 168
  communicative account of 158, 168–70
  costliness of 160, 165, 167–8, 169–70
  deterrence account of 157–8, 159–62, 170
  duties and 161–2, 165
  outcomes and 160–1
  and prison sentences 163–5, 170
  problem of unjust 161, 162
  proportionality 164–5, 166
  retributivist account of 158, 166–8
  see also prison sentences

quotas, affirmative action 63, 74, 76

race/racial discrimination 63, 64, 65, 66–7, 69
  and criminal justice system 158, 159, 170–1
Rawls, John 97–100, 101, 102, 112, 120
reason, human versus animal capacity to 180–1, 182, 183
recidivism 159, 163
reciprocity 226, 227, 228
recreational drug use
  age limits 59
  criminal penalties and 47, 55–6, 59
  deaths 56, 57, 58, 59
  drug licences policy 52
  public education programmes 47, 52, 59
  support and rehabilitation for addicts 56, 59
  taxation policies 47, 49
recreational drugs and paternalism 45–61
  addiction and second-order preferences 52–6, 59
  anti-paternalist arguments 48–50, 59
    autonomy argument 50, 51, 54, 56–7
    better judge argument 50, 51, 54
    disrespect argument 50, 51, 54
  harm issue 45–6, 60
  misinformed choices and 50–2
  overdose argument 56–9
  paternalist argument 47–8
refugees 204, 207–8
Regents of the University of California v. Bakke (1978) 70–1
regulatory chill 38, 39, 41
religion/religious groups 126, 127, 129, 131, 132, 133–4, 137, 138
remittances, emigrant 211
Remmelink Report 25
representative democracy 147, 148–9
reputation 41–2, 43
Responsibility to Protect policy 234

retributivism 158, 166–8
reverse discrimination 7–8, 70–4
rights 142–4
  see also human rights
rights argument for judicial review 144–6, 149–50, 152–4
Robeyns, Ingrid 121
Rwandan genocide (1994) 234, 237, 245

Santeria religion 133
Satz, Debra 90
Scanlon, Thomas 34, 37, 168
schools *see* elite private schools
Schouten, Gina 121
second-order preferences, and paternalist drug policies 52–6
security, and immigration 204, 212, 213, 217
self-determination
  familial 238–9
  see also political self–determination
self-respect 98
Sen, Amartya 101
Sentencing Reform and Corrections Act (2015), US 156–7
Serbs 241
sexism 132
sexual minorities 63, 64, 67, 69, 132
Shared Parental Leave Scheme, UK 110, 115, 116
Sikhs 126, 127, 129, 134, 137
Singer, Peter 174–5, 220
slander 41, 42
slavery, voluntary 20, 21
social integration, and affirmative action 68–70, 76
social justice 97
social primary goods 97–8, 99, 100
social trust, and immigration 216
socially salient groups, defined 64
socioeconomic rights 143, 146
soft paternalism 52
Somalia 245
South Korea
  judicial review 141
  parental leave 119
speciesism 183

stigma
  and affirmative action
    policies 75–6
  external and internal 75, 76
Stilz, Anna 216
suffering
  animal 174–5, 176, 184–5
  human 182–3
sufficiency 101
  intergenerational 192
Sweden, parental leave 119
Swift, Adam 82, 88, 89
Switzerland
  direct democracy 147
  intensive animal farming 173
  physician-assisted suicide 13
syllogism 6–7
Syria 234, 243

taxation
  and basic income 105–7
  and development aid 221
  and prison system 167–8, 169
  see also environmental taxes
technocracies 147
terrorism 213
Tesón, Fernando 242–3
Thomson, Judith Jarvis 69
thought experiments 6, 9–10
three-strikes laws 163–4
tie-breakers, affirmative
  action 76

uncertainty, climate
  change 201–2
unemployment, and
  immigration 214
unemployment benefits 3–4,
  93–4, 103, 107
  conditional 94, 103
  means-tested 93, 96

unemployment trap 96, 103
unfairness, of inequality of
  opportunity 81, 82–3, 85–6
United Kingdom
  Assisted Dying Bill 13, 22
  Citizen's Income Trust 107
  Cremation Act (1902) 135
  development aid 218–19
  Drug Strategy 2017 46
  Human Rights Act
    (1998) 141–2
  Ministry of Justice 157, 167
  Public Order Act (1986) 29, 43
  Shared Parental Leave
    Scheme 110, 115, 116
United Nations, Responsibility to
  Protect policy 234
United Nations Charter 245
United Nations Security
  Council 245
United States
  death penalty 158
  Family and Medical Leave
    Act 123
  freedom of expression 29
  invasion of Iraq (2003) 244
  judicial review 141, 142
  Native American
    Church 127, 134
  physician-assisted suicide 13,
    26
  Sentencing Reform
    and Corrections Act
    (2015) 156–7
  three-strikes laws 163–4
Universal Declaration of Human
  Rights 144
universal values 235–7

Van Parijs, Philippe 100
vanguard democracies 147

veil of ignorance 97, 99
Velleman, David 20–1
voluntary euthanasia 14
  voluntary active 14–15, 16,
    17–26
  voluntary passive 21, 22,
    23, 24
voting rights 143, 147, 154

wages, and immigration 214
Waldron, Jeremy 152–3
Walzer, Michael 238
war
  just conduct in (jus in bello)
    235
  just conduct in aftermath of
    (jus post bellum) 235
  right to (jus ad bellum) 235,
    244, 247
welfare systems, and
  immigration 214
wide proportionality 164
will theory of rights 144
women 63, 65, 69, 132, 133,
  139
  and basic income 95–6
  see also gender
work week 128, 131, 138
World Trade Organization
  227
wrongful discrimination 63–6,
  68
  direct cognitive
    discrimination 64–5
  direct non-cognitive
    discrimination 65
  indirect discrimination
    65, 68

Yugoslavia, Federal Republic
  of 240